WOMEN, LITERATURE, AND THE DOMESTICATED LANDSCAPE

Combining an analysis of literature and art and including more than seventy illustrations, this book contends that the "domesticated landscape" is a key to understanding women's complex negotiation of private and public life in a period of revolution and transition, 1780–1870. As more women became engaged in horticultural and botanical pursuits, the meaning of gardens – recognized here both as actual sites of pleasure and labor and as conceptual or symbolic spaces – became more complex. Women writers and artists often used the subject matter of gardens to educate their readers, to enter into political and cultural debates, and to signal moments of intellectual and spiritual insight. Gardens functioned as a protected vantage point for women, providing them with a new language and authority to negotiate between domestic space and the larger world. Although this more expansive form of domesticity still highlighted the virtues associated with the feminized home, it also promised a wider field of action, re-centering domesticity outward.

JUDITH W. PAGE is Professor of English and was the 2009–10 Waldo W. Neikirk Term Professor of Arts and Sciences at the University of Florida, where she also serves as Interim Director of the Center for Women's Studies and Gender Research.

ELISE L. SMITH is Professor of Art History and Sanderson Chair in Arts and Sciences at Millsaps College.

CAMBRIDGE STUDIES IN NINETEENTH-CENTURY
LITERATURE AND CULTURE

General editor
Gillian Beer, *University of Cambridge*

Editorial board
Isobel Armstrong, *Birkbeck, University of London*
Kate Flint, *Rutgers University*
Catherine Gallagher, *University of California, Berkeley*
D. A. Miller, *University of California, Berkeley*
J. Hillis Miller, *University of California, Irvine*
Daniel Pick, *Birkbeck, University of London*
Mary Poovey, *New York University*
Sally Shuttleworth, *University of Oxford*
Herbert Tucker, *University of Virginia*

Nineteenth-century British literature and culture have been rich fields for interdisciplinary studies. Since the turn of the twentieth century, scholars and critics have tracked the intersections and tensions between Victorian literature and the visual arts, politics, social organization, economic life, technical innovations, scientific thought – in short, culture in its broadest sense. In recent years, theoretical challenges and historiographical shifts have unsettled the assumptions of previous scholarly synthesis and called into question the terms of older debates. Whereas the tendency in much past literary critical interpretation was to use the metaphor of culture as "background," feminist, Foucauldian, and other analyses have employed more dynamic models that raise questions of power and of circulation. Such developments have reanimated the field. This series aims to accommodate and promote the most interesting work being undertaken on the frontiers of the field of nineteenth-century literary studies: work which intersects fruitfully with other fields of study such as history, or literary theory, or the history of science. Comparative as well as interdisciplinary approaches are welcomed.

A complete list of titles published will be found at the end of the book.

WOMEN, LITERATURE, AND THE DOMESTICATED LANDSCAPE: ENGLAND'S DISCIPLES OF FLORA, 1780–1870

JUDITH W. PAGE
ELISE L. SMITH

CAMBRIDGE
UNIVERSITY PRESS

University Printing House, Cambridge CB2 8BS, United Kingdom

Published in the United States of America by Cambridge University Press, New York

Cambridge University Press is part of the University of Cambridge.

It furthers the University's mission by disseminating knowledge in the pursuit of education, learning and research at the highest international levels of excellence.

www.cambridge.org
Information on this title: www.cambridge.org/9781107420236

© Judith W. Page and Elise L. Smith 2011

This publication is in copyright. Subject to statutory exception and to the provisions of relevant collective licensing agreements, no reproduction of any part may take place without the written permission of Cambridge University Press.

First published 2011
First paperback edition 2014

A catalogue record for this publication is available from the British Library

Library of Congress Cataloguing in Publication data
Page, Judith W., 1951–
Women, Literature, and the Domesticated Landscape : England's Disciples of Flora, 1780–1870 /
Judith W. Page, Elise L. Smith.
p. cm. – (Cambridge Studies in Nineteenth-Century Literature and Culture ; 76)
Includes bibliographical references and index.
ISBN 978-0-521-76865-8
1. English literature–Women authors–History and criticism. 2. English literature–19th century–History and criticism. 3. Domestic fiction, English–History and criticism. 4. Gardens in literature. 5. Gardening in literature. 6. Home in literature. 7. Privacy in literature. 8. Gardens–Symbolic aspects–England–History. 9. Women and literature–England–History–19th century. I. Smith, Elise Lawton, 1953– II. Title.
PR115.P34 2011
820.9´928709033–dc22
2010045714

ISBN 978-0-521-76865-8 Hardback
ISBN 978-1-107-42023-6 Paperback

Cambridge University Press has no responsibility for the persistence or accuracy of URLs for external or third-party internet websites referred to in this publication, and does not guarantee that any content on such websites is, or will remain, accurate or appropriate.

In memory of our mothers,
Mollie Marcus Wallick
1926–2008
Elise Lawton Isleib
1924–1992,
and
with gratitude to our daughters by birth and marriage,
Rebekah, Hannah, Katy, and Kelly

Contents

List of illustrations	*page* ix
Acknowledgements	xv
Introduction	1

PART I MORAL ORDER: THE SCHOOL OF NATURE

1	"In the home-garden": moral tales for children	15
2	The "botanic eye": botany, miniature, and magnification	50

PART II THE VISUAL FRAME: CONSTRUCTING A VIEW

3	Picturing the "home landscape": the nature of accomplishment	79
4	Commanding a view: the Taylor sisters and the construction of domestic space	116

PART III PERSONAL PRACTICE: MAKING GARDENS GROW

5	Dorothy Wordsworth: gardening, self-fashioning, and the creation of home	139
6	"Work in a small compass": gardening manuals for women	163

PART IV NARRATIVE STRATEGIES: PLOTTING THE GARDEN

7	"Unbought pleasure": gardening in *Cœlebs in Search of a Wife* and *Mansfield Park*	201
8	Margaret Oliphant's Chronicles of Carlingford and the meaning of Victorian gardens	228
	Epilogue	250

Notes	256
Works cited	288
Index	308

Illustrations

1.1. "The Flower Basket" and "The Cottage Girl," children's gift plates. Riley, *Gifts for Good Children*, #520. — page 16
1.2. Frontispiece illustration in Mary Wollstonecraft's translation of C. G. Salzmann, *Elements of Morality*. Collection of Elise Smith. — 20
1.3. William Blake, "Infant Joy," from *Songs of Innocence*. Library of Congress, Rosenwald Collection of the Rare Book Division. — 21
1.4. Frontispiece illustration by William Blake in Mary Wollstonecraft, *Original Stories from Real Life*. Harry Ransom Humanities Research Center, University of Texas, Austin. — 21
1.5. Illustration in Anna Letitia Barbauld, *Lessons for Children of Three Years Old*, p. 42. Collection of Elise Smith. — 26
1.6. "The Flower Girl," illustration in Maria Elizabeth Budden, *Chit Chat*, p. 134. The Baldwin Library of Historical Children's Literature, University of Florida. — 29
1.7. Frontispiece illustration in Sarah Fielding, *The Governess*, revised edition by Mary Martha Sherwood. The Baldwin Library of Historical Children's Literature, University of Florida. — 33
1.8. Illustration in the pamphlet edition of Ann Taylor's "My Mother." Special Collections, Florida State University Libraries. — 35
1.9. Illustration in Ann and Jane Taylor, *Original Poems for Infant Minds*, p. 59. The Baldwin Library of Historical Children's Literature, University of Florida. — 35
1.10. Illustration in *Peter Parley's First Present for Very Young Children*. The Baldwin Library of Historical Children's Literature, University of Florida. — 36

x   *List of illustrations*

1.11. Illustration in [Jane Elizabeth Holmes Jerram?], *Lucy and Arthur: A Book for Children*, facing p. 143. Collection of Elise Smith. 36

1.12. Frontispiece illustration in Ann Martin Taylor and Jane Taylor, *Correspondence between a Mother and Her Daughter at School*. Collection of Elise Smith. 40

1.13. Title page illustration in the *Child's Magazine, and Sunday Scholar's Companion* 1 (1824). The Baldwin Library of Historical Children's Literature, University of Florida. 41

1.14. Illustration in Jane Taylor, "Come and Play in the Garden," in *The Little Field-Daisy*, p. 3. The Baldwin Library of Historical Children's Literature, University of Florida. 43

1.15. "Miss Sophia," illustration in Elizabeth Turner, *The Cowslip, or More Cautionary Stories in Verse*, p. 38. The Baldwin Library of Historical Children's Literature, University of Florida. 45

1.16. Frontispiece illustration in Maria Elizabeth Budden, *Right and Wrong, Exhibited in the History of Rosa and Agnes*. The Baldwin Library of Historical Children's Literature, University of Florida. 48

2.1. Illustration in Priscilla Wakefield, *An Introduction to Botany, in a Series of Familiar Letters*, facing p. 10. Collection of Elise Smith. 52

2.2. Title page illustration in Lucy Sarah Atkins, *Botanical Rambles*. Osborne Collection of Early Children's Books, Toronto Public Library. 54

2.3. Frontispiece illustration in Mary Roberts, *The Wonders of the Vegetable Kingdom Displayed*. The Baldwin Library of Historical Children's Literature, University of Florida. 57

2.4. "Honeysuckle," illustration in William Curtis, *Flora Londinensis*, vol. 1, pl. 15. Special Collections, Louisiana State University Libraries. 64

2.5. "Girl Botanizing," illustration in Jane Taylor, *A Day's Pleasure*. The Baldwin Library of Historical Children's Literature, University of Florida. 66

2.6. Agnes Ibbetson, *Carex arenaria*. Sketchbook, Botany Library, Natural History Museum, London. 70

2.7. Illustration in Agnes Ibbetson, "On the Structure and Classification of Seeds," facing p. 183. Georgia Institute of Technology Library. 70

List of illustrations xi

3.1. Illustration in Augustin Heckle, *The Lady's Drawing Book*, pl. 4. The British Library Board (c.119.d.24). 83
3.2. Samuel Baldwin, *Sketching from Nature*. Private collection. Courtesy of the Maas Gallery, London. 84
3.3. Jane Taylor, *Flower Baskets*. Suffolk Record Office, Bury St. Edmunds Branch (HD588/13/91). 85
3.4. Jane Taylor, *Woman Sketching*. Suffolk Record Office, Bury St. Edmunds Branch (HD588/5/48–49). 86
3.5. Maria Cosway, *Progress of Female Virtue*, pl. 4. Aquatint by Antoine Cardon after Cosway's chalk drawing. Yale Center for British Art, Paul Mellon Collection. 89
3.6. Maria Cosway, *Progress of Female Dissipation*, pl. 4. Aquatint by Antoine Cardon after Cosway's chalk drawing. Yale Center for British Art, Paul Mellon Collection. 89
3.7. Maria Spilsbury, *Self-Portrait Holding a Drawing*. National Gallery of Ireland, Dublin. 95
3.8. Maria Spilsbury, *Group Portrait in a Wooded Landscape*. Private collection. Photo © Bonhams, London, UK/The Bridgeman Art Library. 97
3.9. Maria Spilsbury, *Group Portrait at a Drawing Room Table*. Private collection. Photo © Bonhams, London, UK/The Bridgeman Art Library. 99
3.10. George Morland, *Domestic Happiness*. Private collection. Yale Center for British Art, Paul Mellon Collection (B1985.36.1388). The Bridgeman Art Library. 99
3.11. Maria Spilsbury, *Family Group before a Thatched Cottage*. Private collection. Photo © Bonhams, London, UK/The Bridgeman Art Library. 100
3.12. Maria Spilsbury, *A Quiet Time – Family Group at the Cottage Door*. Location unknown. Photo © Bonhams, London, UK/The Bridgeman Art Library. 101
3.13. Maria Spilsbury, *After School*. Location unknown. Sotheby's, London. 102
3.14. Thomas Gainsborough, *The Cottage Door*. Cincinnati Art Museum, given in honor of Mr. and Mrs. Charles F. Williams by their children (Accession #1948.173). 103
3.15. George Morland, *The Happy Cottagers*. Philadelphia Museum of Art, The John Howard McFadden Collection, 1928. 103
3.16. Maria Spilsbury, *Four Children in a Landscape*. Location unknown. Sotheby's, London (sale 22 Nov. 2007, lot 50). 106

xii *List of illustrations*

3.17. *Agaricus squarrosus*, illustration in Anna Maria Hussey, *Illustrations of British Mycology*, pl. 8. LuEsther T. Mertz Library of the New York Botanical Garden, Bronx. 107
3.18. *Agaricus caulicinalis*, illustration in Anna Maria Hussey, *Illustrations of British Mycology*, pl. 68. LuEsther T. Mertz Library of the New York Botanical Garden, Bronx. 107
3.19. Richenda Gurney Cunningham, *Earlham Hall from across the Park and Garden, August 1845*. Norfolk Record Office. 114
3.20. Richenda Gurney Cunningham, *View of Earlham Bridge from the Drawing Room Windows, Sep. 6, 1846*. Norfolk Record Office. 114
4.1. Isaac Taylor, *Portrait of Ann and Jane Taylor in Their Garden at Lavenham*, 1792. National Portrait Gallery, London. 118
4.2. Engraving after Jane Taylor's drawing of Castle House, Ongar. Ann Taylor, *The Autobiography and Other Memorials of Mrs Gilbert, Formerly Ann Taylor* 1: 248. Indiana University Library. 122
4.3. Isaac Taylor, view of the Taylors' second house at Lavenham. Ann Taylor, *The Autobiography and Other Memorials of Mrs Gilbert, Formerly Ann Taylor* 1: 173. Indiana University Library. 122
4.4. Jane Taylor, *Cottage with a Man on a Bridge*. Suffolk Record Office, Bury St. Edmunds Branch (HD588/5/52). 127
4.5. Jane Taylor, *Bridge in a Landscape*. Suffolk Record Office, Bury St. Edmunds Branch (HD588/5/53). 127
4.6. Jane Taylor, *Tree with Hills in the Distance*. Suffolk Record Office, Bury St. Edmunds Branch (HD588/13/61). 135
4.7. Jane Taylor, *Path and Stile in a Landscape*. Suffolk Record Office, Bury St. Edmunds Branch (HD588/5/34). 135
5.1. *Dove Cottage, Town End*. Watercolor by Dora Wordsworth after Thomas Green. Dove Cottage, The Wordsworth Trust. 150
5.2. *Rydal Mount*. Watercolor by William Westall from Dora Wordsworth's book. 1831. Dove Cottage, The Wordsworth Trust. 161
6.1. "Bowery Window," illustration in Shirley Hibberd, *Rustic Adornments for Homes of Taste*, p. 193. Mahn Center for Archives & Special Collections, Ohio University Libraries. 167
6.2. Frontispiece illustration in Elizabeth Kent, *Flora Domestica, or, The Portable Flower-Garden*. Collection of Elise Smith. 168

List of illustrations xiii

6.3. "View from the Drawing-Room Window of Lady Broughton's Garden at Hoole House," illustration in J. C. Loudon, "Notes on Gardens and Country Seats. Hoole House," p. 360. A. R. Mann Library, Cornell University. 168

6.4. Illustration in Shirley Hibberd, *Rustic Adornments for Homes of Taste*, p. 335. Mahn Center for Archives & Special Collections, Ohio University Libraries. 171

6.5. Title page illustration in Jane Loudon, *Gardening for Ladies*. Harry Ransom Humanities Research Center, University of Texas, Austin. 181

6.6. Cover illustration of J. B. Whiting, *Manual of Flower Gardening for Ladies*. Museum of Garden History, London. 182

6.7. Illustration in *Amateur Gardening*, 1880s. From Drury and Lewis, *The Victorian Garden Album* (courtesy of Amoret Tanner). 183

6.8. Illustration in P. E., "Ripe Cherries." *Child's Companion* (1824), p. 34. The Baldwin Library of Historical Children's Literature, University of Florida. 184

6.9. "Look at the Carnations which You Gave Me." Museum of Garden History, London. 185

6.10. Victorian calendar illustration. From Drury and Lewis, *The Victorian Garden Album* (courtesy of Amoret Tanner). 186

6.11. "Let Us Go Forth into the Fields," illustration in Anna Letitia Barbauld, *Stories of the Months*, p. 66. The Baldwin Library of Historical Children's Literature, University of Florida. 187

6.12. "The Active Caroline," illustration in Charlotte Anne Broome, *Fanny and Mary*, facing p. 16. Bodleian Library, University of Oxford, Opie A 633. 188

6.13. Ceremonial Free Gardeners' Banner from Lancashire. Museum of Garden History, London. 193

6.14. "A Lady's Gauntlet," illustration in Jane Loudon, *Gardening for Ladies*, p. 17. University of Kentucky Library, Special Collection Library, 634.3 L926. 195

7.1. "Flower-Garden, Valley Field," illustration in Humphry Repton, *Observations on the Theory and Practice of Landscape Gardening*, facing p. 102. Rare Book Collection, Smathers Library, University of Florida. 218

7.2. *Geranium fothergillum*, illustration in Henry Charles Adams, *Geraniums*. LuEsther T. Mertz Library of the New York Botanical Garden, Bronx. 220

xiv *List of illustrations*

8.1. "View from the Window," illustration in Shirley Hibberd, *Rustic Adornments for Homes of Taste*, p. 189. Mahn Center for Archives & Special Collections, Ohio University Libraries. 232

8.2. Frontispiece illustration in E. A. Maling, *In-Door Plants and How to Grow Them*. Rare Book Collection, University of North Carolina, Chapel Hill. 237

9.1. Illustration by Charles Robinson in Frances Hodgson Burnett, *The Secret Garden*. The Baldwin Library of Historical Children's Literature, University of Florida. 252

9.2. Helen Allingham, *A Cottage at Freshwater, Isle of Wight*. Private collection. The Bridgeman Art Library. 254

Acknowledgements

It is hard to pinpoint exactly when and how this project began. Long-time colleagues and friends, we also share a common passion for the garden – the real gardens that we have both created, the gardens of our respective childhood memories, and gardens as they come to life in a wide range of visual arts and garden writing. Although our homes are in the decidedly intemperate American South – in Mississippi and Florida – we have both aspired to the informal English style of mixed borders. As we focused on our shared fascination with nineteenth-century England and women as creative agents in art and literature, our project began to take shape. We hope that our introduction, and of course the book itself, will reveal the range of scholars who have inspired and influenced our work. We also owe a huge debt to many institutions and people for supporting us along the way and making our collaboration possible.

First, we are deeply grateful to Linda Bree for her interest in this project from the beginning and for leading our book through the various stages from initial consideration to publication at Cambridge. She has been an invaluable editor and mentor. In addition, we thank the entire staff at the Press, especially Elizabeth Hanlon and Josephine Lane, as well as Dame Gillian Beer, the series editor. The two anonymous readers for the Press, who responded to our work generously and constructively, helped to make this book stronger.

In the process of conducting our research, we each crossed the Atlantic several times on trips to libraries. We are particularly grateful to have had access to the following institutions: the British Library, the Chawton House Library, the Botany Library at the Natural History Museum, the Lindley Library of the Royal Horticultural Society, the library at the Royal Botanic Gardens, Kew, and the library at the Victoria and Albert Museum. Philip Norman at the Museum of Garden History (now the Garden Museum) was an important source of valuable information, as was Jean Deathridge at the Bury Record Office, Stuart Tyler at the Suffolk Record Office,

Thomas Haggerty at the Bridgeman Art Library, and Maria Singer at the Yale Center for British Art. Judith Page thanks the staff at the Chawton House Library, especially Jacqui Grainger, Sarah Parry, and Corinne Saint, for their generous help during her idyllic month as a fellow there in 2008, which was also made possible through trustees of Chawton House and the efforts of Gillian Dow. Lisa Kasmer, a visiting fellow at Chawton at the same time, enlivened many evenings with conversations about the project. Closer to home, we thank certain key people at the Smathers Libraries of the University of Florida, including Rita Smith, curator of the Baldwin Library of Historical Children's Literature, Nancy Poehlmann, rare book curator, and John Van Hook, humanities librarian, and at the Millsaps-Wilson Library, Tom Henderson, college librarian, and Jan Allison, public services assistant.

For the financial support that made our research possible, we acknowledge at the University of Florida the Sabbatical Program, the College of Arts and Sciences Term Professorships, as well as travel support from the College and the Department of English. At Millsaps College we are especially grateful to Joe and Kathy Sanderson for their generous endowment of the Sanderson Chair in Arts and Sciences, which has provided funds for research trips and for the illustrations.

Each of us has presented portions of this book for invited talks and conferences along the way, and we particularly thank the following: Southeastern College Art Conference, 2005; British Women Writers Conference, 2006; International Conference on Romanticism, 2007; English Research Seminar, University of Southampton, 2008; Chawton House, New Directions in Austen Studies, 2009; Nineteenth Century Studies Association, 2009 and 2010; and the Irish Society for the Study of Children's Literature, 2010.

Many friends and scholars have provided their expertise, support, or challenging questions at crucial moments: Gillian Dow, Pamela Gilbert, Elizabeth Helsinger, Leah Hochman, Kari Lokke, Anne MacMaster, Anne Mellor, Greg Miller, William H. Page, Amy Robinson, R. Allen Shoaf, Steven Smith, Gavin Taylor, Maureen Turim, Charlotte Yeldham, and members of the Millsaps Arts and Letters Works-in-Progress group. Judith Page thanks her students in a graduate seminar at the University of Florida on Women and Gardens in the Long Nineteenth Century (Fall 2009) for reading parts of the manuscript and enlarging on our ideas in their own work.

Most important, we acknowledge our families. Bill, Jason, Steve, and Matt supported our project wholeheartedly, with unwavering confidence in its completion. For their love and encouragement, and in recognition of the influence they have had on our work, we dedicate this book to the women in our families: to our daughters by birth and marriage, Rebekah, Hannah, Katy, and Kelly, and to the memory of our mothers, Mollie Marcus Wallick and Elise Lawton Isleib. The writers and artists that we study in the following chapters understood the crucial role that mother-mentors have in the cultivation of their children's future, and our dedication acknowledges the power of that role in making all of our gardens – and this book – a reality.

An excerpt from an early version of Chapter 1 appeared as Elise L. Smith's "Centering the Home-Garden: The Arbor, Wall, and Gate in Moral Tales for Children," *Children's Literature* 36 (2008): 24–48. An early, short version of Chapter 5 appeared as Judith W. Page's "Dorothy Wordsworth's 'Gratitude to Insensate Things': Gardening in *The Grasmere Journals*," *Wordsworth Circle* 39 (Winter–Spring 2008): 19–23, and a portion of Chapter 7 appeared as Judith W. Page's "Reforming Honeysuckles: Hannah More's *Cœlebs in Search of a Wife* and the Politics of Women's Gardens," *Keats–Shelley Journal* (2006): 11–36. We thank those journals for giving us permission to reprint materials.

Introduction

In Charlotte Smith's *Rambles Farther* (1796), Mrs. Woodfield plans an expedition for the four young girls under her tutelage. Her exemplary daughters Henrietta and Elizabeth are passionate botanists who prefer the idea of a visit to Curtis's Botanic Garden followed by some nurseries in Chelsea; the other two girls, however, seem to require more of what Wordsworth called "outrageous stimulation,"[1] in this case Merlin's museum of mechanical swings, horses, and other amusements.[2] Her brother proposes a compromise: "I will decide for two of these pleasures, since you have time for them; and Ella here will like the miracles of Merlin, as well as your two little disciples of Flora the gardens they are to visit afterwards."[3] Mrs. Woodfield and her daughters are fictional representations of the passion for gardens and botany so prevalent at the end of the eighteenth century, and as we shall see in our *Disciples of Flora*, well into the next. Smith's *Rural Walks* (1795) and *Rambles Farther* illustrate the kind of mental and moral cultivation that could be acquired through gardening and botanizing, differing notably from the frivolous entertainments embodied in Ella and her desire for the more immediate pleasures to be found at Merlin's.

From 1780 to 1870, a period marked by major political, technological, and cultural changes, the domesticated landscape was central to women's complex negotiation of private and public life. Women writers and artists used the subject matter of gardens and plants to educate their audience, to enter into political and cultural debates, particularly around issues of gender and class, and to signal moments of intellectual and spiritual insight. As more women became engaged in gardening and botanical pursuits, the meanings of gardens – recognized here both as actual sites of pleasure and labor and as conceptual or symbolic spaces – became more complex. During this period the home landscape functioned more overtly than previously as a transitional or liminal zone. Often viewed as an enclosed refuge during the late eighteenth and nineteenth centuries, valued for its safe removal from the noise, grime, and moral decay of the increasingly industrialized city, the garden also offered a protected vantage point for engagement with the wider world and the means of expressing one's skills and aspirations to a larger audience than the intimate family circle.

The textuality of gardens – the recognition that they, in the words of John Dixon Hunt, "represent the larger world outside them"[4] – is central to our investigation of both canonical and lesser-known women, and we will see that a study of the domesticated landscape crosses many divides as it reveals unexpected relationships among women. Gardens provided women with a new language and authority to negotiate between domestic space and the larger world. Although this more expansive form of domesticity still highlighted the virtues associated with the feminized home, it also promised a wider field of action. In this way framing devices such as doors and windows, boundaries such as walls and gates, and spatial relationships such as those between the drawing room and arbor become important markers of the dynamic between inside and outside, refuge and prospect. Despite the visual and symbolic constraints of the walled enclosure that was considered the ideal for middle- and upper-class properties, the garden offered expanded possibilities that re-centered domesticity outward. During this period many women writers and artists focused on that spatial progression from the interior of the home into and through the garden.

The idea of cultivating a garden became a foundational metaphor in educational theory and practice. Both the radical Mary Wollstonecraft and the evangelical conservative Hannah More, for instance, use versions of this metaphor of the garden in their writings on women and education. Wollstonecraft opens her *Vindication of the Rights of Woman* (1792) by claiming that women's manners are in an unhealthy state; like flowers that have been planted in an over-rich soil, "strength and usefulness are sacrificed to beauty."[5] More also grounds her *Strictures on the Modern System of Female Education* (1799) in a poetics of cultivation, arguing that pampered women are like the plants of "the luxuriant southern clime," a comparison which encourages indolence rather than industrious attempts at improvement.[6] Both writers prefer the nurturing of unpretentious native plants to hothouse exotics, but most importantly they shift the discourse from seeing women themselves as flowers or gardens – objects to be admired while fresh and blooming – to identifying women as agents, as gardeners involved in the process of growth. They turn the tables on writers like Rousseau, who in his popular *Letters on the Elements of Botany, Addressed to a Lady* (translated into English in 1796) muses to the recipient, "I fancy to myself a charming picture of my beautiful cousin busy with her glass examining heaps of flowers, a hundred times less flourishing, less fresh, and less agreeable than herself."[7] This language of cultivation, with its contested positioning of women as objects or agents, permeates the discussions of gender and education from the 1780s on into the Victorian period. Gardening is both a metaphor for development and itself a form of mental cultivation, an activity that inspires growth for the people who engage in it.

Given this horticultural underpinning of educational theory and practice, it is not surprising that garden settings and botanical instruction appear in many of the children's books and instructional texts of the period, as in *Rambles Farther*. Gardens, greenhouses, and nearby woods and fields become the site and subject matter of much instruction for children and young adults; scientific, moral, religious, and epistemological issues dominate the discussion. Gardens are places where children learn to sympathize with the minutest details of creation – in fact a major theme of botanical writing is the cultivation of sympathy. The traditional association between women and the ethics of care led to the garden being viewed as a school for virtue, evident throughout the children's literature discussed here.

Because of the garden's associations with Edenic myths, intimacy, and childhood, it was often constructed by women writers and artists as an idyllic realm, imbued with nostalgia and memory. As a result, we often see emotional connections with the garden, as it becomes a statement of personality and character as much as a stage for practical action. Women also engaged in a robust practical literature that developed in the early nineteenth century, including gardening manuals and how-to books. These texts cover not only the practical questions of gardening but also, especially in the Victorian period, issues of social propriety. While Dorothy Wordsworth dug in the dirt without commenting on its social acceptability, writers such as Jane Loudon address the question of whether a woman who does so can still be considered a lady. The class-consciousness of practical gardening literature also permeates the novels of Margaret Oliphant, for whom gardens are both important sites for revelation of character and key signifiers of social class and standing in the community. Oliphant's Carlingford novels admirably display the influence of horticultural theory and practice in mid-Victorian England.

Our study draws on a variety of theoretical sources, including early studies of the cultural role of space by Gaston Bachelard and Yi-Fu Tuan, the more garden-oriented writings of John Dixon Hunt, and recent texts by the feminist geographers Gillian Rose, Doreen Massey, Mona Domosh, and Joni Seager. Bachelard's concept of "topoanalysis," for instance, and his discussion of the "dialectics of outside and inside" in *The Poetics of Space*

(1958) inform our understanding of the garden as a bounded but mutable and permeable space. His concern with notions of refuge and enclosure and his interest in thresholds and doors are also important to our analysis. In marking a human tendency to move outward, necessitating an expansion beyond the nest – what he calls an "explosion toward the outside" – his approach undergirds our own.[8]

Tuan's distinctions in *Space and Place: The Perspective of Experience* (1977) between freedom and security also inform our readings and conceptual frame. He asserts that the stable centering of "place" (or home, in our use of the term) should be recognized as a "concretion of value" from which "the openness, freedom, and threat of space" (the world around and beyond the home) can be experienced. Our idea of the domesticated landscape as an arena for practical, political, and symbolic action has roots in Tuan's statement that "Space assumes a rough coordinate frame centered on the mobile and purposive self."[9] Building on Tuan, we argue that women in their various modes of textualizing – whether in their personal lives, intimate letters and diaries, published writings, or visual images – acquired additional layers of private and public meaning by adding the landscape spaces beyond the home to their root sense of domestic place. Both Bachelard and Tuan also recognize the role of memory and nostalgia in the spatial mapping of our lives, a process involving the continual renegotiation of ideas about center and periphery over time.

Stephanie Ross, in *What Gardens Mean* (1998), proposes "enclosure" and "invitation" as two modes of experiencing the garden: the former suggests "comfort, security, passivity, rest, privacy, intimacy, sensory focus, and concentrated attention," the latter, presupposing a long view or prospect, incorporates curiosity and risk as well as ownership and control. Although she does not acknowledge here the ways in which such a dichotomy is overlaid with traditional views of sexual difference, the gendering of protected spaces and open prospects, or, more simplistically, inside and outside, is a commonplace by now.[10] The feminized home of the Victorian period is perhaps the starkest example of this idea of interior removal.

Hunt's *Greater Perfections: The Practice of Garden Theory* (2000) is a key text in theorizing gardens and garden writing, and his basic definition of a garden both as bounded space and as a cultural object that functions rhetorically is also central for us. His statement that "Garden enclosures both define their spaces and appeal across boundaries – by way of representation, imitation, and allusion – to a world dispersed elsewhere" acknowledges the function of gardens as powerful social signifiers. As "concentrated or perfected forms of place-making," they highlight the changing realities of women who were struggling to make meaningful lives within the limited scope of action available to them.[11]

Gillian Rose and other feminist geographers provide us with a different way of interpreting the role of gardens in women's lives. Rose's recognition of "the everyday [as] the arena through which patriarchy is (re)created – and contested" supports our study of the garden as a space in which women both were trained within traditional structures and asserted themselves against those constraints. In her groundbreaking book *Feminism and Geography* (1993) Rose reveals the limitations of humanistic geography as practiced by Tuan, among others, and in its place she calls for a feminist approach that accommodates women "as complex and diverse social subjects." She reminds us that only an essentially masculinist geography could characterize the home-ground so unproblematically as a safe and stable place, and in fact she proposes that female identity in all of its diversity can only flourish through the loss of the constraining "safety" of home. She further critiques the humanistic geographers' concept of "topophilia" as centered on an idealized view of "place" that involves "thoughtless passivity and unthinking immersion in the natural." Rose observes that landscape is more than a cultural construct based on visual perception, but that it also entails a complex system of power relations.[12] As Susan Ford notes in "Landscape Revisited: A Feminist Reappraisal" (1991), the controlling and "unavoidably phallocentric" gaze that surveys the sweeping vistas of a landscape is fundamentally different from the participatory "matriarchal aesthetic." She suggests that the socialized female gaze is "transvestite," in that it has been socialized to take part in the masculine survey but also is rooted in quotidian details. The domestic garden of the late eighteenth and early nineteenth centuries is thus, according to Ford, "a landscape which is heavily feminized," blending "the rational and emotional dimensions of those who participated in it."[13]

Rose presents the notion of "paradoxical space," or "complex and contradictory spatialities," as a way to reorient our understanding of geography away from an exclusive view to one that "speaks of power, resistance and the acknowledgement of difference." She deconstructs the opposition of inside and outside as a Deleuzian "snag or … pleat," rather than as two separate, neatly bounded domains, and we too find that women's movement in and through the garden is a complex mapping that calls for an acceptance of this kind of paradoxical spatial pleating.[14] As Rose argues, "These feminist maps are multiple and intersecting, provisional and shifting,"[15] and the fluctuating nature of this kind of geography lies at the heart of our analysis of garden spaces.

Like Rose, Doreen Massey in *Space, Place, and Gender* (1994) complicates the idea of home as a bounded, secure place and instead proposes that because of the dynamic nature of social relations the identity of home must be "for ever open to contestation": "A large component of the identity of that place called home derived precisely from the fact that it had always in one way or another been open; constructed out of movement, communication, social relations which always stretched beyond it."[16] The garden, we propose, is one of the spaces of greatest flux in the eighteenth- and nineteenth-century view of the home-ground, as it operates as a kind of valve (or pleat) that paradoxically both reinforces and destabilizes the idea of the home as a protected retreat.

Observing that "space is gendered," Mona Domosh and Joni Seager in *Putting Women in Place: Feminist Geographers Make Sense of the World* (2001) assert that "spatial organization and relations are not simply a neutral backdrop for human dramas, but instead help to shape them." Like many geographers, they use the terms space and place as contrasting signifiers, space simply referring to "the three-dimensionality of life" whereas place is "invested with meaning," especially of a personal nature.[17] They recognize that "the geography of daily life" is traversed by – and thus "invested with meaning" by – physical bodies, and "When the 'wrong' bodies are in the 'wrong' places – when women walk into male spaces or vice versa – this is often translated into a challenge to norms of feminine or masculine behavior."[18] Following their lead, throughout this book the question of who belongs in the garden – whose place is it, and how is it invested with meaning? – underlies our exploration of women's texts and images.

Our book also takes into account the groundbreaking work of Ann B. Shteir, *Cultivating Women, Cultivating Science* (1996), although our embracing of gardens in the more inclusive sense is wider; Shteir focuses more specifically on botany, especially on the divide that appears in the early Victorian period between amateur botanists and science, the realm largely claimed by men. More recently, in *Botany, Sexuality and Women's Writing 1760–1830* (2007), Sam George recognizes that the feminization of botany actually begins with such writers as Rousseau, whose *Letters* were influential at the end of the eighteenth century. As we argue here, many women writers in various genres question Rousseau's association of women with flowers, choosing instead to resist such a passive relationship with nature. Furthermore, unlike Shteir and George, we are interested in the broader category of women and domesticated landscape, which includes botanical writing but also texts related to gardening, garden design, and horticulture as well as the more didactic or moralizing approaches found in children's literature and etiquette manuals of the period. Other recent books, such as Jill H. Casid's *Sowing Empire: Landscape and Colonization* (2004) and Beth Fowkes Tobin's *Colonizing Nature: The Tropics in British Arts and Letters, 1760–1820* (2005), also intersect in interesting ways, but both of these studies are centered on colonial gardening or the influence of empire.[19]

Many early nineteenth-century women – living and writing from the inside, quite literally, of this spatial divide – attempted to validate their domestic lives by presenting the small, daily details, unremarkable when considered individually, as a model in microcosm for the larger ideal of a well-ordered society based on duty and devotion. The fictional mother in *Correspondence between a Mother and Her Daughter at School* (1817), co-authored by Jane Taylor and her mother Ann, explains in a letter extolling the virtues of home that "*Men* have much to do with the world without; *our* field of action is circumscribed." But she added in a significant aside, "yet, to confine ourselves within its humble bounds, and to discharge our duties there, may produce effects equally beneficial and extensive with their wider range."[20] These writers and artists often drew on garden imagery to illustrate the ideal of an inner sanctum, characterized by growth, beauty, and meaningful work, within and from which women could influence larger spheres of action. For the popular Mrs. Ellis in her book on *The Mothers of England* (1843), the mother is "enclosed, as it were, in the home-garden with her daughters."[21] Reminding us of Edmund Burke's gendered reading of the sublime and the beautiful, she compares the simple, small events of a woman's life to "the green knolls in a lovely landscape, left out by the painter as insignificant in comparison with the rocky heights, the falling torrents, and the precipitous ravines; yet chosen by the husbandman, and cultivated with particular care, because they alone are capable of yielding the harvest upon which his happiness depends." Her conservative view, in which women should be content with "the freshness, the verdure, and fertility" of home rather than always seeking for the "cold and barren" heights,[22] is balanced, as we will see, by those women who used the garden and near landscape as a zone for experimentation, a place to flex their physical and mental muscles, thus prompting greater freedom and experimentation in their lives.

We have divided the book into four interrelated parts, and in the first of these, "Moral order: the school of nature," we discuss instructional texts in several genres and some of the educational roles that gardens play in the stages of human development. Often these books are set in what we would now call learning communities. In "The visual frame: constructing a view," we present public as well as private modes of apprehending nature through various framing devices – both physical, such as the window, and experiential. The third part, "Personal practice: making gardens grow," includes analyses of those texts that are technically how-to books as well as journals and diaries that function as ways of seeing and interpreting the meaning of gardens. Finally, in "Narrative strategies: plotting the garden," we focus on the ways that gardens are represented and employed to further developments of plot or character in several works of narrative fiction.

Chapter 1, "'In the home-garden': moral tales for children," explores the way in which many of the books written for children during the late eighteenth and early nineteenth centuries use flowers, gardening, botany, and the larger natural landscape as a means of inculcating a range of virtues, both for the young girls and boys who were the primary recipients of these lessons and for the parents who were the educational mentors. Mrs. Ellis's "home-garden," a place of beauty nurtured by women and their apprentice daughters as a haven or retreat, was a common ideal of the period. The cultivated garden was a training ground for children, set apart from the wildness of nature but more flexible, both spatially and socially, than the confined rooms of the home. Operating as a moral as well as physical threshold, the garden separated the refuge of home from the risky freedom of more public spaces while also serving as a transition between the two. Through the lessons learned in that safe, protected realm, children's unruly temperaments could be transformed into the moral order of a virtuous life. The arbor was a key site for the apprenticeship of children into their adult responsibilities, as it enabled experimentation and role-playing, while the garden wall and gate were recognized as clear boundaries, particularly for girls, to demarcate the extent of their domestic domain. Spatial markers connecting the house with the garden (the window, the porch, the arbor) and the garden with the outside world (the gate, the fence) served as physical and moral tropes around which children's lives were structured.

Chapter 2, "The 'botanic eye': botany, miniature, and magnification," looks at botanical texts, many of them designed for children and young adults, through theories of the miniature: Bachelard's idea that "the minuscule, a narrow gate, opens an entire world," as well as Susan Stewart's claim in *On Longing* (1993) that the miniature "presents domesticated space as a model of order, proportion, and balance."[23] In many women's botanical texts from the late eighteenth century through the early Victorian period, the goal of teaching botany is not just – or even mainly – scientific knowledge; instead, botany is a discipline that leads the student to observe nature closely and to imagine the interior world that microscopy and magnification reveal as infinitely expansive. Although the overt goal of such sympathetic apprehension of minute particulars is greater understanding of plant structure and "physiology," an appreciation of the divine underpinning of these insights gives the study of smallness a sense of grandeur and discovery.

As seen in Chapter 3, "Picturing the 'home landscape': the nature of accomplishment," women represented the natural world in a variety of ways during this period, from the amateur hobbies of needlework, flower painting, and sketching the landscape to the more professional skill of botanical illustration. Although authors such as Hannah More scornfully rejected the emphasis on female "accomplishments" — setting the young woman intent on superficial pleasure and admiration in opposition to the sensible, reasonable wife and mother — others recognized the value of seeing and ordering (and thus taming or domesticating) the world of nature through a woman's eyes. The practical, the sensible, the intellectual, and the aesthetic were all components of this new mix of female attributes under scrutiny during this period. The paintings of the successful Royal Academy exhibitor Maria Spilsbury and the botanical illustrations of Anna Maria Hussey will reveal the shifting divide between interior and exterior, near and distant, and amateur and professional. As creative, mobile women operating in multiple spheres, these two artists, like others discussed in this chapter, used their images of nature to acknowledge their actual and metaphorical location in the world. Centered in the home, they were able to apply what we might call domestic confidence to their observation of the landscape, whether in its minute particularities, as with Hussey's study of fungi, or its framing of personal narratives, as in Spilsbury's portraits and cottage scenes.

Ann and Jane Taylor are well known for their children's poetry, such as *Original Poems for Infant Minds* (1804–05), but they also wrote a wealth of letters and other personal texts, as explored in Chapter 4, "Commanding a view: the Taylor sisters and the construction of domestic space." Jane Taylor's *Memoirs and Poetical Remains* (compiled by her brother and published in 1826) and Ann's *Autobiography* (edited by her son and published in 1874) are valuable sources that set up a personal topography, laden with nostalgic and poetic overtones, that allowed them to explore the emotional spaces of home. Boundaries or transitional motifs of various kinds — including doors, windows, porches, arbors, and, in a larger sense, the garden itself — served for them as both linking and separating devices, helping to orient them within the larger domestic refuge. Through their public and private writing the sisters reconfigured the idea of home as an emotional and spatial construction, affected by memory, loss, and nostalgia as well as the ordinary events of lived experience.

Chapter 5, "Dorothy Wordsworth: gardening, self-fashioning, and the creation of home," proposes that the reconfiguration and construction of the garden as a central element of home was the work of both Dorothy Wordsworth's imagination and her hands. Her experiment in gardening and the written record that she kept set the pattern for the way she approached the natural world, as documented in several travel journals in later years. The garden is both a very real place where Wordsworth collects and names native plants and also the textual space where she fashions herself and reflects on what it means to be at home in the world. Dorothy Wordsworth's imaginative labor, including her journals and travel diaries which she shared in manuscript with her intimate circle, stands on its own as a contribution to the history of gardening, garden writing, and the aesthetic and ethical response to the natural world.

According to the early gardening manuals by Maria Elizabeth Jacson, Elizabeth Kent, Louisa Johnson, and Jane Loudon discussed in Chapter 6, "'Work in a small compass': gardening manuals for women," the high standards set for work in the home – including neatness, order, and industry – should not be lowered in the domesticated landscape outside. In Loudon's books, in particular, we find a certain tension among various overlapping and sometimes competing ideas about gardening, in particular about what could be considered appropriate action for middle-class women in the garden. Should they serve only as designers or managers, in their role as arbiters of taste, or was it suitable for them to do some, or all, of the manual labor? As supervisors, they could refine and aestheticize nature from a decorous distance, but when they picked up shovels to dig, did the dirt and sweat of their labor orient them too shockingly toward the masculine? Loudon, Johnson, and other early writers of garden manuals vacillated at times between the rhetoric of social expectations and the practical reality of active women. Though occasionally retreating into the standard language of Victorian discourse about femininity, they enabled their readers to see new possibilities of enterprise and occupation in the garden.

Chapter 7, "'Unbought pleasure': gardening in *Cœlebs in Search of a Wife* and *Mansfield Park*," considers two novels, Hannah More's *Cœlebs* (1808) and Austen's *Mansfield Park* (1814), as representing two different perspectives on the "usefulness" of gardens. For More, the garden is intimately connected to the ideal Christian woman's philanthropic work in the community. Her character Lucilla Stanley uses the garden to launch her philanthropy and to teach others the virtue of charity. She grows plants (or directs her gardener to do so) to serve the poor but is still concerned that gardening is too pleasurable to be good for the soul. In *Mansfield Park* Fanny Price, on the other hand, cultivates a small miniature garden of potted geraniums, anticipating Elizabeth Kent's *Flora Domestica* (1823), for her own health and well-being. In the course of doing so, she succeeds in cultivating her consciousness and fashioning herself as a more confident person. Austen's style, her subtle development of free indirect discourse, captures the meaning of Fanny's private garden world and narratively reveals Fanny's heightened awareness.

Margaret Oliphant's series of stories and novels based in Carlingford (1861–76) focuses our attention in Chapter 8, "Margaret Oliphant's Chronicles of Carlingford and the meaning of Victorian gardens." In these texts, Oliphant uses various styles of gardens and landscape architecture as indicators of status and aspiration and as a revelation of character. The garden becomes a powerful device for Oliphant to further plot and narrative lines. Oliphant develops a narrative geography based on the layout of gardens around the two main residential streets of Carlingford – the walled, secluded gardens and houses of Grange Lane and the more modest and more visible gardens of Grove Street. As we shall demonstrate, Oliphant's fictional gardens reveal many of the issues that engaged garden writers, such as the Loudons and Shirley Hibberd, about the representational qualities of certain styles of gardens and of particular flowers and plants.

Women in this key transitional period from 1780 to 1870 operated within the garden in a variety of ways, using it as a space for digging and weeding, cultivating and training the young, moralizing and contemplating, scientific experimentation, and aesthetic representation. They still typically saw the garden through the lens of their domestic responsibilities and pleasures, however, so the skills as well as the metaphors they used were often borrowed from the more familiar world inside their homes. But the garden, while tied both spatially and rhetorically to the home at its center, also provided women with a new space for active engagement with the world – a space in which to move more boldly and see more clearly. In this way it served as a ground for both social and intellectual experimentation, as we will demonstrate in the following pages.

PART I
Moral order: the school of nature

CHAPTER I

"In the home-garden": moral tales for children

According to Harriet Martineau in her popular book on *Household Education* (1848), it is "instinctive" for a small child to have "a passionate love of flowers." As evidence, she describes a sentimental morning scene in the border with a little girl murmuring to the plants, "Come, you little flower; open, you little flower! When will you open your pretty blue eye?!"[1] A similar image appears on a child's gift plate labeled "The Flower Basket," probably from around the same time (Fig. 1.1): a young girl poses in a garden with flowers blooming around her, suggesting an equation between the charming beauty and innocence of both the girl and the blossoms. Martineau characterizes this association between flowers and children, especially girls, as "charming" but argues that it is "the lowest form of human affection till it is trained into close connection with the higher sentiments."[2] Many of the books written for children in the decades leading up to Martineau's treatise, especially beginning in the 1780s during "the didactic age of youthful literature,"[3] do in fact use what we call the domesticated landscape as a means of inculcating a range of virtues, both for the middle-class girls and boys who were the primary recipients of these lessons and for the parents who were the educational mentors. As Morgan and Richards have suggested, the garden as "'soft' nature ... granted refining and civilizing powers."[4]

Although the rhetorical strategies of many of these didactic stories were rooted in evangelical Christianity, the authors' religious leanings ranged from the conservatism of Mary Martha Sherwood, Sarah Trimmer, and the *Child's Companion* (published by the Religious Tract Society in London) to more liberal dissenters such as Anna Letitia Barbauld and the Taylor sisters. But all agreed that the mother's influence was particularly vital for her daughters: as Sarah Ellis notes in *The Mothers of England* (1843), "If ever, then, the care of a judicious mother is wanted, it is in the opening feelings of a young girl, when branches of the tenderest growth have to be cherished and directed, rather than checked and lopped off." Ellis extends the

Fig. 1.1. "The Flower Basket" and "The Cottage Girl," children's gift plates.

popular metaphor to reinforce her point. The child, being like an "opening flower," must be carefully cultivated so that "weeds of evil growth" are kept at bay. The home becomes "the fair garden" tended by the mother, and, more pointedly, she is "enclosed, as it were, in the home-garden with her daughters."[5] Ellis's "home-garden," a place of beauty nurtured by women and their apprentice daughters as a haven or retreat, was a common ideal of the period.

The garden was a training ground for children, providing a flexible, experimental area for role-playing, safely removed from the dangers of the world beyond but also freer and more expansive than the controlled spaces within the house. And through lessons learned in the garden the roughness of childhood could be tempered and refined into moral order.[6] Applying the kind of topoanalysis found in Bachelard, we recognize that the garden or near landscape in these texts provided a sheltered location for imaginative play and ethical training. As a moral, psychological, and physical threshold, it operated as both a dividing and a connecting device between the safe interiority of home and the risky adventure of public spaces – following Rose's Deleuzian idea of a spatial "pleat" that folds together places in a complex interconnection.[7] Tuan's analysis of "the security and stability" of place, a rooted centrality to which one returns after "the openness, freedom, and threat" of unbounded space, will be relevant to our discussion, although we acknowledge Rose's theory about "complex and contradictory spatialities" that undermine the dualities implicit in Tuan.[8]

We will argue here that the arbor or garden-house became the core of the domesticated virtuous garden, a place for children to experiment with adult roles and responsibilities. The garden wall and gate functioned in turn as clear boundaries to signal the extent of the domestic domain, but also as enticing invitations to a larger world of action beyond the wall. In considering the spatial dynamics of the homestead, Bachelard highlights the symbolic role of the door (or garden gate, in our reading) as a fulcrum between interior and exterior that also opens up possibilities of both security and freedom. The garden (because of, or despite, its malleable spaces) was a model for many of the character traits most closely associated with middle-class women of the period, and by extension their daughters: industry, duty, patience, perseverance, humility, and charity, among others.

In this chapter, then, we will consider the garden as a school for virtue: a site both for modeling appropriate behavior in children, particularly girls, and for contemplating the possibilities – and dangers – beyond the boundaries of that domesticated space. Since many of the central ideas recur throughout the didactic texts of the late eighteenth and early nineteenth centuries, often with only minor variations, we have fashioned our argument thematically rather than chronologically and have drawn from a wide range of texts, both verbal and visual. Children's illustrations, being distilled representations of more complex or lengthy narratives, offer an immediate message to the reader/viewer. Although frequently more simplistic than a nuanced text, they can also transmit the central point powerfully and directly, thus revealing the underlying assumptions and stereotypes about childhood, class structure, and gender expectations.

MOTHERS AND CHILDREN: "ENLIGHTENED DOMESTICITY"

Ann Martin Taylor, author of *Maternal Solicitude for a Daughter's Best Interests* (1813), suggested that children's books should "blend amusement with instruction,"[9] and the garden, with its many pleasures and multiple opportunities for exemplary lessons, provided the location for a number of her poems and tales. The modest but carefully tended and walled garden setting in many children's books attests to the reality of middle-class children's lives and the bourgeois "quest for privacy."[10] These gardens in early children's literature were often contrasted with both the grand estates of the aristocracy, generally presented as examples of ostentation and vanity, and the small plots of the laboring poor (though simple cottage gardens were also frequently used as emblems of modesty and humility). A neat, productive garden reinforces the symbolic power of that liminal zone, transitional between the carefully ordered domestic interior and the world beyond the garden gate.

It is not surprising that the adults most concerned with education, parents and teachers, would be compared to gardeners tending the young like delicate plants, ensuring that they grow in physical and moral strength. Following a long tradition dating back to John Locke[11] and continuing with Mrs. Ellis, the author of *The Pleasing Instructor*, a small booklet published around 1850 by the Religious Tract Society, made this point in both the text and illustration. Just as a "careful gardener looks over his plants, and picks off the snails and grubs," so must the "kind parents or teachers" protect children from their "many naughty ways and ill tempers, which are very disagreeable."[12] In the print's garden setting, a man hands a flower to a young boy with one hand, while his other is raised in admonition. Usually, though, it was the mother who was the earliest instructor of reading, basic factual knowledge, and, most importantly, moral precepts, this being seen as one of the central duties of a woman's life. Mary Wright Sewell, who was grateful to be a woman since it allowed her to have "the first word with the children," worried that many parents spend less time training their children, "our little human plants," than gardeners do tending their plots.[13]

The larger social impact of these views about the mother's role has been disputed in modern scholarship. Mitzi Myers provides a powerful corrective to the argument that in the process of socializing girls writers such as Ann Martin Taylor only strengthened the hierarchy that subordinated women.[14] She proposes instead that Georgian literature for children, "a genre shaped by gender," reflects "maternal and pedagogical power."[15] Referring to Maria Edgeworth but extrapolating more broadly, she characterizes the works written by "mother-pedagogues" as providing "an alternate model grounded in mental development and the accessible heroisms of daily life."[16] Edgeworth herself explained that she wanted to give her young readers "some knowledge and control of their own minds in seeming trifles."[17] Elizabeth Dolan recognizes that Charlotte Smith, in "imagining a professionalized, collaborative version of motherhood for women," similarly insists on training young women in "self-reliance and emotional resilience."[18] This approach – what Myers terms "enlightened domesticity"[19] – may indeed have been seen as empowering by the mothers who bought the books and the children who read them, since despite the sometimes heavy-handed didacticism they were being provided with tools and models for taking control of their own lives (within the limitations operative in their social context). Certainly middle-class girls were being socialized into the virtuous life defined by their parents – as J. H. Plumb notes, these works sold so well precisely because they presented the virtues that parents considered necessary for their children to succeed as adults.[20] But the ideological freight included a large measure of other middle-class attributes that pertained to a girl's process of maturation, the formation of a strong identity, and a developing sense of self-control.

Several illustrations of the relationship between mother/teacher and child from the late eighteenth century will highlight the complex signification of plants and gardens. The frontispiece engraving in C. G. Salzmann's *Elements of Morality* (1791), translated by Mary Wollstonecraft, centers on the sedately dressed mother surrounded by her children in the shade of the garden, while the windows of their home form a reassuring backdrop (Fig. 1.2). The simple ordinariness of this scene, with the rectilinear pattern of the house providing a clear, rational framework for the family group, is markedly different from William Blake's "Infant Joy" (Fig. 1.3) from *Songs of Innocence* (1789). Although Blake also represented the tender care of a mother, his approach is unworldly and imaginative, full of twining tendrils that cradle and caress. The flame-like petals enfold the mother and her infant, watched over by an attentive angel, and the unfurled bud at the right is surely a reference to the baby, so often described as a sweet or innocent bud in the literature of the period. We find an intriguing association between Wollstonecraft and Blake in his illustration for the frontispiece

Fig. 1.2. Frontispiece illustration in Mary Wollstonecraft's translation of C. G. Salzmann, *Elements of Morality*.

of her *Original Stories from Real Life* (1791) (Fig. 1.4). He presents the governess and the two girls under her tutelage in a static, formal composition curiously akin to the Crucifixion, or perhaps more fittingly, the Madonna of Mercy. Blake's teacher, frontal, imposing, and centralized with arms outspread, becomes a savior figure for the two girls who stand under her protection.[21] The gracefully swaying poses of the girls are echoed by the twining vines behind them, reminiscent of the jessamines growing around

Fig. 1.3.   William Blake, "Infant Joy," from *Songs of Innocence*.

Fig. 1.4.   Frontispiece illustration by William Blake in Mary Wollstonecraft, *Original Stories from Real Life*.

the good Mrs. Trueman's windows in Wollstonecraft's story. The symbolic relation between vines and women is an old one, found, for example, in Psalm 128:3: "Thy wife shall be as a fruitful vine by the sides of thine house." An anonymous poet developed this popular analogy in a stanza quoted in the 1828 commonplace book of Mary Young from Essex: "Man is the rugged lofty pine" and "Woman the graceful slender vine" who twines sweetly around his "rough bark."[22] She tempers and softens his strength, but needs his stalwart frame as a support. Thus the vines in Blake and Wollstonecraft take on gendered associations, framing the narrative both literally and metaphorically.

The formative period of children's literature is often characterized in starkly dichotomous terms: the imaginative or fanciful approach, on the one hand, with its roots in early fairy tales, chapbooks, and a Wordsworthian vision of childhood as "the open ground / Of Fancy," and the didactic and moralizing emphasis, on the other, with its "taste for truth and realities."[23] Geoffrey Summerfield, who reinforces this opposition in the title of his book on eighteenth-century children's literature, *Fantasy and Reason*, is particularly harsh in his criticism of these regulatory texts, akin to conduct books in their goal of training the reader's habits: he describes the women authors as "morally shrill" and "stridently enlightened."[24] But like Samuel Pickering and Mitzi Myers, we find that the best of these writers make their moral point in a way that appeals to the imagination through characters and situations drawn from the daily lives of ordinary children and relayed with simple, direct language.[25] Jane and Ann Taylor, Maria Elizabeth Budden, Maria Edgeworth, and Mary Wollstonecraft, among others, will serve as key resources in this chapter as we explore the relationship among girls, gardening, and the construction of a virtuous life.

THE GARDEN AS A SCHOOL FOR VIRTUE

Most women who included garden imagery in their children's books were not interested in the practical aspects of digging, sowing, and weeding, which we will consider in Chapter 6, but instead were searching for suitable metaphors for inculcating virtues in their young readers. In Charlotte Smith's *Rambles Farther* (1796), Mrs. Woodfield's priorities are clear: first, "the affairs of the house," and only after those are attended to can she turn to other "local attachments" such as the garden. Smith describes Mrs. Woodfield and her young charges returning home after an extended time away in London: Ella delights in "the liberty of running upon the grass, and playing without restraint in the fields," while Elizabeth and

Henrietta are both eager to check on their garden. When she next sees her mother, Elizabeth lists the blooms in her little plot and then exclaims, "Oh! mamma, how is it possible you could forebear going into the garden the moment you came home?" Mrs. Woodfield uses this opportunity to instruct her young "disciples of Flora": "Because, my love, I had more important matters to attend to within the house: and you shall recollect, that it has always been one of my rules, as I wish it to be yours, first to fulfil my duty, that I may afterwards enjoy unalloyed pleasure." Having attended to her domestic and charitable responsibilities, she can look forward to enjoying her garden the following morning "while the dew is yet on the flowers. You know how fond I am of a garden at all times."[26] In fact, readers of Smith's earlier *Rural Walks* would remember Mrs. Woodfield reminiscing at some length about the pleasure she took in cultivating her "little spot of ground" as a girl, those being among the "happiest hours" of her youth. She muses to her daughters, "Do you know, girls, that I believe I could now draw every flower, just as they were disposed in my border?"[27] "Rural happiness," for Smith, consisted of the extended domestic realm both inside the house and outside in the garden and nearby fields and woods.[28] Thus, whereas a woman's primary duties centered on the physical upkeep of the house and the social and moral responsibilities to her family (and, depending on class, her servants and charitable dependents), many parents and educators of the period, like Smith, considered a rural setting as particularly advantageous. Because of its peace and beauty, it was the setting best suited for the rearing of children.

For these didactic writers, nature functioned in several ways: as a source of innocent pleasures but also as a sign of God's beneficence and an opportunity for lessons in virtue. A carefully trained sense of sight, especially when turned toward the natural world, was considered particularly useful for aesthetic, ethical, and scientific reasons (as we will develop in Chapter 2 with Maria Elizabeth Jacson's "penetrating eye" and Agnes Ibbetson's "long habit of viewing").[29] Focusing on the aesthetic value of cultivating sight, Smith's Mrs. Woodfield instructs her children how to acquire "a taste for rural beauty," advising them to look at those aspects of nature that might otherwise appear "insipid" with "the eye of a painter or a poet."[30] Budden includes a more fully developed lesson in *Chit Chat* (1825): Kate and Blanche learn under their aunt's tutelage "to use their eyes" when they go on walks, "for each bud and blade of grass might hide something that would pay their search." And most important, "the girls would think as well as talk of what they saw; hence their minds, in time, were full of thoughts, which could serve to please them when they were at home, and sat at work and did not talk. To think is one of our best joys; so we must hoard up, as fast as we can, good and wise and gay thoughts." Later the girls are given their own garden plots, to train them as diligent workers but also in less tangible ways: "This, this is the hour when I must toil with head, and hands, and heart; and think, and work, and feel." In fact a specific place in the garden was constructed for such reveries: "The boughs of trees hung on a seat made of roots, which in the hot months was a cool nook to work and read in, and drink tea in, and more than that, to *think* in." Contemplation of the garden led them to higher thoughts, for "Who could taste the juice of fruits and smell the scent of buds, and not send up their hearts to Him who made fruits and buds?"[31] These girls, like Helen in Budden's *Key to Knowledge* who exclaims to her mother, "how delightful is the power of thinking!," are taught that they must take responsibility for what they see and how they think. As Helen's sister observes, "If people will not look at beautiful prospects, it must be their own faults, not that of the prospect."[32]

One need not have an actual garden to benefit from such moral lessons, as made clear in a letter to "My Dear Children" in the *Child's Companion* of 1829. Regardless of whether they have a plot of their own or not, the writer assures them that each has "a garden of your mind"; but these mental gardens, when neglected, can become overgrown with unwanted plants, like "the weed of *evil passion*, which makes you angry and out of temper."[33] The garden in such analogies is no longer simply the area between the house and the outer world, but instead functions in the mapping of a child's education as a reference to the spirit as well as the mind – a site for training the rational and imaginative powers.

INDUSTRY, NEATNESS, AND MODESTY

Soil requires diligent cultivation to root out weeds, both literal and metaphorical. In line with this, industry was valued as a particularly middle-class principle, emphasized to counteract the indolence associated with young ladies pining for elegance. This crucial character trait, a linchpin of bourgeois values, is highlighted not just in children's literature but also in other texts for women, as discussed in later chapters. Ann Taylor's poem "The Flower and the Lady, About Getting Up" seems to have a very simple message – if flowers can open so regularly and cheerfully in the morning, then so should you – but the class issues raised by her choice of language are telling. The indolent young woman being gently reprimanded by the poet is addressed as "my lady fair" – an aristocrat, then, whose status is reinforced by the appearance of the "noble sun" but who still must learn the lessons of middle-class virtue from the humble flowers, birds, and bees.[34] Andrew O'Malley, in *The Making of the Modern Child*, argues that children's books like those by the Taylor sisters helped to reinforce the particular expectations of the middle class, including industry and perseverance, in contrast to the intemperance of both the unrestrained lower classes and the dissolute aristocracy.[35]

The "mother-pedagogues" of the period believed that the shaping and pruning of the small and pliant child, in particular its moral character, had an effect on the mature growth. Budden, for example, who signed all of her children's books "By a Mother," includes the quotation "As the twig is bent, the tree's inclin'd" on the title page of *Right and Wrong* (1815). This book begins with a child's garden as the context for a moral lesson:

Rosa and Agnes were born and lived in a large and busy town; they had a small garden, however, behind their house, where they could plant seeds, and watch the trees blossom and the flowers bloom. Their father gave each of them a small plot to cultivate for themselves, and told them, by attention and industry, they could there grow various flowers, and, by carefully weeding the ground, might preserve it neat and clean.

But the lazy, inattentive Rosa neglects her garden so that it is overrun with weeds, whereas the obedient, industrious Agnes works hard, and although "her back ached with stooping to weed, [and] she made herself very hot with raking the ground," her little plot of land soon produces an abundance of flowers and fruit. Budden reminds her readers, "It is only by constant endeavours, by patience, and by perseverance that knowledge and virtue are acquired." As with other such authors, here too the character of the child determines the nature of the adult. Rosa's idleness, resulting in an ill-kempt garden, later leads her to "neglect her duties" as a wife. Her house is "disorderly and confused," and just as visitors had "looked on her garden with contempt," they now "viewed her ill-managed, neglected house with disgust and disdain." Agnes, who had learned in her garden that "pleasure follows industry," grows up to be "an active, skilful, useful woman" whose house is "neat and comfortable."[36]

Industry must be directed and trained, however, and its energy used for productive purposes within the limits of class and gender expectations. An illustration included in an 1818 edition of Barbauld's *Lessons for Children of Three Years Old* shows a young mother, well protected from the elements with her bonnet and folded umbrella, encouraging a child who is little more than a toddler to smooth the path with a roller (Fig. 1.5). Tuan's description of the way a path can define a child's perception of space illuminates this image: "A bookish youngster three or four years old can already look at the

Fig. 1.5. Illustration in Anna Letitia Barbauld, *Lessons for Children of Three Years Old*, p. 42.

picture of a footpath disappearing into the woods and see himself as the hero of an impending venture."³⁷ But here, significantly, the path – and thus the child – is bounded by two constraining visual elements: the slim, strong vertical of the mother at one end and a classically inspired gazebo at the other. Ventures and adventures – the movement outward from the stability of the mother as the child's "primary place"³⁸ to the freedom and risk of the larger space beyond – have been curtailed in order to reinforce the sense of safety as the child accomplishes these first steps toward practical and moral responsibility.

Whereas industry as a character trait was especially valued by the middle class, children's stories were also full of references to gardening and the "passive virtues," listed by Hannah More as "fortitude, temperance, meekness, faith, diligence, and self-denial."³⁹ The construction of a set of feminine virtues began in the earliest years of childhood with the books available to young girls. Industry was to be in the service of home and family, never for the purpose of independent action toward what would have been considered a selfish goal. In Budden's *Always Happy* (1814) the young Serena offers to take care of her brother's garden while he is away at school. A model sister, she is eager to help even though the chores will be laborious: "The season is arrived when weeds grow rapidly, and will require constant attention. The young plants, as they increase, will need sticks to support them, the strawberry roots must be watered, and the rose-trees pruned." On his return home Felix expresses surprise at his well-tended garden, now "all neat, all owning the hand of careful cultivation." Serena responds to his praise with humility, as befits the life of service and duty for which she is being trained. Her happiness depends on his: as she explains to her mother, "if I had been idle, my brother's garden would have been unweeded, his socks unfinished, and, instead of being pleased, I should have been discontented, cross, and unhappy." Gardening is thus grouped with sewing as domestic tasks involving dutiful self-sacrifice. Early nineteenth-century attitudes about gender are implicit in her statement, "my industry has pleased you, and I am happy," and also in his final words of praise: "you thought of me when I was far away, and worked for me when I could not work for myself."[40] Here we see a young man who had been raised to expect as his right a home (and in this case a garden) tended by devoted women, to which he could return after his forays into the larger world. One might imagine Felix buying a gift plate for his sister in appreciation: one modeled after an illustration in *The Paths of Learning Strewed with Flowers* (1820), for example, with a girl sewing in a garden setting and the inscription "Ellen works *neatly*, sings *sweetly*, sews *industriously*."[41]

For Budden and the Taylor sisters, as for many other didactic authors of the period, neatness went hand in hand with industry as a way of protecting the domestic realm from the wild disorder of the world beyond. As an extreme example, Mary Martha Sherwood used the words "neat" or "clean" nine times in the first ten pages of *History of the Fairchild Family* (1818) in order to make her priorities perfectly clear. In Agnes and Maria Catlow's *The Children's Garden and What They Made of It* (1865), both Harry and Mary help to clean up their garden after a storm, but the language is indicative of the gender norms: Harry "delighted in hard work" and had "famous fun" repairing the damage, while Mary "neatly tied up everything that had been injured by the wind." Her meticulous care might be construed, in fact, as obsessive: "As Mary did not like to see a single dead leaf, she spent some hours, two or three times a week, in cutting away all that appeared; and having procured a garden basket to carry away rubbish, the garden was thus a picture of neatness and beauty."[42]

A child's garden plot was often used as a training ground, as we saw earlier in the "neatness and good order" of Agnes's garden in Budden's *Right and Wrong*. In *Lucy and Arthur*, probably by Jane Jerram, the two children are given small gardens and a set of tools, but while Arthur loves to play with the tools he often neglects to put them away, leaving them for his long-suffering sister to take to the shed. Modeling the virtues expected of an adult woman – patience and submission as well as moral suasion – the good-natured Lucy, pleased at first to oblige him, soon realizes she has a role to play in teaching him to do better: "she thought it right to oblige Arthur to take his share of the work" in order to train him to be more tidy. Her goodness thus tempers his wildness, though his initial response is revealing: "'Tidy, tidy; you and Susan are always bothering about tidy,' cried Arthur, pettishly; 'boys need never be tidy'." The rift ends in a predictable reconciliation, Arthur kindly but firmly chastised by his parents and Lucy held up as a model of feminine virtue.[43] Her merits reflect the two most important responsibilities outlined in *The Female Aegis; or, the Duties of Women from Childhood to Old Age* (1798): "contributing daily and hourly to the comfort of husbands, of parents, of brothers and sisters ... [and] forming and improving the general manners, disposition, and conduct of the other sex, by society and example."[44] Girls continued to be presented as moral guides for their brothers, as evident in this 1859 article: "The little girl in the nursery is quite ready to set herself up as guide and monitress to brothers two or three years older than herself; girls became mentors at a very early age and how many husbands are kept in good order by the love of training that is in the nature of their wives!"[45]

Among those virtues considered most suitable for young women of the period were modesty, innocence, and simplicity, and wildflowers were frequently identified in children's books as exemplars of these traits. Budden tells a story, for example, about a poor country girl selling violets, primroses, and other flowers that she'd gathered in the woods and meadows. The disdainful Caroline, looking down her nose at both the girl's class and her wares, exclaims, "Pshaw! all nasty wild flowers!," and sniffs that she much prefers garden blooms. Caroline's friend, clearly meant as the model for Budden's readers, tries to explain that all flowers are wild somewhere and that the change to artificially cultivated plants "is not always for the better" – thus gently refuting Caroline's insistence, with an arch smile, that "art produces varieties, endless varieties."[46] Budden associates Caroline with the ornamental, highly bred flowers that she admires, and the reader is led to recognize the greater value of gentle humility and simplicity, whether in the form of wildflowers or simple-hearted, kind-natured girls. The illustration (Fig. 1.6) reinforces the simplistic dichotomy between good and bad actions that is so often found in children's literature: the two girls are presented as if the reader is being given a choice (akin to the myth, popular among neoclassical artists, of Herakles' choice between Virtue and Vice). Caroline and the flower girl are so close in facial type that they could be sisters, or two sides of the same moral coin. They stand side by side as they face outward, Caroline dressed in

Industry, neatness, and modesty

Fig. 1.6. "The Flower Girl," illustration in Maria Elizabeth Budden, *Chit Chat*, p. 134.

fine clothes and an elaborate hat while the country maid with her basket of flowers is in much simpler garb.

Mrs. Woodfield in Smith's *Rural Walks* teaches a similar lesson to her city-bred niece, daughter of "a dissipated woman, related to nobility." This Caroline, too, complains of country life and yearns for "the delightful roses, lilies, and I know not how many charming flowers, for I always forget their names, which one used to have from that delightful man in Bond Street. Mamma used to have them sent her twice a week; and she had such elegant bureaus made of wire, and painted green; our drawing-room used to be quite a little paradise." Smith characterizes Caroline as twice-removed from nature, in associating flowers with the "man in Bond Street" and in seeing little need to learn their names. In this way she is unlike Mrs. Woodfield's daughter Henrietta, her "disciple of Flora," who has just come in from the garden where she was practicing botanical terminology while delighting in the snowdrops. Mrs. Woodfield, hoping to engender in her charges "a taste for rural beauty," chastises Caroline for preferring the luxuries of "an ornamented drawing-room, dressed with flowers procured by art," since "by creating artificial wants, they destroy the enjoyment of natural pleasures."[47]

In "The Violet to the Rose" Jane Taylor holds up two forms of virtue – natural and cultivated – overlaid with a relatively conservative class-consciousness to reinforce the boundaries between the lower classes and the aristocracy. The wildflowers are contrasted with "the splendours at court" where Rosa rules as queen of the garden. The violet, yearning for such gaiety, is invited by the gracious queen to visit, but she soon realizes the folly of such pretensions and recalls her lowly position as "a poor simple peasant": "here, in her hamlet alone, / Violetta will study, unseen and unknown, / Those virtues that sweetly embellish the throne, / And love her fair sovereign – the Rose."[48] The boundary, the garden wall, is thus morally as well as physically permeable – those *within*, the cultured and cultivated, the privileged, must protect themselves from the vulgar encroachers (and here the gardener's loppers play a crucial role) but they can also learn from the best of those *without* (in both a social and economic as well as spatial sense). Taylor, from the vantage point of a middle-class dissenter (someone who is herself both inside and outside the established system), does not advocate any kind of radical reconception: the rose queen is kind and gracious, but the gaiety of her court can and should be tempered with the innocent simplicity of unassuming wildflowers.

Taylor also critiques class pretension in "The World in the House" with a comparison of two homes, one a "modern mansion" with an ostentatiously grand garden enclosed by "nectar'd walls," the other also large, but neat and plain. The daughters in the worldly estate (close to London, notably) are schooled to be "Accomplish'd, artificial, showy, vain": hothouse flowers that Taylor contrasts with the "blooming train" of daughters in the more modest home. Raised to be "Industrious, active, frugal," they have the sweet innocence of wildflowers. She describes them as "the choicest fruit of country air, / – The human plant that buds and blossoms there."[49]

The state of a person's homestead was often used as an analogy for her moral state. A 1755 letter from Elizabeth Montagu comments on the resemblance between her friend Fanny Boscawen and Fanny's garden at Hatchlands, underscoring the common assumption that the garden was considered the woman's domain, reflecting her taste and character: "I walked round the park this morning. It does not consist of many acres, but the disposition of the ground, the fine verdure, and the plantations make it very pretty. It resembles the mistress of it, having preserved its native simplicity, though art and care has improved and softened it, and made it elegant."⁵⁰ Similarly, in Wollstonecraft's *Original Stories from Real Life* Lady Sly's estate, including her large "pleasure-grounds" with "a variety of summer-houses and temples, as they are called," signifies her pretension. Although she takes walks in "her paradise of a garden," she is not inspired by the simple rural pleasures that "lead to the love of God." The character of Mrs. Trueman, in contrast, is conveyed not only by her name but also by her home and garden: her house, small and white, stands near the church, and "the woodbines and jessamins that twine about the windows give it a pretty appearance." Her garden is also small but furnished with "several pretty seats" (a far cry from Lady Sly's temples), from which one can hear the nightingales singing.⁵¹

THE FUNCTION OF THE GARDEN ARBOR

Although the feminine virtues most admired by these didactic authors are those of the unassuming wildflowers, the home-garden formed the most appropriate setting for the education of young girls. The most resonant image of security within the garden during this period was the arbor, bower, or summer-house, since it served so neatly as an extension of the home, as we will see in Chapter 5 with Dorothy Wordsworth's "bower" and "little parlour" and Mary Russell Mitford's "rural arcade."⁵² The arbor can be equated with the interior hearth in terms of its symbolic force as a sign of domestic centering. From this perspective it becomes a key component of the "totalizing space" that enables a coherent view of one's place in a social geography, still possible for children in their more limited world but increasingly difficult for adults in the complex, fragmented mapping of their lives.⁵³ The arbor became a hub of outdoor activities for children, well suited for imaginative play while still typically requiring a measure of decorum – thus providing them with a site for dreaming and escape as well as for experimenting with their adult responsibilities. In a journal entry from 1748 Fanny Boscawen describes the women reading and sewing in their "charming green parlour, stored with chairs," but the rules of the house apply even in this garden retreat: while the children played on a nearby haycock they were made to understand the strict rule "that the hay never peeps out into our green parlour, but stays in the grove, which is full of dead leaves and twigs, so that it could not be kept neat, which the rest of the garden is in an eminent degree."⁵⁴

Much of the conversation, story-telling, and moralizing in Sarah Fielding's *The Governess*, published a year later, takes place in the school's arbor, a place of "Calmness and Content": "Jessamine and Honeysuckle surrounded their Seats, and played round their Heads, of which they gathered Nosegays to present each other with. They now enjoyed all the Pleasure and Happiness that attend those who are innocent and good." The frontispiece illustration in Mary Martha Sherwood's revised edition of *The Governess*, from 1820, portrays the nine girls "united in Harmony and Love": some hold hands or link their arms together while they all gather around a bowl of fruit set out in the arbor (Fig. 1.7). The theme of harmony recurs in the repetition of uniting circles, including the circular grouping of girls and the round table, basket, and fruits. These are supported in turn by the strong vertical of the church steeple in the background, a visualization of moral rectitude, and framed by the twining vines on the arbor, a common emblem of feminine dependence.[55]

The arbor is the site of many tea parties in children's literature and is often described as the favorite location for sewing and reading. The mother in Barbauld's *Lessons for Children of Three Years Old* (1778) arranges a tea party with her son, but having no outdoor furniture she has to recreate the domestic setting with more imaginative play-acting:

We will drink tea out of doors. Bring the tea-things ... But here is no table. What must we do? O, here is a large round stump of a tree, it will do very well for a table. But we have no chairs. Here is a seat of turf, and a bank almost covered with violets; we shall sit here, and you and Billy may lie on the carpet. The carpet is in the parlour. Yes, there is a carpet in the parlour, but there is a carpet here too.[56]

William McCarthy identifies Barbauld's narrator as "an Enlightenment mother,"[57] one who constructs a well-reasoned reality for her child. The world is defined according to her sense of right order, so in this case nature is tamed and brought into the household domain. But like many other late eighteenth-century women writers for children, Barbauld embeds the virtues of work and self-sacrifice within the larger context of pleasure and delight. The garden, like life, requires diligent labor but rewards us with an expanded sphere of comfort. Barbauld's mother uses domestic analogies in order to provide her son with the tools to understand and gradually extend his world.

Arbors are typically associated with girls in the moral tales of the period, however, and when boys are introduced into the narrative it is usually to reinforce gender differences. Edgeworth supports traditional sex roles in her story of the energetic young Frank, who "with vigorous and constant work on his part" and a little help from the gardener's son constructs an arbor for a neighbor while his sister Mary plans to set out roses, clematis, and honeysuckle to grow on it – and in the meantime is busy "sweeping away some litter with a new broom."[58]

The function of the garden arbor 33

Fig. 1.7. Frontispiece illustration in Sarah Fielding, *The Governess*, revised edition by Mary Martha Sherwood.

Other women authors also treated the arbor or garden bench as an outdoor site for practicing domestic skills and virtues. Jane Taylor's "The English Girl" is characterized as humble, pious, and hardworking, enjoying "sporting on the village green" but often seen "beside her cottage neat, / Knitting on the garden seat."[59] An engraved illustration for Ann Taylor's poem "My Mother," which praises maternal love and guidance and calls on young readers to be "affectionate and kind" in return, shows a mother seated in the garden in front of her vine-covered cottage (Fig. 1.8).[60] She has put her work aside to tend to her young daughter's doll, thus acting as a model of tender care, and a plump cat dozes by her side to reinforce the mood of domestic peace. The illustration in an early American edition of the Taylors' *Original Poems* presents a more complex composition (Fig. 1.9). The parents are seated in an arbor shaded by a grape vine with the mother as the central focus, and in an unusual display of physical affection she puts one arm around her husband's shoulder. But it is the relationship between the mother and daughter that best conveys the poet's point: the mother receives a nosegay from the little girl while her son looks away and plays with his hobby-horse, thus confirming that the poem is intended for girls as a kind of primer on how to be good wives and mothers themselves. Similarly, in the illustration for a short story in one of the popular Peter Parley books, one of the two "good girls" sits in the arbor busy with her sewing while the other kneels on the ground by the garden bed. Several tools lie on the ground beside her, along with a pile of uprooted weeds as a sign of her industry (Fig. 1.10). The text (stressing the syllables to encourage young readers) describes them as being "full of joy in their gar-den, El-len with her nee-dle close-ly at work mak-ing a shirt for her grand-fa-ther, and Maud clear-ing out the weeds from the gar-den beds."[61]

In many children's books the garden was an alternate space for training in social and domestic skills, as in the engraving of four well-dressed girls gathering for a tea party served on dolls' dishes in *Lucy and Arthur*. After tea, the author informs us, the girls made daisy chains to decorate the arbor and bonnets of leaves and flowers for their make-believe millinery shop.[62] In the illustration the arbor, softened by vines, serves as a frame for the girls who, enclosed within the small rustic space, play at being ladies (Fig. 1.11). Their ambivalent status is underscored by the contrast between the rough-hewn branches out of which the lattice and furniture are made and the more formal paneling of the back wall, suggesting that their domestic games will prepare them for their duties within a real home one day.

Some of these women writers, in contrast, recognized that the garden is significantly different from interior spaces, more expansive and potentially

Fig. 1.8.   Illustration in the pamphlet edition of Ann Taylor's "My Mother."

Fig. 1.9.   Illustration in Ann and Jane Taylor, *Original Poems for Infant Minds*, p. 59.

Fig. 1.10. Illustration in *Peter Parley's First Present for Very Young Children*.

Fig. 1.11. Illustration in [Jane Elizabeth Holmes Jerram?], *Lucy and Arthur: A Book for Children*, facing p. 143.

liberating. Budden, for example, juxtaposed the tranquility of a tea party outside with the freedom of being in nature. Serena's mother in *Always Happy* allows tea to be set up in a shady bower under a tree "as a great indulgence," and she "permitted Serena to perform the honours of it." When the little girl exclaims how much she's enjoying it, her mother explains, "the balmy air wafting round us, the open view of the surrounding country, the warbling of birds, and the fragrance of flowers, give great zest to our feelings, and invigorate and enliven our thoughts." And she adds, "A room, however airy, cannot bestow these enjoyments, thus pure, thus unbounded."[63] Two sisters in Harriet Martineau's *Deerbrook* (1839) use their dolls as sedate proxies while they play, explaining to a visitor, "We have made arbours in our own gardens for our dolls, where they may sit when we are swinging."[64] But some children managed to bypass the rules of decorum altogether by making their own, wilder shelters. Anna Sewell, recounting her childhood adventures in the swamp, sandpit, and woods around her house, mentioned that a particular wide ditch "was a very delightful place for making bowers to sit in; we used to arch them over, and then make our roof of ivy, which we would strip from the pollard-oaks."[65]

The young protagonist in Edgeworth's story "Simple Susan," from *The Parent's Assistant* (1796), often takes her sewing to her quiet refuge, a "little honey-suckle arbour." But as an embodiment of communal as well as domestic harmony she also works to save the village children's gathering spot: "a little green nook, open on one side to a shady lane," the public equivalent of her private arbor.[66] This commons area, sheltered but accessible to all, was eventually rescued by Susan from Lawyer Case's greedy attempt to enclose it. She can be read as the maternal heart of the community, nurturing her animals and flowers just as she serves her family and friends, and with her charitable spirit she is willing to take a stand for the common good. Her private space, the arbor, is aligned with the communal "green nook," both of them being protected (and protecting) areas associated with the twelve-year-old girl. Myers relates the landscape in this story to Bachelard's concept of "felicitous space," observing that "Susan's miniature garden world is an idyllic landscape of the mind … It is child space, maternal space, family space."[67] On the cusp of womanhood, Susan is wise beyond her years: a young mother figure who recognizes how space can operate in practical as well as symbolic ways.

One of Sherwood's stories in *History of the Fairchild Family* revolves around Mrs. Howard and what she is able to ascertain about children's behavior by overhearing them from the privacy of her bower. This comfortable retreat, where she passes the time with her tea and knitting, stands at the boundary between home and not-home – and, as it turns out, between civility and moral disorder. It was built "at the end of that long green walk, and at the corner of the field; so that anyone sitting in the bower might see through the lattice-work and foliage of the honeysuckles into the field."[68] Mrs. Howard, as moral arbiter, evaluates the children's behavior as she observes them from her leafy garden-house, and she makes decisions about certain coveted prizes to be awarded based on what she sees. The bower is thus perfectly positioned at the spatial and psychological hub, and she must have seemed to the children to have the power of God within this domestic drama, being witness to all and judging all.

Sherwood employs an arbor and grotto as the site for domestic re-enactments and moral lessons in another story about good Lucinda, who hopes to reform her troublesome younger brother by using the garden root-house as a place to train and "soften" him. While she sews he tries to construct a toy hermitage, but this scene of familial harmony is disrupted when he leaves in frustration. It is only much later that he returns to the grotto and repents of his anger. The conclusion to this story is characteristic of Sherwood's approach, and indeed of most didactic children's books of the period, in presenting a model for the resolution of problems and the correction of minor flaws: "The last we heard of Mr. Low's family was that Bernard and Lucilla had furnished the grotto so beautifully that every person in the neighbourhood came to see it; and that this brother and sister were the delight of their parents, and the comforts of every poor old person or orphan child in the parish."[69] Brother and sister play at being husband and wife in that in-between space of the garden retreat, and as is often the case, it is the girl who practices the role of moral guardian for the family.

OUTSIDE THE GARDEN GATE

The pleasures and risks of moving beyond the garden wall are made clear by the way in which children's authors treat the subject of rural walks. Books on the education of girls often bring up the need for physical exercise to balance book-learning and domestic training. Fielding's Mrs. Teachum, associating physical health with mental acuity, encourages walks of several miles during which the girls can run about and gather flowers.[70] Almost a century after Fielding, even the conservative Mrs. Ellis, strong proponent of separate spheres for men and women, advocates life in the country for children because of the freedom it allows them: the benefits accrued from "roaming over hills, listening to waterfalls, and holding converse with the spirit of nature" range from the spiritual (elevation of the soul) to the practical (exercise in the open air). Females, though "naturally and necessarily weak in comparison with man," should be raised to be strong and active and allowed to participate in outdoor activities along with their brothers – "even at the risk of torn dresses, crushed bonnets, and soiled shoes." In writing about the education of girls, Ellis encourages "the indulgence of that wild excitement, that thrilling ecstasy, and that unbounded exhilaration of mind and body, which a free and joyous life in the country can best afford."[71]

The line between suitable exercise and unseemly romping was a fine one, however, differing according to social class as well as the circumstances of the particular writer. Reminiscent of a younger version of Dorothy Wordsworth, Marjory Fleming writes in her journal at the age of seven, in 1810, "Here I pas my life in rurel felicity festivity & pleasure I saunter about the woods & forests," and later she admits that she "dirtied myself" on one of these jaunts. With particularly apt misspelling, she confesses, "I love to walk in lonely solitude & leave the bustel of the nosey town behind me & while I look on nothing but what strikes the eye with sights of bliss." Marjory, who died a year later, was clearly rebelling against some of the feminine codes of behavior that her governess was trying to teach her. She describes herself as "very strong & robust & not of the delicate sex nor of the fair but of the deficent in look."[72]

Many writers and physicians believed that after puberty a girl became more delicate and thus should be shielded from strenuous activities. Although long walks were good for a girl's constitution, care should be taken to avoid damp or cold conditions.[73] Illustrations in children's books tend to confine young girls to sedate activities: the flower in Ann Taylor's "The Little Field Daisy" encourages the "little lady" to "Skip about, but do not tread / On my meek and healthy head," but there is no merry skipping in the print.[74] Instead the girl in the image looks as meek as the daisy: in a long dress and sunbonnet, with a straw basket, she steps daintily through the meadow. The control of high spirits is also seen in the frontispiece of Ann Martin Taylor and Jane Taylor's *Correspondence between a Mother and Her Daughter at School* (1817) (Fig. 1.12), which illustrates a passage from Laura's letter to her mother: "I have been walking in the garden, which is now quite gay with snowdrops and crocuses, violets and primroses. My heart bounded with joy."[75] This emotional energy is nowhere in evidence in the representation, however: two young women slowly stroll in the schoolhouse garden while others, arm in arm, cross the level lawn behind them. The foreground figures embrace with the gentle dependence of schoolgirl friendship, the soft droop of their poses echoed in the wispy delicacy of the

40 "*In the home-garden*"

Fig. 1.12. Frontispiece illustration in Ann Martin Taylor and Jane Taylor, *Correspondence Between a Mother and Her Daughter at School*.

Outside the garden gate 41

Fig. 1.13. Title page illustration in the *Child's Magazine, and Sunday Scholar's Companion* 1 (1824).

surrounding trees. As with many illustrations in early children's books, the artist attempted to capture an essential aspect of the narrative – in this case, sweet harmony – but in doing so toned down some of its complexity. In general, these illustrations fall back on stereotyped gender norms and thus provide a rather simplistic reading of more nuanced, sometimes even mildly subversive, texts.

An even more common image is of a girl reading quietly outside: under a tree in Jane Taylor's "About Learning to Read,"[76] for example, or shaded by a rose-covered porch in the *Child's Magazine, and Sunday Scholar's Companion* (1824) (Fig. 1.13). Sarah Trimmer's point about the power of the visual image on impressionable children, while intended as a warning against the impact of fanciful illustrations in fairy tales, is also true for these more sedate representations.[77] The irony, of course, is that the book could be seen as a sign of empowerment, as we suggest in Chapter 3 in the case of Maria Spilsbury's portraits of cottage women. Here, however, the message seems different: while not particularly memorable as individual prints, the cumulative impact of these repeated portrayals of passive girls – whether demurely standing, gracefully reaching for a flower, or languidly seated – must surely have had a chastening effect on the young readers.

With parental approval, and often with the guidance of an adult, children's walks could extend out beyond their family garden to the landscape surrounding their home for the purposes of exercise, entertainment, and education. Smith's *Rural Walks* and *Rambles Farther* are based on conversations held on such walks, whether short ones in the garden to study the flowers and insects or longer ones to nearby woods and meadows for more botanical lessons from Mrs. Woodfield. The mother in Budden's *Right and Wrong* illustrates the dictum "rational duties lead to rational enjoyments" by contrasting "the fatigue of dancing at a splendid ball" with that felt after "enjoying a long country walk, or a summer day's long country labour" – dancing, though exciting, leads only to a feverish head-ache. She tells her daughter after another walk why they enjoyed their outing so much: "We have not gone blindly along, thinking of what we left behind, but we have amused ourselves with all we saw or met. Such is the proper use of a walk; to give up ourselves to the pleasures that surround us, to examine whatever is curious, and admire whatever is beautiful, and leave our cares at home."[78] In this view, then, nature serves as an antidote to domestic concerns, a carefree zone of exploration that allows women respite from the demands of the home.

While books for and about children from this period often identify the garden and the nearby countryside as a place for imaginative and educational play, the potential for wildness that is always a risk in such free access to nature was carefully and consciously minimized for girls. Often it was the garden fence that marked the boundary between the domesticated, feminized zone of women and children and the world beyond. The significance of this border is made clear in an illustration for Jane Taylor's "Come and Play in the Garden" (Fig. 1.14). The poem warns children always to obey their mother, and the illustration extends the narrative with an imagined scenario of disobedience in which two girls stand on either side of a garden fence, the one on the viewer's side raising her arm to call the other back.[79] The gate, of course, serves as the valve regulating the spatial flow between the two zones of (inner) safety and (outer) danger. Bachelard's discursus in *The Poetics of Space* on the significance of the "primal" image of the door, "an entire cosmos of the Half-open," can be interpreted for our purposes as either the door between house and garden or the gate between the garden and the outer world. He acknowledges that a door can suggest "hesitation, temptation, desire, security, welcome and respect" and asks, "But is he who opens a door and he who closes it the same being? The gestures that make us conscious of security or freedom are rooted in a profound depth of being."[80] These issues are central to our understanding of the garden as an educational site for children in this era.

Fig. 1.14. Illustration in Jane Taylor, "Come and Play in the Garden," in *The Little Field-Daisy*, p. 3.

In the case of most of these moral tales, the adventurous child who moves beyond the prescribed limits, especially a girl, is held up as a cautionary example. The contrast between safety in the enclosed garden and danger in the outer world is sharply drawn in Fielding's *The Governess*, especially in her story-within-a-story, "The Princess Hebe." This fairy tale involves a good queen and her daughter who, forced to flee the court, are taken by a fairy into a hidden refuge. Hebe, though taught by her mother to be vigilant, eventually succumbs to temptation. Fielding vividly highlights the breaching of the boundary between the protected sphere within the wall of impenetrable bushes and the sinful world outside by emphasizing the border or perimeter: Hebe "o'erleaped the Bounds," or in another passage, she was "drawn at last beyond the prescribed Bounds."[81]

We find a similar moral in Wakefield's "The Little Wanderer" from the 1790s, which begins with the telling image of a garden gate left accidentally ajar: Laura "no sooner perceived it, than she felt an inclination to venture beyond its bounds, and in a few minutes found herself at full liberty on a wide extended common." The daily reality of borders, limits, and confinement suddenly, fortuitously, turns into the excitement of freedom and exploration: "Novelty and the pleasure of choosing her own road induced her to walk on, till she had got some distance from home." Such liberty without permission or supervision could not be allowed to go unchecked, however, and Laura is kidnapped by a gypsy woman, a sign of the wild and uncultivated. In this case the story ends well and Laura is finally rescued, but the moral is clear: "Children should not wander beyond the bounds allowed them."[82]

Elizabeth Turner frames a more succinct statement of the dangers of transgressing such physical (as well as social and gender) boundaries in *The Cowslip, or More Cautionary Stories in Verse* (1811):

> Sophia, one fine sunny day,
> Left all her work and ran away;
> When soon she reached the garden gate,
> Which finding lock'd, she would not wait,
> But tried to climb and scramble o'er
> A gate as high as any door.[83]

The result of this rebellion and impatience, dramatically shown in the illustration (Fig. 1.15), is Sophia's headlong fall into the path on the other side. We see a more subtle example of temptation in "The Cottage Girl," one of many nineteenth-century gift plates for children with garden themes (Fig. 1.1): a girl stands at the gate with blooms around and behind her while beyond the fence, contrasting with the lush abundance of the garden, stretches the tantalizing display of a large, empty meadow with another house just visible in the distance. The distant view opening before her, offering new possibilities for action, is in vivid opposition to the close framing of the carefully cultivated garden.

The gravity of transgression is underscored in some of the stories by physical pain, as with little Sophia, and even sometimes by the ultimate punishment of death. In Anna Kent's *York House* (1820) the daring and uncontrollable thirteen-year-old Maria sets the stage for her disobedience by flouting the piety of her older sister: "Religion is very well for old women, who must soon die, but girls have nothing to do with it; give me a doll and a skipping-rope." Tempted by a forbidden fruit at the back of the garden, Maria falls from the high wall and eventually dies from her injuries, lamenting her sinful past and calling for forgiveness.[84] A similar approach is used by the evangelical Mrs. Sherwood, for whom children were born sinners: Mrs. Fairchild reminds her daughter that the only reason she has not been "naughty" recently is because her parents are always there "watching and guiding," "not because there is any goodness or wisdom in you." It is not surprising, then, to find the Fairchilds' beautiful garden as the site of multiple temptations reminiscent of the Garden of Eden. Whether the

Fig. 1.15. "Miss Sophia," illustration in Elizabeth Turner, *The Cowslip, or More Cautionary Stories in Verse*, p. 38.

fruit is a ripe cherry or an apple, the result is the same: the children cannot control their desires and are punished. In one episode they are reminded not to "go beyond the bounds in which they were always allowed to play." Trying their best to be good, they sit for a while and read a story about a little boy stolen by gypsies – clearly an admonition from the author. While the two children aren't kidnapped, they do test their limits by letting their pet magpie out of its cage and chasing it across a fence, over a thatched roof, and finally to the forbidden boundary, the gate. Sherwood increases the tension at this crucial moment, stating that "The children were now in serious trouble," but this time, unlike some previous episodes, they remember to obey the rules.[85]

In Mrs. O'Reilly's mid-Victorian *Daisy's Companions* (c. 1860), Daisy finds herself facing a similar restriction. Hoping that she won't be required to pass her half-holiday by going with her aunt on a round of social visits, she presents an alternative:

May I go and seek my fortune, auntie? Do say "Yes;" quite alone, you know; I must meet with dangers and be unprotected, and Goody never will see the dangers. When I run for my life from wild Indians, or ford rivers, or am nearly starved in desert places, she says my imagination is running away with me. If I set off to seek my fortune with her, and meet with a lifetime of adventures, she will say that it is only two hours, and not a lifetime at all. Please let me go out into the world alone to-day, and then I can be the "wanderer returned" at night.

Daisy's aunt finally agrees that she can go out for a short walk by herself, as long as she doesn't go past the Holt woods. Daisy is distressed by the limitations – "Why, auntie, I couldn't lose myself in the Holt woods if I tried; and it's no fun seeking your fortune unless you can lose your way" – but her aunt insists that she "must be content to keep within bounds." The description of Daisy's room on the next page is particularly revealing, as we consider the contrast between freedom and constraint in a young girl's life: "there was a book-case full of story-books, and above the flower-pots in the window hung a canary's cage. The window was wide open, and so was the cage-door … She kept none of her pets on confinement." The pots and cage are elements of control that flank the window, which suggests flight or openness, while the books provide another means of escape or imaginative release. Daisy's treatment of the canary clearly reflects her desire to be similarly free. But as it turns out, her grand adventure ends with a sprained ankle, a figurative hobbling of her intrepid spirit, and she is compelled to spend a week on the sofa recuperating.[86]

CONCLUSION

The didactic children's literature of the period presents a variety of virtues as moral goals, including industry, neatness, patience, humility, and submission, among others – all of them pointing to the larger ideal of a well-ordered life characterized by restraint and self-control: what Wakefield holds up as "the regulation of the temper."[87] As Marjory Fleming enters into her diary at the age of eight, "Selfe-denial is a good thing and a virtue."[88] Wollstonecraft argues, however, that "the regulation of the passions is not, always, wisdom," and she suggests that men's superiority in certain respects (judgment and fortitude, for example) is due to the fact "that they give a freer scope to the grand passions, and by more frequently going astray enlarge their minds."[89] But the subtitle of Wollstonecraft's *Original Stories from Real Life* (1791) is telling: *with Conversations Calculated to Regulate the Affections, and Form the Mind to Truth and Goodness*. The verbs "regulate" and "form" clearly express her intention to fashion children into worthy individuals. Wollstonecraft was writing two very different kinds of texts, of course – the radical *Vindication* a far cry from her children's stories – but the differences are significant: even one of the most forward-thinking women of the period feels compelled to guide and train children toward a certain moral conformity, believing that through this regulatory process they will be strengthened as individuals acting within a larger social community.

O'Malley proposes that "Teaching children accountability for their actions was an essential part of the late eighteenth-century didactic goal of raising responsible, self-regulating subjects."[90] But the didacticism of this literature for children can be construed in different ways: Steward, in *The New Child*, calls it *re*forming, or denaturing, girls,[91] whereas Myers, with whom we are more in sympathy, considers the approach taken by some of the women authors of the period, in particular Wollstonecraft, a model for empowerment. A middle-class woman who could regulate her own life, both physically and morally, was indeed in a certain position of strength, however dependent and submissive she might have been in other ways. These attributes distinguished her, and her class, from the servitude of the poor as well as the excesses of the wealthy.

Budden emphasizes the central issue of self-control in her story of the impetuous, quick-tempered Rosa who trampled on her sister's carefully tended garden. When her parents discover the truth (not, of course, from the good Agnes), she confesses: "Yes – yes … I believe – I think I did it – but I could not help it: I was in a passion." Her father asks her a series of questions that take her back through the decisions she had made at the time, in this way helping her to see how she could have made better choices. Using himself as an example, he continues the catechism: "And why does my reason govern my passion? because I have made it do so … The child whose passion is permitted to destroy a garden, when grown up, may destroy a fellow-creature." Rosa comes to realize that she has "the power of choosing either to check or indulge" her anger, but through a series of unwise decisions her youthful flaws are magnified in her adult years: "She went on from bad to worse, and the ill-nature and passion that made her destroy her sister's garden, as she grew up, rendered her a perfect fury to her neighbours and a noisy scold to her servants. Instead of trampling on gardens, she gave way to her rage in tearing her clothes, breaking her china, and throwing books and trinkets into the fire."[92] Budden clearly chooses to highlight actions that would be closest to the child's own moral world, the stuff of temper tantrums thus transplanted into the adult sphere in a way that might seem ludicrous to an actual adult but would resonate vividly with a young girl struggling with her own petty outbursts. The seriousness of this kind of emotional and moral disorder is underscored by the fact that the frontispiece illustration represents Rosa's destruction of her sister's garden (Fig. 1.16). The angular twist of her body as she tramples on the flowers is in marked contrast to Agnes's upright stance, reinforced by the columnar

Fig. 1.16. Frontispiece illustration in Maria Elizabeth Budden, *Right and Wrong, Exhibited in the History of Rosa and Agnes*.

vertical of the conifer behind her. Agnes holds one arm up in gentle admonition, echoing the gesture of her mother. With the label "Right and Wrong," we see that order, virtue, and stability are in fact literally on the right, where space is enclosed, secure, upright, and bounded by the mass of the house in the background, unlike the disarray of the more open left side.

As Tuan argues, "From the security and stability of place we are aware of the openness, freedom, and threat of space." Place is constructed, familiar, intimate, "a calm center of established values"; space, on the other hand, being unbounded, is empowering but also potentially threatening. Tuan extends this idea by noting that both are necessary for a "healthy being," which needs "constraint and freedom, the boundedness of place and the exposure of space."[93] But Massey reminds us that spaces are less fixed and more dynamic than Tuan's dualism would suggest. She proposes, instead, that spaces are "open to contestation" and are constructed and reconstructed through the nexus of social relations that operate in those spaces at any given time.[94] For middle-class women and girls of the period under discussion, who typically lived a spatially and experientially stunted existence, their power could only come, with rare exceptions, within the near sphere of the home-ground. Movement outward, that "explosion toward the outside" that Bachelard describes as a natural human tendency,[95] connotes the kind of energy, passion, and aggression viewed as disruptive to the stability of home and thus inappropriate for the female temperament. Kate Flint, in her study of women as readers in the Victorian period, recognizes that while the training of girls through advice manuals and other instructional texts might build a strong sense of individual character, developing individualism was inevitably constrained by the "carefully defined paradigms" of wife and mother.[96] As Myers argues, though, these children's books by female writers present a world of "enlightened domesticity" in which the mother-pedagogues uphold the virtues of "rationality, self-command, and moral autonomy."[97] We have seen how the garden as a transitional zone served as an important training ground for these virtues and in addition how certain images that connect the house with the garden (the window, the porch, the arbor) and the garden with the outside world (the gate, the fence) operated as physical and moral tropes around which children's lives were structured.

CHAPTER 2

The "botanic eye": botany, miniature, and magnification

This chapter considers botanical texts, many of them designed for children and young adults, through theories of the miniature: in particular, Bachelard's idea that "the minuscule, a narrow gate, opens an entire world," as well as Susan Stewart's insight that the miniature "presents domesticated space as a model of order, proportion, and balance."[1] In many early women's botanical texts, the goal is not just – or even mainly – to impart scientific knowledge, but to teach a discipline that leads the student to observe nature closely and to imagine the interior world that microscopy and magnification make possible. Magnification opens up infinite possibilities but does so, paradoxically, through observation of the minute and the commonplace. Although the overt goal of such apprehension of minute particulars is greater understanding of plant structure and physiology, an appreciation of the divine, the extension of sympathy, and the development of intellectual discipline underpin these insights.

Botanical texts by women often participate in a tradition of mother-mentors, in which women are dramatized as teachers through dialogue, usually in a domestic setting.[2] In her study of women's botanical culture from 1760 to 1860, *Cultivating Women, Cultivating Science*, Ann B. Shteir emphasizes the diverse educational goals of botanical texts: to teach plant structures (usually following the Linnaean method) and to use the study of plants as a mechanism for enhancing one's moral and spiritual life. We will demonstrate that a language of growth and process pervades these texts and applies both to the plants themselves and to the lives of those who view and comment on them. Numerous texts make connections between the behavior of plants and the behavior of their human observers: some are selfish, some frugal, some caring, etc. Furthermore, the garden's associations with Edenic myths, intimacy, and childhood also elicit a sense of nostalgia, as we will see again in Chapter 4. Women botanical writers recognize that the minute focus of botanical study comprises a microcosm of the world well suited to teaching about the complexities of life, loss, and recovery.

In domestically based botanical texts, authors often create a miniature world in which the students' adventures in learning take place. Most of them depend on the easy flow between the inside (school room or botanical study) and the landscape beyond. Gardens, greenhouses, and school rooms overlooking the garden become sites and subject matter of much instruction for children and young adults; scientific, moral, religious, and epistemological issues dominate the discussion. Gardens and meadows are places where children learn to sympathize with the details of creation. In fact, a major theme of botanical writing is the cultivation of sympathy for others and for the natural world as a network of living organisms, although this focus on sympathy sometimes conflicts with science: Charlotte Elizabeth Tonna begins *Chapters on Flowers* (1836), in her poetic first chapter on "The Snowdrop," with the sentimental admission, "Botany is doubtless a very delightful study; but … my love of flowers – for each particular petal – is such, that no thirst after scientific knowledge could ever prevail with me to tear the beautiful objects in pieces."[3] Similarly, Jane Loudon in *Botany for Ladies* (1842) laments the need to dismantle the petals of a *Viola tricolor* in order to study the stamen: she begins her detailed instructions with the apologetic phrase, "Commencing this work of destruction, which I always feel remorse at perpetrating, for I love flowers too well not to feel pain at destroying them."[4]

As proposed in our introduction, the idea of cultivating a garden and learning what was needed for productive growth became a foundational metaphor in educational theory and practice. Mary Wollstonecraft and Hannah More, for instance, use the garden as a site for personal development in their writings on women and education. But even though they exploit this metaphor of cultivation, both reject the ornamentality of plants and of women, valuing instead a culture of the everyday and commonplace associated with women writers of the Romantic period. Both of them, we think, would argue against the anonymous writer in *Gentleman's Magazine* in 1801 who claims that "The nurture of exotics not only belongs more particularly to the female province, on account of it being an elegant *home* amusement, but because of there being much delicate work, essential to the welfare of plants, that is more dexterously performed by the pliant fingers of women, than by the clumsy paws of men."[5] One step beyond this association of women with exotics is their actual identification with these plants and, more generally, with the hothouse. But in fact most women botanical authors favor more practical and sturdy plants over the cultivation and collection of exotics.

As Priscilla Wakefield attests in *An Introduction to Botany* (1796), "Flowers growing wild, without culture, are the most suitable for examination,

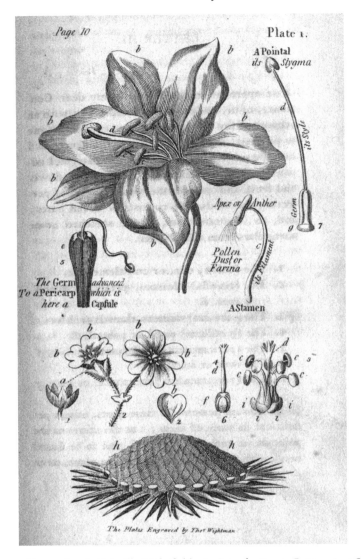

Fig. 2.1. Illustration in Priscilla Wakefield, *An Introduction to Botany, in a Series of Familiar Letters*, facing p. 10.

because those that are domesticated in the rich soil of our gardens, are frequently transformed into something very different from what nature made them" (Fig. 2.1).[6] Even though these texts generally present a privileged world of middle- and upper-class mentors and learners, on the issue of wildflowers there is a democratizing notion that these are not only children of nature but also accessible to all who want to botanize. As young Edward's mother and botanical mentor tells him in Sarah Fitton's *Conversations on Botany* (1817), they will not study geraniums because

> the geraniums in the greenhouse are not natives of England, that is, they do not grow wild in the hedges and fields; and we shall confine ourselves, for some time, to the examination of native plants only. Although these are generally called weeds, many of them are so beautiful that they are cultivated in flower-gardens. A knowledge of the plants of our own country is more desirable for you than that of foreign ones, as it is more within your reach.[7]

Although exotics are prized by collectors and "florists," these botanical writers prefer native plants to the florist's art as being more worthy of their minute studies.[8]

The *Journal of Emily Shore* (1831–39) introduces us to the walks and thoughts of an actual girl interested in botany – particularly in native plants – as one among a number of intellectual pursuits that piqued her curiosity. Exploring multiple voices as she combined both a personal and emotionally responsive approach with the more descriptive and objective mode that she knew to be suited to the public arena, she responded for much of her short life to the closely inscribed world within a three- or four-mile radius of her home. Mary Ellen Bellanca describes the blurring of the boundaries between "home as human sanctuary and nature as messy outdoor world" in the Shore household, and she compares the diaries of Shore and Dorothy Wordsworth in the way that they both write "in the context of daily domestic life, treating household activities and human relationships as important to the same degree as nonhuman nature."[9] Emily's empiricist approach to the acquisition of knowledge leads her to rely on intensive observation as her primary tool. Already as an eleven-year-old she describes herself as "very fond of botany" and uses technical language, describing one find as "a papilionaceous flower, of a yellow colour, and unbranched." Before long she begins to include the Latin names of plants and distinguishes between the botanical systems of Linnaeus, Thunberg, and Withering. She takes particular pleasure in walks where "there are wild flowers for me to find and botanize."[10] These walks take her far afield: to distant woods and cow pastures, over brooks and through thickets, to heaths and bogs.

Emily's description of these adventurous expeditions conveys a very different attitude toward botanical study than that suggested by the title page of *Botanical Rambles* by Lucy Sarah Atkins. The illustration (Fig. 2.2) shows a seated young woman, dressed as if for a morning call; her parasol shields her from the sun and her graceful pose is echoed in the drooping foliage of the weeping willow at the left. The title of Atkins's book also highlights the

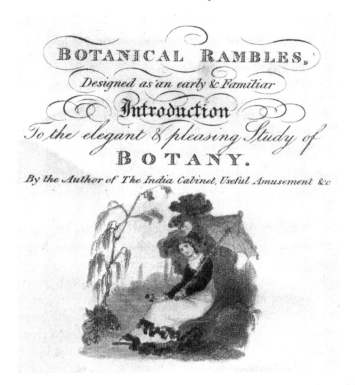

Fig. 2.2. Title page illustration in Lucy Sarah Atkins, *Botanical Rambles*.

ladylike aspects of botanizing: "rambles" connotes a desultory, unfocused stroll rather than a more purposive hike, and the description in the subtitle of botanical study as "elegant and pleasing" is also meant to attract a genteel readership. But given what we know about Emily Shore, she is unlikely to have found Atkins's title page appealing. Although certainly equipped with sufficient knowledge from books, Emily is also not hesitant to make close observations on her own and to trust her own senses: "I gathered some more valerian in the wood, and found that it had not, as I supposed, perfect flowers on stameniferous plants, but sometimes produced four stamens instead of three. Still, however, on my first specimen there are a few perfect flowers, which is very remarkable." At fifteen she determines to "study botany this year in a very different way from that which I have been accustomed to pursue, for I find that I have hitherto been a very superficial botanist, attending to little besides the classification, and not studying the habits, properties, and uses of plants." Several months later she is given the opportunity to use her cousin's microscope and is awestruck by the magnified world revealed to her. Her analogy of jewels, probably the richest and most splendid objects she knew, must have seemed appropriate to her as she struggled for words to describe the sight: "I saw in it the pollen, leaves, and petals of various plants. Their beauty is wonderful; they look like heaps of precious stones. The pollen of the grand scarlet poppy is particularly splendid. The petals of the pink and crimson geranium seem like rubies crowned with amethysts, and those of the spiderwort like a mass of amethysts."[11]

BLESSING SMALL THINGS

Emily Shore expresses just the kind of wonderment in the face of nature that many women botanical writers celebrate. Caroline A. Halstead, for instance, echoes these sentiments in *The Little Botanist, or Steps toward the Attainment of Botanical Knowledge* (1835). She sends a strong religious message, implying that uncultivated nature brings us closer to God than the "productions of the garden and greenhouse." For Halstead, wildflowers, grasses, and weeds "are equally to be admired and more valuable than the gaudy flowers, which have so thrown into shade their unassuming and humbler companions."[12] Although not all botanical writers are so severe on cultivated plants – and indeed both the garden and the greenhouse are crucial to scenes of instruction – the preference for the instructive value of uncultivated nature (often in the form of collected wildflowers brought into the classroom for study) generally adheres.[13]

Some women's botanical texts are much more explicit about the spiritual and religious associations. Shteir has identified several authors (including Priscilla Wakefield and Mary Roberts) who write in the Quaker tradition and share "the delight of the Quaker in the wonders of the natural world."[14] But an interest in spirituality and the interior life seems to cut across religious affiliation. Caroline Jackson-Houlston argues that religious rhetoric provided such authors with a measure of authority – supported by divine sanction, as it were – and thus enabled them to counteract the stigma often associated with women scientists.[15] Botany was in fact the scientific study considered most suited for women: because of the beauty, delicacy, and small scale of flowers, as well as their easy availability in the garden and nearby woodlands and fields, they were the most "feminine" of God's creations.

The pervasiveness of one particular allusion demonstrates this point. In his *Travels in the Interior of Africa* (1799), the Scottish explorer Mungo Park recounts his attempt to follow the course of the Niger River. In a section called "Influence of Religion," Park describes the moment in his journey when he almost gave up hope. Lost, robbed of his belongings, and stripped naked, he recalls that

> At this moment, painful as my reflections were, the extraordinary beauty of a small moss, in fructification, irresistibly caught my eye … [T]hough the whole plant was not larger than the top of one of my fingers, I could not contemplate the delicate conformation of its roots, leaves, and capsula, without admiration. *Can that Being (thought I) who planted, watered, and brought to perfection, in this obscure part of the world, a thing which appears of so small importance, look with unconcern upon the situation and sufferings of creatures formed after his own image? – surely not!*[16]

The delicate perfection of this moss stands in the passage as evidence of God and reason for hope, which is immediately rewarded in the text when Park finds relief from his suffering in a small village. Even given the popularity of Park's *Travels* (which has never been out of print), it is remarkable that at least four of the botanical texts we have studied refer to this passage. Each uses it as an example of how the apparent unimportance of an object in nature can serve as a confirmation of God's presence in the world.

The first instance occurs in Sarah Fitton's *Conversations on Botany*, a text designed for very young children. The major characters are little Edward and his mother, who agrees to instruct him in botany with the warning that, although botany is not difficult, an indolent person cannot learn it (industry, as we saw in Chapter 1, was one of the key virtues stressed in children's literature). Fitton includes several allusions to God's power in creation. In her section on "Cryptogamia," she highlights the discussion of the minute wonders of plants such as mosses, ferns, and lichens with the long quotation from Park's *Travels* on the discovery of the small, delicate moss.[17]

In *The Wonders of the Vegetable Kingdom Displayed* (1822), Quaker Mary Roberts actually uses the reference to Mungo Park in two ways: as a quotation associated with the frontispiece to the volume and, within the text, to reiterate the message. The frontispiece (Fig. 2.3) illustrates the traveler (apparently in considerably less distress than Mungo Park's narrative reveals) delighted with his discovery. The quotation attached to the illustration captures the intensity of the feeling – "At this moment the extraordinary beauty of a small moss caught his eye" – but with no attribution to Park. Roberts, we think, attempts to make this image more archetypal at the outset of the book, something to alert the reader to the idea that the beauty of small things in nature is associated with discovery and transformation. The frontispiece serves as a gateway into the text, as does the

Blessing small things

Fig. 2.3. Frontispiece illustration in Mary Roberts, *The Wonders of the Vegetable Kingdom Displayed*.

(also unacknowledged) epigraph from James Hurdis's *The Village Curate* (1788):

> Not a tree,
> A plant, a leaf, a blossom, but contains
> A folio volume. We may read and read,
> And read again, and still find something new,
> Something to please, and something to instruct.

With this passage, Roberts emphasizes not only the commonplace that nature is a book, but also the idea that the individual parts of nature are themselves folio volumes. So, once again, she alerts the reader to the idea that small objects are worth our attention.

As stated in an advertisement at the beginning of the book, referring to her series of letters to fictional characters, which we discuss in greater detail later in the chapter, Roberts intends "to lead the youthful mind from the minor wonders of creation to the knowledge of their great Artificer." In letter 12, she comments that humans can become overwhelmed by the immensity of the universe and feel insignificant and lost. She proposes that the study of botany is an antidote to this feeling, since God gave so much care to the created world, from the most humble flower to the most complex organism. Once again, she calls upon the example from Mungo Park to reiterate God's concern for humanity and the comforts that nature can provide in times of crisis.[18]

Several years later, Anne Pratt also alludes to Park's *Travels* to introduce the subject of studying botany. In *The Field, the Garden, and the Woodland* (1838), Pratt writes to her nephew John a series of letters to direct his attention (and those of other young readers) to what she calls "interesting facts" about plants. She assures John that the order he will perceive in nature reveals the divine: "Nor should we remark how plainly the wisdom of God is shown to be perfect by the minute parts of his creation … He who has framed the lofty mountain or the huge elephant, has also fashioned the florets of the daisy, and decked with feathers the wings of the moth."[19] In order to elucidate this point, Pratt also relates Park's redemptive story of recognizing the beauty and intricacy of the small moss and, like the other writers we have discussed, attests to the value of small things.

UNDER THE MICROSCOPE

The very popularity and accessibility of the microscope made it possible for women to engage in botanizing at home and to write botanical texts, many of which feature modest microscopes.[20] In "The Microscope and the English Imagination," first published in 1935, Marjorie Hope Nicolson observed that "The Nature that emerged from the microscope was a Nature superabundant and lavish, prolific and creative. No leaf, no stone, no blade of grass but swarms with inhabitants."[21] These early scientists not only emphasized that the microscopic world was alive, but also used the language of discovery to suggest the infinite possibilities of this new way of seeing. If geographical discoveries led to new worlds, and the telescope to an expanded sense of the universe, the microscope suggested a hidden life rich with possibility and meaning. Apprehending the hidden life depends on both seeing with the microscope and imagining the even smaller parts that could not be seen yet, but perhaps would appear with a stronger lens. This dialectic between seen and unseen, sight and imagination, is a constant theme of the mentors in botanical texts. Although the connection with the telescope is not central to early botanical writing, early students of optics would have understood Bachelard's comment that "If a poet looks through a microscope or a telescope, he always sees the same thing."[22]

The world that is suddenly made visible through the microscope is a type of miniature. As Susan Stewart muses in *On Longing*, "That the world of things can open itself to reveal a secret life – indeed, to reveal a set of actions and hence a narrativity and history outside the given field of perception – is a constant daydream the miniature presents. This is the daydream of the microscope: the daydream of life inside life, of significance multiplied infinitely *within* significance."[23] She does not specify botany, but Stewart captures well the spirit of botanical instruction, which, as we have seen, sets out to teach the students not only systems of classification and interesting facts about plants but also their interior, secret lives. Although the vastness of the universe and the sublime objects of nature also attest to divine creation in these texts, the scale of the minute and the details of networks are privileged. Instructors constantly remind us that the tiny leaves of mosses, whose intricacy is visible under the microscope, are equivalent to huge forests. Not only size, but as Bachelard theorizes, "values become condensed and enriched in miniature."[24] The very smallness of the miniature, the microscopic world, makes it even more precious because of the sense of microcosmic wholeness.

It is not a coincidence that Bachelard uses a botanical text as his primary example of miniature and magnification in *The Poetics of Space*: "Botanists delight in the miniature of being exemplified by a flower, and they even ingenuously use words that correspond to things of ordinary size to describe the intimacy of flowers."[25] In order to exemplify this point, Bachelard comments on a long passage from the *Dictionnaire de botanique chrétienne* (1851), in which the writer refers to flowers as "small and delicate" and thoroughly sexualized, the stamens "erect," the pistils "little women" who exercise "great authority in their homes," and the seeds "children swing[ing] in a hammock."[26] This botanist follows Linnaeus and Erasmus Darwin in seeing plant life in socio-sexual terms and revels in the loves of plants in the little heated dollhouse created by the microscope.[27] Bachelard does not comment specifically on the sexually charged description, but he certainly understands the implications of this kind of intimacy. Noting that "no *observer* could see the slightest real feature that would justify the psychological images" in this dictionary, he recognizes that the writer "*entered* into a miniature world and right away images began to abound, then grow, then escape." For Bachelard, the magnified view stimulates the imagination and also releases inhibition, so that the narrator feels free to say what he wants and implies relationships that he would blush to uncover in the real world. Instead of belaboring this point, Bachelard emphasizes the childlike innocence and joy of the writer in uncovering a new reality. Looking through the glass leads the narrator to discovery. Like a child, he sees the world for the first time – "he returns to the garden."[28]

Women writers of botanical texts anticipate this perspective. They avoid critics who would impugn their modesty and by and large offer sanitized versions of plant reproduction. Perhaps, too, by focusing on the spiritual wonder of the small world, women writers displaced the sexualized plants of the male botanists in an acceptable, even admirable, direction. The point, then, was to talk not about plants as if they were promiscuous people, but instead about the very richness and intricacy of plant life as evidence of the plenitude of creation and the possibility of returning to the mythical garden. Both the microscope and the magnifying glass provide the gateway for that journey.

LEARNING HOW TO SEE: MARIA ELIZABETH JACSON'S *BOTANICAL DIALOGUES* (1797)

In addition to references to the microscope and magnifying glass, women's botanical texts often create a miniature world in which the students' learning can be extended and nurtured. Shteir points out that through the 1820s women writers typically use a domestic narrative form and setting to depict this world: the books are written as dialogues among family members, perhaps a mother and child, or personal letters written to a beloved relative or student.[29] Furthermore, the domestic setting of the school room or botanical study adjacent to the garden suggests a small, self-contained world resembling Stewart's description of the miniature as proportional and orderly. This centering in the home functions as balance or counterpoint to the discoveries that the students make in the field and under the microscope, suggesting that those discoveries will always be held in safe bounds. Reiterating class and gender roles, the domestic setting also adds legitimacy to the educational ventures, which are sanctioned as appropriate to the context.

Jacson's *Botanical Dialogues* is "by a lady" and her character Hortensia (the mother-mentor) articulates the roles that her children will play, both in botanical studies and in life. The orderly domestic world is a training ground for the future. Her older son Charles learns that he will be able to devote himself to such "useful and elegant studies" as botany because he will not need a profession. Hortensia, with the Proper Lady looming over her, urges her daughters not to lose sight of their domestic mission even as they become more educated: "a woman rarely does herself credit by coming forward as a literary character." The actual setting of these dialogues, a well-planned estate with garden and greenhouse, reiterates these values: Hortensia has prepared "a little room, which opens into my flower garden, for our study" and thus sets up the perfect relationship between the inside room, where the children examine plates and specimens and learn the botanical language that Hortensia insists on, and the garden, where they collect flowers and observe the beauties of nature. The children venture outside both for fun and for learning; as Henry says, "Now let us go into the garden, and try to put in order what we have learnt, and then we can question each other in turns."[30]

Even though Jacson presents Hortensia and her children in a privileged world, Hortensia nonetheless speaks for the accessibility of science and botanical knowledge. Several times in the text she expresses concern for the expense of plates and botanical books and magazines: "it ought to be a point with every one who publishes on any science, to make their work as easy of access as possible." Calling for more affordable botanical books so that everyone can learn the subject, she praises Curtis's *Botanical Magazine* because it costs only one shilling and therefore "is in everybody's hands and has diffused a general knowledge of plants." So, even though Jacson presents Hortensia and her children as privileged in their studies and their prospects, Hortensia nonetheless embraces a democratic spirit in calling for botany for all. In fact, she sees botany itself as a force for education and democracy, perhaps injecting the subversive into the apparently safe domestic setting.[31]

Hortensia, in fact, sees her primary responsibility as teaching the children to see and to think for themselves. In her epigraph she quotes Martyn's just-published translation of Rousseau's *Letters on Botany*: "'Before we teach them to name *what* they see, let us begin by teaching them *how* to see.'" This passage is important to understanding Jacson's educational mission. Botany or botanical knowledge is not as important in itself to Jacson as is the use to which the study can be put in teaching children the skills necessary for understanding the world and appreciating the power of small things. Unlike some botanical writers, Jacson does not emphasize the religious dimension either, although she certainly points to the idea of the divine plan several times in her text. Although we agree with Shteir in seeing Jacson as somewhat constrained by the backlash of the 1790s in her attitudes toward the education of girls, Jacson is actually quite forceful in insisting that her students think for themselves and not give too much credence to "authority."[32] By framing her presentation in terms of questioning authority, she also subtly suggests that her readers should question her own word as final and should learn different perspectives from the vital form of the dialogue. She tells her children early on that "I never wish you to take anything upon my authority."[33] Jacson models this attitude by endorsing Rousseau's maxim on teaching students how to see, but she also implicitly rejects his ornamental view of girls and women as themselves more beautiful flowers than any they can study. Her frank but not overblown acknowledgement of the sexuality of plants places her in opposition to reactionaries who comment on the "smuttiness" of Linnaeus,[34] and also distinguishes her from other writers who try to avoid sexual content.

Jacson develops two major themes of "seeing" in *Botanical Dialogues*. First, when we are careful to look at the small objects in nature, we see the world anew. Near the beginning of the book, as Charles is learning how to focus on the details, he exclaims, "How carelessly we have often passed by the moss bank in the wood, and complained that there were no flowers!" Through his mother Hortensia's tutelage in observing the minutiae of nature, Charles and the other children learn that such plants as mosses represent miniature worlds of diversity. In studying botany, Hortensia teaches her children a skill akin to the concept of defamiliarization (in which poetry and art reveal common objects in new and startling ways): she models what can be learned through careful observation. Hence, in the second year of study Harriet claims that "We learn daily to see with our naked eyes beauties in the most common plants of which last year we were no less insensible than if we had been blind."[35] Jacson's method also bears some comparison to Wordsworth's idea just one year later in *Lyrical Ballads* that those who are attuned to the world find stories everywhere, as well as to Shelley's argument in *A Defence of Poetry* (1821) that poetry removes "the veil from the hidden beauty of the world, and makes familiar objects be as if they were not familiar."[36] Jacson shares with her poetic contemporaries a value placed on knowledge that leads to sympathetic identification with the human and natural worlds outside of the self.

Second, a related issue actually requires faith in one's own understanding and thus balances the first goal of seeing beyond the self. Jacson tells her readers that they must see and think independently rather than relying on authorities. In the second part of the book, Hortensia and Harriet discuss the merits of looking at plates in botanical books as opposed to viewing the parts of plants through a microscope. Hortensia favors the microscope because in looking through this instrument "we see for ourselves." Although she acknowledges some wonderful reproductions in botanical books, she warns that "Most of our botanical publications are taken one from another; and thus if an eminent botanist has in the course of his researches fallen into a mistake, the error has been propagated." Several times in the text Hortensia uses the example of botanical errors in plates to argue in favor of seeing for oneself, both in terms of microscopy and in relation to larger educational issues. For instance, she notes a repeated error of botanists in assuming that the common fern (*Polypodium vulgare*) does not have an elastic ring around its capsules – but had those botanists not "blindly follow[ed] authority figures" and instead "made use of their own eyes, assisted only by a common magnifier, they must have seen, what had long before their time attracted notice of enquiring botanists." A bit later in the text, she provides the children with several different points of view regarding reproduction in Cryptogamia and suggests that they will need to develop informed opinions for themselves.[37]

That said, however, Jacson, through Hortensia, does praise those botanists who present plants clearly, with close attention to detail. Although she admires Linnaeus for the elegance of his systematic approach to botany, his attention to "minute circumstances," and his "penetrating eye," she also acknowledges "Dr. Grew" because "his investigations made with so accurate and penetrating an eye" contributed to knowledge in the seventeenth century. So Nehemiah Grew, working without system, nonetheless earns Jacson's appreciation because of his precise attention to detail. Curtis's *Flora Londinensis* (1777–98) is also promoted for the "great accuracy" of the illustrations, evident in Fig. 2.4. These drawings are often the first step in minute botanical knowledge, as we shall see with Agnes Ibbetson. An excellent plate can teach the student what to look for in the plant itself – for instance, Jacson's description of the anthers of moss: "This is a beautiful microscopic object, but you must be content to become acquainted with it, and the other parts of fructification in mosses, first by the assistance of plates and afterwards amuse yourselves with viewing them through glasses." While Jacson does not advocate a dependence on authority, she does encourage her children to use and evaluate botanical knowledge and to become a part of the community of botanists by learning the proper language of classification: "I intend strictly to require the use of Linnean terms, as that will be a

Fig. 2.4. "Honeysuckle," illustration in William Curtis, *Flora Londinensis*, vol. 1, pl. 15.

means of imprinting on your minds what you learn, and, as you grow older, will make you ready in the language of botany."³⁸

Jacson's repeated use of the term "penetrating eye" might suggest an interest in getting below the surface of ordinary sight. Although she does acknowledge that microscopy allows for greater degrees of penetration, she is actually more leery than other botanical writers of getting carried away by speculation about the unseen. At one point, Hortensia chides Juliette that "Your imagination went a little too rapidly" as she redirects her daughter back to observing the plants very carefully. And yet, at the same time, Hortensia surely encourages her children to think imaginatively about plants as alive: the natural world takes on human characteristics when

Hortensia tells the girls that their muslin dresses were made from "the soft cradle of seeds" of the cotton plant or speaks of the appearance of ferns in groups as elegant assemblages of "families" in a winter garden.[39] In each instance she invokes an interior life or miniature world that is highly evocative in ways that Bachelard has identified.

Jacson's examples can be quite fanciful at times, but she does not emphasize imagination as an educational value in itself. Instead, she wants the children to be useful citizens. Even when Charles comments on Linnaeus's "genius," Hortensia downplays such terms in favor of praising Linnaeus's usefulness and "his industrious application of his genius." This usefulness – and avoidance of indolence – provides the foundation of her advice to both the boys and the girls, and, as we have seen in Chapter 1, connects Jacson with other educational writers. Even Charles cannot rest on his laurels as the first born, but must train himself for exertion – "cultivate [his] useful and elegant studies" so that he can live a productive life. Henry, who as the younger son must work for a living, can use his botanical studies as the basis of a profession, such as medicine. Hortensia also urges her daughters to usefulness, as Harriet puts it, "in the small duties of life, which daily occur," thus keeping the girls in the domestic sphere. Yet since Hortensia has been promoting the *botanical* small-scale for its ability to open up a wealth of understanding, both scientifically and spiritually, we might be permitted to interpret her exhortation about "small duties" as a positive view of the potential value in mundane domestic life.[40]

Despite the apparent hierarchy of sex and birth order, Hortensia educates the children in the same way by encouraging them to question and talk about the smallest details of plants – a leveling that sometimes seems at odds with her more rigid distinctions. Jacson's credo, "we can do nothing without energy,"[41] applies to all. Her commitment to energy and industriousness is reminiscent of the Taylor sisters' upholding of industry as a primary virtue for children, as discussed in Chapter 1. Jane Taylor centers the moral of her story "Busy Idleness" around "Charlotte the idle flibbertigebet" who is always "flitting from one thing to another without completing anything." Idly picking up *An Introduction to Botany*, she quickly decides, after only reading a page and a half, to go out and botanize: "having found a blank copy-book, she hastened into the garden, where gathering a few common flowers, she proceeded to dissect them, not it is to be feared, with much scientific nicety. Perhaps as many as 3 pages of the copy-book were bespread with her specimens, before she discovered, that Botany was a *dry study*."[42] In the illustration (Fig. 2.5) Charlotte is in the first flush of interest, picking a flower in the garden with the copy-book under her arm, but we

Fig. 2.5. "Girl Botanizing," illustration in Jane Taylor, *A Day's Pleasure*.

would be safe in concluding that this indolent, aimless girl never took the time to study the details of nature that Hortensia and her children admire.

Hortensia's lesson on *Equisetum* (the genus of plants such as rushes that reproduce by spores rather than seeds) brings together several issues of magnification and seeing. She describes the plant in early spring pushing "out of the earth a little club-shaped head; round this head are placed in circles target-form substances, each supported on a pedicle, and compressed into angles, in consequence of their resting against each other before the spike expands." This detailed description, as Hortensia explains, is based on observation with the naked eye: "All this we may see without a microscope; but by the assistance of glasses green oval bodies have been discovered, and attached to them (generally) four pellucid and very slender threads, spoonform, at their ends." When Juliette comments that she would not have suspected such regularity and distinct formations, Hortensia reminds her that "regular organization exists in all the various parts of plants, though from the want of a proper method of investigating them this may not be always visible to us." Hortensia goes on to explain that the threads are in motion and are very sensitive to moist air, adding that they will have to take this point "upon trust" because to see the motion would require greater magnification than they have. She also informs them that a certain German botanist believes the green ovals are seeds, but wisely warns that "Future observations must confirm or refute this opinion" – modern science will not, of course, verify that the *Equisetum* bears seeds.[43]

When Hortensia next has the children examine the capsules from the hart's-tongue fern, the description suggests both the life of the plant and the challenge in viewing the minute world under the microscope:

The warmth of breath ... by occasioning the capsules to open and discharge their seeds, gives them the appearance of something alive. While you are intently looking at one, hoping to observe the operation, the strength and elasticity of the spring, at the moment of discharging, will often carry it out of sight, so that to see the manner of opening requires some dexterous management, and much patience; but we shall be able, I dare say, to overcome the difficulties, and obtain the amusement of viewing through the microscope this curious arrangement.[44]

As this vivid description makes evident, Jacson has Hortensia frame the lesson to teach several different skills and virtues: in addition to keen observation, the children will need patience and dexterity in managing the specimen. Like the green oval bodies and pellucid threads of the *Equisetum*, the delicate leaves of this fern have a story to tell about the "progress" of nature, the constant and unexpected motion of life. The plant specimens are governed by the same "energy" that Jacson values in humans. Magnified objects have, Jacson implies, a secret life, which intense observation can uncover: we are reminded of Stewart's "daydream of the microscope."[45]

"A LONG HABIT OF VIEWING DIMINUTIVE OBJECTS": THE SCIENCE OF AGNES IBBETSON

In the late 1790s, just as Jacson's *Botanical Dialogues* was published, several popular books dealing with women's education mentioned botany as a suitable pursuit if relegated to the level of recreation or entertainment. Erasmus Darwin, in *Plan for the Conduct of Female Education* (1797), cited botany as "a fashionable study for ladies" since it would not only provide them with "amusement" but would also enable them to be better conversationalists with men.[46] A year later Priscilla Wakefield classed botany among the "lighter studies" suitable (again) for the "amusement" of ladies, while Hannah More praised it as a "delightful pursuit."[47] But Agnes Ibbetson took up botany as a serious scientific commitment, and rather than being focused on flowers, which were often connected for aesthetic and sentimental reasons with women, she studied such unladylike subjects as grasses and agricultural crops. Like Anna Maria Hussey (discussed in Chapter 3), she might be seen as transgressing the "limits of modesty and decorum" urged by Priscilla Wakefield in her discussion of women and science, and she certainly stepped outside the realm of "domestic privacy" that Wakefield saw as proper for women.[48] Ibbetson's work introduces another dimension to women's botanical pursuits that were not directly linked to the education of children.

Ibbetson began submitting her findings to scientific journals when she was in her fifties and published more than fifty articles in periodicals such as *A Journal of Natural Philosophy, Chemistry, and the Arts* (significantly, the only woman to do so during this period).[49] Her writing often reveals a blend of humility and confidence, not uncommon in women authors of the period. While she apologizes "for venturing to contradict authors so much superior to me in science," she *does* in fact go on to contradict them.[50] Despite her willingness to engage in scientific debate with male botanists, she asserts that "My part has been that of a reviewer only, it has no more merit than transcribing faithfully what I saw, and drawing exactly what the dissected vegetable offered to my view."[51] But she proudly describes her work as "perfectly original," and in another article states, "I must now mention what no one has before noticed."[52]

Ibbetson emphasizes the importance of careful first-hand examination of botanical minutiae, coupled with the need for confidence in one's findings: asserting that "not one botanist in a thousand has really examined" the inner structure of a tree's buds, she adds, somewhat peevishly, "it is scarcely to be believed how carelessly my work has been noticed, and how little botanists are agreed on the subject, except in the wish to get rid of it, when it is certainly a *new science*, which they have not yet *examined*, but which might prove (if followed up) of the greatest utility to both farming and gardening."[53] She frequently notes the many years of observation and experimentation that lay behind her publications, the dissections repeated over and over again, and the "progressive" nature of her work to offset any criticism of her as a dilettante or of her findings as suspect.[54] Her "Treatise on Botany" (which she hoped would be her magnum opus, but which was never published and remains in manuscript form) begins, "Aweful as it is, as it must be to a woman to present to the Public a work of science," but she goes on to justify her endeavors by emphasizing her "perseverance" and "enduring excessive labour" for sixteen years.

Ibbetson admits that her "presumption" shocks even herself, as she dares to "give hints" to men who are generally considered so much more learned and experienced than she.[55] But she reminds her readers that "in this matter the eyes are the principal judges," which helps us to understand why she considered her drawings to be as important as her text explanations (contrary to the more typical view during this period of scientific illustrations as secondary to the text),[56] and she adds, "a long habit of viewing diminutive objects will detect truth, sooner than much knowledge." Where Hussey writes with a primary goal of entertaining her readers, as we will see in Chapter 3, Ibbetson specifically rejects that approach: "I could have diversified this account, and perhaps made it more amusing, instead of a dry detail of facts; but I write merely to show the *truth*."[57] Her factual language is completely devoid of what would have been called fancy or sentiment at the time. In fact, she argues against the "unhappy custom" of making comparisons between plants and animals and wants to destroy "all those imaginary fancies of feeling and *sensation*, delicate Ladies have indulged till they could weep at plucking a rose." She describes her language as "plain and simple" and one could say the same about her drawing style.[58]

Ibbetson's illustrations are particularly important as evidence of what her eyes have seen, and they vary in style from elegantly simple, beautifully detailed watercolors, like those from her unpublished sketchbook on grasses (Fig. 2.6), to drawings used to illustrate her scientific findings (Fig. 2.7) that were made with the aid of various microscopes, including single-lens, solar, and lucernal.[59] These published drawings have the appearance of simplified line studies with bold contours, seeming at first more like stylized forms than realistic representations of natural objects. She intended to be perfectly clear and unbiased in these images, although they were criticized by one commentator at the time as belonging more in "the regions of fancy" due to "the very high magnifying power she uses, aided by the warmth of her imagination."[60] She responded to such criticism with some pique, stating that she would "stake [her] life" on their accuracy, "since every one has been drawn above 20 times" (and in fact she made it known that her conclusions were substantiated by repeated dissections, sometimes up to two hundred, of different specimens of the same species).[61]

Ibbetson considered herself a dedicated scientist who used rigorous methods and appropriate instruments, especially various kinds of microscopes in addition to "as many different sorts [of tools] as a surgeon."[62] Microscopy revealed to her eyes a world of order and truth that could be understood only through the most painstaking application of her skills. While her writing style tends to be straightforward, detailed, and descriptive, she occasionally resorts to religious language: "It is certainly true, that we are more struck with the power of the Almighty, when we contemplate his small works, than in the view of his larger chefs d'oeuvre: when each diminutive object is so highly finished, it would appear the peculiar care of

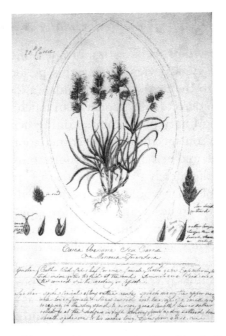

Fig 2.6. Agnes Ibbetson, *Carex arenaria*. Sketchbook, Botany Library, Natural History Museum, London.

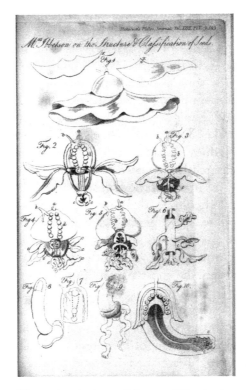

Fig. 2.7. Illustration in Agnes Ibbetson, "On the Structure and Classification of Seeds," facing p. 183.

providence."[63] Nature for her is consistent and clear, above all else, revealing its beauty to those who observe carefully. She "felt convinced, that if I had followed her [Nature] exactly, without exageration [sic], or addition of my own, I might depend that one truth would unfold and explain another, till the whole would be displayed in one grand and beautiful arrangement, simple in its structure, as divine and lovely in its origin."[64] She sometimes personifies Nature as a powerful female agent who "plainly speaks her purpose" and is "alert," who "writes her fair history on my mind," and who has "secret paths" that must be discovered.[65] Arrested by the wonder of small things, Ibbetson even exclaims in one scientific article, "How beautiful the provisions of Nature! What care, what attention, to each minute circumstance!"[66]

NATURE AS AN OPEN BOOK: MARY ROBERTS'S *WONDERS OF THE VEGETABLE KINGDOM DISPLAYED* (1822)

Mary Roberts's *Wonders of the Vegetable Kingdom* celebrates the awe that Ibbetson expresses in that moment of excitement. We have found in Jacson's *Botanical Dialogues* both a commitment to traditions of Enlightenment thought and moral improvement and an understanding of the imaginative and sympathetic dimensions of knowledge. Jacson teaches the children to enter into "the daydream of the microscope"[67] as well as its scientific dimensions. But this daydream, which forms only part of Jacson's vision and is largely absent from Ibbetson's, is the primary mode of Mary Roberts's approach to the subject. "Wonder" is indeed a key term for this book, which is indebted to her religious faith and heritage as a Quaker. Perhaps related to what Robert Ryan has termed the religious reformation of the period, Roberts unabashedly links her work with the divine creation and God's presence in the world.[68] Whereas the connection is evident in Wakefield (also a Quaker) and other earlier writers, Roberts sees the world of nature as God's folio volume and makes the spiritual connection the centerpiece of her text – and of her life's work. Roberts still inhabits a world where religion and science seem complementary and supportive, and her writing combines her two passions without anxiety.[69]

Rather than operating in the domestic setting, Roberts's persona writes a series of letters to such lofty fictional characters as Lælius, Orontes, Timoclea, and Cleora, "designed to comprise, in a small space, a general sketch of the economy, utility, and elegance of the vegetable kingdom."[70] So although the epistolary mode might be common for women writers, the classicism is not.[71] The book is dedicated to William Withering in "esteem for his talents and gratitude for the pleasure derived from his Systematic Arrangement of British Plants," but Roberts is not herself concerned with systematic arrangements.[72] She eschews the domestic setting, we think, in order to emphasize the primary contrast between the small world of botanical study and the vastness of the universe. These two poles interest her more than the personal setting or the give-and-take of dialogue; she is not concerned with gender roles or different educational philosophies. Her use of the formal letter and classical names for her characters promotes a more cosmic sense of the universe, moving between opposite poles of the infinitesimally small and the awesomely grand. We have seen that she opens the book with the frontispiece from Mungo Park, but she also develops Park's spiritual insight in greater depth.

Throughout *Wonders*, Roberts reiterates that "The rapid or gradual unfolding of a leaf, or flower, is scarcely less wonderful, when properly considered, than the formation of a world." She makes the point that we easily appreciate the grandeur of the vast universe but overlook the small and seemingly ordinary objects in nature. As a complement to the association between grandeur and vastness related to the great discoveries of Herschel, Roberts had already introduced the example of the venerable oak tree, which the casual viewer takes in as one massive object. Instead, she encourages her readers to look at the roots through a microscope – to look with what she terms a "botanic eye" – and discover the intricate constellation of vessels and cells that make up "vegetable masses."[73] For Roberts, this intricacy of life is part of the revelation of God and attests to the ongoing process of creation. Another Quaker writer, Sarah Hoare, echoes Roberts's sentiments a few years later in her *Poems on Conchology and Botany* (1831). Hoare presents herself in the preface as a teacher who has led her students to "a more minute examination of the wonderful works of the creator," proclaiming near the end of her collection:

> And not to casual glance display'd
> Alone; – by microscopic aid,
> We view a wond'rous store;
> The cups nectareous now appear,
> The fringe, the down, the gland'lar hair,
> The germ enclos'd with curious care,
> And petals spangled o'er.[74]

Once again, the author contrasts the "casual glance" with the botanic eye that appreciates the wonders of the smallest plant.

Furthermore, Roberts insists that all of creation serves an orderly purpose in the world, and she explains the basic physiology of the plant and the dependency of each stage of development on the one before: roots, stems, leaves, flowers, and fruit. From this analogy, Roberts also suggests a conservative view of the body politic, with the poor associated with the roots all the way to the rich (flower and fruit) who depend on their labor. One of Roberts's fictional characters, Orontes, analogizes the structure of a plant, developing from roots to leaves, to the "progressive stages of education," in which students must establish strong roots in order to develop as strong and healthy beings. Roberts then reports a garden conversation between Orontes and Calista, in which they discuss the various connections between certain types of plants and people; as we saw in Chapter 1 with wildflowers, these comparisons were accompanied by definite moral judgments: whereas "A rose may be considered as the vegetable prototype of some distinguished female, whose worth is far superior to that of gold or rubies," Orontes describes the "Venus-catchfly" as "Dressed in a gay drapery, and flaunting her head to the luxuriant breeze, attracting the summer-flies that skim around her, and blooming only for the vain and gay."[75]

Although Roberts does not arrange her book according to the Linnaean system (preferring instead to discuss plant structure from root to seeds), she does praise Linnaeus for revealing the grandeur in the smallest distinctions of the vegetable world: "In the humblest of his works, in the little flower which a casual observer would have passed by or crushed beneath his feet, he perceived that the characters of Infinite goodness were engraven, too deep to be effaced, too legible to be mistaken." Linnaeus serves also as an exemplar of the "botanic eye," opposed to the casual observer who does not see or appreciate the details of the natural world. Linnaeus's greatness as a botanist derives from his patient observation of small things. He stands in the text as the counterpart of Herschel as discoverer of new worlds, whereas Buffon figures several times as the vain scientist who had his own statue inscribed with "'A genius equal to the majesty of nature'"; Roberts satirizes his pretension by commenting, "A blade of grass was, however, sufficient to confound his impious pretensions."[76]

Roberts presents true botanists as distinguished from landscape painters or searchers for the sublime because they appreciate the small objects in the foreground.[77] In a letter to Eudocia, Roberts had already introduced the sublime in a negative way with a long description of Colebrook Dale, the industrial site that entertained, fascinated, and horrified visitors. Predating Roberts, Anna Seward offered an early ecological response to the violation of nature in her poem "Colebrook Dale," describing the "Scene of superfluous grace, and wasted bloom, / O, violated Colebrook!"[78] Similarly, Roberts tells Eudocia that "There is a sterile grandeur ... in the scenery of Coalbrook Dale, which irresistibly seizes on the imagination. All is wildness and sublimity." The iron works make a kind of sublime parody of the natural processes that Roberts praises in *Wonders*. Instead of roots nourishing stately trees, she projects a vision of hell: "Trees torn up by the roots project their long branches over the broken cliffs." Although Roberts does not offer much commentary on the meaning of this wild vision, she presents it as a scene that cannot be read with a botanic eye. All beauty, connectedness, and intricacy have been uprooted by the crushing power of the industrial sublime. In contrast to this view of the world, Roberts posits "the garden of existence" as filled with abundant variety: "the gay, the pensive, and the melancholy, spring together, and decorate the same parterre."[79] Roberts, thus, does not reject complexity of emotion, but she critiques the violence and disorder associated with the sublime. As we will see in Dorothy Wordsworth and other women writers of the period, the ordinary wonders of creation – for Roberts both wildflowers and parterres – contrast with the spectacle of the sublime.

Roberts devotes most of her text before and after this passage to "the minuter [sic] works of nature" associated with various plants and their intricate parts. She is especially interested in seeds and their "vital principle," which can withstand voyages around the world or burial in the ground for ages. Roberts recognizes that the seed stores the genetic material of life, a notion captured in her description of the strawberry: "The seeds of the strawberry rise from the delicious pulp in which they are enclosed, and, even to the naked eye, present the appearance of strawberries in miniature."[80] The naked eye may be able to see these seeds, but Roberts's imagination conceives of them as precious miniatures that contain the fruit. As Bachelard notes in relation to a fragment from *Cyrano de Bergerac* describing the "heat" of an appleseed, "In this text, nothing stands out, but everything is imagined, and the imaginary miniature is proposed to enclose an imaginary value. At the center is the seed, which is hotter than the entire apple. This condensed heat, this warm well-being that men love, takes the image out of the class of images one can see into that of images that are lived."[81] Seeds for Roberts become just such lived images.

Erasmus Darwin expresses a similar vision of seeds in *The Botanic Garden: The Economy of Plants*, in a passage that Roberts quotes but does not identify:

> Lo, on each seed, within its slender rind,
> Life's golden threads in endless circles wind,
> Maze within maze, the lucid threads are roll'd,
> And, as they burst, the living flame unfold.[82]

As in the image from *Cyrano de Bergerac*, the heart of the seed is imagined as "heat" or in this case "a living flame" that bursts with life. Similarly, Roberts imagines that "Often has Philanthes listened on a calm sunny day, to the crackling of furze-bushes, caused by the explosion of their little elastic pods, or watched the down of innumerable seeds floating on the summer breeze,"[83] with the aural qualities enhancing the image of the seed as a concentrated form of life.

CONCLUSION

A powerful subtext for Roberts and other botanical writers is that the study of botany, including the magic of seeds and generation, is connected to the origins of life in the Garden of Eden. Not literally, perhaps, for all of the writers considered here, but metaphorically all gardens in the Judeo-Christian tradition can be connected to the Garden and hence elicit nostalgia and longing for the past. Even in these texts, where the ostensible purpose is teaching rational systems of plant classification and physiology, the language reveals the intuitive dream world of plants – the flaming seed pod or the slender, barely visible threads of life. In this way, the texts present themselves as rational "discussions" or "conversations," but they often open up the Bachelardian world of the image: the microscopic view of the rational scientist unfolds into that of the dreamer, who sees with a "botanic eye" this world as if for the first time.

Most of these texts, then, have one foot in the Enlightenment, sharing Hooke's ambition that science will uncover the secrets of the world that is *there*, under the microscope, and the other foot in the imaginative dream world that we traditionally associate with the male Romantics – the Wordsworthian seeing "into the life of things" or the Blakean vision of "a World in a Grain of Sand."[84] Like Blake's ideal guardians in the *Songs of Innocence*, these mother-mentors both protect their children and give them the freedom to imagine. Even Jane Marcet, who dramatizes not a mother but a teacher-governess and her two pupils in *Conversations on Vegetable Physiology* and who professes that the study of plant physiology must be useful, employs brilliant metaphorical language to convey, Roberts-like, the marvels of creation. Mrs. B., the teacher, tells Emily and Caroline that "No child has so richly ornamented a cradle as the seed when reposing within the recesses of the flower."[85] This metaphor of the cradle, which we have also seen in Jacson, connects for the pupils and readers the origin and development of seeds with human longing for the security of home. As Bachelard muses, "always, in our daydreams, the house is a large cradle ... Life begins well, it begins enclosed, protected, all warm in the bosom of the house."[86] Mrs. B's seed metaphor becomes a metonym for our desire for warmth and security.

This image of the seed-pod cradle also suggests a miniature, a kind of anthropomorphic dollhouse view of the early childhood of the plant. The appeal to miniature that we have seen throughout, in fact, connects the development of plants to the course of human life. Miniature appeals to young audiences, who can imagine their own lives in terms of the plants. As Susan Stewart has said, the world of childhood "presents in some ways a miniature and fictive chapter in each life history."[87] Think, for instance, of Wordsworth's "best Philosopher" in the "Intimations Ode," a vision of the child as a man-in-miniature.[88] Also, Bachelard posits that "values become condensed and enriched in miniature," which makes such images particularly suggestive. And this richness is especially evident in the miniature when applied to the lives of plants. Once again, Bachelard notes that "Through its attachment to miniaturized forces, the vegetal world is great in smallness, sharp in gentleness, vividly alive in its greenness."[89]

The botanical world, so closely linked with the life of miniature, is also a world of nostalgia, often presented by the mother-mentor in terms of her own botanical and horticultural memories. For instance, in Smith's *Rural Walks* Mrs. Woodfield tells her children that

> I am indeed an enthusiast in my passion for flowers; and I think the happiest hours in which I can carry my recollection in thinking of my past life, are those when I was a girl of ten or eleven years old, and was suffered, nay encouraged, to cultivate myself a little spot of ground, in a part of a garden of my father's, appropriated entirely to flowers. How deep, even at this distance of time, does the impression remain of those simple objects which then charmed my senses![90]

This "little spot of ground," a miniature within the paternal garden, forms the central focus of memory, and the values associated with it – health, happiness, beauty – are ones that Mrs. Woodfield seeks to impart to her children. She goes on to discuss various types of flowers with her children, but has provided them with her memory as a kind of anchor for their botanical and horticultural studies. Like the other mentors we have seen, Mrs. Woodfield teaches her children to observe, to value, and to imagine, as well as to lay the groundwork for the memories that sustain one as the future unfolds. Remembering her flowers, Mrs. Woodfield will always be able to find her way back home.

PART II

The visual frame: constructing a view

CHAPTER 3

Picturing the "home landscape": the nature of accomplishment

Women represented the natural world in a variety of ways – from amateur sketches of flowers and picturesque scenes to more skilled botanical illustrations and landscape paintings – yet despite the range of their artistic interests and abilities there was an underlying ambivalence about the function and value of art-making in women's lives during this period. While authors such as Hannah More scornfully rejected the emphasis on female "accomplishments" – setting the young woman intent on superficial pleasure and admiration in opposition to the sensible, reasonable wife and mother – others recognized the value of seeing and ordering (and thus taming or domesticating) the world of nature through a woman's eyes. Of special interest here will be certain women who used their art as a way to understand their position in the world, with one foot in the home and the other in the natural world beyond. By considering the conflicting attitudes toward drawing as a female accomplishment, we will have a better sense of the background from which these women emerged as active participants in the commercial arena of publication and exhibition. In particular, the portraits, landscapes, and genre scenes of Maria Spilsbury and the botanical illustrations of Anna Maria Hussey will illustrate the shifting divide between interior and exterior, amateur and professional, thus providing us with a way to gauge their art-making as a form of spatial identity. As women operating in multiple spheres, these two artists, like others discussed in this chapter, used images of nature to acknowledge their actual and metaphorical location in the world. Centered in the home, they were able to move outward with confidence to observe and capture the natural scene, whether in its minute particularities, as in the case of Hussey's study of fungi, or its framing of personal narratives, as in Spilsbury's portraits and cottage views.

In Edgeworth's *The Parent's Assistant* (1796), Sophie, who is busy mixing paint for a watercolor, and her nosy brother Frederick enter into a heated debated about word usage that leads Sophie at one point to explain, "I was not disputing, I was reasoning," and Frederick to respond infuriatingly, "Well, reasoning or disputing. Women have no business to do either; for, how should they know how to chop logic like men?" He adds that women should learn useful things like making puddings rather than Greek and Latin, or even drawing, which he asserts is "the same thing": "Women who are always drawing and reasoning, never know how to make puddings." To which Sophie replies that, having learned to mix colors, she could also easily learn to mix ingredients for a recipe.[1] Two years later, however, Edgeworth in *Practical Education* (1798), co-authored with her father, sends a clear warning against "female accomplishments" such as drawing, since they all too often lead only to empty praise: "charming! admirable! and astonishing!" While not devaluing the innocent pleasures to be derived from drawing and music, the Edgeworths encourage women to recognize them as merely pastimes: "We condemn only the abuse of these accomplishments; we only wish that they should be considered as domestic occupations, not as matters of competition, or of exhibition, nor yet as the means of attracting temporary admiration."[2] The difference in tone between the two books may be due in part to her father's participation in the project[3] but is largely, we propose, the result of a shift in approach between pedagogical theories about the education of children, on the one hand, and cultural norms about the roles of young women, on the other. The divide at puberty between childhood, with its greater freedom to explore, and the adult years, which require new levels of responsibility and decorum, was pronounced during this period. Changing attitudes about what was appropriate or necessary for children as opposed to young women – a pushing forward and growing outward (Greek, Latin, drawing, reasoning!) versus a curtailing or constraining (the focus on domesticity and the avoidance of exhibition) – might underlie Edgeworth's views about drawing in these two texts.

Edgeworth may be reflecting this transition out of childhood in several scenes in *Rosamond* (1821), describing the response of two sisters to the landscape during a family trip. Rosamond at this point is between ten and thirteen, so she and her older sister Laura are both at key transitional ages. Excited by the passing views from the carriage, Laura tries to capture them in her sketchbook, "but at every trial she failed in the hope of representing what she saw, and at last gave herself up, as Rosamond advised, to the full enjoyment of the present." A few pages later their brother Godfrey begins speculating about the planting of some land he had inherited. Despite his youth (he had not yet come of age), his father makes plans to assist him. Actively engaged in projecting their mental picture onto the landscape, they serve as a clear contrast to the sisters: Rosamond, though energetically helping with the measurement of various trees, is still primarily relegated in this scene to the position of sympathetic listener, and the more sober and restrained Laura, under the tutelage of a drawing master, is "equally happy in making some rapid sketches of the picturesque groups of trees."[4] While both sisters are "happy," then, they are already conforming to the gendered expectations of the period, and drawing becomes a way of establishing the code of conduct: in the first vignette drawing as a difficult pursuit gets in the way of Laura's direct sensory apprehension of the landscape – and thus serves as an intellectual as well as practical obstacle to the feminine mode of direct sensation – whereas the act of sketching in the second scene is more acceptable both because it is under the aegis of the drawing master and because it sets her apart from the male conversation about controlling or managing the land.

MASTERS AND MANUALS: SKETCHING AS "PROFITABLE IMPROVEMENT"

A new focus in the late eighteenth and early nineteenth centuries on sketching as a skill suitable for women, especially those of the middle and upper classes, prompted some changes in art education. Drawing masters, including such well-known female botanical illustrators as Clara Wheatley Pope and Augusta Withers, were employed by the well-to-do to give lessons in the home.[5] For those unable to afford private lessons – Mary Lawrance, for example, charged half a guinea for each botanical drawing session in 1804 – art was often taught in the schools.[6] The accomplished mother could also provide early lessons in the home, as described in Charlotte Anne Broome's *Fanny and Mary* (1821): the two girls had a sketchbook of their "penciled landscapes," although Mary "coaxed her mama" to fix her mistakes since "her trees looked like sticks with old wigs on them."[7] The importance of the mother's role as instructor was often upheld as a reason for training young women in the arts, thus adding some measure of domesticity to the rhetoric of elegance and taste employed by the numerous instruction manuals in drawing published during this period. Many of these were explicitly oriented to the female amateur, as sketching and painting watercolors of nature, especially flowers, were increasingly viewed by professional organizations like the Royal Academy as fit only for women.[8] While belittled as a lesser form of art, without any higher content and thus more akin to domestic decoration, flower painting, as Ann Bermingham suggests, "allowed women the freedom to embrace the dominant cultural stereotypes of femininity – the overdetermined relationship of women to flowers – while, if they wished, using this relationship to pursue art in a professional way as artists, teachers, authors, and exhibitors."[9]

The very nature of the sketch – its incompleteness, its unassertive scale – placed women in a double bind: while viewed as a particularly suitable feminine "accomplishment" due to its modesty and propriety as an art form, its lack of finish could be interpreted as "an unredeemable sign of moral failing – lack of application, lack of concentration, and lack of discipline."[10] Small in scale and modest in final appearance, sketches perfectly suited the period's expectations for appropriate feminine behavior. In terms of our theory of spatial identity, in which a woman's location in the physical spaces of her home landscape takes on metaphorical associations, the sketch is particularly resonant. Reserved for private viewing and rarely made public, women's drawings and watercolors were typically either framed and hung in the home (as with the "landscapes and flowers" by Jane Austen's Emma) or kept in even greater privacy within the pages of a commonplace book.[11] Richard Sha argues that these sketches "insist upon their own insufficiency" by being "effaced" within these albums, which were compiled from a wide assortment of found as well as original texts and images, often pasted in without attribution.[12] The anonymity of most women's sketches, which were usually neither signed nor exhibited, underscored their low status in the hierarchy of art-making.

The titles of drawing manuals used by women often indicate the nature of the instruction: Thomas Parkinson's *Flower Painting Made Easy: Being a Collection of Correct Outlines after Nature* (1775), for instance, or Anne Everard's *Flowers from Nature, with the Botanical Name, Class, and Order; and Instructions for Copying* (1835). Some give step-by-step instructions while others were intended as simple copy-books, even what we might call coloring books. Such a mechanical approach, relegating women to the role of imitators rather than originators, appalled the fourteen-year-old Emily Shore, who admired the landscape sketches of an older male acquaintance in contrast to the style often recommended for women: "Though boldly, perhaps hastily executed, they are by no means too broad and coarse, but accurate and delicate. It is this style of drawing at which I aim ... I cannot bear what the *Quarterly Journal of Education* calls the neat sampler-like style, practiced by so many ladies."[13] She may have been thinking of the illustrations in Augustin Heckle's *The Lady's Drawing Book* (1753), which start with simple geometric shapes before moving on to the more complex details of natural forms: a full-blown rose, for example, begins as a series of concentric circles (Fig. 3.1). Copy work was a mechanism for keeping women situated in the category

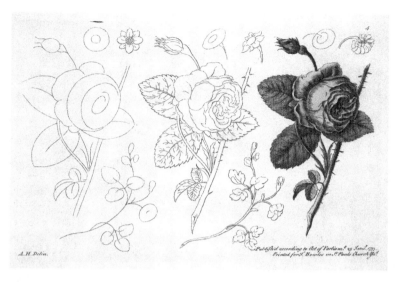

Fig. 3.1. Illustration in Augustin Heckle, *The Lady's Drawing Book*, pl. 4.

of amateur, able to access only with difficulty the level of originality expected of exhibiting artists.[14]

To offset the rote, generic nature of the copy-book approach, some texts, while still offering prints to copy as well as detailed directions for the novice, reminded the reader that the goal was unaffected naturalism. In *Sketches of Flowers from Nature* (1801), Mary Lawrance stated that "Grace or Ease cannot be too diligently sought after" and "natural Appearance ... is the Ultimatum of the Art." Queen Charlotte enjoyed coloring in the outlines of engraved botanical plates, but she and her daughters also spent time sketching plants from life in the Royal Gardens at Kew.[15] Maria Cosway's portrait of the young *Princess Amelia* (c. 1800) presents her in a traditional pose of display, but without the coy glance often found in images of more sophisticated women at this time. Instead the drawing that Amelia holds out for us to see deflects our attention from the girl to her art, thus operating almost like a co-protagonist as it reveals her skill at sketching the landscape.

Fiction, memoirs, and letters from this period often include descriptions of sketching expeditions. Laura in Edgeworth's *Rosamond* stories is always stopping to draw the view, and we might picture her in Samuel Baldwin's *Sketching from Nature* (1857), though somewhat younger and less finely dressed (Fig. 3.2). In Baldwin's conception it is the woman who serves as the primary object of our gaze, not the landscape. She is surrounded by picturesque scenery but turns away from the rocky stream and waterfall

Fig. 3.2. Samuel Baldwin, *Sketching from Nature*. Private collection.

behind her. Her eyes are fixed on something above and beyond the clump of wildflowers in the foreground, leaving us to imagine the view that she is sketching. She is posed more for graceful effect than for the realism of her actions, since an actual young woman would surely be seated on the

Masters and manuals 85

Fig. 3.3. Jane Taylor, *Flower Baskets*. Suffolk Record Office.

stool in order to support the heavy sketchbook on her lap. The air of artificial refinement in Baldwin's painting is entirely absent from Emily Shore's description of a day-long excursion to Bradley Woods in 1837, when she was seventeen: "Some rambled one way, some another; several sketched, and we were all much dispersed. Nearly the first thing I did was to sit down on an edge of rock amongst the gorse, and sketch the profile of a bold rock and part of the valley. Mr. W. sat a little below me, and sketched the same part."[16] Emily shows little regard for where she sat or how she might have appeared to Mr. W. Her focus, instead, is on the "bold rock" that she chose for her drawing.

Jane Taylor's two sketches of flowers arranged in a straw basket (Fig. 3.3), almost identical to each other, could have been drawn from a copy-book. But although they were quickly delineated, without much naturalistic detail, the flowers still exhibit a sense of liveliness, and by duplicating the sketch Taylor was taking the time to practice her skills. The rose in the center might have been based on the geometric underpinning recommended by Heckle, as it was built up from a series of simple circles, but otherwise her touch is light and irregular, avoiding the stiff, lifeless quality often found in novice

Fig. 3.4. Jane Taylor, *Woman Sketching*. Suffolk Record Office.

sketches. Taylor was an accomplished amateur artist (Fig. 3.4), having been taught engraving as a profession by her father. Her brother noted that her drawings, including landscapes as well as still lives, "display a true feeling of the beautiful in nature; and a peculiar niceness and elegance of execution." Although she eventually chose writing over art as a professional pursuit, she continued to draw "for the gratification of her friends" and as a means of strengthening her appreciation of nature: "She retained ... that vivid relish of the beauties of nature which perhaps seldom exists in its highest degree, apart from some knowledge and practice of the imitative arts."[17]

Most women were hesitant about moving outward beyond the home into the public sphere of exhibition and commerce, and female authors were often apologetic about their publications. Even the very popular Edgeworth asked her cousin not to "call my little stories by the sublime title of 'my works,' I shall else be ashamed when the little mouse comes forth."[18] A similar measure of humility appears in many of the prefaces of drawing manuals by women. Priscilla Bury, in her elephant folio *A Selection of Hexandrian Plants* (1831–34), "relies on the indulgences and courtesy of those more able and learned ... who may be induced to patronize the feeble attempts of an Amateur." The concern about women becoming professional artists was also pronounced, since involvement with exhibitions and sales catapulted women out of domestic retirement into a masculine world of display, commerce, and public critique. Women were increasingly entering the professional ranks – in the 1770s just over 10 percent of the works exhibited at the Society of Artists of Great Britain were by women, for example, up from 3.8 percent in the previous decade – but this was often due to exigencies beyond their control.[19] Maria Spilsbury and Anna Maria Hussey, as we shall see, both moved into the public realm at least in part as a result of financial problems.

"TO AMUSE AND INSTRUCT": THE DEBATE ABOUT SKETCHING NATURE

Sketching, in its private, domestic form, was widely regarded as a valuable pursuit for a variety of reasons. Mary Wollstonecraft, who took lessons in flower painting from the botanist James Sowerby, argued that drawing and music could "refine the mind."[20] Drawing was also held up as a harmless amusement "to cheat the lonely hour" and, more practically, as a resource for mothers "to amuse and instruct" their children.[21] Mary Wright Sewell, sister-in-law of Sarah Ellis, argued in her *Thoughts on Education* from the 1850s for a more systematic training in drawing for young girls, especially to prepare them for motherhood: "A lady who has a free use of her pencil, and able to make a ready sketch of any living thing she sees, is sure to attract a group of delighted children round her." Children would benefit in numerous ways as they acquired "the habit of accurate observation" and "the value of correct language and description." Sewell believed that careful observation through the mechanism of drawing could provide, "if the teacher be skilful and cheerful, both moral and spiritual instruction."[22]

The instructional manual *Elegant Arts for Ladies* proposed that drawing and music, unlike the more questionable pleasure of dancing, could "purify the taste and exalt the minds."[23] That manual, like other mid-Victorian ladies' books, offered a much broader range of pursuits than Wollstonecraft might have approved of, but the authors clearly had the same intent: to offset the criticism of such accomplishments as merely a form of vanity. As Wollstonecraft's good Mrs. Trueman professes, referring to her drawings and songs, "I am happy when I can amuse those I love; it is not then vanity, but tenderness, that spurs me on."[24] Many authors warned against flaunting one's amateurish drawings outside the family circle, but some specifically acknowledged their value as simple gifts, thus providing a service to others. In Budden's *Chit Chat*, for example, Kate is given a tulip to depict as a present for a widowed friend, and her aunt explains the value of drawing and painting – first, to preserve nature's beauty and second, to extend that beauty to another in a charitable act: "Thus, by your skill in this charming art, you will not only preserve a picture of this lovely flower, but you will please one who has pleased you, and deserves this mark of your regard."[25]

Priscilla Wakefield, who focused on the value of rational pursuits for young women, had earlier summarized many of the arguments for drawing as a worthy undertaking in *Reflections on the Present Condition of the Female Sex* (1798):

Drawing, not merely for the purpose of making pleasing pictures, and obtaining applause, but for that capacity it gives to a proficient of representing any object with ease and accuracy, is both an useful and amusing qualification; nor are its good effects confined to the exercise of the art alone, it strengthens the habit of observation, and facilitates the acquisition of natural history, which is a study at once delightful and valuable; and it promotes a reverential admiration of the wisdom and goodness of the Great First Cause.[26]

Among Wakefield's most popular books was *An Introduction to Botany* (1796), written as a series of letters between two sisters. In the preface Wakefield establishes the didactic tone by describing botany as an "antidote to levity and idleness," and the lessons are resolutely home-centered as it is Felicia, staying with her parents, who writes about what she is learning to her sister, who is spending the summer away with their aunt. Felicia also occasionally sends sketches to accompany her letters, explaining that it is "difficult to express forms and shapes by writing" and hoping that her drawings "will represent, in a more lively manner, the pleasing objects of our present researches."[27] Shteir's comment about Wakefield's text, that "The sedentary sister at home does not venture beyond the garden and adjacent fields, or beyond domestic ideology,"[28] is an important point to consider as we map the gendered spaces of the home, garden, and near landscape. But Felicia's newly acquired knowledge, expressed through both words and images, and her excitement about scientific learning certainly indicate the ways in which women were more actively engaged with nature – physically, intellectually, and imaginatively.

Maria Cosway's illustrations for *The Progress of Female Virtue* and *The Progress of Female Dissipation* (1800) – Hogarthian moral narratives whose images are supported by Mary Robinson's poems – convey contrasting views of desire, enterprise, and value. Entering the stories of the virtuous and dissipated young women at the same mid-way point (Figs. 3.5 and 3.6), we find significant differences in the way they occupy themselves. Cosway personifies virtue as a woman seated in an austere room, leaning

"To amuse and instruct" 89

Fig. 3.5. Maria Cosway, *Progress of Female Virtue*, pl. 4. Aquatint by Antoine Cardon after Cosway's chalk drawing.

Fig. 3.6. Maria Cosway, *Progress of Female Dissipation*, pl. 4. Aquatint by Antoine Cardon after Cosway's chalk drawing.

forward over her sketching pad as she draws the landscape visible through the window. Having none of the narcissistic self-consciousness of the dissipated woman playing the harp, who turns to study herself in a mirror, the young artist is completely absorbed in the view of nature. Her lack of vanity is made clear by the inscription: "While Nature's beauties her free lines pourtray, / She knows not that she's fairer far than they." It is telling, too, that this young woman is not drawing from a copy-book but is sketching freely from nature, thus responding directly to the rural scene.[29] Lest she be seen as inappropriately yearning for the world beyond the home, Cosway shows us her previous sketch displayed on an easel behind her: a mother leaning over a cradle, the virtue of selflessness in its purest form. And to make the point even more obvious, Cosway turns the mother so she faces inward, toward the deeper recesses of the home, to counteract the orientation outward of the artist.[30] We can read this image as signifying, however subtly, some tension between the two worlds of interior and exterior.

Cosway herself had learned to draw at an early age; as she wrote, "At eight years I began drawing[;] having seen a young Lady draw I took a passion for it more that [*sic*] I had for music."[31] After studying painting in Florence she was elected to the Accademia del Disegno at the age of eighteen, but her marriage while still a minor to the painter Richard Cosway may have required her to revise her artistic goals. In a lengthy letter from 1830 summarizing the events of her life she observed, "his wish was that I should occupy myself as hitherto done in the Arts." But after describing her initial success as a young artist, which she attributed less to the merit of her work than to "the novelty & my Age," she then added a telling comment: "encouraged but never proud I followed entirely the impulse of my imagination[;] had Mr. C. permitted me to rank professionally I should have made a better painter but left to myself by degrees instead of improving I lost what I had brought from Italy of my early studies."[32] From an outside perspective it may be hard to see how her professional life as a painter was curtailed, since she received considerable attention during the first decade of her marriage, in the 1780s, as an annual exhibitor at the Royal Academy.[33] But according to *The Lives of the Most Eminent British Painters, Sculptors, and Architects* (1829–33), Richard Cosway's pride prevented his wife's full professional development: "this no doubt was in favour of domestic happiness, but much against her success in art."[34]

Women like Cosway often received mixed signals during this period about their domestic and professional roles. The issue of usefulness, a recurrent theme in the didactic literature, was also a factor for women artists. Budden made it clear to her young readers in 1814 that "Music, drawing, and dancing, are unnecessary, and must therefore be only thought of as amusements," unlike needlework, which she deemed both amusing and useful.[35] Although middle- and upper-class children, especially girls, were typically taught to draw, the growing bourgeois fear of raising pretentious and luxury-loving young "ladies" led to a rash of sober treatises as well as novels warning against the education of women to be mere dilettantes.[36] Jane Austen, herself adept at drawing landscapes, used sketching as a device in several of her novels, often as a way to satirize leisure-class expectations. In *Northanger Abbey* Catherine Morland's "taste for drawing was not superior; though whenever she could obtain the outside of a letter from her mother, or seize upon any other odd piece of paper, she did what she could in that way, by drawing houses and trees, hens and chickens, all very much like one another." Austen takes an even more caustic tone in *Sanditon*, describing the "very accomplished & very Ignorant" Beaufort sisters who hope to attract "praise & celebrity … curiosity & rapture" with their musical and artistic displays.[37] Jane Taylor, in her scathing denunciation of "patchwork" facility in the poem "Accomplishment," notes the tendency for young women to dabble in botany and drawing: "Thus Science distorted, and torn into bits, / Art tortured, and frightened half out of her wits, / In portions and patches, some light and some shady, / Are stitched up together, to make a young lady." She characterizes this kind of young person as "showy, but void of intelligent grace," and equates her intellectual immaturity with an ill-planned, disordered garden scene lacking in overall harmony: "It is not a landscape, it is not a face."[38] For Taylor the body of nature acquires mature and harmonious form as a constructed and well-ordered landscape, just as human intelligence is manifested in a wise and cultured face.

Jane and her mother, in their *Correspondence between a Mother and Her Daughter at School* (1817), distinguish between "mere accomplishments" and "sterling knowledge," and they clearly put "drawing a flower" in the former category: "Not that I would infer … that all things which are called accomplishments should rank no higher in our estimation, than drawing a flower; since some of them, when properly studied, approach very nearly, in their effects upon the mind, to more solid acquisitions."[39] Hannah More was even more emphatic, pronouncing that a focus on education in the arts is "one grand source of the corruption of women."[40] In her story "The Two Wealthy Farmers," published in 1800 as part of *The Cheap Repository Tracts*, she clearly criticizes the Bragwell daughters who aspire "to be well dressed, to eat elegantly, and to do nothing, or nothing which is of any use" and whose parlor is full of "their filigree and flowers, their embroidery and cut paper." More is referring here to another kind of art-making, often called fancy-work, supported by the influential *Repository of Arts, Literature, Commerce, Manufactures, Fashions and Politics* (1809–29), a monthly periodical primarily for women that was full of advice and patterns.[41] More draws a sharp contrast between the Bragwells and the Worthy family, whose virtues are evident in the state of their parlor: "Instead of made flowers in glass cases ... he saw some neat shelves of good books for the service of the family, and a small medicine chest for the benefit of the poor."[42]

Like fancy-work, flower painting was primarily practiced by women at this time and was identified as a minor art form, charmingly superficial and free from the passions of the human narrative. Middle- and upper-class women were associated with the decorative delicacy of flowers, which lack the utility of plebeian vegetables and the masculine strength of trees. Traditional gender norms were such that this parallel could be viewed as a particularly apt way of complimenting women's beauty. The author of *The Delights of Flower Painting*, for example, uses the familiar comparison to justify the publication: "What more charming Pastime can be found for that Sex, formed to delight and charm; and that, like blooming Flowers, present new Beauties and fresh Scenes of Delight, than representing, in the gayest part of Nature, an Image of their Lovely selves."[43] In her poem "To a Lady, With Some Painted Flowers" (1773), Barbauld contrasts the "rougher tasks" of mighty trees with "Flowers sweet, and gay, and delicate like you," and in the final lines she weaves together the motif of the woman *as* flower, "born for pleasure and delight alone. / Gay without toil, and lovely without art," with the woman *painting* flowers: "Nor blush, my fair, to own you copy these; / Your best, your sweetest empire is – to please."[44] Wollstonecraft, however, resisted the underlying assumption about women's fragility: referring to Barbauld's poem in *A Vindication of the Rights of Woman*, she responded with dismay to the analogy between women and flowers as an "error ... which robs the whole sex of its dignity, and classes the brown and the fair with the smiling flowers that only adorn the land."[45]

Artistic instruction for women, not surprisingly, was oriented around the representation of nature in its small, sedate views. The low, the modest, and the smooth, for example, as embodied in both flowers and women, characterize the feminine "beautiful" in Edmund Burke's *A Philosophical Enquiry into the Origin of Our Ideas of the Sublime and Beautiful* (1757). A simple bouquet, like the basket of flowers sketched by Jane Taylor (Fig. 3.3), was presented in numerous fictional accounts, memoirs, and drawing manuals as the most suitable subject, in terms of both the content of femininized grace and the skill level well adapted to the amateur. Even landscapes, in their full view, could be considered beyond the capability of women: in

Lectures on Female Education and Manners (1794) John Burton recommends that women paint "foliages, fruits, flowers" rather than "apply themselves to Landscape," and Charlotte Smith, in *Minor Morals Interspersed with Sketches of Natural History, Historical Anecdotes, and Original Stories* (1798), also felt that landscapes as well as the human figure "are not proper for a young woman," who should limit herself instead to the more fitting subject of flowers, "the most beautiful objects in nature."[46] The title of her book is telling: before arriving at the final reference to originality the reader is reminded repeatedly of the small scale of the author's intentions with such words as "minor," "sketches," and "anecdotes."

In Smith's *Rural Walks* (1795), Mrs. Woodfield bought for her youngest daughter, one of her "disciples of Flora," art materials and a book of lessons in painting flowers. She explains how the girl's skill will develop by noting, "when she has practiced a little in this, she shall try to draw flowers from nature, beginning with the most simple." Acting as a mentor to her niece, a spoiled city girl who has come to live with them in their rural village, Mrs. Woodfield advises her to develop her drawing skills: "It will now be a constant source of amusement and delight; and who knows, my dear Caroline, but it may hereafter be a resource against the inconveniences of adversity?" Trying to instill in her flighty niece a sense of the value of work and a practical orientation toward life, she continues, "how many derive their support from the little ornamental acquirements of their more fortunate days."[47] Many genteel but impoverished women did, in fact, attempt to make a living by drawing or crafting flowers. We have seen that the Taylor sisters were trained by their father in engraving, an occupation that Priscilla Wakefield listed among the acceptable and profitable employments for women, which also included painting background landscapes and miniatures, designing book frontispieces and needlework patterns, coloring prints, and illustrating natural history books.[48] Among the last group of illustrators were such prolific and respected artists as Mary Harrison, who had to turn to a profitable venture to support her ailing husband, and Matilda Smith, who made more than two thousand botanical illustrations over a period of four decades for *Curtis's Botanical Magazine*.[49] In *The Floral Knitting Book: or, the Art of Knitting Imitations of Natural Flowers*, the anonymous author, a "Lady," advertised in the preface that "Lessons Will be given by the Inventress, on very moderate terms," and she included her address.[50] Mary Howitt, in the children's book *Sowing and Reaping* (1841), described the young Elizabeth supporting herself and her mother by an occupation "that had beguiled many a weary hour even at home – the making artificial flowers." As a family friend remarked, "there is as much art and science, ay, and genius, too, required in the making an artificial flower, as in painting a picture! – and she is quite a gentlewoman too!"[51] In her article on Victorian wax flower modeling, Shteir discusses "the fluidity of knowledge of nature across different areas of culture," including art, science, and commerce, and she describes this particular form of handicraft as "a narrative of malleability," in terms both of technique and of gender norms.[52]

Returning to Smith's Mrs. Woodfield, we might be surprised, given her role as the calm and rational didact, to find that on several occasions she points out to her daughters and niece the picturesque qualities of certain craggy glens and melancholy ruins. She even reminds them that in a drawing the artist can "dismantle one of the most comfortable cottages, till we render it tolerably *picturesque*." But the picturesque aesthetic of the rough and irregular is still, in her rendition, brought back into the domestic realm more suited to the three girls in her charge. Having "composed our little home landscape," Mrs. Woodfield points out "figures appropriate to the scenery": "Three little girls dressing a boy's hat with flowers; and what a quantity of flowers they have got in their baskets!"[53] From the "fantastic" forms of gnarled roots, rocky crags, and wild undergrowth, Mrs. Woodfield thus effortlessly guides her girls back into the tame safety of the domesticated landscape.

MARIA SPILSBURY: FRAMING THE DOMESTICATED LANDSCAPE

While many female landscapists, such as Harriet Green, Amelia Long, Harriet Arnold, and Charlotte Nasmyth, worked in the poetic, atmospheric vein of Claude Lorrain or the naturalistic mode of the Dutch, others preferred a more protected English scene. The paintings of Maria Spilsbury often focused on the garden seen through a window or from within the enclosure of the domesticated landscape – an extension of home that is reminiscent of what Tuan calls the "small, familiar world, a world inexhaustibly rich in the complication of ordinary life but devoid of features of high imageability."[54] More recently, Susan Ford has suggested that the nature of a Victorian garden, with its smaller scale and closely framed details, contrasts with the "phallocentric" dominance implied in the broader sweep of a landscape park,[55] and the same point can be made about the earlier Georgian home-garden. Certainly Spilsbury's views, lacking the drama of romantic landscapes or the immediacy of more realistic scenes, give us insight by their very tameness into the world of women and children.

Fig. 3.7. Maria Spilsbury, *Self-Portrait Holding a Drawing*. National Gallery of Ireland, Dublin.

Spilsbury (Fig. 3.7) was born into a family of artists.[56] Her father Jonathan, a painter and printmaker in London, became the drawing master at Harrow in the late 1780s when Maria was around ten, and later served for several years as the private drawing instructor for the daughters of an Irish widow. He must have at least initially instructed his daughter in art, and she would have received additional encouragement from her mother, who also sketched. While Spilsbury's parents were interested in nurturing her talent, they also had financial concerns, so we must consider whether her choice of subject was affected by what would have been lucrative in the current market. The family lived on such a modest income that Maria had to help out with the laundry, prompting her mother to write, "I beg my dear Maria you would not tire yourself too much – I fear the Washing will be too much for you … When I hear of you I often hear of the Washtub and the Muslins, it is not worth your while to spoil your hand for things."[57] The additional money that Maria provided with the sale of her paintings was an important supplement. Certainly her early specialization in portraiture ensured a steady source of commissions, but she chose a wide range of subjects, including biblical, historical, literary, and genre scenes as well as portraits.

Spilsbury's domestic genre scenes and landscapes, especially those centered on the picturesque cottage, would have been popular in the exhibition hall and also would have sold well to middle- and upper-class patrons. She first exhibited a painting at the Royal Academy as a teenager in 1792, a year after her family moved back to London. Continuing to show her works there each year until 1808, she soon began to attract critical attention: a reviewer for the *Monthly Mirror* in his "Notes on the Royal Academy Exhibition" of 1802 praised her paintings as having a "sprightly intelligence, variety of natural expression and lightness of pencil," though he also spoke rather patronizingly about them as "pleasant ornaments of the Exhibition." Warning "that she is in some points *in danger* of deviating into affectation," he encouraged her to continue "the *naïve* character of expression" for which he found her best suited.[58] One list of the sale of her paintings reveals a price range from four guineas to forty, probably dependent on such factors as the size of the canvas, the number of figures, the subject, and the status of her patrons.[59]

Spilsbury was particularly active around the time of her marriage in 1808 to John Taylor, who was eight years younger than she, in poor health, and without a steady income. Her intense focus on painting, finishing thirteen canvases in 1807 and twelve in 1808, might have been intended to build a solid financial foundation for the upcoming marriage and to provide some extra funds for her elderly parents. On one of her private view days twenty carriages were lined up in front of her door, and she soon became a favorite of the Prince Regent, later George IV, and of the Marquess of Stafford.[60] It has been suggested that the Prince Regent's preference for Spilsbury's paintings was similar to his interest in the novels of Jane Austen,[61] and her domestic portraits and genre scenes might well have reminded him of Austen's perceptive characterization of ordinary life.

Spilsbury's "home landscapes" that dwell on the quieter pleasures of the country seem more suggestive of Maria's own personality than such crowded, festive paintings as *Patron's Day at the Seven Churches, Glendalough*, which includes a barely visible self-portrait, removed from the boisterous action and quietly drawing in a sketchbook. Spilsbury's mother described her just before her marriage as "shy" and hesitant about going to parties, and later her youngest son wrote that she was "of a very retiring disposition, very

Fig. 3.8. Maria Spilsbury, *Group Portrait in a Wooded Landscape*. Private collection.

observing, looking upwards habitually, but inclined to silence, careless of her personal appearance and dress."[62]

Group Portrait in a Wooded Landscape (Fig. 3.8), a scene of the artist and her family, must have been painted around 1818 since the events of that year would explain the ghostly image of a toddler standing by her side in addition to the three older children and the baby on her lap. Despite marrying late at the age of thirty-one she had five children, the last three born in rapid succession in 1816, 1817, and 1818. In a letter dated June 1818 she describes her one-year-old son's death: "During his illness I had neither time nor spirit to take up my pen. The dear child was a sweet patient sufferer." In the same letter she also mentions matter-of-factly that "Johnny, Susy and Sallie have just had the chicken pock and are looking rather poorly but I hope a little country air at Kellyville will revive them."[63] This family portrait was probably left unfinished due to the stress of that year. Although she typically has a light touch with the brush and her landscape settings are often quickly and delicately painted, the background foliage here is so broadly and hastily brushed that she perhaps intended to add more detail later. Her youngest son later wrote that "She painted with great rapidity; too great for she laid too thin colour and began many more works than she could finish."[64] But even in its unfinished state the painting is a charming indication of the family's interaction with each other and with nature. The figures form a linking chain across the foreground, joining the father and older son at the left with the self-portrait of Maria at the right. She uses the landscape as a framing device, the shadowy recess behind John Taylor echoing the black jacket that he wears while the light blue of Maria's gown is picked up in the blue sky just visible through the small opening behind her. This well-ordered scene of a family in harmony with nature, comparable to such Gainsborough portraits as *Mr. and Mrs. John Gravenor and their Daughters* (c. 1754), was disrupted by the death of her son and by her own weakness.[65] She shows herself as frail and weary, with stooped shoulders, and in fact she died two years later at the age of forty-three, after a lingering illness following the birth of her youngest child.

Spilsbury's quiet domestic scenes, whether depicting the sedate middle class or picturesque cottagers, are Austenian in their careful attention to relationships. None of them undermines the gender norms of the period, although Spilsbury often uses the home landscape to provide some openness and spatial flexibility to the women's lives. Her ability to frame the view – to construct, condense, and domesticate it – is reminiscent of Jane Taylor's use of the window as a framing device, as we will see in Chapter 4, and it anticipates what Hunt has called the "clear sense of within/beyond" in a garden.[66] In Spilsbury's small portrait of her future in-laws, Walter and Sarah Taylor with their daughter (Fig. 3.9), the family is gathered around the drawing-room table, the women sewing while Mr. Taylor has just paused from reading.[67] The interior is simply decorated, more akin to the parlor of the Worthy family in More's story, with its "neat shelves of good books for the service of the family," than to the overly decorated interior of the Bragwells.[68] Spilsbury emphasizes the fresh innocence of the daughter by dressing her in white and placing her closest to the blooming houseplant and also to the window itself. The curtain has been pulled back to let in the light and breeze and a vine peeks in through the open window, softening the divide between the shadowy interior and the sunny exuberance of the garden outside. Spilsbury's composition is clearly influenced by the art of George Morland, especially his *Domestic Happiness* from 1789 (Fig. 3.10), readily available in popular prints, but the differences are instructive. By associating the mother visually and spatially with the bookcase behind her, Spilsbury gives her an intellectual weight comparable to that of her husband, and by placing the daughter by the window she not only equates her youthful beauty with the beauty of the flowers, a traditional trope, but

Fig. 3.9. Maria Spilsbury, *Group Portrait at a Drawing Room Table*. Private collection.

Fig. 3.10. George Morland, *Domestic Happiness*. Private collection.

Fig. 3.11. Maria Spilsbury, *Family Group before a Thatched Cottage*. Private collection.

Fig. 3.12. Maria Spilsbury, *A Quiet Time – Family Group at the Cottage Door*.
Location unknown.

also opens up the possibility of extension outward. Morland, in contrast, follows a tradition going back to Jan Van Eyck's *Arnolfini Marriage* (1434) of dividing the space between the masculine zone by the window and the feminine interior.[69]

A mood of peaceful industry permeates Spilsbury's cottage door paintings (Figs. 3.11–3.13), influenced by the treatments of this rustic theme in the 1770s–1790s by Morland, Gainsborough, and Francis Wheatley.[70]

Fig. 3.13. Maria Spilsbury, *After School*. Location unknown.

Gainsborough's approach, like Spilsbury's, is idealizing: in the version now in Cincinnati (Fig. 3.14), for example, he creates an idyllic microcosm of rural harmony symbolically centered on the door as the motif connecting feminine productivity around the home and masculine labor in the fields and forests (in this case hauling firewood). The rhetoric of sensibility (one critic in 1780 described Gainsborough's paintings as "well calculated to move the heart")[71] applies broadly to the popular cottage-door theme, but Spilsbury, while following the lead of Gainsborough, shifts the picturesque, sentimentalized approach more emphatically toward the perspective of the women in the paintings.

Unlike Gainsborough's settings, where the rugged trees, blasted by lightning or pollarded, loom oppressively overhead, nature in Spilsbury's paintings often encircles her female zone in a protective embrace: the dovecote on the roof at the left in Spilsbury's *Family Group before a Thatched Cottage*

Fig. 3.14. Thomas Gainsborough, *The Cottage Door*. Cincinnati Art Museum.

Fig. 3.15. George Morland, *The Happy Cottagers*. Philadelphia Museum of Art.

(Fig. 3.11) and the potted geranium by the door at the right frame the scene and open up a peaceful performative space for domestic activity.[72] In Nead's discussion of women and the English "rural idyll" she recognizes that "The family was seen as a 'natural' and stable unit which should ideally be located in a natural, rural setting."[73] Rose extends her point in a discussion of the "stability, morality and tranquility" of rural England,[74] attributes which are reinforced in Spilsbury's scenes by landscape settings that are reassuring and protective.

Women were at the heart of this idyllic view of the countryside, even as they were seen as standing in for Nature more generally. Nochlin notes that the nineteenth-century French peasant woman, "as an elemental, untutored – hence eminently 'natural' female – is the ideal signifier for the notion of beneficent maternity, replete with historical overtones of the Christian Madonna and Child,"[75] and we can use her analysis to assess these earlier rural images by Spilsbury. Her paintings are less plebeian, being transformed instead into an elegant re-enactment of the rural life by the painter's light brushwork, pastel colors, and willowy figure types. This process of gentrification overlaps with the feminization of the scene, and unlike in many cottage-door representations of the period the sense of familial harmony is not dependent in her works on the return of the male worker. Spilsbury concentrates our attention on the communal interaction of women involved in maintaining order in the family – Nochlin's notion of "beneficent maternity" – and the men, when shown, are minimized in the background. Gainsborough, in contrast, seems to prefer a nostalgic view of pre-enclosure rural labor that balances the male and female roles, giving each its appointed action or duty: the male returning home in the Cincinnati version, c. 1778, serves as a compositional counterweight to the women at the door, and the rambunctious play of the children provides a transition between male labor and female stasis. Gainsborough's approach is echoed in the more popularized and anecdotal paintings by Francis Wheatley and George Morland, such as Morland's *The Happy Cottagers*, c. 1790–92 (Fig. 3.15), where the boys' play with the wheelbarrow mimics their later life as farm laborers and the girl's gathering of straw parallels the maid carrying her bundle of wood. Edwin Cockburn's mid-Victorian *The Return from Market* draws the line between opposing roles even more emphatically as he incorporates the spatial divide of the window: he relegates the woman and children to an interior space of passive dependence as they wait to greet the man of the family, who comes into view through the grid of the window, pushing open the garden gate.[76]

Spilsbury's favorite motif of women sewing emphasizes their active hands; thus, although they also take care of the children who play at their feet or sleep in their laps, child-tending is not their only occupation (as it is in most of Gainsborough's cottage scenes).[77] Also important in Spilsbury's rural idyll is the presence of books, so that manual labor is accompanied by intellectual engagement. The books provide her women with a sense of substance and involvement with the larger world that distinguishes them from Nochlin's "untutored" peasant women as well as from the paintings by Gainsborough and Morland.[78] Although in *Group Portrait at a Drawing Room Table* (Fig. 3.9) the women simply listen to a reading by the paterfamilias while they sew, comparable in that respect to more typical scenes of "domestic happiness" (Fig. 3.10), at other times another female family member or the children themselves do the reading (Figs. 3.11–3.13). In *After School* (Fig. 3.13), for instance, Spilsbury represents a mother and older daughter sewing in an outdoor arbor (a secondary hub of domestic life, as discussed in Chapter 1) while two of the young children, a girl and a boy, read their books nearby. Domesticity is equated with peaceful industry, mental as well as physical, indicated by the repeated motif of heads tilted gently downward to the task at hand.

Spilsbury's portrayal of children, similar to those by Gainsborough, Reynolds, Romney, Morland, and others, reveals the new fascination with childhood in the eighteenth and nineteenth centuries. Works such as *Four Children in a Landscape* (Fig. 3.16) and *Two Children in a Woodland Glade* are probably commissioned portraits, like *Miss Collier in a Wooded Landscape*.[79] But these paintings that we are presuming to be commissioned, clearly differentiated from the scenes of peasant children in a cottage setting, cross over into the realm of genre images in their portrayal of the girls and boys out exploring the forest. Spilsbury emphasizes the darkness of the woodland in each case in order to highlight the innocence of the children with their wide-eyed expressions and light clothes. No adults are in sight, which increases our sense of their vulnerability. The landscape should not be read as a threatening presence, however, nor is it simply a backdrop: it provides motivation for the figural action. In *Four Children in a Landscape*, as in the case of Miss Collier, the children have been collecting wildflowers, and in *Two Children in a Woodland Glade*, the path and rocky stream have beckoned them to explore and now the tired little girl is being carried by her brother safely home. Like the children, the landscape in each case is unspoiled, making the sense of communion between the human and natural world even stronger.

Fig. 3.16. Maria Spilsbury, *Four Children in a Landscape*. Location unknown.

ANNA MARIA HUSSEY: FUNGI, TEA-TRAYS, AND "CHARMING BOGS"

The "home landscape" was also the central setting for Anna Maria Hussey (1805–c. 1877), a botanist who used her art as a primary tool for investigation (Figs. 3.17–3.18). As we have seen with Spilsbury, many women who moved into the public arena were prompted by financial reasons, which was also apparently the case with Hussey. Her husband, the Rev. Thomas Hussey, was an avid amateur astronomer with many publications in the field. These stopped in the late 1830s when he sold his observatory, and her work as a serious illustrator began soon after that, suggesting that the family was in financial need.[80] She commented in a letter to the renowned Northamptonshire mycologist the Rev. Miles Berkeley, expressing concern about the subscriptions for her *Illustrations of British Mycology*, "Your friend's name made the 100 up – from the great expense of the plates that number will only just defray the expenses! So as empty honour is poor compensation for so much time – I hope the number will increase and put a trifle in my pocket" (February 7, 1847).[81] We find a similar concern in an

Fig. 3.17. *Agaricus squarrosus*, illustration in Anna Maria Hussey, *Illustrations of British Mycology*, pl. 8.

Fig. 3.18. *Agaricus caulicinalis*, illustration in Anna Maria Hussey, *Illustrations of British Mycology*, pl. 68.

undated letter to Berkeley, in which she refers to her story "Matrimony," published in *Fraser's Magazine* (1849): "This *pays well* – much better than Mycology!" Hussey was able to work out of her small home in Kent, often in her kitchen and with children underfoot: in another letter she offered to save Berkeley some fungi but added "our house is so small I am afraid of beginning to collect for want of space" (March 27, 1847).

While it can be hard to situate Hussey clearly on the spectrum between amateur and professional, she certainly extended beyond the limited interests of what were known as "lady" hobbyists or Sunday botanists. Shteir has used the phrase "cultivators of science" in reference to those women who observed, collected, and illustrated without making any advances in the field that were considered groundbreaking.[82] One gets the sense from Hussey's published as well as private writings that she was deeply committed to her botanical studies, and had been for years. But her use of language reveals a certain struggle to situate herself in scientific circles, and she seemed very aware of the limitations placed on women actively involved in field botany. During Hussey's years of maturity in the 1840s and 1850s the popular *Elegant Arts for Ladies* encouraged botanizing as a "refining study of wild and cultivated flowers,"[83] but Hussey was outside the norm in several ways: first, in not being interested in botany primarily as an elegant and entertaining hobby, and second, in being focused not on flowers, like Moser, Lawrance, and others, but on fungi. Mushrooms and lichens, including her favorite agarics, certainly lack the connotations of grace and elegance associated with flowers, which were so often connected for aesthetic and sentimental reasons with women, as we have seen. Despite Hussey's home-centered studies, she might have been accused of transgressing the "limits of modesty and decorum" urged by Priscilla Wakefield in her discussion of women and science, and she also stepped outside the realm of "domestic privacy" that Wakefield saw as proper for women.[84]

Hussey's large, two-volume *Illustrations of British Mycology* (1847–55) was a popularizing study of fungi considered by a reviewer for the *Journal of Botany* some years later, in 1886, as "more suggestive of the drawing-room than the study" and recently characterized by Shteir as "a hybrid of fashion and science."[85] Mother of three, Hussey domesticates science by giving instructions that situate her reader in the feminized realm of the home: "plate-baskets" work well for collecting samples, tools can be carried in a "leather sheath with a loop ... reticule fashion," and "tea-trays" are useful for spreading out the specimens at home. She recommends two strong tools ("potent engines," as she calls them), a butcher's knife and a wrenching chisel, but she softens her instructions with the phrase "start not, gentle reader!" Her descriptions of the fungi were often richly, even poetically detailed – about the *Agaricus squarrosus* (Fig. 3.17), for example, she writes, "thrusting forth a snaky mass of heads from the stump of a decaying tree, with strange flexuous serpentine stems, and bristling scaly coat, it is a decidedly repulsive individual" – but a few paragraphs later she employed a more mundane analogy for the same fungus: "if we put an umbrella into a case, which is fastened round the stick, we have no bad illustration of *Ag. Squarrosus*." She extends the analogy at some length, to the point of informing us what part of the fungus is similar to the whalebones of the umbrella. To make a cross-section of a puffball she recommends "those feminine implements, scissors," and she later states that her instructions are suited for "the more delicately constitutioned botanist."[86] Clearly she expected that her audience would consist primarily of upper-class women who could afford the expensive volumes.

Hussey's sensitivity to her own as well as her readers' primary position within the home informs her commentary on *Agaricus caulicinalis* (Fig. 3.18):

The world is full of beauty that we pass by unheeded. There, opposite, is an ugly thatched barn, elsewhere perhaps picturesque, but not when blocking the view from the window; we cannot plant it out, there is a road between – we cannot cover it with ivy, for it is not ours; but look with changed ideas, set aside the prejudiced spectacles, and you will see that every season decks that ragged thatch with beauties of its own; the greenest mosses … [and] the small delicate tufts of *Agaricus caulicinalis*, clasping the straws by their woolly stems; as fantastic and graceful as if Titania herself had created them to ornament her bower.[87]

The view from the window, as we will see with the Taylor sisters, frames the woman's perception of the world, both practically and aesthetically, and Hussey's solution, characteristically, is to join science with sentiment. But for her the home-bower becomes a place as much of intellectual curiosity as of repose. Hussey's approach was quite different, however, from that of the botanist Agnes Ibbetson (discussed in Chapter 2), who insisted on using scientific instruments, especially various kinds of microscopes but also "as many different sorts [of tools] as a surgeon." Also unlike Hussey, Ibbetson wrote in straightforward, factual language in order to destroy "all those imaginary fancies of feeling and *sensation*, delicate Ladies have indulged till they could weep at plucking a rose."[88]

Hussey admits that "delicate ladies" might prefer to avoid collecting in the field and suggests that they could commission the poor to bring in specimens for home study. Although she believes everyone would agree that a certain fungus is "very pretty," she acknowledges the difficulties of collecting it: "it prefers that damp autumnal state of things, when the heavy half freezing dews never rise from the grass all day, when the weather is very questionable, when a lady's gown may be better employed than in sweeping up dead leaves, and her foot instinctively turns into the beaten track away from all those petty difficulties." Hussey herself, however, did not hesitate to explore fairly wild terrain in order to find some of the more unusual fungi, including what she describes as "out-of-the-way wild places, far from carriage tracks, and often where large herds of cattle are pastured." Noting in an aside that "philosophically and chemically we know there is no such thing as *dirt*," she confesses that she takes pleasure in exploring "charming bogs" and roaming through "the warm, reeking, moist atmosphere" of a certain dell where "we bury our foot in the loosened earth." While tramping through autumn fields she recognizes that the "stubble is unpleasant to ladies' ankles ... but who can be troubled with such petty cares? – not we."[89]

Hussey presents a psychological as well as spiritual justification for such botanizing in various comments sprinkled throughout the text. A close study of nature serves, for example, as "medicinal balm" to offset the "apathy" of a "languid duty walk." Dirt, for Hussey (at least dirt acquired in a healthy pursuit like hers), takes on an almost moral significance – a sign of industry, one of the key virtues emphasized by early Victorian moralists to offset feminine lethargy (comparable to what we will see in some of the gardening manuals in Chapter 6). Hussey suggests that if Mama chastises her daughter for getting dirty, then she mustn't complain when the child grows into a "vapid," "repining," "unamusable" young lady. Hussey did have her limits, though: complaining in a letter about a certain foul-smelling fungus, she writes, "I cannot paint it it is so offensive" (August 6, 1845). But she believed that close attention paid to even these "vulgar and humble" fungi can lead to a clearer understanding of what she calls "Infinite Intelligence."[90] Ibbetson had also written about the study of botany as "a *glimpse* of the *agency of the Deity*, an *impulse* of *His* own divine energy," but Hussey's approach is more personal than Ibbetson's, even emotional: she "mourned over" large specimens "crushed in the dusty road," for example.[91] She could also be quite fanciful, even in her published treatise, as when she imagines that squirrels and rabbits might be happier because of nature's beauty, and fairies might bathe in the dew collected in fungi cups. She was clearly focused on entertaining as well as instructing women – even including recipes for puffball omelette and fungus ketchup, though in a characteristically humorous vein "promising that we never use individuals grown on or near dunghills." But she was adamant about the use of scientific language, emphasizing that her "first and last advice will always be, – acquire the terms of strict botanical usage."⁹² Her recommendation may well have been due to the fact that knowledge of this universal language enabled her to reach beyond the limits of her own home life and enjoy a lengthy and mutually beneficial correspondence with Rev. Berkeley.

Her unpublished letters to Berkeley are full of questions about specific fungi, references to specimens that she was boxing up to send him, and comments about drawings that she'd made, but the scientific language that she uses is interspersed with various allusions to her children. She assures him that she'll send "some very characteristic specimens of Nebularis" despite that being "a very anxious period" when her eldest was suffering from inflamed eyes (October 20, 1844), and in an undated letter she confesses, "I am without a cook and Chicken Pox in the house – ! so have plenty to do because the nurses have it." After describing the smell of one fungus she adds that her little girls had just come in exclaiming, "O Mama we have brought you some funny white toadstools" (April 10, 1846). In a later letter from 1849 she notes that they never seem interested in what she knows most about but instead are full of questions about ferns and mosses – and "they cannot understand Mama saying 'I don't know'." She complains at length in an undated letter about having so many distractions that keep her from regular work on her book project: besides being mother and wife she is also "the gardener, the farmer, and just now upholsterer." She also expresses resentment about the time spent with visitors and charity work in the parish and adds that her husband expects her "to help him do everything – I am always under the uncomfortable impression that the thing I am doing is not the right thing to be doing." Puzzled by certain identifications and "weary of enigmas," she sighs, "[I] feel sure Mycology was never intended for women, who love jumping to conclusions better than such patient research" (April 20, 1849). Her plaintive aside is surprising, since Victorian women were more typically characterized as focused on the small details and incapable of grasping underlying theories or reaching general conclusions. Despite her fear of being a "perpetual plague" to Rev. Berkeley because of all her questions, he expressed his admiration by naming a mushroom genus after her (*Husseia*) and also using her maiden name for one of the many new species of fungus he discovered (*Agaricus reedii*).

While often voicing uncertainty about her knowledge of fungi, Hussey was confident of her artistic abilities; writing in an undated letter, she asserts, "I was asked today to state how much I know of Mycology? and could only say very little – but ... I *can* paint – that I am sure of." As Erika Naginski notes in her review of Bermingham's *Learning to Draw*, flower painting (or in this case botanical illustration) "gives women covert access to serious science," although "The paternalism of scientific positivism coincides directly with capitalist culture's feminizing of amateurism"[93] – hence the rhetoric of apology that permeates the prefaces of so many of the female-authored texts of the period, as we have seen. But Hussey was no dilettante. Her obsession is clear: in one letter written during an intense period of work on her book, she mentions having painted fungi for eight hours that day, and in another she laments, "I am so tired of collecting and painting them – I dream of them all night, as well as work all day" (April 10, and August 16, 1846). She often mentions her unhappiness with the lithographs that were made from her drawings. In an undated letter she describes the "great pains" that she took with her drawings, only to find them poorly reproduced by the lithographer, but she ends with an apology for her lengthy complaint: "I should not have scribbled all this but I am sitting watching a sick child (who is thank God shaking off an attack of fever) and so have nothing better to do than to gossip." In another letter she admits, "I do dislike the plates in my work with an 'intense disgust' ... Where they should mark pores they make *smudges* – and there is such a total want of decision in that tiresome lithography – and the artist has no *feeling* of his subject at all" (May 27, 1847). Despite all of these problems with the illustrations (140 in all, most by Hussey and a few by her sister Fanny Reed), they are more professionally assured than the often rather chatty text, which is self-effacing at times and also occasionally derivative (but usually very entertaining).

The published and private writings of Hussey and others like Ibbetson reveal tensions between the personal constraints and professional aspirations of early nineteenth-century women botanists, and they raise crucial questions about the historical and scientific value of those endeavors that were more accessible to women of the period, such as field observations and illustrations. Hussey's large, decorative volumes served an aesthetic as well as scientific function and were directed toward a largely female, upper-class audience to enlist them in this new pursuit of mycology; as such, they differed from Ibbetson's papers, which were published in well-respected scientific journals for the purpose of furthering knowledge in the field. Hussey blended passages that can best be described as anecdotal and sentimental with basic information about the identification and habits of fungi, and, while she was intent that the details in her illustrations be sufficiently precise and true to the object, she also expressed concern that the feeling of her drawings not be lost in the transfer to the lithographic illustrations. Facing a number of significant personal and professional challenges in order to publish her work in two series of plates over a six-year period, she set herself apart from the image of the Sunday botanist or casual watercolorist that was more typical of middle-class women.[94] Hussey operated in a physical and personal space that was both domestic and professional, bringing discoveries from the natural world into her kitchen and sending hints of her private life out into the public arena.

CONCLUSION

Returning to more traditional views of the domestic landscape, a final pair of images — two pencil drawings in Richenda Gurney Cunningham's sketchbook (Figs. 3.19–3.20) — will allow us to consider more fully a woman artist's position in relation to the garden. Cunningham was described as "the most spirited and devoted clergyman's wife," who performed her church duties "with the same enthusiasm with which she continued to enjoy her drawing and other home employments."[95] In August 1845, when she was in her mid-sixties, Cunningham drew Earlham Hall, the home of her youth, from a distant vantage point across the park and garden (Fig. 3.19). The scene is carefully constructed, the house being framed by the foliage of trees. Our access to the view of the building is balanced between the unoccupied bench at the left, well positioned for a clear line of sight through the island beds, and the curving path at the right. The ideology of the home, with its emphasis on stability and order, is the dominant message here. A very different mood informs Cunningham's sketch of the view through the drawing-room window (Fig. 3.20). Here we look past the beds in the lawn to the same simple bench, but now from the other side, and the distant scene is wilder and more disordered. Although the bridge provides a calm focal point, the forest on either side is a confusing tangle of foliage and tree limbs. The curving line of the edge of the lawn clearly separates the carefully tended homestead from the woodland beyond. Though picturesque in the gnarled asymmetry of the trees' growth, the forest seems inaccessible to us; we are cut off by the dense growth, unable to find a path to the bridge. The bench in the two drawings serves as a fulcrum between the garden and the wild growth beyond its clearly marked limits. We can choose to sit facing inward, toward the home, or outward, toward the forest and bridge. The fact that in the later sketch Cunningham situates herself inside the drawing room, using its window as a framing device, further underscores her positioning within the order of the home.[96] Bachelard, noting the "penetrating gaze of the little window," recognizes that "A house that has been experienced is not an inert box."[97] We would add that women's

Fig. 3.19. Richenda Gurney Cunningham, *Earlham Hall from across the Park and Garden, August 1845*. Norfolk Record Office.

Fig. 3.20. Richenda Gurney Cunningham, *View of Earlham Bridge from the Drawing Room Windows, Sep. 6, 1846*. Norfolk Record Office.

experience in and around the house, extending into the near landscape, is the primary enlivening agent.

Bachelard also describes the "dynamic rivalry between house and universe,"[98] which we can see in these two drawings by Cunningham as well as in Hussey's botanical illustrations and Spilsbury's paintings. While these women remained centered in the domestic world, in each case nature provided an opportunity for movement beyond the borders of the home. As their spatial identity expanded, so too did their means of responding to and representing the world around them. To return to Edgeworth's exasperating Frederick, convinced that "Women who are always drawing and reasoning, never know how to make puddings," we offer Spilsbury and Hussey, married with children, as rebuttal: the painter with her laundry and the botanical illustrator with her tea-trays, both of them middle-class women in straitened financial conditions who were able to balance family duties – perhaps even the production of puddings – with their professional work.

CHAPTER 4

Commanding a view: the Taylor sisters and the construction of domestic space

Ann Taylor (1782–1866) and her sister Jane (1783–1824) were among the most popular writers for children in early nineteenth-century England; we still recite Jane's "Twinkle, twinkle little star" even though the author's name is largely forgotten. The sisters were praised by Robert Browning, Maria Edgeworth, and Sir Walter Scott for their collections of poems, most notably *Original Poems for Infant Minds* (1804–05) and *Rhymes for the Nursery* (1806), which Browning described as "the most perfect thing of their kind in the English language."[1] Leonore Davidoff's research on the Taylor family provides much-needed context for Ann and Jane's strongly held religious beliefs as evangelical dissenters as well as their social conservatism about gender roles, at least as professed publicly in their poems, stories, and essays.[2] But the Taylor sisters also wrote letters and memoirs that reveal some tension between their sense of domestic duty and their personal ambitions. These private texts set up a personal topography in which the garden plays a key spatial role. Not just as a setting for the house or a site for practical action, the garden for Ann and Jane took on nostalgic and poetic overtones in their writing as they explored the physical and emotional spaces of home.

We will consider in this chapter the way in which boundaries, both spatial and temporal, affected the mapping of the Taylor sisters' lives. The window, for example, which operates as a valve between the inner sanctum of the house and the external landscape, was a key trope for both of them. More generally, transitional motifs of various kinds, including doors, porches, and arbors as well as windows and, in a larger sense, the garden itself, served for them as both linking and separating devices – permeable boundaries that helped women and children negotiate their movements from one area to another within the larger domestic refuge. In a similar fashion – in fact much like the configuration of a view through a window – memory and the deep-rooted nostalgia associated with it were temporal filters that colored their sense of place, as we saw in Chapter 2 with Smith's Mrs. Woodfield. The construction of domestic space through the Taylors' writing created a mobile, fluid shaping of the terrain as well as a re-centering of the core notion of home. Stephanie Ross's identification in *What Gardens Mean* of two distinct but interconnected modes of relating to the garden – the security and intimacy associated with "enclosure" and the compelling but risky adventure associated with "invitation" – provides a useful framework for our consideration of the Taylors.[3] In a sense, the Taylor sisters will stand as another test case for some of the issues raised in the previous chapters, bringing our themes into sharper focus. The idea of personal mapping – of spatial centering and extension as a means of framing personal narratives – will remain important. Understanding the ways in which women's lives were largely enacted within a domestic landscape enables us to view the personal as well as published texts of the Taylor sisters in a new and more nuanced way.

CONSTRUCTING MEMORIES

Ann and Jane were born in London to devoted middle-class parents, but because of their father Isaac's career as a successful engraver and Independent preacher, the Taylor family moved four times before Ann's marriage in 1813.[4] It is not surprising, then, that the issue of memory, overlaid with the sentiment of nostalgia for childhood homes, crops up repeatedly in the sisters' writings.[5] What does "home" consist of when you move so often? For Jane and Ann, their memories were often related to the landscape setting, in particular the near garden. In Ann's poem "To Memory" (1805) she looks back on the landscape of her youth, symbolized by spring flowers now withered by "the wintry blast" (though she herself was only twenty-three at the time). She calls on Memory to "Command this Eden of my youth to bloom" and then describes the scene as a landscape painted by this same personification:

> With pencil moistened in thy clearest hues,
> Still o'er the thatch these truant ivies fling;
> The bower's wild rose with softest blush suffuse,
> Sweet with the fragrance of a distant spring.

Rose-covered bowers, views through casement windows, and vines twining over thatched roofs are components of the domesticated landscape that play a role in this poem and also recur frequently in other writings by the Taylors. These iconic images of the garden are crucial elements for Ann and Jane in their idealization of the home as refuge: "O paint them fair," the poet beseeches Memory.[6]

Fig. 4.1. Isaac Taylor, *Portrait of Ann and Jane Taylor in Their Garden at Lavenham*, 1792. National Portrait Gallery, London.

Their father painted a portrait of the two sisters in the large garden of the family home in Lavenham in 1792, when Ann was ten and Jane a year younger (Fig. 4.1). They seem caught between their close-knit family, gathered in the background arbor, and the unknown future as they stand facing forward, somewhat apprehensively, with identical sober expressions. Inspired much later in life by this painting, Ann wrote a poem for her sister in 1806 that contrasts the permanence of the sisters' relationship, visualized in their clasped hands and matching dresses, with the changing rhythms of the garden around them:

> Spring, summer, autumn wind their dance,
> Old winter hobbles near,
> And verging round the blue expanse
> Declining suns appear;
> The seasons vary, – but we stand
> Dear girl, as ever, hand in hand.

In the second stanza Ann describes the ephemerality of nature as the seasons make their rounds, concluding with a shift from the timeless portrayal of the girls in the oil painting to a more active, volatile image that acknowledges the inexorable passage of time:

> And hand in hand we travel on,
> The lovely change to trace;
> To mark when one sweet flower is gone,
> Another fill its place;
> And with a rapt delight pursue
> Each simple line that nature drew.[7]

Flowers were often used as emblems of transience and mortality, as we have seen, and Ann employs this popular topos to reinterpret her father's more straightforward portrait. Perhaps the expressions of the two little girls, looking at her so seriously across the divide of those fourteen years, prompted her verses, along with the metaphorically suggestive setting of the family garden.

When the family moved to Colchester in 1795 their new house, though now in the center of a bustling town, had a garden that Jane cherished as the site of "her happiest hours." One of Jane's later poems, "On Visiting an Old Family Residence," describes the cultivated landscape around it as an "embowered retreat" and, even more romantically, as "fairy ground."[8] Her nostalgic idealization of the childhood terrain in Colchester does not lend itself to detailed description but instead gives us a feeling for her deep-rooted emotional attachment. Bachelard suggests that such memories lead us back to "the land of Motionless Childhood," where "we comfort ourselves by reliving memories of protection." He adds, in a statement as relevant for the home-garden as for the building itself, "For the real houses of memory, the houses to which we return in dreams, the houses that are rich in unalterable oneirism, do not readily lend themselves to description."[9] In "Birth-Day Retrospect" (1809) Jane Taylor remembers the happiness of her youth through a sentimental veil – "I trod enchanted ground"[10] – and we find a similar idealization of the childhood garden in her essay "Spring Flowers." Here she plays the role of a retired gentleman musing about the pleasures and lessons gained from his simple, well-ordered life. Proposing that the children and the elderly are particularly able to appreciate a small flower garden, he is led into a nostalgic reminiscence of his childhood: "My paternal garden seems still to me like enchanted ground, and its flowers like the flowers of Paradise. I shall never see the like again, vain as I am of my gardening! – Those were *poetry*, these are *botany*."[11]

As Jane suggests in this essay, such poetic and nostalgic associations are often made between the idea or ideal of home and the landscape in which the house itself is situated. The move away from Colchester in 1811, after sixteen years there, was particularly hard on the two sisters, even though they were in their late twenties by that time. Ann notes in her autobiography, "Jane and I went, as we felt for the last time, to every memorable spot within reach, sending loving looks in every direction. Colchester was very dear to us" – and many years after writing this passage she adds, "Colchester to me is dear still." She describes walking to the "Springs," the "Wild Mount," the "High Woods" – "every spot to which a single association was attached."[12] We find a similar commemoration of specific beloved sites in the journal of Emily Shore, who acknowledges at the age of nineteen, shortly before her death in 1839, that "I was much happier as a child than I am now, or ever shall be." The melancholic tone that appears in her journal after she moved to Madeira for her health is based in large part on her nostalgic memories of the English landscape that she loved as a child: "Oh, there are moments when visions start up before me of sweet well-known spots – woods where the anemone and bluebell grow; streams shaded with ash-trees and hawthorn, where I have wandered alone in early spring mornings, on violets and primroses and grass drenched with dew, myself the happiest of the happy ... all these, and other spots full of a thousand sweet recollections."[13] In Harriet Martineau's *Deerbrook* (1839), the governess Maria Young suggests that "The imagination is a better medium than the eye" for appreciating nature, for "the remembrance is purely delicious, – brighter in sunshine, softer in shade." The beloved landscape seen through the summer-house window takes on special meaning for Maria and her friend Margaret, soon to marry and move to London, in the last chapter of the novel. Deciding not to transplant bulbs from the country to "the little balcony of a back drawing-room" in London, Margaret already feels the force of the loss to come as she gazes nostalgically out on "these delicious green meadows." But she promises to return for visits: "We shall come and look upon your woods sometimes, you know. I am not bidding good-bye to this place, or to you."[14] For these women, as for Emily and the Taylors, home was as much about the landscape as about the friends and furnishings that were left behind.

The Taylor sisters' desire to commemorate the home place and its natural and cultivated surroundings prompted them each to pick a strand of ivy "as a memorial of many of our happiest, gayest, or most agreeably melancholy hours."[15] Before their departure the sisters went for a moonlight stroll: "As it was late we could not go far; we only went to the bridge at the entrance of the meadows, and to a few familiar spots thereabouts, talking of Colchester, of Ongar, of all the dear friends who had walked with us here, and of the last moon we should see upon those woods, those meadows, and that stream!" The solemn, melancholic mood is palpable, as they commit to preserving as best they can the sense of a home soon to be lost. But you only have to turn the page in this letter to a friend and the tone shifts dramatically, now infused with excitement about the new countryside that awaits them: "And, now, follow us ... till we turn into the *Ongar* Road at Chelmsford. It was a fine afternoon; quite new country opening upon us at every step, and expectation, which had begun to doze, was all alive again."[16]

Place, as a "concretion of value"[17] as well as a literal configuration of beloved objects, was important to the Taylors. An album or scrapbook begun in 1813 includes a series of views of their homes depicted by various family members.[18] Jane's drawing of the Castle House at Ongar where they moved when she was twenty-eight is loosely brushed, suggestive rather than descriptive, emphasizing the long sweeping curve of the drive and fences (Fig. 4.2). The house itself, set back at a distance and surrounded by soft washes that give the sense of foliage, is well protected from the viewer's intruding gaze – quite different, in that respect, from the map-like details in her father's aerial view of their second house at Lavenham (Fig. 4.3). Tuan differentiates between these two types of perspective: the aerial view is objective, neutral, "God-like," whereas the central, frontal angle is an "egocentric viewpoint," one that invites action and involvement.[19] We are pulled into Jane's scene by the long curve of the road and are led back to a home that has the quality of a refuge or retreat. An intriguing variation is found in another print of Castle House, probably the work of Jane or one of her brothers, in which the Taylor home, easily identifiable by the distinctive gables, is again set far in the distance.[20] Here, though, the great sweep of the landscape has been brought within the domestic realm of security – Jane's "safe, happy affectionate *home*"[21] – by the presence of a young woman seated under a gracefully arched tree in the foreground. She is reading, with her small

Fig. 4.2. Engraving after Jane Taylor's drawing of Castle House, Ongar. Ann Taylor, *The Autobiography and Other Memorials of Mrs Gilbert, Formerly Ann Taylor* 1: 248.

Fig. 4.3. Isaac Taylor, view of the Taylors' second house at Lavenham. Ann Taylor, *The Autobiography and Other Memorials of Mrs Gilbert, Formerly Ann Taylor* 1: 173.

dog beside her, and her calm presence provides feminine oversight of the domestic territory.

The Taylors were in the habit of capturing the image of family homes in drawings, watercolors, and engravings, and as they moved away from each other they continued the practice of sending sketches and descriptions of their new locations. Ann, for example, constructed a paper model of the parlor in the house at Rotherham where she lived as a young married woman and drew in all of the furniture and decorative objects, as well as the curtains at the windows and the landscape beyond.[22] The view or prospect was thus considered part of the furnishings of a home. This degree of detail about the particularities of their daily lives is coupled, as we have seen, with a romanticized, nostalgic recollection of earlier homes. In the midst of packing for another move, Ann insists that she is "not subject to dangerous excesses" of sentiment, noting that there is "a sufficiency of common-place about chairs and china, and bread and beer, and cheese, and string, and straw, to reduce the fine edge of romantic suffering," but she distills her memories of former homes down to certain personally meaningful highlights: "Oh, that low white porch where the vine leaves cling! I shall never forget it." In a similar vein, Jane describes her "dear paternal home" at Ongar in a letter to a friend, and beyond a general reference to the house as "an old-fashioned place, with a pretty garden," the only detail she mentions is that "at the door is a rural porch, covered with a vine."[23]

THE WINDOW AS VALVE: TRANSITIONAL DEVICES BETWEEN INTERIOR AND EXTERIOR

The porch, the door, the window – those points of entry, or perhaps more fittingly in this context, of exit, those membranes that allow the home and the garden to flow together – were often used by the Taylor sisters as literal or metaphorical images related to the safety and intimacy of the home and the freedom and risk of spaces outside those walls. In Ann's autobiography, which she addressed to her children and entitled "Domestic Recollections," she moves from a description of the family workroom at Lavenham to a view of the garden through the large window:

One wing of the premises seen from this window was covered with a luxuriant tea tree, drooping in long branches, with its small purple flowers; – on a bed just opposite was a great cinnamon rose bush, covered with bloom; a small grass plot lay immediately under the window, and beyond were labyrinths of flowering shrubs, with such a bush of honeysuckle as I scarcely remember to have seen anywhere.

Once past the ordering frame of the window her memories then seem to pile together, a rich jumble of description without any spatial logic: "Then there were beds of raspberries, gooseberries, and currants, espalier'd walks, ample kitchen garden, walls and palings laden with fruit, grass and gravel walks, a honeysuckle arbour, and an open seated summer-house; flourishing standard fruit trees, and no end of flowers and rustic garden seats." But at the end of this lengthy description she again returns to the open relationship between interior and exterior: "all this world of vernal beauty, all to be enjoyed only by stepping into it."[24] She provides her children, then, with a view of the home that is extensive in its boundaries, incorporating the lush confusion and delight of cultivated nature.

The Taylors' next house at Colchester was situated in a busy part of town, so the distant prospect of the countryside took on more resonance than the near view of the garden. This point is evident in Ann's description of the workroom where the sisters studied such diverse subjects as anatomy, geography, fortifications, drawing, and engraving. As at Lavenham, this room was the hub of family activities, and although Ann exclaimed over the "Happy days, – mornings, evenings, Happy years!" passed there she also dwelled on the view outside, as if she had spent considerable time through the years dreaming about the landscape beyond that enclosed space: "From the windows we could just see over the garden, and beyond the roofs, Mile End church and parsonage in the pretty distance, reminding us of the evening walk by which the day's business was so often closed."[25]

We find a similar movement outward, mixed with an overflowing jumble of details side by side with more general descriptions, in Ann's account of the new home at Ongar. Beginning with a short sentence about the history of the building that is followed immediately by details about the hall door, she then organizes our view by setting up the cardinal axes: at the center, the vine-covered façade of the house, a flower garden in front, a view of the church at the right, and trees on a hill at the left, the whole encircled by a moat. This mapping of the spatial logic of the home universe is followed by a very brief list of the specific rooms in the house. The home being visually and conceptually ordered, brought within the imaginative and emotional grasp of the new inhabitants, the exploration outward could begin. The opening forth required some clearing away of the vines around the windows so that this membrane between interior and exterior spaces was negotiable: "We had to *saw* the ivy from the back parlour window before we could see it, but some still remains to fringe the mullions; we have beautiful walks in every direction; and we have placed our garden seat at the end of a retired field."[26] We can expand our understanding of

Ann's account by applying the ideas of Tuan, who explains that "Space assumes a rough coordinate frame centered on the mobile and purposive self." Developing the point that the structure and stance of the human body constitute the "fundamental principles of organization," he notes, "Upright, man is ready to act. Space opens out before him and is immediately differentiable into front–back and right–left axes in conformity with the structure of his body." This space, however, is centered in a secure and stable place, so that a natural hierarchy is established which is built on the "prestige of the center."[27] For Ann Taylor, then, the center was the house, but not the interior rooms as much as what we might call the skin of the house: the windows and the vine-covered front.[28] This centering allowed her to move as Tuan's "mobile and purposive self" out to the distant field and the walks beyond. Gillian Rose would emphasize, instead, the paradoxical nature of the spaces described by Ann Taylor, noting the verbal descriptions that shift from one view to another even as the eye might flit in a non-linear fashion, taking in small details as well as larger visual composites.[29] Feminist geographers like Doreen Massey would also highlight the relational aspect of Ann's understanding of her home-ground – the "we" who deal with the ivy, take long walks, and make decisions about garden design. Movement in, around, and beyond the home, in Massey's view, is not enacted by Tuan's "mobile and purposive self" but is facilitated by the very openness of the reality of home, "constructed out of movement, communication, social relations which always stretched beyond it."[30]

Ivy was a recurrent motif for the Taylor sisters, as a sign both of nature's softening effects and of civilization's taming hand. The give and take of co-existence is illustrated by this simple image: while a luxurious vine can mask the hard bones of a house, the rampant disorder of vegetation run wild can in turn be pruned and tamed by a civilizing hand. So humans can live in harmony with a domesticated nature. But Jane is not above little digs at picturesque pretensions. She spoofs this kind of sentimental nostalgia in a poem about an idle, well-to-do young man who decides to sell the family home and move instead into a small cottage: "The tasty trellis o'er the front is seen, / With rose and woodbine woven in between: / Within, the well-paid artist lays it out, / To look ten times more rural than without." Predictably, the listless young man finds no happiness in this faux-rural retreat: "poor *Felix*, sits and yawns, / In spite of paper trees and painted lawns."[31] Good-hearted Emily, the protagonist of Jane's only novel, *Display: A Tale for Young People* (1815), is as industrious and charitable as Felix is lazy and pretentious, but she too falls for the picturesque vine. Searching for a way to help a poor widow about to be evicted from her house, she finds "a little building covered with ivy, which had formerly been a pleasure-house, but was now disused, and falling into decay." Overseeing the renovation, Emily makes sure that the workmen protect what she considers the most charming aspects – the thick ivy covering the windows and the overhanging tree branches – and she adds other picturesque touches: "To adorn the entrance, she contrived to form a rustic porch, with a seat, of mossy logs and branches; and she led over it a wild honeysuckle and a white Jessamine, which had long grown there, and crept over the front of the building." Widow Jones is initially taken aback by the darkness of her new cottage, only reassured by the sight of her "puss" sleeping on the hearth, but Emily blithely assures her that "you'll look so pretty sitting to knit in the porch! and be sure ... that you do not tear down the ivy that grows over your little window."[32] This is just the sort of cottage, in fact, that Jane portrayed in a simple ink and wash sketch, presumably from life (Fig. 4.4). Richard Sha questions how women, associated with the soft and the smooth, could use a picturesque style that was noted for its rough irregularity, and he concludes, "The solution to this paradox seems to be that women were encouraged to delineate domesticated versions of the picturesque, that is, thatched cottages."[33] In *Essays in Rhyme*, however, Jane Taylor acknowledges that "a tattered cottage" roofed with thatch and covered in moss might present "quite a picture to poetic eyes," but when seen up close "The picturesque is vanished, and the eye, / Averted, turns from loathsome poverty."[34]

While poems, hymns, and stories for adults as well as children written during this period often contained references to nature's beauty as evidence of God's bounteous love, Jane presents an interesting corrective to this approach in her poem "Poetry and Reality." She wonders why we, who love nature, shouldn't worship "The God of nature in that green recess; / Surrounded by His works, and not confin'd / To rites adapted to the vulgar mind?," but she goes on to warn "the fond enthusiast" against making a temple of nature. While those who don't respond to the beauty of the landscape "Possess but half a soul," there's a greater danger in "Confounding picturesque, with moral taste." The Christian gospel, she argues, is found in the small, thankless, daily gestures of good will toward the poor and oppressed, not in "Poetic musings on a church-yard flower."[35] Here Jane Taylor seems to question the Wordsworthian faith that love of nature leads to love of humanity.

Jane's poetry for young children is less caustic, however, and the picturesque vines in her poem about "The Industrious Boy" clearly function as positive signs of moral virtue and domestic security. Diligent William, who

Fig. 4.4. Jane Taylor, *Cottage with a Man on a Bridge*. Suffolk Record Office.

Fig. 4.5. Jane Taylor, *Bridge in a Landscape*. Suffolk Record Office.

loves his toys but cares even more for his books and other "rational pleasures," grows up to be a cheerful, contented man. His wife and baby by his side, he enjoys the rewards of those habits of industry:

> His garden well loaded with store,
> His cot by the side of the green,
> Where woodbines crept over the door,
> And jessamines peep'd in between.[36]

The portrayal of a well-ordered life is combined with images of fertility that underscore the prospect of abundance and prosperity. Particularly important in this respect are the vines framing the cottage door: although requiring careful training to subdue their rampant tendencies, when tended properly their lively and energetic nature works in harmony with the stable lines of the house. This, of course, serves as an apt metaphor for childrearing and the harnessing of youthful imagination in the service of adult rationality, a thematic image that we will see again in Hannah More's honeysuckles in Chapter 7.

Jane frequently included references in her letters and other, more public writings to views of nature seen through a framing device such as a door or window, as if taking particular pleasure in the sense of connection provided by that motif. In one letter she reveals, "We have not indulged in one walk yet, though the country and weather have been beautifully inviting; but we sit at the bow window next the garden; and quite enjoy ourselves."[37] The suggestion of physical passivity is aligned here with the simplest kind of pleasure, simply sitting and enjoying the view, although Jane's mother responded with "No exercise! … Shame on you!" Jane replied by reassuring her parents, who advocated a long walk every day, that they had plenty of exercise "in the house and garden, where the children play continually."[38]

The window also played a prominent role in the sisters' private studies where the hard work of writing was accomplished. In those passages the view often provided a mental stimulus for their work. Given small rooms of their own, the sisters took full advantage of their separate work spaces. As Ann writes, "What, either of mental improvement or of personal piety, can be expected to flourish where numbers are crowded into one room? How much may not be expected from those happy ones who enjoy the luxury of a chamber, or a closet to call their own?" She observes about Jane's study at Colchester that it was in "a not very desirable attic" so the window, providing "a peep of landscape over the roofs," was an important point of release.

Jane was prompted, in fact, to make a sketch of the prospect, unfortunately now lost.[39]

Writing to her sister Jane explains, "When I am low in spirits, weary, or cross; or especially when worried by some of the teazing realities of life, one glance at the landscape from the window of my attic, never fails to produce a salutary effect on me." She also relied on the view for inspiration, as she notes at the beginning of a poem written for a friend's birthday: "I went to the window, since nature's green vest / Some feeling poetic is wont to suggest."[40] On the morning of her own twenty-first birthday Jane describes opening her eyes and looking at "the beautiful frost-work on my window," which she then uses as the basis for an essay in which she ponders the passage of time. She recalls a similar experience seven years earlier, as she lay in bed picturing her future enacted in "the fantastic coruscations of the frosty panes": "I could imagine groves, spires, cascades, and wide spreading landscapes, representing the bright scenes of life through which I was about to pass."[41] Here the window operates as a lens into the future, a thin film on which her future is enacted. The house serves as a container, both comforting and constraining, the window as an opening, and the landscapes in her imagination as realms of dream-like possibilities.

Jane's attic room, once full of stored lumber before she cleared it out and equipped it as a study, becomes an intellectual and professional retreat – her "consecrated attic,"[42] similar, as we shall see in Chapter 7, to Fanny Price's attic retreat. But Jane still feels the need for that valve into the outer world. She writes to a friend about her workroom, "though my study cannot boast the elegance of yours, it possesses one advantage which, as a poet, you ought to allow surpasses them all – it commands a view of the country; – the only room in the house, except one, which is thus favored; and to me this is invaluable." Commenting on the fact that she'd already written a whole page even though it was just after six o'clock in the morning, she attributes this "chiefly, to the sweet fields that are now smiling in vernal beauty before me."[43] Later, just before moving out of this house, Jane finds comfort in the thought of "the moon and sunshine that will still irradiate its walls."[44] Even given the familiarity of the near landscape, the opening out of the prospect through the window, beyond the darker interior spaces of the home, fostered a feeling of creative possibilities for Jane, as for many women writers and artists of the period.[45]

In their next house in Ongar Ann also had an attic study, a place of both refuge and prospect (reminiscent of Dorothy Wordsworth, as we will see in Chapter 5) and an early version of Woolf's room of one's own: "My own room was one I had requested on the attic floor commanding a beautiful country view, and having the advantage of a closet where I could sit and write. This was to be my 'sanctum'; here a new life was to begin, and the employment more delightful to me than any other, was henceforth to be mine without let or hindrance." Although the phrase "commanding a view" was not unusual, and in fact matches her description of the main part of the house – "From every window in front we command a rich and beautiful valley" – in the context of the sisters' own rooms it takes on a new resonance. Here for Ann is her "sanctum," the site of her new life with the promise of work that will bring her great joy. Her language is centered in the self – "my own room," "I had requested," "my sanctum," "to be mine" – so as a result we feel more strongly that *she* is in control of that view, conjuring it up as a muse for her work.[46]

Before her marriage Ann wrote that "none but the fully occupied can appreciate the delight of suspended, or rather, I should say, of varied labour ... Life cannot be made up of recreations, they must be garden spots in well farmed land."[47] Work with all its variety is visualized as a landscape, all of it requiring labor of some kind, the gardens as well as the farms, and each component in its own way being both productive and beautiful. After her marriage, however, Ann allows herself at times to express her frustration, admitting that her writing could only be done in her "limited leisure," not as the real work of her day.[48] The independence so evident in the description of her attic "sanctum" is markedly at variance with her later attitude, when she describes "that waiting, and watching and solicitous dependence for happiness which a wife must feel towards one who is appointed to rule both over and in her. In him, most emphatically, her desires centre ... She cannot enjoy an independent pleasure, for the very thought of its independence prevents it being pleasure." She associates the tasks of gardening at times with those of housekeeping, both being opposed to the intellectual focus needed for writing, and explains in a letter to her siblings in 1814, written soon after her marriage: "Whenever I can, – but there is always 'some bed or some border to mend, or something to tie or to stick,' – I endeavour to get to writing about eleven, and write during the morning, more or less, as I am able." But the garden was also a refuge for her. Lamenting the "din" of a child-filled home and the "pressure of daily employments," she recommends that "every burdened mother" should get away periodically for some quiet time alone: "She will look at herself and her proceedings, as from a distance, and sometimes in the solitude of the chamber, or the garden, will find it no unhealthy exercise to describe herself *aloud*."[49] Finding a space for herself, whether in the innermost recesses of the home, her bedchamber, or the outer extensions of her domestic realm, the garden, she has the chance to reinscribe herself. By describing herself out loud she confirms her individual voice, becoming once again her own woman rather than the wife, mother, and mistress of the family conjured in her mother's treatise on womanly duties.

We are reminded here of Ann's mother, also a writer and gardener, who sent a telling letter home when she was away on a rare visit to London, in which she seems at first to be more concerned about the plants than her own children:

> I hope you take care of Dickey and ye trees, mind I can tell whether they have had justice done them by their looks. I am not sure if those two beautiful geraniums will do well where they are, if they look less healthy than they did, by all means remove them to their old situation in ye best parlour window, telling the new maid to mind she don't break them when she shuts the windows; and pray forsake not the poor rose-tree in ye pot in ye garden; if it is too much trouble there, have it in among ye rest. And pray tell me how you individually are in health.[50]

Unlike the mother in Smith's *Rambles Farther*, who sets up a clear hierarchy with a woman's oversight of the house as her primary duty and her activities in the garden as a secondary pleasure,[51] Mrs. Taylor allows her pressing concern for the plants to take precedence over her responsibilities as a mother, if only temporarily. But she was still operating within a carefully circumscribed domain, the potted geraniums and garden roses having been planted, most likely, in the service of domestic beauty and order.

Jane, unlike her sister, never married and always lived with her parents or brother; as she reveals, "I find that *home* is the place that suits me best."[52] Returning one year from an extended trip during which her typical daily pattern had been to spend the evening in social engagements rather than "some kind of mental exertion" (the latter being her more usual pattern), she writes, "my mind never had so long a holiday; and I feel it is time to send it home." Home for her, then, was equated with work, not domestic chores but intellectually engaging pursuits, thus significantly different from most women's view of home life at the time. Jane explains her work in a letter to her mother: "I do actually, what you describe as so desirable – 'sit down composed and unembarrassed in my study'."[53] Unembarrassed about her preference for a quiet life, she characterizes herself as having "a taste for retirement" – partly for practical reasons, to safeguard her time for writing, partly because of an innate shyness that her family often remarked on, and partly because of her deep religious feelings and her need for what she describes as "daily, constant, private prayer."[54] Compared to her sister, Jane was able to concentrate on her profession more fully throughout her short life, but she too acknowledged the difficulties of dividing her time between domestic duty and writing. As she admits in a letter of 1809, "In truth, Jane Taylor of the morning and Jane Taylor of the evening are as different people, in their feelings and sentiments, as two such intimate friends can possibly be. The former is an active, handy little body who can make beds or do plain work, and now and then takes a fancy for drawing, etc. But the last-mentioned lady never troubles her head with these menial affairs; – nothing will suit her but the *pen*."[55] Carol Shiner Wilson recognizes the "tortured debates" between these two personae, reflecting Jane's desire for a life of the intellect and her sense of duty to the home – in other words, "what she thinks and what she feels she ought to think."[56] Both sisters, then, experienced what Leonore Davidoff describes as a "tension between work and domesticity" that surfaced repeatedly in their private writing although it was carefully submerged in their published texts, especially their poems and stories for children.[57]

TWO VIEWS OF NATURE

The primary trope of our book, the lens through which we are viewing the texts and images, is the domestic, or domesticated, landscape, referring to nature that is near at hand, tended, cultured, and nurtured. This trope has provided us with a new analytical tool for studying the Taylor sisters, and it also enables us to draw crucial distinctions between them. Ann is caught up in home life, as wife and mother, whereas Jane's world is both simpler, being more solitary, and also more complicated, revealing a complex array of responses to the natural world. Ann focuses on the small, the particular, the mundane; Jane, in contrast, is more aligned with the romantic sublime in her sensibility, although most of her writings and drawings are still centered in the home in some way, thus distinguishing her from the masculine tradition of the sublime.

Jane characterizes herself and Ann as hanging "like twin buds on a stalk, / (We may call ourselves flowers in song),"[58] but they often describe their personalities, writing styles, and adult lives as differing in significant ways. Ann writes to Jane in 1817, recognizing the ideal of conjoining intellectual and domestic pursuits:

[W]hat different lives we lead! There are some things I regret, but I feel daily that mine is the lot for me, and yours for you, and we must take them as they are. If your fame, and leisure for the improvement of your mind, could be combined with the comfort and pleasures of a larger domestic circle; and if, with a husband

and children, I could share a glimmer of your fame, and a portion of your reading, we should both perhaps be happier than it is the usual lot of life to be, and at least happier than it seems good for us to be.[59]

Ann was the outgoing, social one, but with a strong domestic streak that caused her son to portray her as "ever a home bird [who] enjoyed especially the more simple features of a home landscape." Jane was more shy and diffident; as she writes to a friend, "My love of quiet and retirement daily increases."[60] Her humility often caused her to deflect attention away from her own contributions in order to elevate her sister's role. In a poem written for Ann on her birthday in 1809 and published in *The Associate Minstrels*, Jane uses a metaphor from nature to make her point, as she often did. While Ann is a flourishing plant "spreading sweet fragrancy wide," Jane pictures herself as "blighted and pale, at your side," and adds, "I hang down my head in the shade."[61] In reference to this book of poetry, which was written by a close circle of friends that included the two Taylor sisters, Jane apologizes for her "morbid humility" but suggests that "in comparison with my blooming companions in this garland, I allow my pieces to rank as the leaves."[62]

Ann loved to write about the small details that make the home a beloved retreat, while Jane was continually drawn to the larger world of nature and its mysteries. Ann's son Josiah Gilbert noted, "Ann Taylor dealt with the facts of life, and Jane with those of nature."[63] He used as evidence their best-known poems: Ann's "My Mother," a sentimental tribute to maternal devotion, and Jane's "Twinkle, twinkle little star," the simplest of rhymes that distills the profundity of nature into language suitable for young children. As Ann puts it, "My mind likes to walk in a defined path, with a close fence of particulars," and although she writes to her husband in 1818 describing nature as her "first love," she clads her personification in the clothes of a demure young woman: "O beautiful nature, how lovely thou art / In thy bonnet of blue and thy mantle of green!"[64]

Jane, on the other hand, was often inspired by the more sublime aspects of the landscape. In her poems for children she usually draws a close circle centered on the garden or on the familiar aspects of nature experienced on ordinary walks, but she also has a romantic streak that battles with what she describes as her rational side. During her walks, whether "a solitary turn around our pretty garden" or longer jaunts through the countryside, she seems more intent on a general imaginative or spiritual response than on the kind of careful attention to detail that would characterize a botanizer. "Not at all intimidated by rain or wind," she is drawn to the North Devon coast and describes it with particularly remarkable language for an otherwise calm and sensible young woman: "We had traveled several miles over a high, wild, and dreary tract of country; – giving the idea of traveling over the world as a planet, and rendered still more desolate in appearance by torrents of rain." Her brother characterized her as having "a fine sense of the beautiful and sublime in nature," so in different periods of her life and different locations she could delight in the "cheerful" face of nature as well its more awe-inspiring aspects. In Colchester in 1806, for example, she writes about "the smiling landscape, and the clear sky, and all the beauties of a country walk," while six years later in Ilfracombe she realizes that "our rambles among the rocks I enjoy most; though at first they excited sensations of awe and terror, rather than of pleasure."[65]

Ann's son explains the difference between the two sisters' love of the countryside in this way:

[N]ature with its peace, its pathos, and its infinite suggestiveness, was [Jane's] chosen refuge. Ann was fond of nature, but it was chiefly in relation to domestic incidents – she dwelt upon the cottage, the stile, the footpath, the garden and domestic animals – while Jane looked upon the larger landscapes, and her mind floated into dreamy reveries over the expanse of sea and sky, partaking more of the contemplative, and curiously inquiring character of her brother Isaac.[66]

Ann is firmly centered in the domestic habits of the home, although she sometimes wearies of its tedium and constraints, whereas Jane, though also preferring home life, allows herself to dream more freely. The near landscape is thus a comforting buffer for one, an entry into new imaginative terrain for the other.

In a letter from 1809 Jane observes, "That I have an eye to see, and a heart to feel the beauties of nature, I acknowledge with gratitude; because they afford me constant and unsatiating pleasure; and form almost my only recreation."[67] Her sketch of a great sweeping bridge gives us some idea of her approach to nature: surprisingly modern in its elegant abstraction, the bridge is flanked by a steep, forbidding cliff to the left and lighter, more gently sloping hills at the right (Fig. 4.5). The loose, "dreamy" washes act as a foil for the calligraphic elegance of line seen in the tallest tree, its vertical emphasis working to balance the broad curve of the bridge. The patterns of light and dark also create a skillful compositional harmony, most notably in the contrast between the stark white bridge and the inky wedge projecting out into the water below it. But Jane was also attracted to the near view more typical of the unassertive modesty associated with women's sketches of the period[68] – a single picturesque tree (Fig. 4.6), for example, or a country path and stile leading to a sunlit field (Fig. 4.7). None of these gives us

Fig. 4.6. Jane Taylor, *Tree with Hills in the Distance*. Suffolk Record Office.

Fig. 4.7. Jane Taylor, *Path and Stile in a Landscape*. Suffolk Record Office.

close descriptive detail, but instead we are left with the sense of an artist who was interested in the general mood of the scene: the atmospheric shifts, the patterns of light, the undercurrents of energy, the organic rhythms of growth and decay.

In her drawings Jane created images through which we move – over a bridge, across a stile, down a lane – but we are most often given a point of security or home base from which to operate. We are positioned on the near side of the fence or right before the sunlit spot at the base of the spreading tree, but still there is the suggestion of a larger world to explore. Similarly, spatial indicators often took on added layers of significance for the Taylor sisters in their writing: personal, gendered, moral, or metaphorical associations complicate the movements back and forth between interior and exterior, window view and garden enclosure, cultivated landscape and distant prospect. Windows, doors, porches, paths, and lanes assume new roles in the domestic landscape, acting as barriers and boundaries as well as passages and directional axes that shape a woman's life. As we shall see in the next chapter, in creating and writing about her garden in Grasmere Dorothy Wordsworth makes the garden itself the focal point of her life, both a place of refuge and an invitation to a larger world of imagination and thought.

PART III

Personal practice: making gardens grow

CHAPTER 5

Dorothy Wordsworth: gardening, self-fashioning, and the creation of home

On Christmas Eve, 1799, Dorothy and William Wordsworth wrote a long letter to Coleridge, describing their new home in the Lake District where they settled after a lonely stay in Germany.[1] In William's words,

> D is much pleased with the house and *appurtenances* the orchard especially; in imagination she has already built a seat with a summer shed on the highest platform in this our little domestic slip of mountain. The spot commands a view over the roof of our house, of the lake, the church, helm cragg [*sic*], and two thirds of the vale. We mean also to enclose the two or three yards of ground between us and the road, this for the sake of a few flowers, and because it will make it more our own. Besides, am I fanciful when I would extend the obligation of gratitude to insensate things?[2]

This brief description encapsulates much of what the Wordsworths will do to and for the property they rented around Town End, Grasmere, now known as Dove Cottage. The letter reveals no grand plans or theories of design (that will come later, especially for William), but it does indicate the ways that the Wordsworths imagine making the space their own and the value they place on "insensate things." Although they like their commanding view of the vale of Grasmere and towering Helm Crag, emphasis actually falls on the domestication of the spot as a refuge from the larger world – the imagined summer-house or shed (which would finally be completed in 1805) and the enclosure of the garden for the sake of privacy and cultivation, as well as a sense of ownership. As Dorothy writes to her old friend Jane Pollard Marshall the following September, "We have a boat upon the lake and a small orchard and a smaller garden which as it is the work of our own hands we regard with pride and partiality. This garden we enclosed from the road and pulled down a fence which formerly divided it from the orchard. The orchard is very small, but then it is a delightful one from its retirement, and the excessive beauty of the prospect from it."[3] In the course of making the garden, then, the Wordsworths re-imagined the space, building a wall where needed, but also tearing down an unnecessary fence.

In this chapter, we propose that the garden as a central element of home was primarily the work of both Dorothy's imagination and her hands, as William acknowledges in the very first sentence quoted above. As we shall see, Dorothy's primary role in the garden also becomes evident in the journal, where we learn that she does most of the gardening (and other domestic work) while William composes poetry.[4] The Wordsworths spent an extraordinary amount of time at home outside and clearly viewed the garden as an extension of the tiny house. Not only the garden but also the orchard and surrounding woods, mountains, and lakes were subject to Dorothy's home-making aesthetic. Furthermore, her experiment in gardening and the written record that she kept set the pattern for the way she approached the natural world, as documented in several travel journals in later years.

THE CROFT OF MEMORY

Dorothy Wordsworth's attraction to images and objects of refuge in nature – nest-like summer-houses, natural bowers in a mountain scene, protected and secluded slips of ground – all reveal her domesticating impulses, her desire to make the unhomelike places and objects of the world accessible and welcoming.[5] When she sees a threatening scene, she attempts to find a way to redeem it with an image of protection or hope. In Burkean terms, Dorothy rejects the boundlessness and grandeur of the sublime, transforming the landscape by either domesticating it or re-imagining it in terms of the picturesque, as several other writers have argued. In this regard, she shares an aesthetic with women artists such as Maria Spilsbury, as we saw in Chapter 3. Commenting on this issue, William Snyder suggests, "Perhaps because their message tends to privilege intimacy over spectacle, domesticity over transcendence, women artists of the late eighteenth and early nineteenth centuries find more compatible the understatement, subtlety and integrative qualities of the picturesque."[6] But rather than simply endorsing standard views of the picturesque as valuing variety, attention to detail, and the evidence of passing time, Dorothy insists on home-making as the primary value.[7] This impulse in part represents a rejection of that alienation from the natural and human worlds that is often the burden of sublime visions, but we can also see Dorothy's choice in terms of gardening history – as an embracing of small spaces at a time when the reigning aesthetics preferred the grandeur of the sweeping views in a landscape park.[8] Dorothy's commitment to her "small orchard" and "smaller garden," her diminutive garden-making, was both a financial necessity and an imaginative desire: she found her way of being a gardener – and her way of *being* – in a smaller space. As her brother will later claim in his sonnet "Nuns fret not at their convent's narrow room," there is an advantage to working within a "scanty plot of ground" – in this case, "two or three yards between us and the road."[9] Smaller spaces inevitably open up the world of detail to the imagination and inspire reverence for those details in nature, such as the "few flowers" alluded to in the first letter. Akin to the reverence for the miniature or magnified life in botanical texts discussed in Chapter 2, Dorothy's narrow plot actually becomes a gateway to a larger life.[10]

Dorothy Wordsworth repeatedly emphasizes the nested or secure aspects of her environment. In *Romantic Visualities*, Jacqueline Labbe has related Dorothy's preference for protected places to Jay Appleton's habitat theory, which argues that there are two primary impulses for desirable habitats: prospect and refuge. According to Appleton in *The Experience of Landscape*, "the ability to see and the ability to hide are both important in calculating a creature's survival prospects. ... Where he has an unimpeded opportunity to see we can call it a *prospect*. Where he has an opportunity to hide, a *refuge*."[11] Bringing the category of gender to this analysis, Labbe quotes studies that argue that women have a preference for habitats of refuge, concluding that women such as Dorothy "can display their dissatisfaction [with the openness of prospect] by transforming their immersed position into an advantageous site of peculiarly feminine power."[12] We have seen in Chapter 1 a comparable preference for refuge in children's literature of the period, evident in the centrality of the garden arbor for domestic role-play as well as for surveying the larger scene. Similarly, while Dorothy finds creative advantage in habitats of refuge, she never gives up the prospect, the wider perspective, entirely. Often she views the distant landscape from the perspective of a safe or hidden place, as her allusion to the imaginative shed overlooking the vale of Grasmere suggests. Her ideal garden implies a private retreat that includes a high platform from which to observe the valley below.

As we have noted, Bachelard's meditation on what he calls "simple images of *felicitous space*" proposes that we as humans are attracted to such spaces of intimacy, memory, and dreams as houses, rooms, nests, shelters, and corners.[13] We will return to Bachelard to illuminate Dorothy's desire to recapture a lost intimacy associated with the safety and comfort of home. But Dorothy's experience reveals that home can also be a fraught concept, reminding us of Rose's critique of this unproblematic association between women and the "safety" of home.[14] The difficulty of Dorothy's life after her parents' death, when she was still a girl, is well known in Wordsworth scholarship, but it is worth emphasizing that Dorothy's losses fostered a need to recreate the home-that-might-have-been.[15] Writing to Jane Pollard in 1793, Dorothy confides that she dreams of the time when she might have a home with William in "Retirement and rural quiet." She reminds Jane, "you remember the Enthusiasm with which we used to be fired when in the Back-Kitchen, the Croft, or in any other of our favorite Haunts we built our little tower of Joy."[16] The images in this list move from inside the house (the coziness of the back kitchen) into the croft or kitchen garden and beyond to unspecified haunts – all scenes for the "little tower of Joy," the state of mind of this remembered idyll of childhood. Dorothy's letter is one of many attempts to "build" the place that can be home. We are reminded here, in the imagined trajectory outward and the strong tone of nostalgia, of the Taylors' descriptions of home in Chapter 4. Dorothy's croft of memory will become the small garden in Grasmere and its related shelters. As she writes to Lady Beaumont in 1804, "I must tell you that we have been busily employed about finishing a little hut or shed, a sort of larger Bird's nest (for it is lined with moss) at the top of our Orchard."[17] This attraction to images of shelter and nesting is also related to Dorothy's preference for the domestic and the intimate over the sublime, as we shall see both in her gardening and in the way that she writes about it. Furthermore, Dorothy's language – she uses such words as "hut," "shed," "nest," and "summer house" interchangeably for the outdoor spaces she constructs or imagines – implies a close relationship between these humble structures and the natural world, as well as the paradoxical fragility of home.

BEANS AND ROSES: THE GRASMERE JOURNALS, 1800–03

Although Dorothy Wordsworth distinguishes between her garden and the uncultivated nature that she and her brother so admire on their walks, her attitudes toward both are guided by her home-making impulse. Continually during the Grasmere period and into later years, when Dorothy records her thoughts while on various tours, she views the natural world in terms of her domestic aesthetic.[18] She finds even in lonely or desolate parts of nature a tree that can serve as a shelter and constructs that shelter in her imagination. Or, in the familiar holly woods around Dove Cottage, "The Hollins," she writes on April 30, 1802:

After dinner we took up the fur gown into The Hollins above. We found a sweet seat and thither we will often go. We spread the gown put on each a cloak and there we lay. William fell asleep … I did not sleep but I lay with half shut eyes, looking at the prospect as in a vision almost I was so resigned to it … When we turned the corner of our little shelter we saw the Church and the whole vale. It is a blessed place. The Birds were about us on all sides.[19]

The Hollins, then, becomes another home-site for Dorothy, a place for rest and retreat but also a spot that stirs her imaginative vision of the world around her, both natural and human. Dorothy is so engaged in the moment (though in a more passive, receptive sense, given her use of the word "resigned") that she describes the experience as a vision – while William sleeps. In the next day's entry, she continues to meditate on the significance of the holly woods:

Rose not til ½ past 8. A heavenly morning. I sowed the flowers William helped me. We then went and sate in the orchard till dinner time. It was very hot. William wrote the Celandine. We planned a shed for the sun was too much for us. After dinner we went again to our old resting place in the Hollins under the Rock. (May 1, 1802)[20]

The rhythm of the day is contained in this description: from work in the garden, to temporary refuge in the orchard, to planning the shed, to retreat to the cool shade of the woods that have become so homelike and welcoming. The passage also moves out from the house, from levels of cultivated to uncultivated nature, a spatial scheme that occurs throughout the journal.

Thinking of nature as a continuum based on various degrees of human intervention is central to Dorothy's idea about the garden, as is the natural cycle of seasons and work. The cyclical pattern of nature also establishes the textual rhythm of the journal and its relentless dailiness. While some have found coherence in the patterns of repetition in the journal, others have argued that the text is most meaningful as a narrative. Susan Levin, for instance, has written of the journal as Dorothy's (ambivalent) story of William's courtship of Mary Hutchinson and subsequent marriage.[21] We agree with Levin that thinking of the journal in terms of narrative structure is justified, and her interpretation of it as a romance plot is intriguing. But this plot locates Dorothy as an outsider-observer, the one who is also so distraught about losing her beloved that she cannot attend his wedding. We propose to shift the focus so that Dorothy occupies the center of the narrative: her vision of nature, the garden, and home frames the journal from beginning to end, even as we are aware of William's courtship of Mary. In fact, the journal essentially ends with Mary's entry into the home-garden after her marriage to William, but it is the state of the garden and its ability to nurture a new "plant" that absorbs our interest.[22] Throughout, Dorothy has defined her experience through the garden, not, as Levin correctly reminds us, through explicit analysis but through the accumulation of painstaking detail and through metonymic association of those details with herself, as, for instance, she describes a columbine as "a graceful slender creature, a female seeking retirement and growing freest and most graceful where it is most alone."[23] The journal tells the story of the garden – how it was made, how it relates to the human and natural world beyond, and how it expresses Dorothy Wordsworth's idea of home.

Beginning in mid-May, the journal is perfectly timed to chart the spring planting of both vegetables and flowers, including seeds and transplants from the wild or from other gardens. Although the garden is a communal enterprise (Dorothy receives help from William, their brother John, and various neighbors and servants), Dorothy is the center of activity. She describes numerous solitary "rambles" during which she gathers plants and flowers for the garden. On June 7 she eagerly waits at home for her brothers' return to Grasmere after they have been away. It is 11 p.m. before William returns and Dorothy reports, "We did not go to bed till 4 o'clock in the morning so he had an opportunity of seeing our improvements." Although she describes numerous times sauntering in the garden by moonlight, in this case the siblings perhaps wait until 4:00 because in early June that might have meant the first light of day. Dorothy in fact writes that the "birds were singing."[24]

Although Dorothy spends much time hunting the countryside for specimens of plants and flowers, she is careful to maintain her respect and reverence for uncultivated nature. She often laments the way that construction and development are changing the countryside, and ever attentive to detail, she will not pick flowers if she thinks her action will do the flower or the site some harm. On January 31, 1802, for instance, she describes a walk around Grasmere and Rydal lakes: "I found a strawberry blossom in a rock. The little slender flower had more courage than green leaves, for *they* were but half expanded and half grown, but the blossom was spread full out. I uprooted it rashly, and felt as if I had been committing an outrage, so I planted it again. It will have but a stormy life of it, but let it live if it can." Dorothy may be using the blossom as a substitute for talking directly about her own fate (uprooted then replanted in her home region), but the passage also demonstrates her ethics of caring for uncultivated nature, a theme to which she returns near the end of the journal: "We stopped our horse close to the hedge opposite a tuft of primroses three flowers in full blossom and a Bud, they reared themselves up among the green moss. We debated long whether we should pluck [them] and at last left them to live out their day, which I was right glad of at my return the Sunday following for there they remained uninjured either by cold or wet."[25]

Implicitly, Dorothy also seems to understand that her gardening paradoxically breaks down the boundaries between the cultivated and the wild. She naturalizes wildflowers and mosses, making them part of her home-garden, which in fact raises the question of whether they are then still wildflowers. As Harriet Ritvo asks in relation to this practice of transplanting, "At what point did a species cease to be wild? Was the simple incorporation within a cultivated setting enough to establish that a line had been crossed?" Ritvo goes on to suggest that "if a species could be simultaneously cultivated and wild – perhaps these appropriations subtly redefined the taxonomical status of the garden itself. That is, the garden wall might cease to function as the boundary between cultivated land and the wilderness."[26] Similar questions and implications apply to Dorothy Wordsworth's project of transplanting native plants from the wild. While she does not address the questions directly, Dorothy indicates her uneasiness in uprooting and conscripting plants that are happy in their wild state.

Whereas the garden houses wildflowers, human intervention also changes the wilderness. Dorothy typically writes about the way she and William construct domestic space out of what they find in nature, an activity that in turn influences their work in the garden. For instance, Dorothy describes an excursion that she, William, and Coleridge took on April 23, 1802, under Nab Scar, climbing among the austere rocks. At one point, William makes "himself a seat in the crumbly ground" and begins to recite his poetry. The episode culminates in the description of Coleridge

in search of something new. He called to us and we found him in a Bower, the sweetest that was ever seen. The Rock on one side is very high and covered with ivy which hung loosely about and bore bunches of brown berries. On the other side it was higher than my head. We looked down upon the Ambleside vale that seemed to wind away from us the village *lying* under the hill. The Fir tree Island was reflected beautifully. We now first saw that the trees are planted in rows. About this bower there is mountain ash, common ash, yew tree, ivy, holly, hawthorne mosses and flowers, and a carpet of moss. Above at the top of the Rock there is another spot – it is scarce a Bower, a little parlour on[ly] not enclosed by walls but shaped out for a resting place by the rocks and the ground rising about it. It had a sweet moss carpet. We resolved to go and plant flowers in both these places tomorrow.[27]

Even in this wild, rocky spot, Dorothy frames the scene in a way that softens it and makes it habitable. With the detail of the overhanging ivy and berries, she creates a picturesque moment amidst the sublime austerity of the mountains. By repeating the word "bower," too, Dorothy highlights the element of refuge. The term "bower" has clear poetic associations, of course, with the biblical and Spenserian "bower of bliss" (celebrated in book III of *The Faerie Queene*), an idealized place of love and fulfillment. It is also associated with the artificiality of pastoral literature. But Dorothy reclaims and transforms it – both the word itself and the possibility that it can be found in nature or constructed out of natural elements. Dorothy reserves the term for a place that is covered and enclosed by trees and vegetation, as well as carpeted. There must be a protected quality, such as Scott will describe in the natural bowers of *The Lady of the Lake*, "The primrose pale, and violet flower, / Found in each cliff a narrow bower," or William Wordsworth in "Lines Written in Early Spring," where the narrator refers to his place in a grove as a "sweet bower."[28] Dorothy is careful to distinguish the bower, the truly protected and enclosed spot, from the other resting place that is more like a "little parlour" or outdoor room. In both instances, though, Dorothy finds the places compatible and welcoming and hopes to make them more so by planting flowers in the wild, a reversal of her usual pattern of seeking flowers for her own garden at Town End.[29]

Dorothy includes a description of the view from this bower of the vale of Ambleside. The sight of the village under the hill seems rather commonplace, but Dorothy does reveal that patterns become clear when seen from a distance – the trees are planted in rows, for instance, that are only now discernible. The journal entry follows the progress of Dorothy's thought from this private retreat out into the vale and back again. Rhetorically the passage privileges the bower, since the view is literally framed by and dependent on it.

So attractive was this secluded spot under Nab Scar that in the following month Dorothy and William construct a bower behind Dove Cottage, art imitating nature.[30] Located in the orchard, it becomes the center of Dorothy's consciousness for the garden and the surrounding area. So inspired, it seems, by the perspective of the new bower, Dorothy writes in the present tense, unusual in the journal and a signal of the intensity of the experience that she records in a vivid descriptive shorthand: "It is a nice cool shady spot. The small birds are singing. Lambs bleating. Cuckow calling. The thrush sings by Fits. Thomas Ashburner's axe is going quietly (without passion) in the orchard. Hens are cackling. Flies humming, the women talking together at the doors: Plumb and pear trees are in Blossom – apple trees greenish the opposite woods green, the crows are cawing."[31]

This passage exemplifies the power of detail in Dorothy Wordsworth's imagination. Her consciousness is magnified, alert to details that at other times might simply register as part of the background. A familiar passage from Bachelard's *The Poetics of Space* (discussed in Chapter 2) glosses this point: "Thus the minuscule, a narrow gate, opens up an entire world. The details of a thing can be the sign of a new world which, like all worlds, contains the attributes of greatness."[32] Through both the present tense and the minute detail, then, the moment comes vividly to life and the garden bower forms the center of it all. Several descriptions that follow reiterate the way the bower focuses attention on details and creates the fiction that the world around it will remain forever young.

After the bower is constructed and functioning as the center of the garden, Dorothy notes that William finishes "his poem on Going for Mary," which Dorothy writes out on May 29, 1802.[33] Thus for the first time in the journal Dorothy mentions (albeit obliquely) that the marriage is imminent and that the dynamics of home will have to change. Several events in the garden mark the change. First, the swallows' nest, which Dorothy had observed being constructed for ten days, falls down: "Poor little creatures they could not themselves be more distressed than I was."[34] The ruined nest is particularly disturbing to Dorothy, it seems, because it represents the potential destruction of the security of home and a betrayal of the hope that a nest represents. As Bachelard explains, "Would a bird build its nest if it did not have its instinct for confidence in the world? If we heed this call and make an absolute refuge of such a precarious shelter as a nest … we return to the sources of the oneiric house."[35] Dorothy has heeded this call in constructing her garden, which, like all gardens in this world, enjoys a precarious existence but is even more intensely valued because of its potential loss.

Then as if her confidence in home-making is restored, Dorothy exults on June 29 that "my swallows are on their nest. Yes! there they are side by side both looking down into the garden."[36] Given the emotion with which Dorothy records this event (especially in relation to her matter-of-fact tone at other times) and Bachelard's commentary on the symbolic significance of nests, the return of the swallows could have signaled her hope for refuge. At the same time, her descriptions indicate that she is still ambivalent about the coming changes – first the trip to France with William and then William's marriage to Mary. Emotional turmoil finds its analogue in the garden. Following a stormy night on Sunday, July 4, Dorothy records that "The Roses in the garden are fretted and battered and quite spoiled the honey suckle though in its glory is sadly teazed. The peas are beaten down. The Scarlet Beans want sticking. The garden is overrun with weeds." Dorothy's language is both violent and anthropomorphic here, suggesting the disruption and danger to the garden: fretted, battered, spoiled, teased, beaten down. Anticipating her long absence, as well as the change that absence will bring, Dorothy describes a garden in need of preventative care that she may not have time to provide. Although she rallies after this description, her final note on the garden comes in the form of an elegiac apostrophe: "I must prepare to go. The Swallows I must leave them the well the garden the Roses, all. Dear Creatures! they sang last night after I was in bed – seemed to be singing to one another, just before they settled to rest for the night. Well, I must go. Farewell. —." Upon her return to Grasmere on October 6, 1802, with the married couple, Dorothy is eager to see how the garden fared in their absence: "We went by candle light into the garden and were astonished at the growth of Brooms, Portugal Laurels, etc. etc. etc."[37] What a world must be included in those etceteras, for they indicate that the garden-home has survived, even thrived, amidst the precariousness of change.

John Worthen reads the poem that William wrote to commemorate "going for Mary" as both announcing his commitment to Mary Hutchinson and affirming his dedication to the sister who had been so instrumental in making the garden their home.[38] In this reading, Mary's journey will be like that of the mosses, herbs, and flowers that have been transplanted to make the garden – she will come to the "little Nook of mountain ground" and, after settling in, will "love the blessed life that we live here."[39] While there certainly is emphasis on Mary joining their family (the twosome referred to by the "we" in the text), the poem is a direct address to the garden itself:

> Dear Spot! which we have watched with tender heed,
> Bringing thee chosen plants and blossoms blown
> Among the distant mountains, flower and weed,
> Which thou hast taken to thee as thy own,
> Making all kindness registered and known;
> Thou for our sakes, though Nature's child indeed,
> Fair thyself and beautiful alone,
> Hast taken gifts which thou dost little need.[40]

Written over the course of several weeks, William's poem tempers the emotions that well up in Dorothy's more immediate farewell to the garden. While William has the leisure to praise the beauty of the garden and its kindness for accepting the strangers and making them at home, Dorothy commands herself twice: "I must go." She will return to live with William and Mary, but she knows that the journey to "fetch" Mary marks a significant change in her life.

Although not quite the conclusion of her journal, Dorothy's farewell is for all intents and purposes the end. As we have seen, she marks the return to the garden with her brother and his wife, but the journal dwindles away after October 1802, as if the marriage plot has finally caught up with the cyclical life of the garden and the gardener, the chaste bower transformed into a bower of bliss. Dorothy's extended writing about the garden ends with the Grasmere journal and the celebration of its resilience during the ongoing process of construction and rejuvenation. Although specific references to this garden come to an end, except for a few allusions in later letters (especially concerning the completion of the shed and the family's subsequent use of it as a retreat), the aesthetics and ethics that Dorothy formulates with regard to the garden and the natural world guide her future work.

SITUATING THE GARDEN AT TOWN END

How does Dorothy's garden fit into the meaning of gardens and their history? As we have seen, Hunt argues that "Gardens are privileged … because they are concentrated or perfected forms of place-making."[41] For Hunt, the garden, a subset of landscape architecture, is a constructed place that always involves some type of enclosure, even if only that implied by the concentration of effects. As an enclosed and constructed space, the garden involves an interplay of within and without, a preoccupation with the meaning of real and implied boundaries. This interplay is central to Dorothy's version of place-making, or more precisely, home-making. She yearns for the protection of bench and bower, but she is also keenly aware of the world outside her garden and of herself and her garden as objects of interest: "A coronetted Landau went by when we were sitting upon the sodded wall. The ladies (evidently Tourists) turned an eye of interest upon our little garden and cottage."[42] Sitting on the wall that she and William have made, the boundary between inside and beyond, Dorothy participates in both worlds at the moment that the pricey carriage goes by. She seems not only aware of but also amused by her status as a tourist attraction. Her comment also demonstrates that the garden is a text to be read and interpreted by curious tourists and friends alike. Her niece Dora Wordsworth's later illustration of Dove Cottage (Fig. 5.1) indicates just how close the Wordsworths would have been to the road when sitting on the wall, and it also reveals the informality of the homestead: the cottage is supplemented by several lower outbuildings set at odd angles to follow the curve of the road, and the tiny front garden is tightly packed with plants, shrubs, and

Fig. 5.1. *Dove Cottage, Town End*. Watercolor by Dora Wordsworth after Thomas Green. Dove Cottage, The Wordsworth Trust.

a corner tree with little regard for formal balance, matching the charming irregularity of the fence palings.

The situation of the garden and cottage was indeed notable. As John Murdoch explains, "Until Humphry Repton published views of his own house, the Hare Street Cottage, in 1816, the idea that the cottage, especially in a constricted site, close to a road and with other houses pressing in, could be the creation of an aesthetically sophisticated sensibility, was not widespread." He adds that there was an earlier history of the cottage aesthetic, but "the deliberate construction of a cottage and garden adapted to the existence of scholar-gentlemen was a characteristic development of the early 19th century. The work of the Wordsworths at Dove Cottage in 1800 was therefore highly original."[43] The Wordsworths' "construction" of a cottage and garden was also striking in the role that Dorothy played in imagining its shape and significance. Of her near contemporaries, she was perhaps closest in this regard to Mary Russell Mitford, whose letters and published writings such as *Our Village* attest to her central role in the garden. Like Wordsworth, Mitford viewed gardening at Three-Mile Cross, the cottage she shared with her parents near Reading, as a form of home-making. On July 11, 1824, Mitford writes to Benjamin Robert Haydon to describe her garden:

my little garden is a perfect rosary – the greenest and most blossomy nook that ever the sun shone upon. It is almost shut in by buildings; one a long open shed, very pretty, a sort of rural arcade where we sit ... All and every part is untrimmed, antique, weatherstained, and homely as can be imagined – gratifying the eye by its exceeding picturesqueness, and the mind by the certainty that no pictorial effect was intended – that it owes all its charms to "rare accident."

Mitford thus emphasizes not the studied pictorial effect of some gardens but what she presents as the unplanned homeliness that makes the garden her own nook of ground, her secure spot. As Mitford's letter to her friend Emily Jephson (July 10, 1824) makes clear, the garden substitutes for other forms of power, passion, and fulfillment denied to single women: "I am so glad you have a little demense [sic] of your own too; it is a pretty thing to be queen over roses and lilies, is it not?"[44]

Stephen Daniels observes that women's gardening in the early nineteenth century had "a new inflection, both more limiting, in emphasizing ornamental rather than useful plants, and more liberating, in offering an arena of independence."[45] While we agree with Daniels in general, there are a few noteworthy exceptions to his generalization. As we shall see in Chapter 7, Hannah More, for instance, felt guilt over emphasizing the ornamental and pleasurable aspects of gardening, and in her life and fiction she emphasized the utility, spirituality, and discipline of work in the garden. Dorothy Wordsworth (uninhibited by the kind of guilt that More expressed) was focused on both the utility and beauty of her garden, as evidenced in her intertwining of beans and roses, peas and honeysuckle. Work is pleasure; pleasure is work. Dorothy's ideal garden is the kitchen croft of her childhood, as we saw in her early letter to Jane Pollard Marshall reminding her friend of their "little tower of Joy."[46] As a mature gardener she will ignore the stylistic and functional barriers between types of gardens, conceiving of the one at Town End as decidedly non-hierarchical, a mixed genre uniting beauty and utility: a re-imagined kitchen garden.[47]

Dorothy's aesthetic bears some resemblance to Maria Elizabeth Jacson's position in *The Florist's Manual* (1816). We recall Jacson's work as a botanical writer from Chapter 2, and in *The Florist's Manual*, as we shall see, she extends her talents to horticulture and landscape design, assuring her middle- and upper-class female audience that "A Flower-Garden is now become a necessary appendage of every fashionable residence." While that class-consciousness and the whiff of the ornamental do not cohere with Dorothy's views, Jacson's endorsement of "the Mingled Flower-Garden," which displays repetition and unity rather than "the prevalent solicitude for rarity and variety," is supported by the "mingled" quality of the garden at Town End – the preference for steady accumulation and repetition of native plants rather than a quest for rarity.[48] Although Jacson is more concerned with the view of the garden from the house than Dorothy, who rarely mentions it, she is quite attuned to the particular problem of building a new cottage and garden near a public road – and she offers a practical solution. Rather than situating the house and garden on high ground and a flat surface, she advocates "removing the earth until a hollow [is] produced":

the artificial little valley retreat was secured, completely secluded from the public eye, and between the banks there was placed a rustic seat formed of dried branches of trees, entwined by honeysuckles, and other sweet ornamental climbers, well calculated for the retirement of a solitary student, and sufficiently spacious for the accommodation of a social party, who might equally wish to escape the observation of the idle or inquisitive traveller.[49]

That description is not so far from Dorothy's rustic garden situated close enough to the road to be visible to that curious traveler, although Jacson values the privacy that the topography of her "artificial little valley" provides for the cottage.

Dorothy was constructing her garden at the same time that William was working on the second and third editions of *Lyrical Ballads*, when he expanded the Preface in 1800 into a poetic manifesto and added an appendix on poetic diction in 1802. As a poet, of course, William's medium was language and the Preface is famously about language and culture. But for Dorothy, language was not limited to her journal. The garden was also Dorothy Wordsworth's text, telling a story for those who learn to read it and understand its paradoxical vulnerability and power. It appeals to the sympathy and imagination of the reader or viewer. To borrow William's analysis of his own work, Dorothy creates the taste by which her garden can be enjoyed and shuns traditional poetic diction (in the form of elaborate decoration) in favor of fresh combinations of plants and benches and arbors. Like her brother, she prefers the "plain humanities of nature" to "a motley masquerade of tricks, quaintnesses, hieroglyphics, and enigmas."[50] And like Jacson, Dorothy knows that once the basic garden is in place, "a more extended variety may be superadded."[51] Her garden contains no allusions to classical mythology and no statuary; instead she imagines the landscape itself as alive. Frequently personifying the flowers in her garden and in the wild, Dorothy suggests a kind of natural animation, as in her description of the daffodils that she and William come upon in Gowbarrow Park on April 15, 1802: "some rested their heads upon [the] stones as on a pillow for weariness and the rest tossed and reeled and danced and seemed as if they verily laughed with the wind that blew upon them over the lake."[52]

Dorothy's down-to-earth attitude is also evident in the books she consults. The first botany treatise that she and William acquire is William Withering's *An Arrangement of British Plants* (1796), a book that adopts the Linnaean system but adheres to the common, English names of plants. This emphasis must have suited Dorothy, who in her journal wants to identify and name plants in their common English forms. Dorothy's perspective is close to Mitford's narrator in "A Great Farmhouse," who comments that "One is never thoroughly sociable with flowers till they are naturalized, as it were, christened, provided with decent, homely, well-wearing English names."[53] As a companion to Withering, Dorothy also had access to John Abercrombie's *The Gardener's Pocket Journal* (1789), a popular and unpretentious horticultural guide, a gardening how-to book with a strong emphasis on the kitchen garden.[54] Abercrombie's practical appeal and Withering's highly influential book countered the widespread interest in exotic plants among horticultural enthusiasts at the time. Dorothy expressed no interest in show plants, exotics that might be collected to impress others or to represent one's acquaintance with the far-flung parts of the empire.[55] And as we saw in Chapter 2, most women botanical writers rejected the association of women and hothouse plants as well as the excesses of collecting exotics. Since Dorothy was especially interested in cultivating local transplants from the wild, her garden was a kind of reverse colony in which native plants found a home.

The democratic spirit of Dorothy's garden extended to her work habits: she worked unabashedly outside, with no concern for a gendered division of labor. She accepted help, but she also dug in the dirt herself. Social propriety was not a concern for the Wordsworths in the early Grasmere days; they were not bound by conventional behavior.[56] Dorothy roamed the countryside at all hours of the day and night, scavenging for plants, observing the moon, or listening for the mail coach. As far back as 1794, she responded to her aunt Mrs. Christopher Crackenthorpe's criticism that she had walked rather than taken a coach: "I cannot pass unnoticed that part of your letter in which you speak of my 'rambling about the country on foot.' So far from considering this as a matter of condemnation, I rather thought it would have given my friends pleasure to hear that I had courage to make use of the strength with which nature has endowed me ... but was also the means of saving me at least thirty shillings."[57] Young Dorothy sets the tone for her future rambling and for her attitude toward conventions of various kinds. She moves seamlessly from the garden into the house and over to the neighbors, with not a whit of concern for proprieties of dress or that she is spending too much time indulging herself in the garden or lying in the orchard – or sitting on the wall observing lady tourists observing her. Because Dorothy was not – and did not aspire to be – a conventional lady, she became a more creative gardener and observer of the natural world. Like Hussey tramping through the bogs for fungi, Dorothy focused on plants, her beloved mosses, for instance, and not on the effects of dirt or stubble on her hemline. And like Austen's Elizabeth Bennet in *Pride and Prejudice*, who slogged through the mud to see her ailing sister, Dorothy did not care what people would think.[58]

Rather than questions of propriety, Dorothy was more interested in the practical and theoretical implications of the relationship between her garden and the outside world, between cultivated nature and the "wilderness" beyond. Although we agree with Jacqueline Labbe that the small space of the garden is "potentially empowering" for Dorothy, we see her extended challenge as an attempt to understand how her garden relates to the world of objects and ideas beyond her cultivated home landscape. In regard to this relationship of the garden to other forms of nature, Hunt reminds us that "All natures have been culturally constructed," a pronouncement that includes both the wild and the cultivated. In fact, Hunt reiterates the tripartite categories – wilderness (first nature), agriculture (second nature), and gardens (third nature) – deriving from Italian Renaissance theorists. According to Hunt, "To retain this habit of thinking has many advantages: it actively discourages the belief that nature is normative rather than culturally constructed, it allows place-making to be seen as essentially related to its immediate topography, and by virtue of its emphasis on graduated modes of mediation, it urges more subtle adjudications of landscape architecture than the habitual ones of 'formal' and 'informal'."[59] In Dorothy Wordsworth's practice and in her writing, horticulture and agriculture, beauty and utility, overlap: the scarlet runner beans get tangled up in the roses climbing the wall, yet both are constructed products of her imagination and work.

Also, from the outset both William and Dorothy designed their garden with careful attention to the site – the position of the cottage bounded by the road, backed by the orchard and the gradually rising land. Rejecting any given sense of propriety for the garden, they set about to make the place work without doing violence to its nature. As William proclaims to Sir George Beaumont in his now-famous letter of 1805, not even the grandest scheme for a landscape can compensate "for violation done to the holiness of nature."[60] By "nature" in this context, Wordsworth means the topography of the site. In *A Guide through the District of the Lakes*, he reiterates this position: "The rule is simple; with respect to grounds – work, where you can, in the spirit of nature, with an invisible hand of art. Planting, and a removal of wood, may thus, and thus only, be carried on with good effect; and the like may be said of building, if Antiquity, who may be styled the co-partner and sister of Nature, be not denied the respect to which she is entitled."[61] In his implicit objection to the homogenous style of the landscape park, Wordsworth aligns himself with the picturesque theorists and against Capability Brown. As Tom Williamson states, "When applied to garden design, the 'picturesque' was less about rugged grandeur, more about the creation of variety, surprise, and interesting detail, in reaction to the formulaic simplicity of the Brownian park."[62] And, indeed, no detail of Dorothy's garden was ever too small to magnify and record. Her narrow plot of ground was ever-expanding, an aesthetic that she also applies to the landscape of Scotland.

PATCHWORK: RECOLLECTIONS OF A TOUR OF SCOTLAND (1803)

Having gone on the tour of Scotland with William and (part of the time) with Coleridge in the summer of 1803, Dorothy struggled to find the motivation and time to record her recollections – she did not keep a diary during the trip, although she took some sketchy notes for future reference.[63] It took her twenty months to record the *Recollections* and copy the manuscript, and her work was temporarily derailed by the tragic death of her brother John at sea on February 5, 1805. Significantly, the summer-hut provides the retreat for her to complete this task and to heal. Dorothy writes to Lady Beaumont on June 11, 1805, that

I have been engaged in finishing a copy of the journal of our Tour of Scotland – this was at first beginning a very painful office, – I had written it for the sake of Friends who could not [be] with us at the time, and my Brother John had been always in my thoughts, for we wished him to know everything that befell us. The task of re-copying this journal, which at first when it was proposed to me after his death, I thought I could not do, I performed at last and found it a tranquilizing employment. I write to you from the Hut, where we pass all our time except when we are walking – it has been a rainy morning, but we are here sheltered and warm, and in truth I think it the sweetest place on Earth – .[64]

Carol Kyros Walker concludes that "Had the shed – the 'moss Hut' – not been erected above the cottage, Dorothy, without a retreating spot, might have taken even longer with her journal."[65] Instead, Dorothy finds the strength and shelter on the very spot that she had celebrated when she first arrived in Grasmere and "in imagination [had] built a seat with a summer shed on the highest platform in this our little domestic slip of mountain." The imagined – and now realized – garden hut becomes the agent that makes Dorothy's writing possible.[66]

Several writers have noted that when touring, Dorothy, as Susan Levin puts it, "reveal[s] her dependence on and joy in domestic life in nature."[67] But the significance of this domestication has not been appreciated. In fact, another critic, Rachel Brownstein, disapproves of this tendency when, commenting on the *Recollections*, she notes that Dorothy "seeks out nooks in which she can build a fantasy cottage to be happy ever after with William and flowers; and when nooks and islands are lacking, a picturesque Scotsman, wrapped cozily in a plaid, pleases her by lending a requisite lie to a harsh, alien scene. In part this is simply the fashion of the time, workaday Romanticism, and in part it is spinsterish and insular, the less attractive side of her personality."[68] Brownstein dismisses Dorothy's domesticating instinct as a troubling "lie" and a product of her narrow, "spinsterish" point of view; we see it, rather, as part of Dorothy's coherent mode of constructing nature as homelike and inhabitable by the imagination. This perspective provides Dorothy with a way to humanize nature and to make the prospect of the wildness appealing. Walker notes that Scotland, with its barren and starkly sublime scenery and its remote villages, could strike the English traveler as being "as alien as France or Germany."[69] Dorothy's *Recollections* reveals an observer trying to become less of a stranger – in the process she tames and controls nature by using familiar comparisons or by imagining the "*inhabited* solitudes" of Scotland as being more like England and her idea of English natural beauty.[70] In terms that Domosh and Seager have outlined, Dorothy invests the spaces of Scotland with meaning: "we might say that 'spaces' become 'places' when we have some personal association with them."[71]

Dorothy reserves her highest praise for those places that she can imagine inhabiting herself, or that she can see William enjoying. She recalls such a place near Loch Lomond:

How delightful to have a little shed concealed under the branches of the fairy island! the cottages and the island might have been made for the pleasure of each other. It was but like a natural garden, the distance was so small; nay, one could have forgiven any one living there, not compelled to daily labour, if he did not connect it with his dwelling by some feeling of domestic attachment, like what he has for the orchard where his children play. I thought, what a place for William! he might row himself over with twenty strokes of the oars, escaping from the business of the house, and as safe from intruders, with his boat anchored beside him, as if he had locked himself up in the strong tower of a castle.[72]

In this passage, Dorothy imagines the landscape in terms of her ideal in Grasmere: "a little shed" just like the one in which she works from her notes in order to memorialize the journey. She uses a series of diminutives to envision this space as snug and comforting: the shed is little, the garden is small, and the island is fit for fairies. Further domesticating the scene, she brings in an image of children at play in the orchard, and the security of her imagined substitute for home is also evident in her final account of William's boat. This description of a domestic refuge – and the deference to William's comfort even in imagination – is typical of Dorothy's attitude in her journals, as we have seen.

But Dorothy also develops some more distinctive ways of presenting the Scottish landscape. One of her most interesting images compares the appearance of the village of Wanlockhead to a patchwork quilt:

Every cottage seemed to have its little plot of ground, fenced by a ridge of earth; this plot contained two or three different divisions, kail [*sic*], potatoes, oats, hay;

the houses all standing in lines, or never far apart; the cultivated ground was all together also, and made a very strange appearance with its many greens among the dark brown hills, neither tree nor shrub growing; yet the grass and the potatoes looked greener than elsewhere, owing to the bareness of the neighboring hills; it was indeed a wild and singular spot – to use a woman's illustration, like a collection of patchwork, made of pieces as they might have chanced to have been cut by the mantua-maker, only just smoothed to fit each other, the different sorts of produce being in such a multitude of plots, and those so small and of such irregular shapes.[73]

Employing her "woman's illustration," Dorothy frames the scene for her readers and opens up the possibilities of an aesthetic that sees the variety of agricultural crops as if they were in gardens for display (although there were neither trees nor shrubs, much less flowers). An English cottage and kitchen gardener such as Dorothy would have expected flowers and crops mixed together, as her scarlet runner beans and roses grew in tandem back home. Rather than a close inspection of the details of the plots, Dorothy provides a more panoramic view of the quilt-like effect. Paradoxically, though, seeing the plots as a patchwork actually provides another kind of detail. William Snyder sees in this passage Dorothy's association of nature with the female "craftsperson," "pattern-maker," or "integrator" who works with a "certain visual and tactile intricacy" compatible with the variation and irregularity of the picturesque.[74] Although Dorothy does not personify nature explicitly (as we discussed in the case of Agnes Ibbetson in Chapter 2), we see her as working in a similar way to Nature the quilter: she composes her overall image by fashioning her recollections into a design drawn from the variety of natural and experiential materials at hand. The passage thus serves as a description of Dorothy's craft as a writer who can shape variety and intricacy into a whole, stitching together her journal from the various pieces of her experience: more of a patchwork effect than a unified narrative, which is in turn more suited, perhaps, to conveying the disjunctive, episodic quality of travel.

In another instance, Dorothy focuses minutely on the intricate patterns, finding horticultural qualities in a simple potato patch:

We passed by one patch of potatoes that a florist might have been proud of; no carnation-bed ever looked more gay than this square plot of ground on the waste common. The flowers were in very large bunches, and of extraordinary size, and of every conceivable shade of colouring from snow-white to deep purple. It was pleasing in that place, where perhaps was never yet a flower cultivated by man for his own pleasure, to see these blossoms grow more gladly than elsewhere, making a summer garden near the mountain dwellings.[75]

Seeking the familiar summer garden, Dorothy transforms the blossoms of the potato patch, an agricultural plot, into varied and colorful flowers – a horticultural display. Not only does she view the garden-like qualities as exceptional, but she creates in her recollection a substitute flower garden and a more domestically welcoming scene. Through her frame, Dorothy helps her readers transform this commonplace plot into a garden, both extending our sense of what qualifies as a garden and blurring the boundaries between second and third nature, agriculture and horticulture.

In the Scottish tour, Dorothy also approaches inhospitable scenes by making them English, another form of domestication. For instance, she describes a spot that seems deserted:

At the lower end of this new reach of the vale was a decayed tree, beside a decayed cottage, the vale spreading out into a level area which was one large field, without fence and without division, of a dull yellow colour; the vale seemed to partake of the desolation of the cottage, and to participate in its decay. And yet the spot was in its nature so dreary that one would rather it was left to waste and solitude. Yet the encircling hills were so exquisitely formed that it was impossible to conceive anything more lovely than this place would have been if the valley and hill-sides had been interspersed with trees, cottages, green fields, and hedgerows.[76]

Reversing the pattern of William's meditation on the ruined cottage in the poem of that name, Dorothy does not want to speculate on the ruin and decay: she is almost ready to consign it to "waste and solitude." But the surrounding hills remind her of what might be, and instead of leaving the sight in desolation, she imagines it transformed into an English valley, a little community complete with cottages and hedgerows, superimposing the absent hallmarks of Englishness onto the barren countryside. This emphasis on Englishness, the constant comparisons with the beauties of the English Lakes, provides a unifying note in Dorothy's *Recollections*. When experiencing and writing about a strange place, Dorothy keeps herself centered, as if the summer-house or shed where she composed herself and her recollections were the center of the world. Similarly, the natural beauties of Grasmere are Dorothy's standard for what gardens ought to be.

Elizabeth Bohls argues that Dorothy Wordsworth resists the aesthetic impulse of picturesque framing by including descriptions of natural beauty matter-of-factly in her journals.[77] Although we agree that Dorothy's descriptions "erode picturesque detachment,"[78] in the *Recollections* she does bring her domesticating aesthetic to Scotland. Her version of the picturesque reveals her delight in the detail, variety, and intricacy of the scene, while at the same time valuing the commonplace and everyday and transforming the rough and decrepit into the ordered and inhabited – perhaps like the intricate design of a quilt for everyday use. As we have seen, she views one garden in terms of a patchwork quilt, transforms a potato patch into a vibrant flower bed, and imagines another scene to conform to the English countryside. Her approach implicitly critiques the disinterestedness of aesthetics, as Bohls argues. But Dorothy does not abandon control, although she does not frame a scene to exercise power. Rather, she imagines new possibilities and ways of seeing to make a strange land familiar, or, sometimes, to critique a style that seems resistant to her imaginative transformation.

CONCLUSION

After her physical decline in 1829, when Dorothy could no longer travel with ease, her mind often returned to Grasmere and to the home the Wordsworths had left in 1808 to accommodate the growing family. The house and garden at Town End became the home of her dreams, the croft of memory, a place associated with shelter and protection that was valued even more than the greater comforts of nearby Rydal Mount. In "Grasmere – A Fragment" (1829), for instance, Dorothy recalls the "sheltered hold" of the valley, the "shelter of those trees" that screen the cottage, and, most of all, that in "a sheltered chink / The foxglove's broad leaves flourished fair."[79] Rydal Mount, the Wordsworths' home from 1813, was relatively spacious and graced with a beautiful garden that William renovated, as we see in a watercolor by William Westall from Dora Wordsworth's commonplace book, which shows the house elevated above extensive plantings (Fig. 5.2). The sketch emphasizes the way that the foreground bed curves around in a gentle embrace of the lawn beyond, but the woman walking on the path seems small and insignificant in relation to the grand scale of the landscape. It is not surprising, then, that in her need Dorothy Wordsworth returns to the memory and imagination of Grasmere for the comforting intimacy of home – her little "tower of Joy": "That Cottage with its clustering trees / Summons my heart; it settles there."[80] If the house and garden that she built at Town End fulfilled her girlish dreams, then the permanent move to Rydal Mount signals an inevitable loss of intimacy. Because Grasmere, with its bowers and nests, was so associated with Dorothy's deepest dreams, she recalls it most strongly later in life – a deep nostalgia that we have also seen with the Taylors' descriptions of their childhood home and with Emily Shore's memories of England from the distant perspective of Madeira.[81] Bachelard explains that "the places in which we have *experienced daydreaming*

Conclusion 161

Fig. 5.2. *Rydal Mount*. Watercolor by William Westall from Dora Wordsworth's book. 1831. Dove Cottage, The Wordsworth Trust.

reconstitute themselves in a new daydream, and it is because our memories of former dwelling places are relived as daydreams that these dwelling-places of the past remain in us for all time."[82] As early as 1800, Dorothy notes, "Grasmere was very solemn in the last glimpse of twilight it calls home the heart to quietness."[83]

Besides her record of the Grasmere years, Dorothy extended her thoughts to the larger world in her travels. But she never strayed far from the perspective that was shaped by her work and thought in Grasmere. A scene from her Continental tour of 1820 captures Dorothy's imagination:

I can hardly conceive of a place of more solitary aspect than the lake of Chiavenna: and the whole of the prospect in that direction is characterized by melancholy sublimity … In our descent we found a fair white cherub uninjured by the explosion which had driven it a great way down the hill. It lay bedded like an Infant in its cradle among low green bushes. W. said to us "Could we but carry this pretty Image to our moss summer house at Rydal Mount!" yet it seemed as if it would have been a pity that any one should remove it from its couch in the wilderness, which may be its own for hundreds of years.[84]

The cherub, a displaced sculptural object "bedded like an Infant in its cradle," suggests the most profound image of protection and warmth. But it is an image at odds with the setting – a "couch in the wilderness." Perhaps identifying with this cradled infant, Dorothy does not agree that it would be best to carry the sculpture to the summer-house. Rather, it belongs to this hillside in Italy. Like the wildflowers from around Grasmere that would be injured by transplanting, this object belongs to the place where it has been nurtured in the wilderness. Dorothy implicitly suggests that it would be out of place, not at home, at Rydal Mount, a looted object rather than an integral part of the garden. In the wilderness, however, it is at home.

As these examples demonstrate, Dorothy Wordsworth brought her particular perspective to both cultivated and uncultivated nature. In Grasmere, her garden became her way of making a home for herself and William, but she carried this domestic ethic into her travels too. When she found comfort and intimacy there, she wanted only to protect it from the forces that would disturb its integrity. Her writing, which she never thought of in public or professional terms, nevertheless contributes an important episode to the history of women in the garden as designers, workers, and dreamers – as home-makers in the highest sense of that word.

CHAPTER 6

"Work in a small compass": gardening manuals for women

Instructional manuals for women were published in great numbers in the late eighteenth and early nineteenth centuries, including general guides to comportment as well as practical handbooks on domestic duties. Because the home was so often buffered from the outside world of commerce by a garden – whether the rural peasant's cottage garden, the suburban plot, or the upper-class estate – early manuals on floriculture and botany reveal the extent to which ideas associated with domesticity began to move beyond the interior spaces of the house. An ongoing debate about women's desires, expectations, and capabilities extended to the gardening manuals written by women that we will consider in this chapter, including those by Maria Elizabeth Jacson, Louisa Johnson, and especially Jane Loudon.

Michael Waters, in *The Garden in Victorian Literature*, has identified three primary functions for fictional females in the garden that reflect certain deeply rooted assumptions in Victorian culture: they can perform light tasks that emphasize their graceful femininity; they can supervise or delegate, thus showing their innate aesthetic insight; and they can simply serve as ornaments, amplifying the natural beauty around them.[1] Sarah Bilston argues in "Queens of the Garden," however, that the gardening manuals, by "authorizing women to engage in physical labour, aesthetic debate, and technological innovation" and by participating in the process of breaking down class, gender, and geographical distinctions, "turn[ed] the performance of gardening, as well as the experience of reading and writing about it, into self-consciously political acts." But Bilston suggests that the political insights gained in the garden were safely contained by the rhetoric of the early manuals and by the relative isolation of the individual women who practiced their small acts of cultural rebellion: "Unorthodox female behavior – sweating, debating, self-making – becomes possible in the garden because it is (apparently) a space outside culture ... The garden's claim to 'natural' status works to depoliticize the activities of the women who operate in it."[2] While Bilston's argument is primarily grounded in the later

Victorian period, we will see that the politics of social transgression was also certainly a subtext in some of the earlier nineteenth-century manuals, which begin to question the standard dichotomies of feminine and masculine, inside and out, nature and culture, intuition and artifice, art and science, and physical labor and intellectual design.

The first significant English book on gardening written by a woman was Maria Elizabeth Jacson's *The Florist's Manual; or, Hints for the Construction of a Gay Flower Garden* (1816), followed in quick succession by several other key works: Elizabeth Kent's *Flora Domestica, or, The Portable Flower Garden* (1823), Louisa Johnson's *Every Lady Her Own Flower Gardener* (1839), and a series of books by Jane Loudon, beginning with *Instructions in Gardening for Ladies* (1840).[3] Both Jacson and Johnson used the word "passion" to refer to women's intense and growing interest in gardening, and by 1846 the editor of an American edition of Loudon's works described "lady gardeners" as "a class of amateurs which, in England, numbers many and zealous devotees, even among the highest ranks."[4] Clearly early nineteenth-century women were attracted to the idea of the garden as a forum for action, as we have seen in Chapter 5 with Dorothy Wordsworth, but the degree of seriousness with which they approached the intellectual, creative, and practical aspects of gardening varied widely – due in part to personal differences, of course, but also to social pressures and expectations.

Jane Loudon (1807–58) was eager to move beyond the idea of gardening as merely an amusing pastime for ladies, as she often used serious, practical, scientific language to educate her readers. But even though she was one of the most successful authors on gardening in the nineteenth century, she still felt the need to introduce her major work on *Gardening for Ladies* with the kind of apologetic justification so often employed by women writers of the period. After dedicating the book to her husband, the well-known horticulturist J. C. Loudon, "to whom the author of the following pages owes all the knowledge of the subject she possesses," she begins her introduction in a similar vein: "When I married Mr. Loudon, it is scarcely possible to imagine any person more completely ignorant than I was, of every thing relating to plants and gardening; and, as may be easily imagined, I found every one about me so well acquainted with the subject, that I was soon heartily ashamed of my ignorance."[5] Loudon was probably not as ignorant as this passage suggests, however, since she did some gardening as a teenager, and her introduction was almost certainly constructed for a calculated effect: to inspire readers by her own example.[6]

Although Loudon occasionally mentions her husband's publications or turns to experts for verification or support, more often she relies on her own experience.[7] After that humble preface her tone throughout *Gardening for Ladies*, with few exceptions, is knowledgeable and unapologetic. Recognizing that handbooks "intended for professional gardeners are seldom suitable to the wants of amateurs," she still frequently brings in technical and scientific language. Noting that fine distinctions of interest to the botanist might be "of little or no use" to the practical gardener, she persists in including explanations that would have little relevance to an amateur.[8] In this way Loudon presents gardening as a difficult but worthy pursuit rather than an occasional diversion. Her central maxim, in fact, was "that which cannot be grown well, ought not to be grown at all."[9] According to Loudon and other women writing about the English garden, the high standards set for work in the home, based on domestic skill and knowledge, should not be lowered in the landscape outside.

Despite a desire to situate the garden, with all its pleasures and demands, firmly in the domestic scene, in many of these early manuals, especially Loudon's, we find a certain tension among various overlapping and sometimes competing ideas about gardening. Should it in fact be viewed primarily as a science or would it be devalued if presented as a decorative embellishment for the home? If the former, would it be more suited, then, for professionals than amateurs, and more closely allied with botany than with the hobby of floriculture? Should gardening for "ladies" be restricted to ornamental flowers, or could it also incorporate the functional uses of plants without lowering the status of middle- and upper-class gentlewomen? Should these women serve only as designers or managers in the garden, or was it suitable for them to do some, or all, of the manual labor? How could women justify moving outside into the garden if there were (as so many writers assured them) ample opportunities for work and pleasure inside the house? In short, did the definition of home during this period include the garden as well as the interior spaces?

"THE VERY EMBLEM OF HOME": GARDENING AND DOMESTICITY

Jacson recommends in *The Florist's Manual* that the flower garden serve as "an ornamental appendage to the house," thus explicitly incorporating it into the domestic sphere.[10] Louisa Johnson is even more forthright in her discussion of gardening as a domestic art: the cultivated garden "surrounds home with an unceasing interest; [and] domestic scenes become endeared to the eye and mind." A garden could act upon young women as a powerful attractant, helping to reconcile them to the restrictions of their daily lives. According to Johnson, in fact, "it attaches them to their home."[11]

The increasing popularity of greenhouses and conservatories as accessible sites for middle- and upper-class women to display their feminine taste as well as to develop their gardening skills helped to bridge interior and exterior spaces. In calling the greenhouse "the prettiest and most gratifying apartment in the whole establishment," the author of *Every Lady's Guide to Her Own Greenhouse* (1851) reinforces this link.[12] Even without such a room, a transition to the garden could be formed by creating strategic lines of sight. Jacson gives specific instructions for laying out the garden to be viewed in the best light "from the windows of a house," and this pictorial strategy of using the window as a frame is repeated later in her statement of intent: referring to "my sister gardeners," she writes of "my earnest desire to lead them from the pleasure they receive in the superficial view of a profusion of gay and varied colours before their windows, to the investigation of the habits and properties of these elegant playthings."[13] Similarly, Shirley Hibberd encourages his readers to create a "bowery window," thus making "a choice garden within and without, such at least as may give a lady full employment, and add vastly to the grace and pleasure of the home."[14] In the illustration (Fig. 6.1) the large window is indeed the central focus, flanked by vine-covered trellises and fronted by the low rustic fence of the balcony, and the space is clearly marked as feminine by the presence of a young woman in a loose morning gown who tends her plants.

The garden as a carefully cultivated site – whether a small area by the window for potted plants or an impressive array of beds and borders – presented nature as safely tamed and thus sanctioned for women's presence. The domestication of nature led to a comparable shift in the language used. Just as Jacson presents flowering plants as "elegant playthings," Loudon refers to a suburban garden under the management of a lady as a "domestic pet."[15] Elizabeth Kent chose a different rhetorical strategy, but one that functions in a similar way. Like many women authors at the time, she borrowed maternal images to underscore her points: in giving cultural instructions for raising auriculas, for instance, she notes that the directions would "equally apply to those flowers raised at home, and to such as are only adopted children." Kent introduces the theme of domesticated (and domesticating) flowers in her title, *Flora Domestica, or, The Portable Flower-Garden*, and carries it through her discussion of individual plants. To give just one example, she calls daisies "the very emblem of home ... the *robin of flowers*," thus doubling the connotations of nostalgic innocence.[16] Her

Fig. 6.1.   "Bowery Window," illustration in Shirley Hibberd, *Rustic Adornments for Homes of Taste*, p. 193.

focus on potted plants of all kinds, in fact, serves as an apt analogy for early nineteenth-century women: constrained, nurtured, and protected, as seen in the frontispiece illustration in her book (Fig. 6.2). The setting is an exuberant but carefully ordered greenhouse, with paved floor, pots of blooming plants, and a grapevine rambling overhead. The perspectival line of the bench on which four pots are neatly placed leads our eyes back to a young woman in a pink dress and bonnet with a girl beside her. They occupy the middle ground of the well-tended mixed border, caught within a network of visual signifiers that restrict their options, although the view of a mountain in the distance does suggest a larger world beyond their tidy home. This home space might seem secure and stable to Bachelard or Tuan – a nostalgic ideal, fertile, blossoming, and neatly composed – but

Fig. 6.2. Frontispiece illustration in Elizabeth Kent, *Flora Domestica, or, The Portable Flower-Garden*.

Fig. 6.3. "View from the Drawing-Room Window of Lady Broughton's Garden at Hoole House," illustration in J. C. Loudon, "Notes on Gardens and Country Seats. Hoole House," p. 360.

Massey sees the vitality of a meaningful place as being constituted not by "the security of a (false, as we have seen) stability and an apparently reassuring boundedness" but instead by "its interactions with 'the outside'."[17] The mountain view, for Massey, would provide a crucial outlet from the "potted" life of the women on display, although for middle- and upper-class English citizens of the nineteenth century the removal of the homestead from the world outside, not its open accessibility, would have been of paramount concern.

This well-defined home-ground, stopping at the outer boundary of the garden, finds expression in a small, early nineteenth-century plot in Birmingham owned by the middle-class Luckcock family: an outdoor bench situated close to one of the windows, picturesquely framed by a rose-covered trellis, was inscribed with a verse contrasting the noisy, gaudy "World without" and the calm pleasure of "the World within."[18] The garden, thus included in the inner sanctum, was controlled and embraced by multiple domesticating devices: window, trellis, bench, and inscription. In the typical homestead, such as the Luckcocks', the window operated not only as a frame but also as a passage or valve from sheltered interior to the landscape outside. We see this again in 1853 when Charlotte Yonge equates the beauty of the garden with the order (moral as well as physical) of the home: "see the dark red China [rose] cluster round the cottage window, almost a sure token that content and cleanliness are within."[19]

Several times in *The Ladies' Companion to the Flower-Garden*, Loudon uses the breakfast-room window as a transitional device. She notes the value of the grape vine "for covering a bower or veranda, or training around the window of a breakfast-room" and adds that "Nothing can, indeed, be more beautiful than a Vine in the last-mentioned situation, forming a framework, as it were, to the garden beyond."[20] Visual as well as physical access to the natural world provided women with opportunities to expand their limited field of action. "Flora" wrote an article for the *Ladies' Magazine of Gardening*, edited by Loudon, describing her small garden "which I manage myself by the help of a man-servant." She mentioned in particular a border "just in front of the windows of the room in which I usually sit."[21] The view was clearly a matter of some pride to this woman, whom we imagine spending many hours dreaming, planning, and sewing in that carefully designed spot. Her pose by the window was surely repeated by many house-bound women, who would have considered the garden as both a form of escape and a new source of beauty for a dark interior. One poor widow, for example, who brightened her cottage by opening it up to the garden, was held up by Loudon as an example to her readers:

> For the window she made a curtain of coarse white muslin, lined with pink glazed calico; and on the outside she planted a nasturtium and a major-convolvulus or two, which, as she watered them every morning with the soap-suds in which she had washed herself, grew luxuriantly, and being carefully trained, soon made a kind of framework of leaves round the window, which had a very pretty effect when seen from the room. She sowed a few annual flowers in the little garden behind the house, and a few of these gathered occasionally, and arranged tastefully on plates with water, or a little wet sand, were placed on the table. Thus, at the expense of only a few shillings, and a little female industry tastefully directed, a miserable abode was changed into one that looked perfectly enviable.[22]

Flowers thus became the medium for the transformation of this small home, made possible with the virtues of industry, taste, and economy that were touted during this period as particularly praiseworthy in women of all classes.

At the opposite end of the social spectrum was Lady Broughton's extensive and elaborate garden at Hoole House, near Chester.[23] J. C. Loudon included an illustration of her flower garden as seen from the drawing-room window in his article on her estate (Fig. 6.3). In the distance we see a series of circular beds, past which are the shrubbery and rockwork, but in the foreground the terrace acts as a transitional zone between interior and exterior, carefully arranged with objects that reinforce its use as an outdoor room: two chairs, across one of which a cloak has been draped, several large books, a basket of cuttings, and a potted lily. A massive vine-clad arbor stands at one corner of the terrace but is brought into scale by the woman on the lawn seen through, and framed by, its arch. The tools resting nearby on the grass are clearly not hers – she is dressed for a stroll rather than for work – but they, along with the ladder, convey a sense of the ongoing labor necessary to tame such a large estate. The terrace, which reappeared around 1800 as a practical and aesthetic link between home and garden,[24] could serve, according to Jane Loudon, as "an admirable medium for uniting the architectural stiffness of a mansion with the beautiful wildness and grace of nature."[25] In an illustration in Shirley Hibberd's *Rustic Adornments for Homes of Taste* (Fig. 6.4) we look out onto the garden as if from a window of the house, past a young woman seated on the terrace step with her dog, and down to the fountain and distant statue, the view forming "from the windows of the dwelling a picture *complete in itself*."[26] A glimpse of the garden could thus offer enticing opportunities for an extension of the home but also – through freeze-framing, as it were – could relegate women and the

Fig. 6.4. Illustration in Shirley Hibberd, *Rustic Adornments for Homes of Taste*, p. 335.

spaces they occupy to an aestheticized realm of static display rather than allowing them meaningful room to explore.

In *The Lady's Country Companion* Loudon advises her newly married friend Annie to situate "a little sheltered place where flowers would delight to grow" right outside the morning room, and later she makes her instructions more specific: "I should like to have those cedars, the remainder of those gloomy firs, cleared away, which I see close to your house in your sketches, and your flower-garden so placed that you could step into it at once from the windows of your usual sitting-room." She then recommends a geometric plan for this garden, "so as to produce something of the effect of a Turkey carpet when looked down upon from the windows of the house." Here we find a telling parallel with her proposal that Annie's drawing room have a carpet with a pattern "chiefly of flowers."[27] The boundaries between interior design and garden planning are blurred, so the woman of the house can use her taste to good effect in both areas.

When Loudon encourages this same young friend to "throw open your window,"[28] her choice of the active verb conjures up an image of the window being flung open by a woman eager to get to work. A garden, for Loudon, is participatory, calling for energetic action. Based on the various gardening operations described in her *Gardening for Ladies*, one can move with her from the innermost heart of the home, the kitchen, where potted seedlings are stored before being put out on display; to the breakfast room, where one can take a few moments to view the garden, sitting in relaxed enjoyment of the prospect; to the garden itself, where there is the opportunity for active participation in designing and maintaining the "pleasure-grounds"; to the world outside the garden boundary, where one can purchase tools, plants, and seeds from a variety of reputable nurseries, and visit private or public gardens. In fact, Loudon makes the point that while French gardens are "chiefly calculated for being seen from the windows of the house," English gardens are designed "for being walked in."[29] Action, whether in the form of strolling, designing, or digging, is crucial for her sense of a woman's involvement in the garden, as we will see.

While Loudon's books are clearly centered on the demands and pleasures of the garden itself, she creates a line of connection that links the private interior world with the larger public realm. She enjoys hearing about the renovation of her friend Annie's new home and garden in the country but worries that she is too constricted: "It is well to love home, and to take a deep interest in all relating to it; but it is not well to live entirely in so confined a sphere." She warns that the mind could become "contracted by dwelling only on a limited number of objects" and encourages Annie to "seek nature": "leave your trim flower-garden, and your tame poultry, and wander in the woods, admiring the poetry of forest scenery."[30] We found in Chapter 2 that women botanists used much the same argument to justify their explorations. Perhaps Loudon realized how easy it would be for women's serious gardening efforts to be belittled or dismissed as merely domestic. Her own husband, for example, in his introduction to the first volume of the *Gardener's Magazine* (1826), stated that gardening allows men to display their wealth, offers them enjoyment after hard work in the city, and in fact lies at the very root of civilization, being one of the "first arts attempted by man on emerging from barbarism," but for women, in contrast, gardening is merely an "agreeable domestic recreation." Jane, unlike her husband, hoped that women would use gardening as a springboard to a more meaningful life, although one that remained separate from the traditionally male sphere. She states as her primary goal for the weekly magazine *Ladies' Companion at Home and Abroad* "mental cultivation … ; not to make women usurp the place of men, but to render them as rational and intelligent beings." The spaces for this intellectual activity are clearly home-centered: "in the drawing-room; in the study; in the dressing-room; in the housekeeper's room; and in the garden."[31] The "abroad" of the magazine's title is what she terms, rather loosely, "nature," so a sort of green buffer is provided for the home by the garden and landscape beyond.

Despite the typical domestic centering, only rarely did women writers during this period refer in their gardening manuals to a plant's culinary value. Whereas women's gardening before the eighteenth century had been associated to a large extent with culinary and medicinal plants, by the later eighteenth and early nineteenth centuries aesthetic or scientific considerations were more prominent. As we have seen, one common view was that floral and female beauty were naturally related, both being considered purely ornamental and in a sense non-functional. Jane Loudon would hardly have aligned herself with this view, but although she continually emphasizes the scientific basis of gardening, she also occasionally acknowledges the domesticity implicit in its practice by women. She notes, for example, that the flowers of the Judas tree, *Cercis siliquastrum*, "have an agreeably acid taste, and when fried in batter make excellent fritters" – a simple statement that brings us abruptly back into the warm kitchen, away from the rarefied air of scientific discourse that permeates most of her handbook. Other minor points of connection between the home and garden are spotted throughout Loudon's works: darning needles pierce pasteboard for sifting seeds, hair pins peg down verbenas, and a knitting needle makes holes to plant cuttings.[32]

"THE SIMPLEST AND PUREST OF PLEASURES": CONSTRUCTING A RATIONALE FOR GARDENING

The benefits enjoyed by the worthy Agnes in Budden's *Right and Wrong* (including the virtues of patience, neatness, and industry, as discussed in Chapter 1) were also cited by Loudon and others as justifications for women gardeners. If the plot produced food for the table it could at least be seen as practical, as in Martha Bradley's *The British Housewife* (1756), but the purely ornamental flower garden required a domestic rationale of a different sort. Loudon's readers, in contrast to Bradley's, considered gardening a pursuit worthy of attention less for its utilitarian advantages than for its more intangible benefits. As Maria Edgeworth explained in a letter written in 1832, "I find the love of garden grows upon me as I grow older more and more. Shrubs and flowers and such small gay things, that bloom and please and fade and wither and are gone and we care not for them, are refreshing interests, in life, and if we cannot say never fading pleasures, we may say unreproved pleasures and never grieving losses."[33]

The pleasure-garden was increasingly viewed as a feminized space untainted by plebeian or masculine practicality. Loudon writes of harmony and "artistical feeling" in the garden, but she also refers to neatness and order as aspects of good taste. Many writers of the period noted that beauty, in the domestic realm, was found more in careful attention to details than in the grand overview. Ellis, for example, concentrates on "*the minor morals of domestic life*," among them the virtue of neatness, and reminds her readers that "the sphere of a domestic woman's observation is microscopic."[34] This attribute of home life extended into the garden and was taught to children as one of the most admirable habits to develop, as we have seen. Johnson observes that "Nothing is so unbecoming as weeds and stones in parterres, where the eye seeks flowers and neatness." Although she admires the abundance of a "Plaisaunce" filled with flowers of all kinds, she reminds her reader that the garden should be orderly: "If it is not beautifully neat, it is nothing."[35] Loudon also upholds a well-tended garden as "essentially requisite, and any departure from it is exceedingly offensive."[36] It might seem that tending a garden was not in fact so different from housekeeping – sweeping, dusting, and polishing were replaced by raking, deadheading, and staking, while building a good loamy soil could be seen as comparable to the intricacies of following a recipe.

The creation of a sphere of beauty to surround the house, like a buffer to protect it from the noise and grime of the working world outside, probably needed no additional justification in the context of early nineteenth-century ideas about the home. But those who encouraged women to take on the new challenges of an ornamental garden did often cite various benefits in order to inspire their readers. Jane Taylor praises gardening as "wholesome and innocent,"[37] both characteristics being significant elements in the nostalgic view of rural life voiced during this increasingly urbanized period. In part to counteract the dissipation of urban culture, as well as the listlessness that was seen as particularly dangerous for middle- and upper-class women, gardening was touted by numerous authors as being a particularly healthy pursuit. Loudon certainly must have been aware of the concern expressed by many of her contemporaries about the weak constitutions of indolent girls, and in her book on children's gardens she presents gardening as an antidote.[38] After describing in *Gardening for Ladies* how a woman might do all of the digging necessary in a small garden with only a light spade, she notes that the exercise, along with "the reviving smell of the fresh earth," will improve both "her health and spirits."[39] In light of widespread fears about the possible ill effects of dirt, dampness, and fatigue on a lady's delicate constitution, Louisa Johnson offers the practical solution of a good gardening apron and a pair of rubber boots: "In these protections, a lady may indulge her passion for flowers at all seasons, without risk of rheumatism or chills, providing it does not actually rain or snow; and the cheering influence of the fresh air, combined with a favourite amusement, must ever operate beneficially on the mind and body in every season of the year."[40]

Mental and moral benefits were also presented as encouragement for women gardeners, helping to justify this as a worthy pursuit – an important consideration for an audience of women reared on such books as Hannah More's *Strictures on the Modern System of Female Education* (1799), in which even "innocent" amusements might lead to softness and dissipation.[41] The moral struggle between industry and indolence was much discussed in books for children and young women, as we have seen. Gardening also provided the opportunity for developing additional virtues such as patience and perseverance, which are "necessary in most affairs of life," according to Loudon, but "particularly so in gardening, as nature cannot be hurried in her operations."[42] Both of these virtues were often cited in comportment books of the period, including *The Young Lady's Book* (1829),[43] which included a chapter on floriculture as the first major section after "Moral Deportment."

Loudon also believed that gardening fostered strength of mind, counteracting the characteristic view of women's delicacy. She advised her readers to move beyond the simplest gardening procedures and take on more difficult challenges, asserting with unladylike zeal that "the pleasure will be great, in proportion as these difficulties appear at first sight to be insurmountable."[44] Johnson, like Loudon, recognized the value of rational deliberation as well as physical exercise, pointing out that "the mind ranges with singular pleasure" over the "vast and interminable field of observation" offered in a garden.[45] Both authors, aware of the opportunity in gardening for intellectual development, remind us of Wollstonecraft's view that "Gardening, experimental philosophy and literature would afford [women] subjects to think of and matter for conversation, that in some degree would exercise their understanding."[46]

Mental as well as muscular flexing is needed for successful gardening, but since both were considered somewhat suspect attributes for a lady at the time women writers had to make their case carefully. Johnson, for example, concludes her introduction with a powerful but cautiously worded presentation of the benefits of gardening:

> It is a passion most blessed in its effects, considered as an amusement or a benefit. Nothing humanizes and adorns the female mind more surely than a taste for ornamental gardening. It compels the reason to act, and the judgment to observe; it is favourable to meditation of the most serious kind; it exercises the fancy in harmless and elegant occupation, and braces the system by its healthful tendency. A flower-garden, to the young and single of my sex, acts upon the heart and affections as a nursery acts upon the matronly feelings. It attaches them to their home; it throws a powerful charm over the spot dedicated to such deeply-interesting employment; and it lures them from dwelling too deeply upon the unavoidable disappointments and trials of life, which sooner or later disturb and disquiet the heart.[47]

Johnson carefully fashioned this strong statement so as to avoid antagonizing her readers with an argument that might seem overly bold. The intensity of "passion" is softened by the promise of "amusement," and the feminine appeal of "adornment" balances the historically masculine traits of "reason" and "judgment." As soon as she sets forth the possibility of "serious meditation," she retreats into less controversial language for a lady's manual: "reason" is set aside for "fancy" and "serious" is replaced by "harmless and elegant." Most significantly, all of these advantages are not intended for display in the larger world but instead "attach" women even more firmly to their domestic lives. In a similar vein, Mary Russell Mitford describes her garden as her "passion," but then quickly minimizes the impact of that powerful emotion by adding, "But you will forgive me for overrating it. It is, at least, a mistake on the right side, to be too fond of one's own poor home."[48]

Johnson summarizes the benefits of gardening in her conclusion, as she reviews the activities for each month: "There is something to be done in every week of the year, – something to be attended to, which amuses the mind, interests the imagination, and benefits the general tone of mental and physical health."[49] In *Cœlebs in Search of a Wife*, More's Mr. Stanley – a gardener himself and father of the admirable Lucilla, who was also "passionately fond of cultivating a garden" – employs a similar set of terms as he praises this "amusement" as being "so pure, so natural, so cheap, so rational, so healthful, I had almost said so religious."[50]

Johnson's introduction includes several references to God and Providence, but in general she seems to have been more concerned with the reality of the garden than with the spiritual benefits it might provide – although she, like Jacson, Loudon, and others, had no compunction in using those benefits to entice ladies into their gardening boots. For Johnson the main reason to garden is a simple one: gardening is a pleasure, a joy, a delight. She begins her manual with the statement that "a garden affords the purest of human pleasures," and Loudon's introduction to *The Ladies' Flower-Garden of Ornamental Annuals* (1840) is equally simple and blunt: "The love of flowers is calculated to improve our best feelings, and subdue our bad ones." And then couching this view in the religious sentiment that was so prevalent at the time, but almost as an afterthought, she adds that "we can hardly contemplate the beauty and richness of a flower-garden without feeling our heart dilate with gratitude to that Almighty Being who has made all these lovely blossoms, and given them to us for our use."

As we discussed in Chapter 2, for many women the idea of witnessing God's hand at work in the natural world must have been understood as a given: a foundational assumption so pervasive in the literature that they hardly needed to dwell on it. Much more of a concern for them were the practical questions of *who* could garden, and how, which we will consider in the following sections dealing with issues related to class, management, and labor.

MANAGING THE GARDEN: WOMEN AS SUPERVISORS

Many women seemed to take pride in their own work, but we do often find references in children's books, novels, and essays to "the gardener," a staple of genteel households with a plot of land. Almost always male, the gardener would do the heavier manual labor, although women were sometimes hired for menial chores. In a letter written in her forties (c. 1815–17), Maria Edgeworth expressed delight in her garden – "I am glad I have acquired this taste for a *gay* or even a shabby garden … it is a *rest* to the mind and at all times a relief" – but she had to rely on one of her "dear little undergardeners – Sophy" to do the planting when her father was unavailable.[51] Certainly Loudon in her later gardening manuals and magazines recognized that her audience – generally educated middle-class women – could afford to have help, especially for jobs that required a great deal of physical strength or that might simply be too discouraging for a novice.

In her entry on "Gardener" in *The Ladies' Companion to the Flower-Garden*, Loudon states directly that "To keep a flower-garden in perfection, it is necessary to have a good gardener, unless the amateur understands how the various operations of gardening are to be performed sufficiently well to be able to direct an indifferent gardener, or a common labourer, how to execute them." She is not referring here to the kind of small cottage garden that could be tended by the woman of the house in her free time, but instead is describing a larger "show-garden" associated with a middle-class suburban villa or even an estate. For those with a small garden she admits that the expense of hiring a "first-rate flower-gardener" (amounting to £70–80 a year)[52] might be too great, and although she recommends maintaining a close connection with a nurseryman to supply plants and "to keep the garden constantly in order," she reasserts her primary intention to encourage and instruct lady gardeners:

> The great enjoyment of gardening, however, in my opinion, is only to be obtained by the amateur who gardens himself, and who understands the principles or reasons upon which each operation is founded; and, therefore, I should recommend all persons fond of gardening, and especially ladies who have sufficient leisure, to manage their gardens themselves, with the assistance of a man to perform the more laborious operations.[53]

The key concept in this passage is the lady as *manager* – she directs, she oversees, she does some of the light work, but she is not the sole worker. By the early Victorian period when Loudon was publishing her books it was assumed that genteel women of the burgeoning middle class were at one remove from the actual labor, in the garden as in the home or nursery. They were overseers of the domestic realm, resulting in the curious reality of daily lives based on a combination of responsibility and leisure. For Loudon, at least in this passage, the requisites for a lady's garden are *leisure* and *assistance*. Thus the issue of class goes hand in hand with the more explicitly addressed issue of gender in her gardening manuals. We should not be surprised, then, by Loudon's observation in her monthly "Floral Calendar" for 1842 in the *Ladies' Magazine of Gardening* that planting dahlias, being "a rather more serious affair," is suited for the gardener whereas working with seedlings is "more adapted to a lady."[54] Here she seems to distinguish between male seriousness and female delicacy, thus reinforcing the gender stereotypes of the period and contradicting some of her advice published elsewhere.

Doing one's own work, unless clearly for entertainment or edification, was demeaning and jeopardized one's social status (though we will return to this issue in the next section and find conflicting views in Loudon's publications). Gentility required the help of servants, and gardening manuals had to take such issues into consideration. As Davidoff and Hall observe about Victorian assumptions, "To be large, or loud, or strong, was to be ugly and carried with it notions of moral collapse as well as physical failure to conform."[55] Children's books also helped to reinforce expectations about women, work, and class, as discussed in Chapter 1. In Budden's *Always Happy*, for example, the mother emphasizes the value of a strong constitution by telling her daughter about a lady who "fancied herself unequal to any exertion" but eventually became "the healthiest and happiest woman of my acquaintance." This transformation was the result of a radical change in attitude: "She made a good resolution, and very wisely kept it – she altered all her plans – she rose early, she took long walks, she superintended her garden, assisted in the education of her children, and overlooked the business of her house."[56] The verbs used by Budden are noteworthy – "superintend," "assist," "overlook" – since they echo Loudon's passage in focusing on management skills rather than physical labor. Both Loudon and Budden associate such skills with the ability to create domestic pleasure: as Loudon observes, "Suburban gardens generally give more pleasure to their possessors than gardens of more importance; principally, perhaps, because they are seldom, if ever, under the control of a master gardener; but are managed by the lady of the house; and thus a suburban garden becomes a kind of domestic pet, for we always love things that are partly our own creation." Here the idea of female power – being in control of one's "creation" – is softened by the analogy of the garden to a pet. And Loudon assures her readers that this power will be put to good use to create a retreat from the world outside: "surely the delight of turning from a dusty and dirty street, and rows of formal houses, to gaze upon fresh green leaves, and to smell the fragrance of flowers, are pleasures that may well compensate for the amount of time and trouble bestowed upon them."[57]

Some ambivalence about the necessity of employing a gardener can be found in Loudon's epistolary book, *The Lady's Country Companion*, in which she sympathizes with her friend Annie's difficulties with "a cross old gardener, who cannot be displaced." She clearly assumes, however, that Annie, recently married and newly settled in a country house, will soon have more professional help, since in her seventh letter she notes in passing, "I believe you have not yet a regular gardener." Still, Loudon must have intended that her instructions about the garden be put to good use by Annie herself: later in the same letter she admonishes, "you must not mind going upon the [wet] grass, if you are to be a real gardener, and to attend to the flowers in the regular beds."[58] "Real" gardeners do not have to do all the work themselves, according to Loudon, although neither should they shy away from at least some measure of active involvement in the daily tasks. Loudon herself, after her husband's death in 1843, did all of the work in their Bayswater garden with only the occasional help of her sister-in-law; faced with sizable debts, she was unable even to hire a part-time gardener.[59]

Having help in the garden, although clearly an advantage in many ways, was not always a boon. Middle-class women often had trouble supervising male servants, since they were usually more inexperienced at asserting their authority than upper-class women on larger estates.[60] It is especially easy to understand how a true novice aspiring to be a lady gardener could be intimidated by the knowledge and experience of a hired professional, or even what was known as a jobbing gardener. The anonymous female author of *Every Lady's Guide to Her Own Greenhouse* (1851) recommends hiring "a man who does not know too much," one who will "attend to what he is told, and not act on his own opinion." This advice was for the woman's "own comfort ... for it is unpleasant to be subject to the invisible sneers of a man who considers you wrong." Even being subject to the gaze of a male servant could be unnerving, so this author advises her reader to be mistress of her own greenhouse or conservatory rather than allowing a male servant to be the master. In this way the reader can "do as you please; your will is not disputed; there is nobody to question your judgment, nor condemn your acts." Dispensing altogether with a man to help with the more demanding physical jobs was not recommended, but an assistant should be chosen who would do no more than follow directions, unlike a professional gardener who would act like a "monarch": "I declare I know ladies who submit to black looks, impertinent remarks, rude sneers, and other uncouth behaviour, in a manner that I would not submit to even from my husband – that is, if I could help it." "Directing" and "managing" and "supervising" were still the primary skills of this author, who called herself "'monarch of all I survey,' and perfectly mistress of my own greenhouse," although she did not skirt around the necessity of hard work. In describing her pleasure at having visitors admire her winter flowers, for example, she admits that their delight "sweetens the labour – for sometimes gardening amounts to this – in the service of my plants."[61]

"STIRRING THE SOIL": WOMEN AND MANUAL LABOR

The image on the title page for Loudon's *Gardening for Ladies* (Fig. 6.5) conveys something of the tricky balance she is advocating between labor and decorum. A woman and a young girl, probably her daughter, stand between a rose-covered arbor and a small flower bed. Holding a rake and hoe, they are surrounded by other garden implements, including a wheelbarrow, spade, and watering pot. What appears to be the handle of a trowel sticks up out of the dirt of the circular bed. The image is thus full of gardening signifiers, although the woman and child seem incapable of

"*Stirring the soil*" 181

Fig. 6.5. Title page illustration in Jane Loudon, *Gardening for Ladies*.

any actual labor. They stand gracefully on their tiny feet, wearing clothes that point more to their gentility than to their contact with the dirt of the garden. Contrary to Loudon's own advice, the woman wears no gloves, and her bonnet is more decorative than functional. A similar scene is portrayed on the cover of J. B. Whiting's *Manual of Flower Gardening for Ladies* (1849), a book that seems to be capitalizing on the growing interest in this niche market (Fig. 6.6). In sharp contrast to these images of women that emphasize the grace and refinement of their gardening activities is an illustration from the 1880s on the cover of the popular weekly magazine

Fig. 6.6. Cover illustration of J. B. Whiting, *Manual of Flower Gardening for Ladies*.

Amateur Gardening (Fig. 6.7). This scene of a family in the back garden of their suburban house might well have surprised Loudon, despite her own experiences, because of the gender reversal: one woman in a bustled dress pushes a lawnmower and another kneels on the path with her pruning shears, trimming some flowers, while a gentleman in his suit stands passively beside her with a watering can.

Earlier in the century, though, a crucial question for many readers of these gardening texts must have been how much of the actual work they could do themselves. The Tudor housewife in Thomas Tusser's *A Hundreth Good Pointes of Husbandrie* (1557) could work in the garden, hoeing and planting, but could the Victorian "angel in the house" also dig in the dirt? Even before the publication of Coventry Patmore's poem in 1854 the mores of the burgeoning middle class were affecting gender stereotypes, in particular related to feminine decorum and the issue of work. Although many women were turning to the garden as a productive site for healthy exercise as well as aesthetic pleasure, the physical actions involved in this pastime were often construed as coarsely plebeian for any but the working poor. The early nineteenth-century British were ambivalent about the appropriateness of women's labor in the garden. On the one hand, such work could be held up as evidence of moral worth, as in a poem from 1825 by James Luckcock, a provincial businessman of modest means: here the adoring wife is full of

Fig. 6.7. Illustration in *Amateur Gardening*, 1880s.

praise for her husband, "Who shun'd the giddy town's turmoil, / To share with me the garden's toil, / And joy with labour reconcile."[62] On the other hand, however, the garden could be seen as distracting a woman from her domestic duties. Anne Cobbett in *The English Housekeeper* (1835) maintains a clear divide between inside and out, as she places the man in the garden doing the chores while his wife stays within the home, taking "the same pains with all that belongs to the inside of the dwelling."[63]

Young girls as well as boys were encouraged to tend their gardens themselves, since during this period pre-pubescent girls were allowed to join their brothers in healthy physical activities in order to counteract any tendency to listlessness or dissipation.[64] A short story published in the *Child's Companion* in 1824, for example, describes two siblings hard at work in their garden plots, explaining that "William and his sister thought they should never be tired of gardening."[65] But adolescent girls were expected to exhibit more propriety in their activities, and in fact physicians warned that their delicate frames could be in danger from any activity more vigorous than a walk.[66] In line with this view, the same author in another story gave the active role of digging to a boy while his sister was relegated to the role of entertainer: "After playing for some time, William took his spade and began to dig his garden, while Jane sat down and read to him out of a pretty new book."[67] In the illustration (Fig. 6.8) Jane, constrained by a ladylike

Fig. 6.8. Illustration in P. E., "Ripe Cherries." *Child's Companion* (1824), p. 34.

long dress and bonnet, concentrates on her reading while her brother energetically shovels dirt. The potted plant beside the girl also serves as a visual metaphor for her more constricted state: she, like the plant, is being tended and trained. As J. C. Loudon remarked, potted plants are "thoroughly domesticated."[68] Expanding on his association between female virtue and houseplants, Davidoff and Hall explain that the Victorian woman was "limited and domesticated, sexually controlled, not spilling out into spheres in which she did not belong nor being overpowered by 'weeds' of social disorder."[69] An engraving from the early nineteenth century (Fig. 6.9), with the inscription "Look at the Carnations which You Gave Me," reinforces the standard gender ideology of the period: the women are presented for our viewing, carefully dressed and trimmed out, just as the flowers are arranged for display in decorative pots on a tiered stand. The implication, of course, is that women *are* flowers, carefully cultivated and trained – a common view of the period, as we have seen. Here the most active work they might be involved in is watering, evident by the sprinkling can in the foreground.

This gender construction continued even in many later Victorian images (Fig. 6.10), in which younger girls gardening in short frocks are generally limited to watering their flowers, their brothers being the ones who wield the shovel.[70] As gentle nurturers rather than diggers, they could remain neat and clean while still benefiting from the virtues associated with gardening. Lucy Sarah Atkins allows the sisters in *Botanical Rambles* (1822) to be "actively engaged" in the greenhouse, arranging the pots, deadheading, and

Fig. 6.9. "Look at the Carnations which You Gave Me." London, Museum of Garden History.

Fig. 6.10.   Victorian calendar illustration.

training the "delicate tendrils," but when their botanical curiosity prompts a desire to study a potato, they are helpless: "If Frederic were but a little older, he could dig some up for us to examine."[71] Similarly, in Barbauld's *Stories of the Months* (1850) the illustration for her hymn in praise of God – "Let us go forth into the fields; let us see how the flowers spring" – includes a boy pushing a wheelbarrow in which a girl rides, while other boys with tools and a romping dog lead the way (Fig. 6.11). Behind the demure girl in the wheelbarrow stands a more enigmatic figure: upright, with billowing drapery, this young woman looks assertively out while holding a rake in one

Fig. 6.11. "Let Us Go Forth into the Fields," illustration in Anna Letitia Barbauld, *Stories of the Months*, p. 66.

hand and propping up a large basket of garden produce with the other. Is she a personification – an allegory of Spring, perhaps, since the same illustration appears in Barbauld's story for May – or might she be a peasant girl just back from the field, watching this little parade of middle-class children play-acting as gardeners?[72] In either case, whether intended by the illustrator or not, the reader might follow the clues of contrast and placement in construing her as the powerful alter ego of the girl in the wheelbarrow and thus perhaps a challenge to convention.

Young Caroline, a "merry little romp" in Broome's *Fanny and Mary* (1821), describes as her happiest memory the freedom of running about her uncle's new homestead while it was still under construction: "The house was all in confusion, and the grounds were all in confusion, and I had a whole week of confusion … I scampered about all day long; for there was nothing I could hurt in the garden, and nothing that I could hurt in the house." The illustration (Fig. 6.12) shows "The Active Caroline" lifting a heavy shovel to construct a pile of rubble, while her uncle hangs a swing for her. The point of the book, however, is not to sanction such rambunctious play, but instead to control and limit "the evils of idleness and self-indulgence."[73]

Fig. 6.12. "The Active Caroline," illustration in Charlotte Anne Broome, *Fanny and Mary*, facing p. 16.

But we can turn to a real girl in the 1830s and find an assertive personality that contradicts the views expressed in some of the popular fiction and conduct books. Emily Shore, whom we introduced in Chapter 2, was hardly a typical middle-class girl, however. From a liberal and learned family, she reveals an extraordinary voice in her journals, one in which curiosity and confidence intermingle. In March of 1833, when Emily was thirteen (well past the age of acceptable girlhood romping), she wrote about transplanting wildflowers to her two garden beds. Using the verb "work" to convey the labor involved ("I worked at my garden, which mamma has lately given me"), her descriptions remind us of the effort involved in such intensive gardening: "I cut away the earth pretty deeply in one part … I then went with a spade and wheelbarrow to the bottom of the garden … I have dug up a few young trees, and planted them with my flowers."[74] Here is a girl who pushed her own wheelbarrow rather than riding sedately as a passenger, and whose energy was not curtailed by social restrictions.

Despite her comments about women as managers and supervisors in the garden, Loudon would surely have approved of Emily's use of the spade. In her manual for children, *My Own Garden*, she expects the children to be fully involved in the actual labor, with few exceptions, without differentiating between specific tasks according to sex.[75] She is also willing to encourage grown women to take on some of the heavier gardening tasks, within reason. The first chapter of *Gardening for Ladies* is entitled "Stirring the Soil," making the arduous task of digging sound like no more work than stirring a pot of soup. But she is convinced that with the proper precautions (especially "a little attention to the principles of mechanics") even the heavy work could be handled by women. Although she acknowledges that the normal system of digging is "peculiarly unfitted to small and delicately formed hands and feet," she goes on to explain that lesser force exerted over a longer period of time could often accomplish just as much. So a woman using an appropriately designed spade might do all the work in her small garden by shoveling smaller amounts of dirt at a time, and she assures the reader that digging could be "done with perfect ease," requiring "skill more than strength."[76] Loudon might have been influenced by her husband's general belief that gardening depended "more upon the labour of the brain than of the body,"[77] although she is willing to apply that precept to women as well as men. She recognizes that a woman's mind and body can work together to accomplish much of the mental and physical work associated with gardening. It is revealing that she considers digging more important than any other work in the garden, and even gives it moral overtones: "I do not know any single operation in gardening so illustrative of personal character as digging." She feels able to distinguish between "an idle, careless man" and a "useful, handy" one based on whether he can "dig well," and she goes on to propose that "no young gardener ... ought to despise the spade."[78] Given these strong feelings, it is not surprising that she encouraged women to do their own digging when possible, and to do it properly.

Loudon must have known how shocking such advice would have seemed to some of her readers, however. A woman like Dorothy Wordsworth, free from middle-class conventions while at Grasmere, could roam freely through the countryside in search of wild plants to dig up for her garden, but many of Loudon's readers would have been raised on the platitudes in such popular publications as *The Young Lady's Book* (1829) and *The New Female Instructor, or Young Woman's Guide to Domestic Happiness* (1834).

In the chapter on "The Florist" in *The Young Lady's Book* the author warns that women should not dig, make compost, or even "study the modes of manuring," and for the sake of "health and pleasure" the lady should confine herself to sowing seeds, transplanting young plants, training, watering, and light weeding – all "light and graceful occupations to a young lady." A young woman's delight in flowers is described in this book as "natural," for "there is something peculiarly adapted to feminine tenderness in the care of flowers." In fact, if one were to find a woman with "a total disregard" for flowers she could be accused of being "unfeminine," exhibiting "a deficiency of taste in general."[79] This, of course, would be a serious accusation at a time when good taste was considered one of the major indicators of a gently reared lady.

The gender implications are clear. Although a young woman who doesn't love flowers is "unfeminine," any eagerness to engage physically in the more difficult tasks of gardening would be characterized as "masculine." A woman's delight in the beauty of cultivated nature was socially prescribed as being primarily reflective. That is, her delicacy, innocence, and purity are reflected in and enhanced by those same traits in flowers, but they would be tainted by involvement in the actual work needed to create and maintain a garden. *The New Female Instructor* warns its readers to "avoid every thing that is masculine, either in your dress or your behavior." Softness and delicacy are upheld as key female charms: "However valuable may be the blessings of health, it is indelicate in a lady to boast of it; to talk of her great appetite or her strength; to say she eats heartily, can walk several miles, or can bear a good deal of fatigue." Digging in the dirt would surely have been ruled out by the author of this manual, especially since he (or she?) considered it "indelicate and exceedingly illiberal for a young lady to talk of being hot, or to say she sweats."[80] A similar concern surfaces in a letter written in 1815 by a Devonshire woman to her sister: her promotion of gardening as a healthy pursuit is tempered by her fear that digging might have gender repercussions, evident in her description of a neighbor who is seen "digging and hammering away" as "rather a masculine woman" – although she did concede that she "looks in a good state of preservation."[81] The question of masculinity had surfaced earlier in Wakefield's *Reflections on the Present Condition of the Female Sex* (1798), in which she transcribes an account of Sarah and Mary Spencer, sisters left destitute by family fortune, who "took a farm, and, without ceasing to be gentlewomen, commenced farmers." Although many of their neighbors scathingly referred to them as "captain Sally" and "her man Mary," thus bringing into question their very nature as women, other more enlightened gentry respected their labors: "not seldom, in one and the same day, have they divided their hours in helping to fill the dung-cart, and receiving company of the highest rank and distinction." And, Wakefield's source adds, "they even handled the dung-fork with an air of elegance."[82]

Almost fifty years later, Loudon seems unconcerned with this widespread fear of appearing masculine – or, to shift from gender to overlapping class considerations, the fear of appearing low-class – when she describes digging in the garden as "a fine healthy occupation, not only from its calling the muscles into vigorous action, but from the smell of the new earth being particularly invigorating."[83] But in light of the attitude expressed in *The New Female Instructor*, Loudon's encouragement may not have converted many of the young ladies who read such books in hopes of acquiring genteel accomplishments. Part of the difference in viewpoint was due, undoubtedly, to a largely urban as opposed to rural readership, but it was also probably the result of complex and shifting attitudes toward female capabilities in the mid-nineteenth century. For Loudon, digging was not just confined to lightly turning over the topsoil; in addition to "loosening the soil," she lists "burying manure; exposing the soil to the action of the weather; trenching; [and] ridging," although the latter three she later acknowledged were "operations too laborious to be performed by any one but a gardener's labourer," at least when done "on a large scale." Other digging operations listed by Loudon – planting, transplanting, and removing plants of all kinds, including trees and shrubs – could presumably be handled by her women readers, although large trees should only be planted or moved by a "professed gardener."[84]

The topic of women's work in the garden, clearly a controversial one, is raised in the first volume of the short-lived journal the *Gardener and Practical Florist*, from 1843. Advising ladies to devote their attentions to the delicate jobs of watering, staking, and "regulating the petals" of carnations, the anonymous author continues: "We do not imagine that females are to wheel barrows about, nor to dig the ground as directed by Mrs. Loudon, but we presume that a man servant is at least an attendant for all unfeminine operations."[85] He considers even the lightest contact with the soil inappropriate for ladies, unlike Peter Mackenzie, who a year earlier sent a short paragraph to the *Gardeners' Chronicle* entitled "Gardening Practised by the Fair Sex." Mackenzie expresses admiration for two young women whom he had observed working in their garden, "one with a Dutch hoe, and the other with a rake." He notes that many professionals "could not have used these tools to better purpose" and adds: "It was delightful to witness the graceful manner in which they performed their work; for they appeared far more pleasant and happy than in the stiff and starched manner in which they are generally seen." He then ends with a quotation from Milton, in which Adam calls on Eve to join him in caring for "our tended plants."[86]

Mackenzie's brief paragraph prompted two strong rebuttals. Spoofing the idea of these women gardeners as graceful ladies, one critic suggested that they must instead have been the housemaid and the cook brandishing a ladle and broom. Surely, he continued, the mistress of the household would have been doing her needlework inside while overseeing her servants, thus keeping the proper hierarchy intact: "The man to the plough, and the maid to the loom, / And the mistress watch early and late." A Miltonic Paradise, this author argued, consists of *Adam* delving while Eve is busy at the spinning wheel, creating "a nice tidy home" in Eden.[87] A second rebuttal to Mackenzie appeared a week later, making the case that lady gardeners "will never be the fashion while men are so plentiful, and that ladies can be better employed 'in harmony with the design for which they were intended'."[88] In an editorial aside John Lindley, author of *Ladies' Botany* and head of the horticultural section of this periodical, remarked that "if he means that delving, and hoeing, and raking, are not employments for the fair sex, we have no doubt that the ladies will generally agree with him." In the same year, however, "A Lover of Gardening" expressed her delight in the new periodical *Ladies' Magazine of Gardening*, edited by Jane Loudon, noting that lady gardeners "are, I think you will find, a very numerous class."[89]

The idea of women digging in the dirt was clearly a problematic one. The prelapsarian activities of Adam and especially Eve could be interpreted in different ways, as seen above, although in general during this period Edenic gardening was cited as the ultimate justification for the purity and innocence associated with this pursuit. Mackenzie's use of Milton was thus a clever rhetorical strategy, and a similar approach can be found in the design of an intriguing mid-nineteenth-century ceremonial banner from Lancashire, painted on silk (Fig. 6.13). This painting was made for one of the early associations of Free Gardeners, initially begun as organizations of professionals but by the early nineteenth century turning into more general mutual-aid societies. The Free Gardeners drew their lineage from the first garden in Eden, which explains the prominent position given here to the figures of Eve with a rake and Adam with a spade, flanking an escutcheon with the serpent twined around the tree of the knowledge of good and evil.[90] Although Eve is given equal visual weight with Adam on this banner, she was actually no more than an adjunct in the Free Gardeners' mythology.

Fig. 6.13. Ceremonial Free Gardeners' Banner from Lancashire. London, Museum of Garden History.

Adam, considered the first gardener, was the founding figure: the letters ANS on the columns here stand for Adam, Noah, and Solomon, believed to be the three original or Grand Master gardeners. But Eve with her rake can serve as a useful counterbalance to the conservative image of Eve at her spinning wheel. Thus Mackenzie's graceful lady gardener wielding a rake becomes a descendant of the Free Gardeners' Eve, both of them helping to expand the early Victorian definition of a "nice tidy home."

Tools, in fact, being the instruments of the profession, were important indicators of serious commitment. Both Loudon and Johnson encouraged women to equip themselves properly. In Loudon's entry on "Implements" in *The Ladies' Companion to the Flower-Garden* she lists a variety of gardening tools, from the "ordinary" (a spade, fork, rake, hoe, trowel, pruning knife and shears, watering pot, syringe, basket, fumigating bellows, wheelbarrow, scythe, and roller) to those more suitable for gardening on a large scale.[91] For Loudon, in particular, the right kind of tool (as well as the right shape and weight) was crucial. Although she grants that pruning might seem to be "at first sight, a most laborious and unfeminine occupation," she characterizes it as being in actuality one of the easiest of garden chores for a woman. A personal testimonial underscores her point: "With the aid of a small, and almost elegant pair of pruning shears, which I procured from Mr. Forrest, of the Kensington Nursery, I have myself (though few women have less strength of wrist) divided branches that a strong man could scarcely cut through with a knife."[92] She is very practical in her advice, suggesting that the wheelbarrow should be designed with long, curved handles so the weight is transferred down to the wheel rather than borne by the gardener's arms, since "few ladies are strong enough" to transfer heavy dirt from one place to another without one.[93] Not only did she specify *what* tools to use, she also told her readers how to use them, and women responded in large numbers to her advice, often requesting information about how to find the ladies' tools that she described.[94]

The authors of these manuals also realized that practical dress as well as appropriate tools were necessary for successful gardening. The lady gardener should wear clogs or Indian rubber shoes, and thick gloves to protect the hands were also crucial. An illustration in Loudon's *Gardening for Ladies* of "A Lady's Gauntlet of strong leather, invented by Miss Perry of Stroud, near Hazlemere" (Fig. 6.14) is simple but telling: while the hand is encased in a stout glove that reaches up to the elbow and holds a leafy sprig to show its particular function, the rest of the body (from what little one can see of it) is dressed in a soft and apparently rather delicate fabric. From the context of Loudon's manual as well as the details of the illustration we are able to identify the gardener as a gentlewoman, in contrast to the working-class woman who was provided with steel-tipped gloves when she was hired in 1823 to weed and kill slugs and snails at Aubrey Hall.[95] The issue of class was paramount, of course. While poor women were considered strong enough for physical labor, middle-class women (or those living on the borders of gentility) were hesitant to risk their status as "ladies."[96]

The number of letters Loudon received from women gardeners must have been prompted at least in part by the relative lack of seriousness with which they were treated in publications by male authors. Loudon's husband, for example, alludes rather derisively to women's tools in his opus, *An Encyclopaedia of Gardening* (1822): describing a French "rose-gatherer"

"*Stirring the soil*"

Fig. 6.14. "A Lady's Gauntlet," illustration in Jane Loudon, *Gardening for Ladies*, p. 17.

he notes, "Of course, this instrument, like a number of other horticultural toys manufactured by the Parisians, is chiefly *pour les dames*."[97] Women here seem to be grouped with children as merely playing with their gardens (although there's also certainly a nationalist as well as sexist tone in his comment, the French often being dismissed as weak and effeminate by the English male).[98]

Certainly Jane Loudon knew that many middle- and upper-class women were perfectly capable of working in the garden, and happy to do so. She not only had her own experiences in Bayswater to draw on but also those of the women she met on gardening tours and the many others who wrote to her as editor of the *Ladies' Magazine of Gardening* (1842) and *Ladies' Companion at Home and Abroad* (1849–50). Loudon responded to letters about gardening matters sent to *Ladies' Companion* and signed by "Diana," "Kate," "Alpha," and "Francesca," among others, and women were also mentioned in the same magazine in notices of horticultural exhibitions. That these women were not anomalies can be seen by even a superficial perusal of such periodicals as the *Transactions of the Horticultural Society of London* and the *Floricultural Cabinet and Florists' Magazine*. In the former, women from various backgrounds were occasionally cited for their prizewinning flowers and fruits – from the Duchess of Dorset, the first female winner of the society's prestigious Banksian Medal in 1823 (along with forty-two men), to Mrs. Goose of Horsham Saint Faith's[99] – and although the Duchess certainly had a team of gardeners to follow her directions, Mrs. Goose probably did not. Letters and short articles by women frequently appeared in the *Floricultural Cabinet*, especially in the 1840s and 1850s. Some were merely signed "A Lady Amateur Gardener," "A Lady Florist," or "A Clergyman's Daughter," but others gave their first name, allowing us to track the course of their correspondence. Lucy, for instance, began in 1843 by sending in questions – when to transplant gentianella and how to sow penstemon seeds – but by 1845 she was bold enough to offer a brief comment about a proven method of steeping seeds in sulfate of ammonia, and from 1846 to 1849 she published seven longer articles ranging from tips about propagating and growing specific species, to botanical studies, to a more general article "On the Disposition of Flowers in Masses."[100]

The question of women's work in the garden was in part a matter of gender expectations (especially regarding problematically "masculine" behavior) and in part related to class (with a bourgeois fear of being too closely associated with the dirt and sweat of lower-class labor). Intermixed with these overlapping concerns was the stark reality of money, connected with gender through issues of control and authority and with class through issues of wage-earning. Some women writers directed their instructions explicitly to the lady gardener on a small income, without the benefit of any professional assistance. Jacson criticizes those women who merely follow the fashion of installing a flower garden but then leave everything up to a gardener. Although she describes flowers as "elegant playthings," her intentions in *The Florist's Manual* are less lofty: "I attempt only to assist in the humble path of exhibiting to the best advantage the moderately-sized flower-garden" so that "any one may be enabled to form a gay and well-mingled garden through the spring and summer months at a small expense."[101]

Louisa Johnson was even more emphatic than Jacson in insisting that women need not have a large budget or extensive help and are themselves perfectly capable of the hard work required to make and maintain a garden. The title itself, *Every Lady Her Own Flower Gardener: Addressed to the Industrious and Economical*, is a clear indication of her approach. Her short book, published in 1839, provides a very different kind of instruction than Jane Loudon's *Instructions in Gardening for Ladies* (1840; the title was shortened to *Gardening for Ladies* in later editions) and especially *The Ladies' Companion to the Flower-Garden* (1841) in length, consistent simplicity of language, emphasis on economy, and focus on the small garden. Johnson includes in her preface a quotation summarizing what she had been hearing from her acquaintances: "We require … a work in a small compass, which will enable us to become our own gardener: we wish to know how to set about everything *ourselves*, without expense, without being deluged with Latin words and technical terms." Sprinkling the preface with adjectives such as "practical," "useful," "simple," and "economical," she sets the stage for a new kind of manual for women with small gardens. Her readers could not be expected "to take more than common pains" to grow flowers, since they were probably only able to "command the services of an old man, a woman, or a stout boy."[102]

Johnson offers various suggestions for making a garden that could be handled by a woman with only a minimum of assistance. In comparing the merits of gravel or grass walks, she notes that grass, while beautiful, requires a great deal of attention in the form of mowing, rolling, and trimming (discussed in detail by Loudon in her entries on "Lawn" and "Mowing" in *The Ladies' Companion*). Gravel walks, on the other hand, "only require an old woman's or a child's assistance in keeping them free from weeds" (and they have the added advantage that "a lady has not the same fears of taking cold, or getting wet in her feet"). She permits a lady gardener whose "physical powers are not equal to the fatigue of planting" to superintend the planting of shrubs by an employed laborer "or a stout active girl," but a few paragraphs later, in describing the actual process of planting, she assumes that the reader would be the one doing the digging: "when you wish to transplant or plant a shrub, dig a circular hole sufficiently large to receive the roots of the plant, which must be laid neatly down, while some person holds the shrub in its proper position." It is instructive to highlight the verbs used by Johnson in her last chapter, in which she summarizes the activities for each month: cut, lay, roll, dig, plant, transplant, prune, support, protect, spread, sow, water, sweep, weed, move, stake, tie, propagate, trim, hoe, train, stir, mow, clip, gather, prepare, examine, look. In short, as she states on her final page for the month of December, "Take care of everything."[103]

We have seen considerable ambivalence in the gardening manuals and other texts about what was considered appropriate action for women in the garden. Widely recognized as arbiters of taste and morality, middle-class ladies could fashion a cultivated garden so as to bring it securely within the embrace of the home circle. As designers and supervisors, they could promote a taming, refining, and aestheticizing of nature. But did the gender scales tip dangerously toward the masculine when they picked up a shovel to dig in the dirt – or to stir the soil, as Jane Loudon phrased it, searching for a balance between feminine domesticity and manly physicality? Loudon herself was caught between rhetoric and reality, between the constraints of social expectations and the practical lives of active women. Though occasionally retreating into the standard language of Victorian discourse about femininity, she, like Jacson and Johnson, enabled female readers to see new possibilities of enterprise and occupation in the garden.

PART IV

Narrative strategies: plotting the garden

CHAPTER 7

"Unbought pleasure": gardening in Cœlebs in Search of a Wife *and* Mansfield Park

Both Hannah More and Jane Austen thought about gardens and gardening in literary and textual terms. Echoing Milton, More writes to Horace Walpole: "I spend almost my whole time in my little garden, 'which mocks my scant manuring.' From 'morn to noon, from noon to dewy eve,' I am employed in raising dejected pinks, and reforming disorderly honeysuckles."[1] Austen tells her sister Cassandra that "I could not do without a Syringa, for the sake of Cowper's line."[2] In this chapter we will explore what gardening means for both of these authors and two of their characters, Lucilla Stanley and Fanny Price. Although Austen and More have been linked, it is usually in terms of distinguishing Austen (appreciatively) from the more didactic More. When the topic under consideration is gardening, however, the distinction between the two authors actually reveals different but complementary approaches to the meaning and use of gardens and gardening.

More's *Cœlebs in Search of a Wife* (1808) focuses on gardening in both literal and metaphorical ways. Fashioning her text as a conduct book in narrative form, More, a prolific evangelical Christian writer, educator, and activist, presents gardening at the center of the proper middle- and upper-class woman's domestic life.[3] The garden is not merely an ornamental space for More, however; it is useful and productive, tied to work and most importantly to charitable activity. Unlike the landscape parks still popular at the time that More was writing, the gardens of *Cœlebs* attain value in proportion to their practical use. By linking them to women's charitable projects such as growing plants and produce for the poor, More proposes a public function for what might have been regarded as a private leisure activity and assigns value to the work in which women engage. What might look like a conservative proscription actually becomes a challenge for women to turn domestic labor into public good.

In contrast, Austen sees the usefulness of gardening more in terms of Fanny Price's personal development.[4] Like More, however, she also critiques the merely ornamental and the rage for fashion in gardens and landscape design. We will focus here on the garden as a private (female) space, an idea that appears as early as Austen's *Catharine, or The Bower* (1792) and develops in *Mansfield Park* (1814) into a place that fosters Fanny Price's introspective consciousness. Working in limited space, Fanny creates and nurtures a green world, a miniature garden in the form of potted geraniums – in her own room. In *Mansfield Park*, written just a few years after the publication of *Cœlebs*, Austen positions her narrative, Fanny Price, and the various landscapes and gardens in the novel in relation to More's work. Interesting in itself, More's novel also, then, provides a rich intertext for Austen's.

REFORMING HONEYSUCKLES

In recent years, several critics have turned their attention to More: to the role of Christian philanthropy in her writing and to her position vis-à-vis the ideology of separate spheres.[5] We suggest that women's gardens and the practice of gardening in More's writing support the position, best argued by Mitzi Myers, Anne Mellor, and Dorice Williams Elliott, that More's concept of women's work "posed an inherent challenge to that ideology's confinement of women within the private sphere of the home by making their participation in publicly useful activities outside the home seem to be simply an extension of their domestic role."[6] Our analysis of gardens in *Cœlebs*, then, contributes both to the complication of More, often treated dismissively as a moralist, and to the ongoing re-evaluation of the ideology of separate spheres, especially in relation to gardens and gardening.

In *Cœlebs*, furthermore, Hannah More uses the garden, part of the extended site of women's domestic work as well as a source of public charity, as a basis for criticizing the consumer economy, the fashionable market for landscape improvement, and the association of landscape with male power. In general, women writers wanted to free gardens and landscape from the male obsession with manipulating nature for the sake of the prospect, as well as from masculine ways of viewing women as cultivated landscape, a form of control and power.[7] More herself writes in *Strictures in Female Education* that "A woman sees the world, as it were, from a little elevation in her own garden, whence she makes an exact survey of home scenes, but takes not in that wider range of distant prospects, which he who stands on a loftier eminence commands."[8] Thus the freedom from prospect paradoxically becomes a source of women's strength. Anticipating feminist critiques of the masculine gaze, More develops an epistemology of the garden rather than the landscape park to explain the way a "woman sees the world."

Whereas the garden embeds the viewer in the scene, the landscape park requires an "eminence" in order to "command" a view.[9]

The garden is not only a site of literal work and "home scenes" but also carries the metaphorical implication of improvement achieved through mental cultivation. More's novel extends the physical cultivation of land to include a "social or educational sense," as Raymond Williams explains.[10] Gardening, a discipline in which disorderly honeysuckles are reformed, is also a figure for the redemption possible in this world. For More, then, there is a spiritual as well as social or educational dimension to gardening. *Cœlebs* interweaves the literal and the metaphorical poles in order to emphasize the similarity and to validate both forms of cultivation. Although More does use flowers in fairly conventional ways, including as a symbol of passion, her careful emphasis on women's gardening as active work resists the conventional objectification of women as the cultivated land. As Jacqueline Labbe has argued, More develops "the idea of the female *gardener*, active instead of passive, creative instead of created, self-fashioning instead of other-fashioned or *cultivated*."[11]

As a mark of confidence in her own voice in *Cœlebs*, More frames the narrative in terms of Milton's *Paradise Lost* and what she sees as the perfect model for her domestic gardener, Eve. On the surface this frame may seem to be an endorsement of a limited role for women, but More subtly uses allusions to *Paradise Lost* to assert a more radical reading, in which Eve becomes the center of the epic as the character who takes on an actively redemptive role as a figure of charity. More implies that while Eve lost the Garden of Eden, modern women can reclaim cultivation by linking it both to the public good and to spiritual reformation. Thus More provides a proleptic refutation of Virginia Woolf's later argument in *A Room of One's Own* (1929) that "Milton's bogey" cast an oppressive shadow over women writers for centuries.[12]

In this chapter, we argue that gardening, as a material occupation, a subject in literature, and a trope for human development, spirituality, and sexuality, is central to understanding More's deceptively static novel and its articulation of women's roles, as well as Austen's more celebrated treatment of these issues. More perhaps poses the greater challenge: on the one hand, she revises patriarchal tradition and embraces the possibilities of women's power, but on the other, the very structure of the novel, narrated by a man in search of a wife and including many discussions by men on proper female behavior and attitudes, sets up a dynamic unfavorable to women's agency. This conflict, as well as the association of gardens with both passion and restraint, luxuriance and pruning, provides an ongoing tension in the novel.

Cœlebs in Search of a Wife charts the search of a young evangelical man, Charles, for the perfect Christian wife. Following a tour of the fashionable sites of London, as well as various country seats, Charles, the bachelor-narrator (hence *Cœlebs*, as in "celibate") visits Stanley Grove, the home of the pious Stanley family. It is no surprise to the reader that Charles soon falls for the lovely Lucilla Stanley, the eldest daughter, and after some delay of gratification, marries her. The perfect Lucilla unites the love of domestic serenity with a passion for helping others, and the main outlet for her aesthetic pleasure in domesticity and for her charitable work is the garden, which she cultivates primarily in order to produce plants to bestow on worthy members of the working class. In this relatively uneventful plot, descriptions of gardens and gardening enliven the narrative, often forming miniature narratives themselves that focus on Lucilla's goodness and the efficacy of her work. This brief summary, although accurate, does not capture another complexity in the novel: the remarkable fact that both Lucilla and Charles have been educated on similar principles, reading widely in "good" literature (i.e., not novels), including Latin. In fact, More implies that Lucilla cultivates the garden so well because she has cultivated her mind, having read Latin with her father every morning since she was nine years old. As a gardener, Mr. Stanley trains the minds of his daughters based on "the genius of the soil"[13] and not rules of gender, even though he is quite aware of the prevailing educational prejudices.

IN SEARCH OF OUR FIRST MOTHER'S GARDENS: EVE AS GARDENER AND PHILANTHROPIST

On first reading, More's approach to Milton appears almost worshipful, but her admiration should not obscure her inventive use of *Paradise Lost* in *Cœlebs* or her emphasis on the redemptive qualities of Eve as a model for women in the fallen world. Even though most of the quotations from *Paradise Lost* focus on Eve in the garden, the extension of the analogy between Eve and Lucilla Stanley suggests that More was also inspired by the ending of the epic in which Eve takes on the role of mother of humankind, proclaiming, "By mee the Promis'd Seed shall all restore."[14] But whereas Milton sees Eve's redemption in terms of her reproductive function, More expands on this power, suggesting instead that her modern Eve finds her strength and makes her contribution in her charitable work. So, even though More frames the novel with allusions to Eve in the garden before the Fall, she rewrites the narrative to allow her a productive as well as reproductive role.

This change is crucial because it uncovers the critique implicit in More's seemingly conventional support of Milton in the opening chapter, where the narrator defends Eve's devotion to "household good"[15] and domestic economy, when in reality More reshapes this notion of good to include charitable works. Ironically, her Eve comes to embody the Angel Michael's injunction to Adam:[16]

> only add
> Deeds to thy knowledge answerable, add Faith,
> Add Virtue, Patience, Temperance, add Love,
> By name to come call'd Charity, the soul
> Of all the rest.[17]

More embodies her Eve in the figure of Lucilla Stanley, who not only avoids the errors of Milton's Eve but fulfills the active Christian life that the Angel Michael imagines for Adam in *Paradise Lost*. Lucilla's functional and creative gardening, furthermore, reclaims a part of the Edenic legacy – "not nice Art / In Beds and curious Knots, but Nature boon."[18] Throughout *Cœlebs*, Lucilla is associated with the Miltonic garden, almost always transformed into useful communal space and work – not the curious knots of the ornamental garden.

As in women's dress, More is suspicious of the merely ornamental in the garden: hence, even garden beauty has a moral purpose of uplifting the gardener to the spiritual life – to the contemplation of God's goodness in creating the plenitude of nature. In supporting poor families, the Stanleys also encourage gardening among them. Lucilla's sister Phoebe explains that "'We have always … a particular satisfaction in observing a neat little flower-garden about a cottage, because it holds out a comfortable indication that the inhabitants are free from absolute want, before they think of these little embellishments'."[19] Presumably, the rationale is that such cottage gardens serve an economic function for the cottagers, but there are also aesthetic or spiritual benefits in being "free from absolute want." Although this passage might strike the modern reader as patronizing, it also reveals Phoebe's concern to preserve these families from crushing poverty.

More prepares the reader for this scene by establishing earlier that Lucilla's passion for gardening is connected to her acts of charity. On inspecting the grounds at Stanley Grove, Charles has discovered that near the "ladies' flower garden" is "a small nursery of fruit trees," not at all stylish or ornamental. It turns out that Lucilla cultivates this nursery so that she can supply those who are less fortunate with trees for their new gardens when they marry:

> She begged this piece of waste ground of her father, and stocked it with a number of fine young fruit trees of the common sort – apples, pears, plums, and smaller fruits. When there is a wedding among the older servants, or when any good girl out of her school marries, she presents their little empty garden with a dozen young apple trees, and a few of the other sorts, never forgetting to embellish their little court with roses and honeysuckles. These last she transplants from the shrubbery, not to fill up the *village-garden*, as it is called, with anything that is of no positive use.

Hence, in addition to running a school for young girls in the village, Lucilla also contributes to the lives of the cottagers. With the help of only a "poor lame man in the village," Lucilla raises a stock through cutting and grafting, all done at her own expense. She transforms a "waste ground" into a useful plot, highlighting the redemptive power of gardening in the fallen world. As several commentators have noted, in addition to Lucilla's own work in the garden, More emphasizes that she actually oversees the whole process, even after the gardens are planted, because part of the role of the charitable lady is surveillance: "She makes … periodic visits of inspection, to see that neatness and order do not degenerate."[20]

Lucilla's surveillance extends to her own activities as well. Mrs. Stanley explains to Charles that Lucilla's pleasure in her flower garden was so great that she began to regard the activity as a guilty indulgence, and even considered giving it up:

> she said that her gardening work so fascinated her, that she found whole hours passed unperceived, and she began to be uneasy by observing that all cares and all duties were suspended while she was disposing beds of carnations, or knots of anemones. Even when she tore herself away, and returned to her employments, her flowers still pursued her, and the improvement of her mind gave way to the cultivation of geraniums.

Instead of urging Lucilla to give up this pursuit, Mrs. Stanley suggests that she hang her watch in the conservatory "to keep her within her prescribed bounds."[21] Emblematic of time and restraint, the watch guides Lucilla's pleasure in the garden. The watch is also a reminder that this Eve gardens in a world dominated by time and loss.[22] In her portrayal of Lucilla as under the control of her passion – "her flowers still pursued her" – More may have been thinking of her own struggle to curb her passion for the garden, which she feared detracted from her spiritual life: "I feel in finishing my garden that I have too much anxiety to make it beautiful; that it occupies too much of my attention, and tends to give worldly thoughts a predominance in my mind."[23]

Lucilla is associated not only with her own gardens, then, but also with the gardens of the poor whom she befriends. A key episode in the development of her relationship with Charles occurs in and around the cottage of a poor woman whom Lucilla and Phoebe attend. Charles comes upon the cottage while on a walk and is struck by the beauty of the roses. Unaware that Lucilla and Phoebe are inside, he decides to enter the wicket and pluck some blossoms for Lucilla; he then goes inside to offer "compensation" for his "theft." Guided by the sound of "a soft-female voice," he ascends the stairs and comes upon an arresting scene of the two young women ministering to an emaciated patient. Charles feels entitled to enter the house because of his superior social standing to "the rank of the inhabitants," a seemingly unexamined assumption in the novel.[24]

In *Cœlebs*, the scene Charles intrudes upon confirms his notions of Lucilla as a charitable benefactor, but the way he frames and re-imagines it adds a deeper dimension to his reading of her charity. Placing her in the context of the needy cottager, Charles describes Lucilla as an Eve-like figure:

Her voice was inexpressibly sweet and penetrating, while faith, hope, and charity seemed to beam from her fine uplifted eyes. On account of the closeness of the room, she had thrown off her hat, cloak, and gloves, and laid them on the bed; and her fine hair, which had escaped from its confinement, shaded that side of her face which was next the door, and prevented her from seeing me.[25]

This passage echoes Milton's description of Eve's luxurious locks, her "wanton ringlets."[26] Charles's narrative perspective is voyeuristic, paradoxically somewhat akin to Satan's longing view of paradise in book 4. But although the passage (and the very action of plucking the rose) is charged with eroticism (even Phoebe's "disheveled hair" and "deep flush"), Charles purifies the image with the Christian virtues of "faith, hope, and charity" that Lucilla also embodies, thus placing eros in the context of caritas.

Furthermore, More appeals to the image of Eve at the end of *Paradise Lost* as the figure who demonstrates faith and hope, those virtues that the Angel Raphael urges on Adam and the future of humankind; in this way More once again places Eve's redemptive role in the forefront. Earlier in the novel Lucilla's mother had told Charles that

"Charity is the calling of a lady; the care of the poor is her profession. Men have little time or taste for details. Women of fortune have abundant leisure, which can in no way be so properly or so pleasantly filled up, as in making themselves intimately acquainted with the worth and the wants of all within their reach."[27]

Through the Stanley women, More deflects emphasis from Eve/woman as erotic object in favor of her as embodiment of the cardinal virtues. Even so, the image of Lucilla as a latter-day Eve with her fine hair escaping its confinement suggests an undercurrent of freedom, or at least the notion that women's "confinement" is more complicated and difficult to maintain.

PRUNING EXCESS: CONSUMPTION AND CULTIVATION

Throughout *Cœlebs*, More uses scenes relating to gardens to frame commentary and discussion about numerous issues, including literature, landscape, and gender. For instance, earlier in the novel the two daughters of Lady Aston, both of whom have benefited from the tutelage of Lucilla and Phoebe, commission a Temple of Friendship to be built in honor of their teachers. When family and friends visit to dedicate the Temple, Charles offers a detailed description of it and the surrounding grounds. But more significantly, the set-piece on the Temple becomes the occasion for an extended discussion among Mr. Stanley, Charles, and others – one of the devices used by More to critique a variety of topics.

In the course of this discussion, Charles reports that he was much disappointed with the society of London because the people and their conversations seemed superficial. A lively meta-conversation ensues on the topic of literature and landscape. Charles's point is that poetry celebrating gardens is only compelling if there is a human interest. While the Abbé de Lille's *Les Jardins* is well written, Charles finds it uninteresting because the garden has no cultivators or inhabitants. In turning to *Paradise Lost*, Charles asserts that "The gardens, even of Paradise, would be dull without the gardeners."[28] More here offers a lightly veiled critique of landscape poetry that merely describes the plants or aesthetic effects rather than focusing on the moral dimension of the garden – what it teaches and inspires in the human mind. Although Erasmus Darwin is unnamed he is the obvious object of discussion, as Sir John Belfield claims that

"We had, indeed, some time ago, so much of this gorgeous scene-painting, so much splendid poetical botany, so many amorous flowers, and so many vegetable courtships; so many wedded plants; roots transformed to nymphs, and dwelling in emerald palaces, that, somehow or other, truth, and probability, and nature, and man, slipt out of the picture, though it must be allowed that genius held the pencil."

More the moralist speaks through Sir John and argues for what she sees as "truth" and "nature" in representation. In contrast to Darwin's fancy in *The Botanic Garden* (1791) (and we have to assume More's opposition to his emphasis on the sexuality of plants), Sir John praises the moral and religious landscape poetry of James Thomson and William Cowper, whose scenery "is perpetually animated with sketches of character, enlivened with portraits from real life, and the exhibition of human manners and passions."[29]

Whereas Thomson and Cowper are master literary moralists in ensuring that description is subservient to moral teaching, More sees women as the moralists of actual gardens. Not only are women's gardens put to good use in *Cœlebs*, but women such as Lucilla understand the workings – and not just the beauty – of nature. For instance, when Charles tells Lucilla that he fears life in the country might be a bit dull in the winter, she responds that a gardener understands the importance of the winter work behind the garden: "'The pleasure is in the preparation … When all appears dead and torpid to you idle spectators, all is secretly at work; nature is busy in preparing her treasures under ground, and art has a hand in the process'."[30] For Lucilla, the beauty of the garden needs to be validated by connecting it to God's work in all creation – otherwise natural beauty becomes just another form of vanity.[31] Lucilla also points to the moral lesson in patience and preparation. But she speaks this part in private conversations with Charles – More reserves the longer and more varied conversation for the men who temporarily occupy the Temple of Friendship. And yet this passage presents a playful inversion of the expected roles, with men (represented by the uninitiated Charles) labeled "idle spectators" and the women gardeners (represented by the experienced Lucilla) as the "professional people," understanding the value of winter. This playfulness not only demonstrates the importance of Lucilla's work, but also shows on this upper-class level that a woman may indeed have more meaningful work to accomplish in terms of the community than mere dilettantes could appreciate.

A central critique that emerges from this conversation is that "overflowing commerce" has introduced "excessive opulence" into the culture, which has "debilitated the mental energies" at the same time that it has promoted art and "mechanic ingenuity." This commerce "has given perfection to our mirrors, our candelabra, our gilding, our inlaying, and our sculpture, but it has communicated a torpor to the imagination, and enervated our intellectual vigour."[32] Through Sir John, More launches a trenchant appraisal of a consumer economy that sounds remarkably like an earlier critique – that of Wordsworth in the 1800 Preface to *Lyrical Ballads*. Wordsworth sees the mind blunted by "gross and violent stimulants" as reduced "to a state of almost savage torpor."[33] Like Wordsworth, More prefers a kind of natural austerity and simplicity – in poetry as in gardening. Throughout *Cœlebs*, there is a preference for gardens that reveal not "excessive opulence" but well-organized usefulness for the public good.[34]

More questions the easy commerce among aesthetics, economics, and sexual possession expressed by Addison: a "Man of Polite Imagination ... feels a greater Satisfaction in the Prospect of Fields and Meadows, than another does in the Possession. It gives him, indeed, a kind of Property in every thing he sees, and makes the most rude uncultivated parts of Nature administer to his Pleasures."[35] Furthermore, More rejects the association of women with a nature that is to be dominated: Lucilla, although she excites chaste passion in Charles, is not objectified – and her gardens are not valued as property or possession. In fact, Lucilla's goal of giving her produce away subversively denies the patriarchal model of landscape as possession.

More has prepared for these discussions of excess by her running commentary on and criticism of "accomplishments" in women, which she sees as a "superfluity of enterprise" without the guiding hand of reason – the "shreds and patches of useless arts."[36] As if to parallel the gilded interiors of upper-class homes, mere accomplishments, as discussed earlier in Chapter 3, turn women into commercial objects. Like Wollstonecraft and other feminists of the period, More is wary of these accomplishments and uses a true knowledge of nature and the garden as an antidote to this superfluous enterprise that smothers the imagination of women.[37] As Anne Mellor has argued, "In an era of greatly expanding imperialism and consumption, she *moralized* both capitalism and consumption."[38]

In contrast to the excesses of consumption, the garden represents for More a well-regulated economy, which has nothing to do with financial gain or wasteful spending. As Mr. Stanley proclaims, "I will venture to pronounce, that not all the anxious cutting out of pleasure, not all the costly indulgences which wealth can procure, not all the contrivances of inventive man for his darling youthful offspring, can find out an amusement so pure, so natural, so rational, so healthful, I had almost said so religious, as that unbought pleasure connected with a garden." More's theory of economy is based on the well-tended garden, judiciously but not overly pruned, and she brings into dinner conversation at Stanley Grove examples of women who managed the domestic economy poorly, using garden analogies. Mr. Stanley, for example, uses the language of pruning to argue that "The true economist will draw in by contracting the outline, by narrowing the bottom, by cutting off with an unsparing hand costly superfluities, which affect not comfort but cherish vanity." In *Cœlebs*, excess is justified only when it is divine, as Mr. Stanley explains regarding the existence of flowers: "These flowers are of so little apparent use, that it might be thought profuseness in any economy short of that which is divine, to gratify us at once with such forms, and such hues, and such fragrance."[39]

IMPROVEMENT AND IMPROVERS

Related to horticultural economy is the proper attitude toward landscape improvement. Readers of *Mansfield Park* will recall the scene in which the characters discuss proposed "improvements" to the Rushworth estate, Sotherton. Mr. Rushworth imagines that a landscaper such as Humphry Repton – "or anybody of that sort" – would be sure to do away with the avenue of trees at Sotherton in order to improve the prospect. In response to Rushworth's cavalier attitude toward the destruction of ancient trees, Fanny Price responds, " 'Cut down an avenue! What a pity! Does not it make you think of Cowper? "Ye fallen avenues, once more I mourn your fate unmerited" '."[40] Several Austen scholars, most notably Alistair Duckworth in *The Improvement of the Estate*, have identified Austen's ambivalence about improvement, especially if it leans toward "innovation" and a "radical attitude to a cultural heritage."[41] Such readers have seen lines of Burkean influence in Austen's narratives, and of course many others mention Austen's love of Cowper, especially of *The Task*, where Cowper criticizes the depredations of landscape improvers.[42]

Raymond Williams points out about the word "improvement" that while the more general usage of improving oneself or "making something better" became the norm, it still maintained its "underlying connection" to making a "monetary profit, where it was often equivalent to *invest*, and especially to operations on or connected with the land, often the enclosing of common or waste land." When applied to landscape, "improvement" also takes on class connotations. Austen is of course aware of the complexities of the word. Williams quotes her comment about the landowning Musgrove family in *Persuasion* that they were "in a state of alteration, perhaps of improvement."[43]

While Austen expresses reservations about improvement, she complicates the issue of landscape by focusing her narrative on the more general notion of an individual's development or cultivation. As Duckworth has argued, improvement becomes the major trope of *Mansfield Park*. One's attitude toward unthinking changes to the landscape – tearing down ancient avenues of trees for the benefit of the prospect – becomes, as it were, a mark of one's mental culture and cultivation. When Austen incorporated these debates into her novels, she did so with full awareness that the term represented contested values.

Likewise, improvement is a major theme in *Cœlebs* and the key to the way Charles's initial sense of Maple Grove develops.[44] It is no coincidence, in fact, that More calls the Stanleys' estate Maple Grove, the name itself evoking the association of the Stanleys with pastoral calm. But even more telling is the fact that Charles identifies the grounds as largely untouched by modern revisions:

> The park, though it was not very extensive, was striking from the beautiful inequality of the ground, which was richly clothed with the most picturesque oaks I ever saw, interspersed with stately beeches. The grounds were laid out in good taste; but though the hand of modern improvement was visible, the owner had in one instance spared
>
> The obsolete prolixity of shade,
>
> for which the most interesting of poets so pathetically pleads. The poet's pleas had saved the avenue.[45]

Unlike Austen's boorish Mr. Rushworth, Mr. Stanley is an improver, but a respectful one. Like Austen, More defends her respect for landscape by referring to one of her favorite poets, Cowper. In fact, a later discussion in *Cœlebs* on the meaning of improvement takes place in the context of Cowper and literary style. According to Sir John Belfield, one of Mr. Stanley's guests, Cowper's followers need to bear in mind that "deviation is not always improvement; that whoever wants to be better than nature, will infallibly be worse; that truth in taste is as obvious as in morals, and as certain as in mathematics."[46]

In honor of her gardening, Mr. Stanley refers to Lucilla as a "little Repton of the valley,"[47] but her gardening is an act of redemption rather than improvement. She redeems, we recall, a bit of waste ground from its uselessness for the benefit of others. Finally, in fact, More justifies Lucilla's pleasure in gardening because it is an activity linked to moral reform as well as spiritual redemption, related to what Carole Fabricant has termed "the myth of restoration": "The very act of shaping and cultivating a garden, of course, inevitably evoked associations with man's paradisal existence and his first occupation on earth. Religious and mythic sanctions were thus readily available to elevate the role of landscape designer and to suggest that he was capable not only of improvement but of redemption as well."[48] What distinguishes More from the designers that Fabricant identifies in the Augustan period is that she places her Eve in the center of the garden as the *agent* of redemption. More does not focus on the glorified (male) landscape designer who feminizes the landscape as his pliant Eve.

A final scene in *Cœlebs* brings the theme of improvement as redemption together with More's other preoccupation with Christian charity.

Sir John and Lady Belfield, who plan to build a conservatory on their estate, Beechwood, in Surrey, have been guests of the Stanleys for six weeks and have absorbed the Stanley ethos: they have determined to devote themselves more fully to evangelical religion, to forgo "the world" except for a brief stay in London, and to use their riches in a more charitable way. Because of this determination, Lady Belfield begins to have doubts about her desire to have a conservatory attached to their house. She talks instead of building a charity school to educate their less fortunate neighbors. Her husband, though, proposes that "we will adopt Lucilla's idea of combining charity with an indulgence – we will associate the charity-school with the conservatory. This union will be a kind of monument to our friends at the Grove, from whom you have acquired the love of plants, and I of religious charity."[49]

Mr. Stanley approves Lucilla's plan and of course offers a mini-sermon in explanation. While he sees "expensive gardens" and conservatories as "infatuations of opulence" for people who live elsewhere for most of the year, when the estate is truly the home such expense is justified: "And where a garden and greenhouse are to supply to the proprietor the place of the abdicated theatre and ballroom, and especially when it is to be a means in her hands of attaching her children to the country, and of teaching them to love home, I declare myself in favour of the conservatory."[50] Typical of the values of *Cœlebs*, he sets the world of London and fashion against what he sees as the purer pursuits of the country. In this context, a conservatory passes muster as a way to connect the family with home and to enhance the education and piety of the surrounding community.

More seems to be playing on the double meaning of a conservatory as a building to nurture plants and protect them from harsh weather and also as a place where students are educated. The Stanleys and the Belfields can thus happily erase any differences between the indulgence of a hothouse and the founding of a charity school. Both are regarded as acceptable forms of improvement linked to home, nurturing, and cultivation of virtue (in direct contrast to the hothouse in *Northanger Abbey*, where General Tilney "forces" exotic fruit trees to bloom).

More's gendered treatment of gardening in *Cœlebs* confirms the assumption that women were more associated with flower and kitchen gardens, as well as conservatories, than with landscape parks. As Tom Williamson states in *Polite Landscapes* (and as we have seen throughout our study), "At this social level [the elite], women had been active gardeners for centuries – William Lawson's *Country Housewife's Garden* of 1617 was addressing an established audience. But the evidence suggests that as the park grew in importance in the course of the eighteenth century the garden, and especially the flower garden, was increasingly viewed as a female space."[51] In her essay reclaiming that space in garden history for women, Susan Groag Bell argues, too, that gardens are gendered, that men are associated with the monumentalism of the landscape park and women with the commonplace of the flower garden. The contrast between the monumental and the commonplace is useful, but does not absolutely hold. More demonstrates in *Cœlebs* that women can also re-imagine the monumental space, such as the Temple of Friendship, "carved with the initials of Lucilla and Phoebe" that the Miss Astons construct. This temple serves as the sisters' version of the temples at Stourhead, but instead of the tribute to male heroism and classical virtue, the Aston girls have immortalized their affection for their young mentors, Lucilla and Phoebe Stanley. In place of classical grandeur, readers find a "pretty temple" and "little rustic window," the diminutives feminizing the monument as the appropriate place for girls.[52]

This form of monumentalism, the female-centered "temple," actually fits well into More's idea of the garden and its functions, for her monument makes public the commitment to charitable works and usefulness over ornamentation: in this case, the good work that Lucilla and Phoebe have done for the Aston girls. This particular monument pays tribute in an unassuming way, also in line with the emphasis on simplicity and lack of pretension in human relationships. Placed in the garden, the temple helps to define the space as appropriate for nurturing both women and their flowers, and it is an apt emblem for More's gendered garden in *Cœlebs* as well as for her re-imagination of what gardens mean for middle- and upper-class Christian women in the early nineteenth century. More uses the garden to place these women in their proper sphere: not a secluded domestic space but a working, productive, and sustaining plot of ground.

FANNY PRICE'S POTTED PLANTS

No such monuments appear in *Mansfield Park*, but Austen nonetheless takes up a garden theme that she had begun in her juvenilia. Margaret Anne Doody has connected the manuscript notebooks in which such early works as *Catharine, or The Bower* (1792) were written and the mature novels from 1809–11, the last date being the year that she began *Mansfield Park*. Doody follows Deirdre Le Faye in theorizing that Austen "rediscovered her earlier manuscript notebooks when she unpacked the family belongings at Chawton in July 1809."[53] We will argue that there are further thematic and narrative connections between *Catharine* and *Mansfield Park*, specifically regarding the topic of gardens and the response of Kitty and Fanny Price to the need for such private, restorative spaces. For young Catharine, or Kitty, her bower in the garden has strength-giving qualities despite her great-aunt's claim that it is dangerous and unhealthy. Similar issues arise in *Mansfield Park*, a novel in which several gardens and garden-like enclosures appear, although it takes an imaginative leap to see Fanny Price as the inheritor of Catharine's bower.[54]

Austen also seems to have been thinking of *Cœlebs* when she added an allusion to More in a revision of *Catharine* after her move to Chawton: she has Aunt Percival chide Kitty, after discovering her in the bower with Edward Stanley, by remonstrating, "I bought you Blair's Sermons, and Coelebs in Search of a Wife, I gave you the key to my own Library, and borrowed a great many good books of my Neighbors for you, all to this purpose."[55] Rather than question Kitty about her actions, Aunt Percival imagines the worst and moralizes about Kitty's downfall. After having read *Cœlebs*, it seems, Austen recognized something of More in the extreme didacticism of Kitty's aunt. Austen, furthermore, had great fun at More's expense. In a letter to Cassandra, she reacts to being corrected about her reference to "Caleb": "I am not ashamed about the name of the Novel, having been guilty of no insult toward your handwriting; the Diphthong I always saw, but knowing how fond you were of adding a vowel wherever you could, I attributed it to that alone – & the knowledge of the truth does the book no service; – the only merit it could have, was the name of Caleb, which has an honest, unpretending sound; but in Coelebs, there is pedantry & affectation. – Is it written only to Classical Scholars?"[56]

Austen shifts the focus in *Mansfield Park* from More's attention to the intersection of private and public in the garden to the garden as a purely private place where consciousness is nurtured. As Mary Waldron persuasively argues, Austen's fiction counters the overt didacticism of a writer such as More: "*Mansfield Park* aims to counteract an increasing tendency for fiction to sermonize through ideal object-lessons." Furthermore, "Mansfield Park is a version of More's Stanley Grove, brought into the real world and mercilessly exposed."[57] In revealing what she regarded as the shallowness of such fictional sermonizing and certitude, Austen also rewrites the evangelical garden of *Cœlebs*. Austen's garden is not the site in which her female characters find their social usefulness or the author comments on proper behavior; in other words, it is not a testing ground for conduct and philanthropy. Instead it is often a space of introspection and personal growth for her female characters – paradoxically a more spiritual dimension than the evangelical More captures in her overtly didactic novel. In Austen, then, unlike More, the garden is tied not so much to acceptable philanthropy as it is to private restoration and the kind of introspection that makes a developed consciousness possible.

Austen rewrites More's story primarily from the point of view of the outsider, Fanny Price. Although *Cœlebs* is narrated by Charles, the focus is on Lucilla, the privileged oldest daughter of the Stanley family who has access to the land and directs its cultivation. In making Fanny the poor relation who lives at Mansfield Park in a precarious position, Austen complicates the way in which she imagines garden space. Like her precursor, Kitty, who lived as an orphan with her aunt and built her bower with her two female friends in her aunt's garden, Fanny must construct her own place within the larger estate. She does not have her own bower in the garden or a plot of ground or an assistant to help her cultivate her plants, but she does nonetheless tend a garden in the place she appropriates, the place that no one else in the family seems to want: the East room. Without direct access to the land, then, Fanny brings the garden into her indoor bower.

THE BOWER

There is precedent in Austen (and also in other women writers, as we have seen) for connecting indoor and outdoor space. In *Catharine*, composed in 1792 but revised shortly after the move to Chawton, Austen not only suggests that the outdoor bower has the power to heal Kitty when she is disturbed, but also draws a connection between the bower in the garden and Kitty's bedroom. Clara Tuite, in analyzing the sexual and transgressive qualities of the bower, has noted the connection between outer and inner sanctums, claiming that "an early nineteenth-century lexical shift from bower to bedroom is not a new development but a reversion to an originally Anglo-Saxon meaning of inner chamber, recess, retreat or sanctum."[58] Hence, when the narrator notes that Kitty went to her bower in the garden out of habit instead of her bedroom, she draws a connection between the traditional functions of the two spaces:

To this Bower, which terminated a very pleasant and retired walk in her Aunt's Garden, she always wandered whenever anything disturbed her, and it possessed such a charm over her senses, as constantly to tranquillize her mind and quiet her spirits – Solitude and reflection might perhaps have had the same effect in her Bed Chamber, yet Habit had so strengthened the idea which Fancy had first suggested, that such a thought never occurred to Kitty who was firmly persuaded that her Bower alone could restore her to herself.[59]

The narrator imagines both the bedchamber and the bower as a feminine space associated with tranquility and renewal – for Catharine, the place where she is most herself and not some false representation that she reveals to the world.

Although connected, then, to a long tradition, the association of bedroom and bower gains additional meaning in this period because of the newer configurations of indoor and outdoor space. Eighteenth- and early-nineteenth-century gardening theory drew a connection between the arrangement of a garden into discrete areas – later what came to be called "rooms" – and the arrangement of indoor space. Mark Laird sees this social mirroring of indoor and outdoor space as a significant development, as he refers to the "interesting correlation between the circuit arrangement of Georgian interiors – saloon, library, drawing room, dining room used for diverse simultaneous activities – and the circuit arrangement of the grounds."[60] Contemporary garden writers also recognized such divisions: for instance, in *The Garden Vade Mecum* (1790), John Abercrombie refers often to the division of the flower garden into various "compartments" and writes in terms of "boundary districts" that reflect the various areas of the house.[61]

In his *Observations on the Theory and Practice of Landscape Gardening* (1803), Humphry Repton describes the different outdoor spaces at Bulstrode as if they make up the various rooms of a large structure: "the leisure-ground is perfect as a whole, while its several parts may furnish models of the following different characters of taste in gardening: the ancient garden, the American garden, the modern terrace-walks, and the flower-garden." Repton's aesthetic connected the individual parts of the garden, devoted to different traditions, styles, and plantings, to the grand scale of the whole. He goes on to describe the more naturalistic relationship of the "flower-garden" and the "natural landscape" at Nuneham, and makes a particularly interesting comment about the estate Valley Field:

where the flower-garden is in front of a long wall, the attempt to make the scene natural would be affected; and, therefore, as two great sources of interest in a place are variety and contrast, the only means by which these can be introduced are in this flower-garden, which, as a separate object, becomes a sort of episode to the general and magnificent scenery.

No longer just a room, the flower garden is now an "episode" that introduces the larger story. As such, the flower garden displays the variety that the grand, uniform scene avoids. Repton also writes that "A flower-garden should be an object detached and distinct from the general scenery of the

Fig. 7.1. "Flower-Garden, Valley Field," illustration in Humphry Repton, *Observations on the Theory and Practice of Landscape Gardening*, facing p. 102.

place" and that it should be protected and enclosed, as is the garden at Valley Field (Fig. 7.1).[62]

This enclosure and privacy become the focus of *Catharine, or The Bower*. In her opposition to the bower, Kitty's Aunt Percival distrusts the privacy of the space and its effect on Kitty. Aunt Percival constantly threatens to have the bower torn down, although she never carries out this action. Ridiculously, she associates the bower with catching colds and toothaches, as well as with unhealthy independence on the part of a young girl. Furthermore, she distrusts Kitty's reading in the bower, another act of independent thought and action, as discussed in Chapter 1. In a typical scene, "the Bower began to have its usual influence over her Spirits, she contributed towards settling them, by taking out a book, for she always had one about her, and reading."[63]

Austen attributes so much importance to the bower that she includes it in the title of the work, the apposition seeming to suggest that the structure itself is on a par with Catharine in importance. The narrator also lets us know why Catharine originally became so attached to the structure: because she had built it with the help of two dear friends, the Wynne sisters, who lost their parents and were forced to leave their comfortable home life for, on the one hand, an arranged marriage in the East Indies and, on the other, exile in Scotland as a dependent on another family member. The bower therefore represents a happier time when the Wynne family was intact and Catharine enjoyed the intimacy of these female friends. Although, as Tuite argues, Aunt Percival feared this intimacy as well as the sexual overtones of a young man's visit to the bower, the narrator and Kitty see the bower as a place of healing and rejuvenation.

FANNY'S NEST OF COMFORTS

Given that Kitty is lively and enthusiastic, we might not immediately link her with the more subdued Fanny Price. Indeed, she is more often connected to the naïve and overly imaginative Catherine Morland of *Northanger Abbey*. But we will argue that Fanny's creation of a bower-like space in the East room connects her to Catharine, the heroine whom Austen had recently rediscovered as she began work on *Mansfield Park*. The East room functions as Fanny's retreat, her secluded indoor garden space in Mansfield Park, the only place where Fanny feels completely safe. Recalling Catharine's faith in her bower's restorative powers, Fanny repeatedly returns to the East room to "try its influence on an agitated, doubting spirit."[64]

It might seem eccentric to read the East room, high up in Mansfield Park, as a garden, but if we keep in mind Hunt's definition of gardens as "concentrated or perfected forms of place-making"[65] there are some strong connections. In some ways, Fanny's small grouping of potted plants, a miniature garden, fulfills Hunt's definition quite well: concentrated, bounded, and enclosed. Fanny does not have access to her own outdoor space, so the East room becomes a substitute garden, which she fills with potted plants. In *Flora Domestica*, Elizabeth Kent's poetry-laced book on growing potted plants, Kent assumes that people who live in town may have to rely on potted plants for their gardens: "A lover of flowers, who cannot have a garden or a greenhouse, will gladly cherish any thing that has the aspect of a green leaf."[66] Fanny may not live in a cramped urban space but her circumstances are as constrained as someone who does, and her desire to nurture potted plants fits the category of cherishing "any thing that has the aspect of a green leaf." For Kent, writing less than a decade after the publication of *Mansfield Park*, the portable flower garden makes a good substitute garden for those without access to land.

Not only does the narrator repeat several times that Fanny likes to "visit" her plants, but the reader also learns that Fanny grows geraniums (more accurately pelargoniums), a variety that gained great popularity in the 1790s and into the new century. Furthermore, Fanny clearly connects horticulture

Fig. 7.2. *Geranium fothergillum*, illustration in Henry Charles Adams, *Geraniums*.

with the culture of her mind and mental restoration. At one point when she retreats to the East room, she hopes that "by giving air to her geraniums she might inhale a breeze of mental strength herself."[67] Why geraniums? They had by Austen's time become one of the many widely grown exotics in English gardens, although they needed extra care in the colder climate. They were also popularly represented, as Fig. 7.2 from Henry Charles Adams's *Geraniums* (1805) exemplifies. Mary Russell Mitford, Austen's contemporary and, as we have seen, an avid gardener, writes to a friend that she does not fear for her "double row of rich geraniums" because "Mrs. Reeve has promised to house them for me during the winter."[68] With its morning sun in cold weather, the East room functions as a kind of greenhouse for Fanny, but also in warmer weather it becomes an open-air garden that benefits from the breeze. Austen suggests a connection between Fanny and her need for careful cultivation and this botanical transplant from warmer regions.

Furthermore, as window gardens became more popular in the nineteenth century, they also became the subject of garden and health writing. As early as 1815, Charlotte Smith has her character Mrs. Talbot teach her children the value of growing plants: even "the humblest inhabitant of a garret has a few springs of mint or angelica ... in his wretched abode" for spiritual and physical health.[69] Jane Loudon advises her readers to "have a few plants in pots in the east window": "Two rather tall and spreading geraniums" will be a perfect substitute for someone planning but not yet able to realize an outdoor garden.[70] Although Loudon notes that rooms with plants require more ventilation than usual, Elizabeth Twining, in "A Few Words about Window-Gardens," also explains that plants "help to purify the air" and are thus beneficial to the health of residents. Twining is especially eager to demonstrate that potted plants are invigorating to the working people of London living in cramped and poorly ventilated conditions. In the second part of her essay she invents a story demonstrating that window gardening promotes family life, cleanliness, and Christian piety. In a factory town, a working-class family cultivates their window garden, which extends out from the home to the small, modest flower border below the window and inspires their neighbors to improve their lives through gardening. When the landlord comes to inspect his property, he finds, instead of the usual dirty and dreary space, "A few scarlet geraniums in pots at the windows, a sweet scent of mignonette from the border under the parlour window, which was bright and clear and wide open."[71] Although the countryside that Fanny inhabits is rarefied in comparison, her window garden serves an analogous function in promoting physical and spiritual health.

Without access to a private space outside, Fanny makes the East room serve as her garden, the place where she is most at home in Mansfield Park. Austen specifically describes this room as if it were a protected outdoor refuge:

The aspect was so favourable, that even without a fire it was habitable in many an early spring, and late autumn morning, to such a willing mind as Fanny's, and while there was a gleam of sunshine, she hoped not to be driven from it entirely, even when winter came. The comfort of it in her hours of leisure was extreme. She could go there after any thing unpleasant below, and find immediate consolation in some pursuit, or some train of thought at hand. – Her plants, her books – of which she had been a collector, from the first hour of her commanding a shilling – her writing desk, and her works of charity and ingenuity, were all within her reach; – or if indisposed for employment, if nothing but musing would do, she could scarcely see an object in that room which had not an interesting remembrance connected with it.[72]

Without a fire (Mrs. Norris's orders), the East room actually functions as an outdoor bower, dependent on the weather. Furthermore, although it is primarily associated with meditation and renewal, it is also the place where Fanny engages in "works of charity and ingenuity" – a more meditative version of Lucilla Stanley's plan to cultivate plants and fruit trees for charity. But whereas Mr. Stanley grants Lucilla the ground to cultivate, Fanny is forced through her tenuous position in the family into a more imaginative creation of a safe haven, a home within the larger structures of Mansfield Park. Instead of a plot of ground she has her potted geraniums, which she airs and nurtures in the breeze of the open window. Her unspecified works of charity do not seem associated with the plants, but her mental health does.

Arguing that Austen's mature work was transformed by her reading of the canonical Romantic poets, William Deresiewicz develops the connection between memory in the East room and in "Tintern Abbey." The connection arises because a view of this ruin is represented in one of the three "transparencies" left on the windows of the East room, "where Tintern Abbey held its station between a cave in Italy, and a moonlight lake in Cumberland."[73] The subjects of all three transparencies feed Fanny's imagination – her respect for British tradition, her desire for cave-like seclusion, and her attraction to nature. These images emphasize that the East room is associated both with Fanny's dreams and also with her quest for mental composure. It is the place where Fanny brings the world to herself, in miniature – pictures from others' travels and even her geraniums, which originated in South Africa. As we have seen in earlier chapters, Bachelard conceptualizes the miniature as "a narrow gate [that] opens up an entire world."[74] Referring to miniature gardens, John Mack theorizes that "carefully cultivated spaces are sometimes conceived as small worlds in their own right."[75] Through the portal of the East room and through her reading, Fanny imagines this world. When Edmund visits her room, he notices what she is reading: not novels, like so many of her fictional predecessors, but Lord Macartney's book on China, Crabbe's *Tales*, and the *Idler*. While the first reference links Fanny to adventurous travel in her imaginative life, the latter two refer to two authors admired by Austen herself: George Crabbe and Dr. Johnson.

A closer look at Bachelard's analysis of nests elucidates the connection, noted by several critics, between Fanny's "nest of comforts" and Bachelard's theory:[76]

> If we go deeper into daydreams of nests, we soon encounter a sort of paradox of sensibility. A nest – and this we *understand* right away – is a precarious thing, and yet it sets us *to daydreaming of security*. Why does this obvious precariousness not arrest daydreams of this kind? The answer to this paradox is simple: when we dream, we are phenomenologists without realizing it. In a sort of naïve way, we relive the instinct of the bird, taking pleasure in accentuating the mimetic features of the green nest in green leaves ... The nest is a lyrical bouquet of leaves. It participates in the peace of the vegetable world.[77]

Bachelard's association of the nest with the green world further supports our understanding of the East room as Fanny's garden bower. It also suggests the precariousness of Fanny's existence at Mansfield Park, because as comforting as her nest could be, it is also subject to invasion and danger when others intrude upon her. Although Edmund is always welcome, other visitors are more troubling or ambiguous. For instance, when Mary Crawford visits the East room, she compromises Fanny's beliefs with her requests – first for Fanny to practice *Lover's Vows* with her and then when she forces Henry's necklace on her. Most dangerous to Fanny's peace and health, though, is the visit from Sir Thomas when he attempts to persuade Fanny to marry Henry Crawford. These incursions into Fanny's bower are akin to Aunt Percival's threats to tear the bower down in *Catharine*, but they are more menacing.

As if in tacit recognition that his visit has deprived Fanny of her retreat, Sir Thomas recommends that she take a walk in the shrubbery "to reason [herself] into a stronger frame of mind."[78] The restorative powers of the shrubbery (a plantation of trees and shrubs near the house) are well documented in *Emma*, in a fine piece of narration which sets the scene for Mr. Knightley's proposal: "Never had the exquisite sight, smell, sensation of nature, tranquil, warm, and brilliant after a storm, been more attractive to her. She longed for the serenity they might gradually introduce ... she lost no time hurrying into the shrubbery."[79] The narrator does not give us such a poetic glimpse of Fanny hurrying into the shrubbery, but we do learn that she has done so when Aunt Norris begins to complain about her absence. Although Sir Thomas comes to her defense by admitting that he himself recommended the walk, Aunt Norris persists with the argument that Fanny "does not like to be dictated to; she takes her own independent walk whenever she can; she certainly has a little spirit of secrecy, and independence, and nonsense, about her, which I would advise her to get the better of."[80] This scene serves to show once again that Fanny cannot find the habitual comfort of the East room in the garden as long as a guardian such as Mrs. Norris, like Aunt Percival in *Catharine*, attempts to regulate and circumvent her privacy – which to the eyes of Mrs. Norris looks like perverse secrecy.

When Fanny is banished to her former home in Portsmouth, she feels even more acutely the loss of her privacy and her space for renewal: "The smallness of the rooms above and below indeed, and the narrowness of the passage and staircase, struck her beyond her imagination." Here smallness does not open up a world in miniature, but instead the noise and dirtiness combine with enclosed spaces to suffocate and stifle. Even so, she tries to replicate the East room with her sister Susan, going so far as to choose books from the circulating library so as to "inspire a taste for the biography and poetry which she delighted in herself." But despite the pleasure that Fanny takes in this newly found intimacy with her sister, there is no place for restoration at Portsmouth, even in the spring. In fact, Fanny realizes the delight she had taken in that season at Mansfield Park, when for the first time in years she cannot experience it:

What animation both of body and mind, she had derived from watching the advance of that season which cannot, in spite of its capriciousness, be unlovely, and seeing its increasing beauties, from the earliest flowers, in the warmest divisions of her aunt's garden, to the opening of leaves of her uncle's plantations, and the glory of his woods. – To be losing such pleasures was no trifle; to be losing them, because she was in the midst of closeness and noise, to have confinement, bad air, bad smells, substituted for liberty, freshness, fragrance, and verdure, was infinitely worse.

In the memory of spring, Fanny imaginatively possesses the outdoor spaces of Mansfield Park, demarcated by gendered "ownership" – Lady Bertram's flower garden and Sir Thomas's plantations and woods. Her memory also seems to have deepened her feeling for nature beyond her rather lame panegyric to the evergreens in Mrs. Grant's shrubbery: "How beautiful, how welcome, how wonderful the evergreen!"[81] In the narrator's construction of the idyll of rural England, Fanny associates Mansfield not only with health but with the liberty of the country – an idealized reconstruction of her own experience without the intervention of Mrs. Norris or the pressure of Sir Thomas.

FANNY IN THE ROSE GARDEN

Although critical emphasis has been on the larger landscapes of Mansfield Park and Sotherton, several scenes that involve the East room and other less grand spaces reveal Fanny's inner life and her status in the Bertram family.

Austen introduces the reader to the history and details of the East room after two important outdoor scenes have taken place. The first of these occurs during the day trip to Sotherton, where Austen allegorizes and prefigures the transgressions of Maria Bertram and Henry Crawford as they escape into the vast park; on this same expedition Austen establishes Fanny's disapproval of the kind of improvement that would lead to the destruction of an ancient avenue of trees.[82] Before this revealing day trip, an important but often neglected episode takes place in the rose garden at Mansfield Park. Whereas the scene at Sotherton introduces proper and improper responses to the patriarchal landscape, the rose garden suggests a different issue. In keeping with the tradition of flower gardens being associated with ladies, the rose garden at Mansfield is Lady Bertram's domain. But given that she is a habitué of the sofa, we can expect no active role in gardening from her – in More's terms, Lady Bertram would be the target of severe criticism in that she "owns" a purely ornamental garden in which she does no work herself.

In *Mansfield Park*, we actually get no direct presentation of the garden, but we learn what happened through a scene in the drawing room. One evening Edmund and Julia Bertram return after dining at the parsonage to find Fanny on the sofa rather than working at the table on her sewing or the "poor basket." In an extended dialogue that follows, we learn that Fanny had cut roses for an hour in the heat of the day at the bidding of her Aunt Norris, who found refuge with Lady Bertram in the shade of the "alcove." Not only did Fanny gather the roses, but she also made two trips on foot to her aunt's house in order to deliver them. In developed paragraphs of indirect narrative discourse, we learn what both Edmund and Fanny think after this event: Edmund is incensed that Fanny would be treated in this way and angry with himself for neglecting her as he pursued Mary Crawford. Fanny, in turn, has been "struggling against discontent and envy."[83]

The flower garden, which should be a refuge for the women in the family, becomes another site that represents Fanny's second-class status. In a novel that alludes uncomfortably to slave labor in Antigua, the rose garden scene reinforces Fanny's dependency on Sir Thomas and his family. This passage also highlights the dark side of ornamental gardens on huge estates – they are dependent on the intense labor of those who are barred from the deeper enjoyments and renewal of the garden.[84] Unlike Lady Bertram, Fanny has no claim to the land or to the leisurely enjoyment of it. Mrs. Norris's desire for the luxury of the roses is dependent on Fanny, whose enforced labor in the garden in the heat of the day literally makes her sick. With her delicate constitution, she must retreat to her attic bedroom and the East room in order to regain her strength and equilibrium. We generally agree with

John Wiltshire's assessment of Fanny's illness as psychosomatic, linked to her powerless status in the family,[85] although in this case the hot sun does play a role.

Austen also implies recognition of the underside of ornamental gardening, as had been clear in *Northanger Abbey*, particularly in regard to General Tilney's quest for exotic fruits. The General is not a gardener himself but he takes a commanding interest in the elaborate kitchen garden on his estate. In an attempt to impress Catherine Morland, whom the General mistakenly thinks a potential heiress, he personally takes her for a tour of his kitchen estates on her first morning at the Abbey. After a long paragraph in which the General questions Catherine about her presumed guardian's hothouses, Austen presents the scene through Catherine's point of view:

> The walls seemed countless in number, endless in length; a village of hot-houses seemed to arise among them, and a whole parish to be at work within the inclosure. The General was flattered by her looks of surprize, which told him almost as plainly, as he soon forced her to tell him in words, that she had never seen any gardens at all equal to them before.[86]

Tyrannical in his relationship to his children, the General also lords it over his workers in the hothouses, although he does not seem to dirty his own hands. He is a veritable Kubla Khan, with his hordes of workers, his enclosures, a village of hothouses magically rising up within the walls. He extracts Catherine's response to gratify his vanity, and then goes on in false modesty to explain that "The pinery had yielded only one hundred in the last year," which he knows would be an extraordinary number of pineapples. Although there is no such condemnation of the rose garden in *Mansfield Park*, Austen does reveal its limitations for an outsider such as Fanny – it becomes a place of oppressive labor rather than renewal, illness rather than health.

CONCLUSION

One of the paradoxes of the ending of *Mansfield Park* is that Fanny Price, in being absorbed more fully into the family when she returns from Portsmouth and of course following her marriage to Edmund, loses the East room as her beloved private space, the place where Austen's narrative technique has allowed us to see her mental struggles and, at times, her renewal. We might be tempted to say that this room, associated with the east, with morning sunlight and warmth, is the place of her youth, which she must leave in assuming her new role in the family. But we get no real assurance that Fanny will find a way to duplicate this green world of nest and bower in the safety of marrying Edmund. Whereas in More's evangelical tale Lucilla will continue to work in the garden of her married home, as she had in her parental home, Fanny in gaining the park loses her secret refuge.

In entering the inner circle Fanny will perhaps no longer suffer the mental turmoil and threats to her health associated with powerlessness. But will she sacrifice the introspection and growth associated with her bower when she becomes Mrs. Edmund Bertram? Austen leaves that question open. One might argue that Fanny will have her own gardens now, so she does not need the East room – there is certainly some truth to that point. She will also be able to preserve the most important function of the East room garden: finding a nurturing and comfortable place within the larger world by making a home.

Both of Fanny's future homes, Thornton Lacey and the Mansfield Parsonage, will have respectable gardens. In fact, the question of Thornton Lacey arises when Henry Crawford announces, after a visiting, that he has a plan for its "improvement." But Edmund rejects Henry's grand proposal: "'And I have two or three ideas also … and one of them is that very little of your plan for Thornton Lacey will ever be put into practice. I must be satisfied with rather less ornament and beauty'."[87] Even so, Edmund agrees that the farmyard must be removed from the front and replaced with a garden. So, at the end of the novel we know that when Fanny marries Edmund and moves to Thornton Lacey she will have access to her own garden, as of course she will when they move yet again to Mansfield Parsonage. But what she will make of them remains a mystery.

Austen's idea of a garden, then, is finally related to the potential for a character like Fanny to cultivate herself and to live most fully in her private life. Unlike More, she does not determine that the garden is best served for philanthropic purposes – a kind of staging-ground for charitable acts and piety. Instead, Austen leaves open the possibility that characters such as Fanny, as well as Emma Woodhouse and Anne Elliot, will discover in the garden, in the shrubbery, or in an extensive walk in nature a depth of feeling and knowledge that they would otherwise not have experienced. Whereas Austen explores, then, a more complex psychological terrain in her gardens, More demonstrates a more nuanced negotiation of the relationship between private life and the larger world.

CHAPTER 8

Margaret Oliphant's Chronicles of Carlingford and the meaning of Victorian gardens

Recent readers of Margaret Oliphant's series of stories and novels, the Chronicles of Carlingford,[1] have noted that material objects and human actions represented in her fiction often function as powerful signifiers of the norms of class and gender in mid-Victorian society.[2] Oliphant observes and critiques the culture in minute detail, noting the significance of such varied concerns as dress, décor, speech patterns, and religious allegiances of the inhabitants of Carlingford, the small fictional town near London. One of the most interesting topics, and a subject curiously overlooked in criticism, however, is Oliphant's use of various styles of gardens and landscape architecture as indicators of status and aspiration, as well as a garden setting to further plot and narrative lines. Oliphant, in fact, develops a narrative geography based on the layout of gardens around the two main residential streets of Carlingford – the walled, secluded gardens and houses of Grange Lane and the more modest and more visible gardens of Grove Street, the less desirable location. In this chapter, we argue that the construction of space in the series, particularly of gardens as imagined from inside and out, from within and beyond walls, provides a key to the world that Oliphant represents in the series in general and in *Miss Marjoribanks* in particular.

Of all of the Carlingford novels, *Miss Marjoribanks* (1866) has been the subject of most recent critical attention. Works that analyze Oliphant's use of the "queen" metaphor for Lucilla Marjoribanks are particularly relevant to our discussion of gardens because of the connection between Ruskin's "Of Queens' Gardens" from *Sesame and Lilies* (1865) and the composition of the novel. Melissa Schaub, in fact, argues that Oliphant uses the queenly allusions in order to distinguish Lucilla from Ruskin's idealized and mythologized domestic queens and the feminine essentialism associated with them. Schaub demonstrates that Oliphant surely read the essay when it was published and refers to the book in her *Blackwood's* article of 1868, "The Latest Lawgiver," concluding that "Oliphant uses her depiction of Lucilla to support an anti-idealist position, deconstructing the garden wall that provides an absolute (an unworkably abstract) boundary between male and female spheres."[3] Although others have argued that Ruskin actually blurs the boundaries between public and private by extending the queens' influence into all of England,[4] the crucial point from our perspective is that Ruskin idealizes both women *and* their gardens. He presents the gardens as largely mythic, not the plots and crofts where real women dig in the dirt and write about their experiences in practical ways, as Dorothy Wordsworth, Jane Loudon, and others had done.[5] Although Oliphant uses some mythical allusions in *Miss Marjoribanks* and other novels, she is primarily concerned with actual gardens and what they mean in the culture. They are constructed spaces that carry the weight of meaning from the fragrantly blossoming apple trees in one text to the mignonette gone to seed in another. She deftly incorporates issues relating to the domesticated landscape to enrich narrative and character and to present and critique cultural norms, although she does not display an active interest in botany or horticulture herself – there are no gardening manuals, for instance, among her voluminous publications, nor have extended references to her own garden come down to us in journals or letters. Less interested in the epistemology of the garden than such earlier writers as Dorothy Wordsworth and the Taylors, Oliphant fully exploits the social and cultural meanings of Carlingford's cultivated terrain.

Focusing on the house rather than the garden, Andrea Kaston Tange has recently written on the drawing room in *Miss Marjoribanks* as the place where Lucilla "expand[s] the boundaries of her cultural space."[6] Tange argues that Oliphant uses it as a kind of staging-ground for Lucilla to fulfill both her feminine responsibilities and her unconventional projects. Thus Lucilla, installed in the feminine center of the home, becomes a powerful figure and manipulates the spatial containment to her own advantage.[7] This reading is compelling, but it omits the relationship between the interior spaces and the various gardens in the novel. We first glimpse Lucilla's consciousness through the garden, which she enters with a glance of "reorganising genius" (27) even before she moves into the drawing room.[8] In exploring the ideological implications of the garden, this chapter complements the earlier focus on the interior of the house in the critical literature on Oliphant. Looking at various gardens in the Carlingford series, we are interested in the dynamic between inside and outside, house and garden, but also inside and outside from the narrative and phenomenological perspective of characters who are either included or excluded, who look out from windows into the garden or who look into the garden from beyond the walls. What does inclusion or exclusion mean?

In *Greater Perfections*, Hunt argues that gardens inherently involve us in questions about the relationship between within and without. Hunt, as we have seen in earlier chapters, formulates a definition of gardens as "concentrated or perfected forms of place-making," emphasizing the elements of both enclosure and construction. Gardens are made, culturally constructed, not born. Hunt is interested in "not just how cultures express themselves through place-making, but how places, envisaged or made, determine social activity in their turn."[9] As he proposes in an earlier essay, "The Garden as Cultural Object," gardens are particularly prone to "invented" historical traditions because they "provide spaces and forms of a ritual or symbolic nature that inculcate certain values and norms of behavior having an implied continuity with the past." In the nineteenth century, for instance, an age of rapid technological transformation, "'new' traditions bolster the social aspirations of an emergent middle class."[10]

For our argument about Oliphant's fictional use of gardens, we reiterate Hunt's point in "The Garden as Cultural Object" that gardens "represent the larger world outside them" and that components of the garden serve as signs.[11] Oliphant exploits the potential of architecture and the construction of gardens, as well as her knowledge of gardening styles, to help tell her stories of life in Carlingford: the elements of the various gardens function as signs as surely as dress, manners, or décor do. Oliphant recognizes the textuality of gardens – that certain styles of gardening or types of flowers operate like a language to be read and interpreted. Her gardens tell stories and enhance the larger narrative of which they are a part.

Hunt's theory implicitly reinforces the notion of gardens as liminal zones for women who often have to negotiate appropriate relationships between the domestic and public spheres, although he is not explicitly concerned with gender. Rose's recognition of "the everyday [as] the arena through which patriarchy is (re)created and contested"[12] once again supports our notion that the garden is a key place where the constraints of patriarchy simultaneously assert themselves and are challenged. Two books on Victorian gardens have also been particularly useful in our work on Oliphant: Brent Elliott's *Victorian Gardens* and Michael Waters's *The Garden in Victorian Literature*. With sensitivity to issues of class, Elliott notes that the multiplicity of styles in the Victorian period – from displays of exotic plants to self-consciously revivalist traditions such as cottage gardens – were inspired by "rapidly changing technology, a new professional group to administer it, and an artistic ferment spread by the proliferating gardening magazines."[13] Waters extends similar insights to various literary representations of garden styles and to the relationship between textual space *of* a narrative and the represented spaces *within* a narrative.

Although Waters acknowledges that a more wild and naturalistic style will develop later in the period with William Robinson and Gertrude Jekyll, he emphasizes the earlier Victorian preference for gardens that display their artifice: what he calls the "trim" garden, after Trollope.[14] He traces the nineteenth-century genealogy of this garden style to Humphry Repton and later practitioners such as the Loudons, who (as we saw in Chapter 6) value the artfulness in garden design. An important mid-century voice for this perspective is that of the prolific Shirley Hibberd, although many of his ideas are found earlier in Maria Elizabeth Jacson and Jane Loudon. Aiming "to set forth something like a code of taste in gardening," Hibberd confidently states in his well-known *Rustic Adornments for Homes of Taste* (1856),

modern taste requires that a garden should be a garden, not a wilderness, nor a prairie, nor a "boundless contiguity of shade." It is an artificial affair, or wild weeds would be allowed to riot in it; it is trim and bright, and in some sense a picture, and hence a framing or boundary of some kind is essential. If a boundary is essential why should it not be visible, and in its way ornamental.[15]

No fan of the ha-ha or sunken fence popular half a century earlier, Hibberd argues that a garden should reveal its artifice and structure. Like Jacson and the Loudons, Hibberd sees the garden in relationship to the house and is aware of the dynamic interplay between the two. One of the prints in his chapter on "Floral Ornaments" (Fig. 8.1) illustrates his praise of light in a domestic interior: "Without it no flowers, no colours, no life, so 'open the shutters and let in more light,' that it may come in through chequered leafiness and tinged with rainbow colours."[16] The artist uses a symmetrical composition in order to underscore the balance between dark and light, interior and exterior, and leafy foliage, soft drapery, and hard architectural lines. The center of the scene is occupied by a Wardian case that creates a carefully enclosed artificial landscape in miniature, although the open window, letting in light and air, entices us out into the garden. But the vantage point is from within: according to Jacson, the garden should be "an ornamental appendage to the house," and Hibberd expands on this view when he writes that "Near the house, the artificial tone should be highly cultivated, for here at least the garden is but an amplification of the house itself."[17] Jane Loudon uses windows as framing devices, as we saw in Chapter 6, and Hibberd wants to see "from the windows of the dwelling a picture *complete in itself.*"[18] These authors' emphases on well-managed and bounded spaces close to the house align well with the standard of taste in the Carlingford

Fig. 8.1. "View from the Window," illustration in Shirley Hibberd, *Rustic Adornments for Homes of Taste*, p. 189.

novels, where gardens not answering to these specifications often appear as eccentric, new-fangled, déclassé, or bohemian.

GARDENS FROM GRANGE LANE TO GROVE STREET

One consistent pattern in the Carlingford series is the distinction Oliphant draws between Grange Lane and Grove Street, the elite neighborhood and the lower-middle-class area. Although Oliphant does not provide many details about the topography of Carlingford (several critics have commented on the difficulty of mapping out the town),[19] she does describe several of the gardens in relation to the houses. From the outside, Oliphant uses the walled image of the homes on Grange Lane to express the longings of particular characters for a higher status or for their greatest desire. In *The Doctor's Family*, for instance, told from the point of view of the young

Dr. Rider, an outsider who is trying to build a practice in Carlingford, the walled gardens represent a world and a life to which Rider aspires: he thinks of "the bowery seclusion of Grange Lane, and Mr. Wodehouse's famous apple-trees holding tempting clusters over the high wall" at several moments in the text.[20] Or, in *The Perpetual Curate*, Mr. Wentworth "gave a wistful lingering look down the long line of garden-walls, pausing upon one point where the blossomed boughs of an apple-tree overlooked that enclosure."[21] For the curate, the longing is associated not so much with class fulfillment as it is with his frustrated desire for Lucy Wodehouse, the woman he loves but cannot marry in his current position. Similarly, Oliphant expresses the frustration of the Dissenting minister Mr. Vincent, in his hopeless passion for Lady Western. In *Salem Chapel*, Vincent stands in front of the half-open door to Lady Western's garden and feels alienated from the "sweets of spring."[22] His vision is of a paradise that he cannot enter. The idealized garden is part of his fantasy and the manifestation of his unrequited love.

In *The Rector*, one of the earliest novels in the series, Oliphant had established that the walled gardens were among the most distinctive characteristics of the old country towns:

The high brick walls, all clothed with fruit-trees, shut in an enclosure of which not a morsel except this velvet grass, with its nests of daisies, was not under the highest and most careful cultivation. It was such a scene as is only to be found in an old country town; the walls jealous of intrusion, yet thrusting tall plumes of lilac and stray branches of apple-blossom, like friendly salutations to the world without; within, the blossoms drooping over the light bright head of Lucy Wodehouse underneath the apple-trees.[23]

The key to this description is the interplay of within and without – the walls are "jealous of intrusion" but at the same time they send out "friendly salutations to the world without." Thus the walls are the ambivalent meeting place of the secluded home and the public world. The apple trees, reminiscent of the tempting fruit in Eden, are crucial to this blossoming paradise; although they entice passersby, only those within the garden participate fully in their bloom. The description also reveals an old-fashioned garden, with lilacs and apple blossoms representing years of fragrance and production – "careful cultivation." Evoking a present indebted to the past, this garden represents the enclosed world of Carlingford and its traditions.

In contrast to the stability of Grange Lane, the rectory in *The Perpetual Curate* represents the encroachment of the new world where Mrs. Morgan has to plant Virginia creeper, an aggressive climbing vine, "to shut out the sight of the railway." In fact, *The Perpetual Curate* begins with a view from the rectory's drawing room:

> It was, as we have said, a very pretty drawing-room, and the windows opened upon as pretty a bit of lawn as you could see, with one handsome cedar sweeping its dark branches majestically over delicious greensward; but some people did think it was too near Grove Street and the railway. Just at that moment a puff of delicate white vapour appeared over the wall, and a sudden express-train, just released from the cover of the station, sprang with a snort and bound across the Rector's view, very imperfectly veiled by lime-trees, which were thin in their foliage as yet.[24]

The not-quite-genteel positioning of the rectory and the connection with the railway make it an interesting borderline place in the novel – in terms both of geography and of class. Perhaps, too, Oliphant suggests that a rapidly changing world of express trains challenges the church itself, represented in this tale by the very imperfect Rector. After establishing a pleasant view from the drawing-room window, the narrator brings us up short with the image of the thinly clad lime trees. Furthermore, Oliphant injects a note of gossip – "some people did think" – to suggest the precarious social positioning of the rectory in relation to Carlingford society. Mrs. Morgan makes the best of it, but the ambiguous view from the window mirrors the constraints and complexities of her life.

Despite the variety of gardening styles and developments in technology in the Victorian period, the gardens of Carlingford – both the fine enclosures of Grange Lane and the more modest open plots of Grove Street – are predominantly old-fashioned, evoking a fragile world of country traditions and stability. In the Chronicles of Carlingford, these gardens have endured the many changes in fashion and taste. More innovative or technologically advanced plantings stand out like sore thumbs. When a gardener takes a more scientific or forward-looking approach, the narrator remarks on it, as in *Miss Marjoribanks*:

> [Mr. Woodburn] was a great amateur of flowers and fruit, and had his garden lined on each side with greenhouses, which were no doubt very fine in their way, but somewhat spoiled the garden, which had not in the least the homely, luxuriant, old-fashioned look of other gardens, where, for the most part, the flowers and shrubs grew as they liked, and were at home – whereas Mr. Woodburn's flower-beds were occupied only by tenants at will.

The controlled environment of Mr. Woodburn's garden is metonymic of the character's controlling personality. When his wife, the town's incorrigible mimic, wants to speak secretly to her brother Mr. Cavendish, she chooses the only spot in the garden that does not fit in with her husband's regime – "a little arbour, so covered up and heaped over with clematis that even the Scotch gardener had not the heart to touch it."[25] The luxuriant arbor provides Mrs. Woodburn with a refuge apart from Mr. Woodburn's greenhouses – a place associated with romance and secrecy, and the garden spot most closely aligned with women in their enlarged domestic sphere, as we have seen. Furthermore, the characterization of the flowers as "tenants at will" suggests their impermanence and dependency (unlike leaseholders) at the whim of the landlord: they may be uprooted at any time. As such, these plants represent the vulnerability that Mrs. Woodburn and her brother Mr. Cavendish feel after misrepresenting their class origins. The tenacious clematis covering Mrs. Woodburn's arbor, which protects their secret, seems to be the only firmly anchored plant in the garden.

Throughout the Carlingford fiction, Oliphant uses gardens and plants as markers of class and gender. *The Rector*, for instance, begins in Mr. Woodhouse's upper-middle-class garden, which is safely enclosed behind walls and a green door off Grange Lane. The two Wodehouse daughters are in the garden on a beautiful spring day, with the younger daughter Lucy engaged in light gardening chores appropriate to a lady:

She had great gardening gloves on, and a basket and huge pair of scissors on the grass at her feet, which grass, besides, was strewed with a profusion of all the sweetest spring blossoms – the sweet narcissus, most exquisite of flowers, lilies of the valley, white and blue hyacinths, golden ranunculus globes – worlds of sober, deep-breathing wallflower. If Lucy had been doing what her kind elder sister called her "duty," she would have been at this moment arranging her flowers in the drawing room.[26]

As many of the gardening manuals discussed in Chapter 6 make clear, light pruning and collecting flowers were the least contested kinds of activities for ladies. Lucy is fitted with gloves and other paraphernalia, so there is nothing untoward here. But, in modest transgression against her duty, she lingers outside, rather than carrying the fruits of her labor into the drawing room and composing herself for dinner. Lucy's "rebellion," however, is tempered by the Edenic description of the spring flowers and the general sense that she presides appropriately over this profusion, as well as over the two clergymen who visit and respond differently to the abundance of nature. Furthermore, such language as "sweet," "exquisite," and "sober" does double duty here, applying not only to the flowers but to Lucy herself, such an ideal Victorian lady. A latter-day Eve before the Fall, Lucy belongs in this enclosed and protected garden off Grange Lane.

In the last Chronicle of Carlingford, *Phoebe Junior*, however, Oliphant uses a garden off Grange Lane to very different effect. In this novel, old

Mr. and Mrs. Tozer have recently moved to the neighborhood, having bought the former property of Lady Weston[27] following Mr. Tozer's retirement as the town's prosperous butterman. Mrs. Tozer prefers her previous position, living over the shops in High Street "where she saw everything that was going on" and had day-to-day contact with people of her class and religious affiliation as a Dissenter. But even though Lady Weston's house is somewhat rundown and out-of-date, it is attractive to Mr. Tozer with its "aroma of high life about it" and its "delightful garden charmingly laid out." Oliphant explains that "Tozer himself soon took a great interest in this little domain out of doors, and was for ever pottering about the flowers, obeying, with the servility of ignorance, the gardener's injunctions."[28] In a reversal of the scene from *The Rector*, here Tozer overturns the convention; instead of his giving orders to his gardener, the gardener directs him as if he were a serf in his own domain. Here and in many other scenes in the novel, Oliphant points to the social ineptitude of the Tozers, who do not really belong in Grange Lane. They are encroachers, moving into a ready-made upper-class garden in which they are never quite at home.

The gardens of Grove Street also signal certain class allegiances or limitations. For instance, at the home of the former Dissenting minister and his wife, Mr. and Mrs. Tufton, there is a small garden in front and a vegetable patch in the back with the family's plebeian cabbages. Inside, Mrs. Tufton's potted geraniums are depicted as almost grotesque: "A low parlour with two small windows, overshadowed outside by ivy, and inside by two large geraniums, expanded upon a Jacob's ladder of props, which were the pride of Mrs. Tufton's heart and made it almost impossible to see anything clearly within, even at the height of day."[29] Whereas potted plants in the window were generally considered decorative and good for one's health, as noted in Chapter 7, Mrs. Tufton's beloved geraniums constitute a running joke in the novel because they are overdone and cultivated without taste. In this respect they are clearly unlike the refined window plants illustrated in the frontispiece of Miss E. A. Maling's *In-Door Plants* (1862) (Fig. 8.2), intended for ladies who must revise their gardening practices while living in town. Providing a delicate screen for the window while still leaving plenty of glass for looking outward (and in), Maling's design incorporates the foliage of ferns along with a few flowering plants – but nothing as heavy-handed as Mrs. Tufton's blooms, which more closely resemble the plants that Shirley Hibberd describes in *The Town Garden* (1855): "Geraniums pass a torpid life on window-sills and in dark parlours, where none but the housekeeper can aver they are geraniums."[30] Too much of a good thing, Mrs. Tufton's beloved geraniums have grown out of control and require an ugly system of

Fig. 8.2. Frontispiece illustration in E. A. Maling, *In-Door Plants and How to Grow Them.*

propping. They literally overshadow each of the visits of the current minister, Mr. Vincent, and like the cabbages near the house, reveal the Tuftons as déclassé. Their plants give off a whiff of the lower class because of the way in which the Tuftons grow them, not because there is inherently anything questionable about geraniums. As we saw in Chapter 7, they are prized by Fanny Price and other English gardeners, and Hibberd exclaims, "How doatingly does the dear old granny in her white cap cherish the huge geraniums, that make her alms-house window a bower of greenery and bloom!"[31] But Mrs. Tufton's plants are oppressively overgrown, suffocating Mr. Vincent rather than contributing to the healthy atmosphere that better-tended plants would have provided.

In *The Perpetual Curate*, in contrast, Mrs. Morgan busies herself at her husband's rectory with her ferns, which form a comic backdrop to some of the action but are also identified as appropriate plants for a lady to tend and collect. Mrs. Morgan disapproves of her husband's silly curate, who constantly intrudes on her plants and her life, and Oliphant uses the ferns to put Mr. Leeson in his place by showing the way he pretends to understand their cultivation.[32] A later joke in the *The Perpetual Curate* centers on Mrs. Morgan's fern album, which the despised know-it-all curate fingers in her drawing room, and her Wardian case, an early terrarium popular for growing ferns and other suitable plants. Hibberd includes several illustrations of these containers in his *Rustic Adornments for Homes of Taste*, as in Fig. 8.1 with the heavy Victorian drapery pulled back to reveal the case, sculptural in its imposing stature. Such elaborate terraria were magnificent statements of the leisure-class love of these "leafy pets."[33] Mrs. Morgan has to endure a pseudo-discussion of plants with the curate, who "pretended to know about ferns on the score of having a Wardian case in his lodgings (which belonged to his landlady), though in reality he could scarcely tell the commonest spleenwort from a lycopodium."[34] Oliphant establishes the curate's social inferiority by emphasizing his pretenses about ferns and Wardian cases, when in fact his landlady knows more than he does about their botanical history and cultivation.

MISS MARJORIBANKS: CULTURE AND CULTIVATION IN CARLINGFORD

Miss Marjoribanks, Oliphant's comic masterpiece in the Carlingford series, builds on similar assumptions about location and class in the town. This novel focuses on the life of Lucilla Marjoribanks, the society doctor's daughter, and her attempts to rule Grange Lane as a kind of benevolent dictator. Linked to both Austen's *Emma* and More's *Cœlebs in Search of a Wife*, it traces Lucilla's various attempts to play the part of social, political, and philanthropic arbiter of the town. As such, the gardens, houses, and geography of Carlingford play an important role in Lucilla's career, as well as in the lives of several other characters. Hunt's idea that gardens determine social activity is particularly relevant in this novel since Lucilla orchestrates several social scenes around the garden.

When Lucilla returns home to Carlingford after school and European touring, she sets herself up as manager of her widowed father's household. In order to impose her imprint on the house, she has "converted" the main room "from an abstract English drawing-room of the old school into Miss Marjoribanks's drawing-room, an individual spot of ground revealing the character of the mistress." The narrator's language of landscape ("spot of ground") for such an important indoor room suggests both a deliberate cultivation of a particular style (the green wallpaper selected to match her eyes) and a connection between the drawing room and the garden, which Lucilla in fact views as an extension of her domain. When she first assesses the drawing room, Lucilla sees it in overblown terms as land that needs to be claimed for civilization: "a waste and howling wilderness." The intertwined drawing room and garden complement the strategic placement of the house itself, which "command[ed] ... all Grange Lane," a conclusion Lucilla is pleased to reach on her first "tour" of the town as triumphant "young sovereign."[35] We are reminded of Mitford's ebullient response to Miss Jephson: "I am so glad you have a little demense [sic] of your own too; it is a pretty thing to be queen over roses and lilies, is it not?"[36]

Lucilla fulfills her role as lady of the house by instructing the gardener in the particulars of cultivation (in contrast to Mr. Tozer, who in the later *Phoebe Junior* is ordered around by his). Although she does not dirty her own hands, she is very interested in the arrangement of the walled garden and how it relates to the house. When she has a special party, she compensates for having only one room appropriate for music (the drawing room) by opening the windows and setting up seating arrangements outside in the garden, with one spot illuminated by lamps and moonlight under the large lime tree (so different from the thin effect of Mrs. Morgan's limes). Lucilla's guests thus listen to the music under the windows, enjoying the permeable boundaries between inside and outside. This outdoor space in the walled garden has been constructed in the most intimate way, giving the guests the privilege of being part of a particular social world from which those outside the walls are excluded: "whenever anybody was tired of the music, there were quantities of corners to retire into, not to speak of that bright spot full of yellow light under the lime-tree."[37]

In contrast, the gardens of the more modest houses on Grove Street are generally open to the world and available to the gaze of passersby on the street. After arriving home in Carlingford, Lucilla begins her tour on the "plebeian side" of Grove Street "where the straggling chrysanthemums propped each other up, and the cheerful Michaelmas daisies made the best of it in the sunshine that remained to them." No longer in her beautifully secluded garden on Grange Lane, with its velvety lawn and well-maintained shrubs, Lucilla walks on Grove Street by the cottage of the local drawing master ("in front of a little garden where a great deal of mignonette had run to seed, and where the Michaelmas daisies had taken full possession"), and she is arrested by a lovely contralto voice coming from the house. Lucilla sees no reason not to call on the Lakes without warning, and as she stops to ask Barbara Lake to sing at one of her Thursday evenings, the narrator completes a description of the cottage and garden: "And in the little garden in front, half-buried among the mignonette were some remains of plaster-casts, originally placed there for ornament, but long-since cast down by rain and neglect."[38] The Lakes' garden (there is no gardener here!) matches the shabby-genteel artiness of their home and their slightly bohemian existence on the fringe of Carlingford society. With the introduction of the Lakes, the reader is no longer in the world of trim middle-class gardens behind the old brick walls of Carlingford, the kind of garden that Hibberd had recently celebrated: "all must be trim as the Corporal's boots; no ugly branches straggling out of the line, no rampant growth to shut out light and suggest that you can't afford to keep a gardener."[39] On Grove Street, the flowers, though cheerful, are uncontrolled, lacking the tidy order of a well-tended garden, and the sculptures have fallen from their pedestals.

Lucilla responds to the Lakes' bohemianism with bourgeois snobbery, but she cannot compete with either the superiority of Barbara's voice or the artistic spirit of Rose, the younger sister. Although Rose's artistic ambitions are finally thwarted, Oliphant gives her more attention and credence than the good people of Carlingford do.[40] The Lakes' house and garden betray not so much a lack of taste (like the Tuftons' in *Salem Chapel*) as a lack of money. Hibberd would understand that they clearly cannot afford to keep a gardener. Nor does their garden fulfill the requirements that Louisa Johnson had set out in *Every Lady Her Own Flower Gardener* (1839): "I cannot lay too great stress upon the neatness in which a lady's garden should be kept. If it is not beautifully neat, it is nothing."[41] Lucilla observes that the Lakes need improvement, but she does not see them or their garden as a "project" because they are marginal, not destitute.

Perhaps Lucilla's greatest project involves the cottage and garden that she renovates for Mrs. Mortimer, a widow whom she befriends in a very proprietary way. If, as several readers have noted, Oliphant's Lucilla is related to More's earlier character of the same name – the perfect charitable lady whose projects are finely tuned to the needs of the poor – then the sequence involving Mrs. Mortimer is the key.[42] Lucilla inadvertently brings Mrs. Mortimer back together with her former love, the visiting Archdeacon, when she takes him to see the way she has set the widow up in the cottage, which is also being used for a small school. But whereas More's Lucilla objectively examines the meaning and efficacy of her philanthropy, Oliphant's Lucilla displays a comic frustration when her friend is reunited with Mr. Beverly and does not need her charity any more. The garden is central to these chapters, as it helps to define Lucilla's privileged position in relation to a poor widow and also reveals the limitations of her charity.[43] Mrs. Mortimer does not find the old-fashioned cottage garden to which she has been consigned as picturesque or comforting as Lucilla does, and she refuses to play the role of the satisfied cottager to Lucilla's Lady Bountiful.

The episode at Mrs. Mortimer's cottage begins with a chance meeting. Walking in a lane between Grove Street and Grange Lane, Lucilla comes upon Mr. Beverly and invites him to visit Mrs. Mortimer with her: "Opening from this lane was a little door in the wall, which admitted to a little garden very bright with flowers of the simplest old-fashioned kinds, with a little house planted at its extremity, which had pretensions to be an old-fashioned and quasi-rural cottage, on the score of being very rickety, uncomfortable, and badly arranged."[44] From the outset of this scene, then, the narrator approaches the quaintness of the cottage and garden ironically, and locates it as neither in Grove Street nor in Grange Lane, but in an unnamed lane between the two. Whereas the Lakes' house and garden is at odds with Grove Street because of its bohemian feel, this cottage is a misfit for a different reason: more staged than homelike, it serves Lucilla's plan for a quaint scene, with Mrs. Mortimer as the grateful cottager in her surrounding garden.

Thinking that she would display her protégé to the Archdeacon, Lucilla is perturbed to find her charity upstaged by the previous relationship. She is an unwilling witness "here, in this spot, which she had, so to speak, created" to "a revolution so unlooked-for and disagreeable" – the renewed affection between the Archdeacon and Mrs. Mortimer. The intimacy of the reunited lovers is signaled by the Archdeacon's hat touching the foliage in this embowered feminine space: "It was Dr. Marjoribanks's gardener, under Lucilla's orders, who had arranged and planted the garden, and trained the embowering foliage which had just brushed the Archdeacon's clerical hat as he went in."[45] Even though Mr. Beverly had shown some interest in Lucilla before this moment in the garden, Lucilla is most concerned to see the possible loss of her cottage project and protégé – not the loss of a possible husband.

The disarray of her plans is symbolized in the scene by the disarray of the garden. Although at first the garden presents a conventionally pretty sight to Mr. Beverly and Lucilla in the bright summer sunshine, when Lucilla is left on her own after the initial meeting she notices all the problems, beginning with the wisteria "sprawling all over the front of the house uncared for." This space that she created with the help of her gardener is decidedly not as trim as a Corporal's boot. But a stroll around the garden "restored her more and more entirely to herself," not because she is pleased with everything but because she sees the need for improvement. Detached espaliers, dead verbenas, and fallen dahlias call her back to her mission:

> Miss Marjoribanks could not help observing that the branches of the pear-tree, which was all that the garden contained in the shape of fruit, had come loose from the wall, and were swaying about greatly to the damage of the half-grown pears, – not to say that it gave a very untidy look at the corner … It was nearly a week since Miss Marjoribanks had been round Mrs. Mortimer's garden, and in that time the espalier had got detached, some of the verbenas were dead in the borders, and the half of the sticks that propped up the dahlias had fallen, leaving the plants in miserable confusion.[46]

There is still work to be done, even after the unexpected conjunction of Mrs. Mortimer and Mr. Beverly. If Lucilla can no longer prop and prune Mrs. Mortimer, at least she can continue to redeem fallen dahlias and restore the garden to its quaint cottage-garden order.

For Mrs. Mortimer, however, the story is very different. Because she has heard the rumor of an attachment between the Archdeacon and Miss Marjoribanks, she feels guilty at the prospect of a renewed relationship with him. Her emotions find an objective correlative in the rain that comes on after the encounter: "A little garden may look like a little paradise in the sunshine, and yet feel like a dungeon when a poor woman all alone looks out across her flowers in the rain, and sees nothing but the wall that shuts her in, and thinks to herself that she has no refuge nor escape from it." Feeling "like a creature in a cage, helpless, imprisoned, miserable," Mrs. Mortimer looks out of her window and sees not a charming garden but a reflection of herself and her state of mind. After presenting the garden and entire situation from Lucilla's point of view, then, the narrator takes us into Mrs. Mortimer's consciousness: "the rain poured down fiercer than ever, the bricks of the uncovered wall grew black with the wet, and the Westeria [sic] crouched and shivered about the porch as if it wanted to be taken indoors."[47] Furthermore, Oliphant attributes a kind of anthropomorphic suffering to the wisteria as a reflection of the widow's own mood.

Lucilla laments the efforts that she put into planning the garden and cottage renovation when the former lovers reconcile, but she does not examine her own feelings and motivations too carefully. Oliphant suggests that Lucilla had tried to create an artificially quaint home for Mrs. Mortimer in line with her own noblesse oblige, but then she does not understand the implications of her failed charity. The cottage and garden that Lucilla had constructed for Mrs. Mortimer speak to a nostalgic vision – both of charity and of gardens – that Lucilla cherishes. She thinks that she can stage the perfect scene in which Mrs. Mortimer acts out her drama as an educated widow fallen on hard times but redeemed by the simplicity of the cottage, garden, and eager students. But the narrator has already warned us that the happy cottage life is either a fiction or a charming anachronism in Carlingford in the 1860s. Michael Waters argues that "the survival of the cottage garden idea(l), both as an imaginatively compelling visual image and as a concentrated store-house of old-fashioned values," was frequently represented in Victorian literature. According to Waters, garden writers "applauded novelists and poets for keeping alive [the] names and charms" of old-fashioned plants and flowers.[48] Oliphant may accomplish this effect, but she fully exploits the constructed quality of such nostalgia. She acts less as an antiquarian or preservationist than as a canny author revealing the gap between the ideal and the reality of cottage life a century after Austen does something similar in *Sense and Sensibility* (1811).[49] Even at the beginning of the century, as we saw with the cottage-door paintings of Maria Spilsbury and others, the ideal of the cottage and surrounding garden was already a fiction – so much so that in referring to the Victorian period Brent Elliott asks, "to what extent was it [the cottage garden] a genuine feature of the ancestral English past, and to what extent a nineteenth-century invention?"[50]

This is not to say that cottages and cottage gardens per se did not exist, of course. As we saw in Chapter 5, Dorothy Wordsworth re-imagined the space at Town End as a working cottage garden. But even at Town End she recognized, with elegiac intimations, that this experiment in living and gardening on the edge of a public road would not last, since the cottage was already being framed as tourist attraction. And just a little bit later than the period of Wordsworth's *Grasmere Journals*, Mitford was already presenting the cottages and the countryside, in Elizabeth Helsinger's words, as a picture or "cultural artifact" in the self-conscious and self-reflexive rhetoric of *Our Village*.[51]

In her 1854 article for *Blackwood's* entitled "Mary Russel [sic] Mitford," Oliphant comments on Mitford's idyllic vision of cottage gardens and village life. Mitford, according to Oliphant, works with an "invented" tradition, what Hunt would later identify as the "ritual or symbolic nature"[52] of gardening:

You shall find nothing fairer in all England than the sweet quiet of Our Village, with all its blossomed orchards round it, with its warm banks of turf, its flowers, and wooing bees, and running stream. Not a bit of hedgerow or greensward in it that is not true as the daylight which overspreads it all. The labourers are all a-field, the good wives at home; the cottage maidens, trim in the afternoon sunshine …

Nor do you fail to perceive the hall overseeing this bright domain from among its stately trees – nor the rectory, peeping out from its embowered gate – nor the patrician cottage, with its sunny lawn and gay gardens.

Although Oliphant wants to believe "that it is not all an illusion,"[53] she is aware of the fictive quality of Mitford's village that other Victorian commentators noted and that Mitford herself in her self-consciousness recognizes. Mitford's visitors particularly marked the contrast between the sunny persona of Mitford's sketches and letters and the difficult life that she actually led, much of it caused by her father's gambling and irresponsibility. Forced to leave a comfortable, well-appointed house because of her father's financial profligacy, the family moved to Three Mile Cross, a small cottage outside of Reading. Although Mitford writes glowingly of her garden and eccentric cottage in her letters and sketches, visitors were more likely to report the hardship of living in a cramped, damp house, its tiny garden crammed with flowers.[54]

But Mitford nevertheless constructed her home and garden in her writing as a representative of the true old English style, most memorably at the beginning of *Our Village* (1824):

A cottage – no – a miniature house, with many additions, little odds and ends of places, pantries, and what not; all angles, and of a charming in-and-outness; a little bricked court before one half, and a little flower-yard before the other; the walls, old and weather-stained, covered with hollyhocks, roses, honeysuckles, and a great apricot-tree; the casements full of geraniums (ah, there is our superb white cat peeping out from amongst them!); the closets (our landlord has the assurance to call them rooms) full of contrivances and corner cupboards; and the little garden behind full of common flowers, tulips, pinks, larkspurs, peonies, stocks, and carnations, with an arbour of privet, not unlike a sentry-box, where one lives in a delicious green light, and looks out on the gayest of all gay flowers-beds. That house was built on purpose to show in what an exceeding small compass comfort may be packed.[55]

Mitford includes a litany of old-fashioned flowers to express the value that she places in the familiar. These flowers are "common," and thus in some way her garden is also democratic and forward-looking as well as traditional. Like the cottage, the garden is diminutive and as such serves as a microcosm of the larger world. But whereas Mitford dramatizes herself within her common garden, Oliphant maintains more distance from her imagined cottage garden and uses it in part to represent Lucilla Marjoribanks's self-presentation as the charitable lady to the poor widow. Lucilla is most content when she can supervise and direct, and the cottage and garden are the perfect stage for her action.

The single-minded Lucilla cannot understand that Mrs. Mortimer is unhappy as the recipient of her charity. Oliphant reveals the subjectivity that Lucilla cannot appreciate by placing Mrs. Mortimer by the window looking out at the garden walls. What in Lucilla's mind should give her protégé a sense of security actually closes her in and makes her feel the hopelessness and isolation of her position:

And if it was a tedious business looking out of the window when the rain was drenching the four walls of the garden and breaking down the flowers, and reducing all the poor little shrubs to abject misery, it could not be said to be much more cheerful in the sunshine, when pleasant sounds came in over that enclosure – voices and footsteps of people who might be called alive, while this solitary woman was buried, and had nothing to do with life. Such a fate may be accepted when people make up their minds to it; but when, so far from making up one's mind, one fixes one's thoughts upon the life outside, and fancies that every moment the call may come, and one may find one's place again in the active world, the tedium grows more and more insupportable. As for Lucilla, naturally she could not see any reason why Mrs Mortimer should sit at the window – why she could not content herself, and eat her dinner instead.[56]

Whereas in other parts of the novel the garden walls prevent the outsiders from coming in (Lucilla's moonlight party, for instance), in this case they form Mrs. Mortimer's prison, because the real life, the active life, is beyond. We are reminded here of the walls that so often enclose and constrain the children in late eighteenth- and early nineteenth-century didactic stories, as discussed in Chapter 1, and of the girls who yearned for the freedom outside the garden enclosure. Here Mrs. Mortimer, a grown woman, finds herself in a similar state of psychological entrapment. But Oliphant is sensitive to her constricted life as a dependent widow – even if Lucilla cannot imagine her protégé's subjectivity.

Similarly, Oliphant portrays the boundaries of gender and class in Barbara Lake, a young woman with talent but limited by circumstances. Oliphant reveals Barbara's feelings through her relationship with Mr. Cavendish, a man who changed his name and social aspirations when he inherited a small fortune. Cavendish is drawn to Barbara, even though his class aspirations would make an alliance with Lucilla more useful to him. After flirting with Barbara but then attempting to resist her appeal, Cavendish nevertheless seems drawn like a magnet to Grove Street:

when he looked at the lights that began to appear in the parlour windows, and breathed in the odours from the little gardens, it is not to be denied that he asked himself for a moment what was the good of going through all this bother and vexation, and whether love in a cottage, with a little garden full of mignonette and a tolerable amount of comfort within, was not, after all, a great deal more reasonable than it looked at first sight?"[57]

Oliphant uses his sensitivity to the scent of the gardens, particularly the Victorian cottage-garden favorite, mignonette, to highlight Cavendish's attraction – never mind that in the earlier scene Lucilla had noticed the mignonette going to seed.[58]

Oliphant makes fun of Cavendish's "love in a cottage" fantasy by having him rather improbably imagine Barbara as Tennyson's Mariana at her window, longing for her lover and surrounded by a decaying garden (despite the sweet odor of the mignonette). Barbara is perhaps like Mariana in being isolated and abandoned, but she quickly distinguishes herself from that figure by dashing out of the house, greeting Cavendish in the garden, and then inviting him inside, all the while planning her imagined wedding.

Later, when Cavendish returns to Carlingford after a ten-year absence, he imagines Barbara as "a Rosamond, dilapidated indeed, but always ready to receive and console him in her bower."[59] Oliphant here incorporates another ironic allusion: this one to Henry II's betrayal of Queen Eleanor in his relationship with Rosamond, who is poisoned by the jealous queen. In Oliphant's version, Cavendish leaves the queen (Lucilla) and takes up with a diminished and older Rosamond, who nevertheless exudes the attractions of a bower and thus the promise of passion.[60] So even though Cavendish does not go for "love in a cottage" as a young man, as a now-aging lover he opts for Barbara's bower of bliss, thus rescuing them both from loneliness and from Carlingford's gossiping intrusion. Since both of them have "gone off," they make a perfect match.

MAKING THE DESERT BLOOM

The ten-year gap that finally resolves the relationship between Barbara Lake and Cavendish also brings Lucilla's life into sharp relief. The virginal Lucilla, who had vaguely considered both Mr. Beverley and Mr. Cavendish, succumbs to the proposal of her long-suffering cousin, Tom Marjoribanks, who races back to Carlingford from India when he learns of her father's death. But the narrator highlights Lucilla's feelings in the final chapters, not Tom's triumph. After a decade of managing her father's house and garden in Carlingford, Lucilla finds herself at his death in possession of a "ripe female intelligence" but without a "'sphere'" in which to act and in a difficult financial situation. In accepting Tom, Lucilla has decided that they will use what little money they have to reclaim the family's interest in the country estate of Marchbank, which Tom remembers visiting as a child: "Tom seemed to see himself a little fellow, with his eyes and ears wide open, trotting about with small steps after the Doctor, as he went over the red brick house and neglected gardens at Marchbank: it was only to be let then, and had passed through many hands, and was in miserable case, both lands and house."[61] Lucilla offers Tom the prospect of "improving" the land, although she does not think of improvement in the eighteenth-century sense of reinventing the landscape in aesthetic terms, but rather as agricultural cultivation. And, she imagines, while he is busy with the crops she will improve the people.

For Lucilla, who thinks she has outlived her usefulness in the town of Carlingford, the village near Marchbank becomes a new sphere for her imagination:

It gave her the liveliest satisfaction to think of all the disorder and disarray of the Marchbank village. Her fingers itched to be at it – to set all the crooked things straight, and clean away the rubbish, and set everything, as she said, on a sound foundation. If it had been a model village, with prize flower-gardens and clean as Arcadia, the thought of it would not have given Miss Marjoribanks half so much pleasure. The recollection of all the wretched hovels and miserable cottages exhilarated her heart.[62]

Although the narrator wryly provides us with the literal description of the village from Lucilla's point of view, in this instance Lucilla is not interested in the real state of the Marchbank house and gardens or the nearby village as much as she is in the figurative potential. The narrator turns the horticultural references into metaphors to capture Lucilla's way of seeing: "Lucilla's eyes went over the moral wilderness with the practical glance of a statesman, and, at the same time, the sanguine enthusiasm of a philanthropist. She saw of what it was capable, and already, in imagination, the desert bloomed like a rose before her beneficent steps, and the sweet sense of well-doing rose in her breast."[63] The language Oliphant uses to represent Lucilla's thought echoes Ruskin's language in "Of Queens' Gardens," which is framed by an epigraph from Isaiah (35:1), "let the desert be made cheerful, and bloom as the lily," and a reference to "a whole world in wilderness" outside the garden gate. Ruskin urges his queens to exert their moral influence and sympathy in this world beyond the garden gate and drawing room. Oliphant's echo of Ruskin (and the Bible via Ruskin) serves both to legitimize Lucilla's project *and* to critique its impracticality in a world where, in Elizabeth Helsinger's words, "social, legal and economic power [is] in the hands of men."[64]

Margaret Homans argues that Lucilla becomes a more private and emotional heroine after the death of her father, but unlike Homans we do not see her, even in mourning, as a "psychologically deep heroine whose emotions create and justify the perpetuation of a separate private, domestic sphere."[65] Lucilla is not permanently transformed by her mourning, nor does she retreat to private life in marriage. Having exhausted Carlingford and given grief its due, Lucilla creates a new sphere of interest for herself.[66] In contrast to Austen's Emma, whose moral and imaginative development is gauged by her heightened sensitivity to the natural world ("Never had the exquisite sight, smell, sensation of nature, tranquil, warm, and brilliant after a storm, been more attractive to [Emma]"),[67] Lucilla does not grow or respond to nature in the same way. She appreciates the potential of nature as an abstraction that relates to her "career," not as a site of meditation and beauty. The shabbiness of the projected village attracts her moral sensibility precisely because it needs improvement and is not aesthetically appealing. Like the neglected drawing room that she renovated in her father's Carlingford home, Marchbank village, Lucilla imagines, will provide her with a project to organize. Oliphant recognizes Lucilla's skill but distances the narrative voice from Lucilla's supreme self-satisfaction.

Nevertheless, Lucilla's project to "redeem" the cottagers of Marchbank is in line with the perspective of a writer and garden activist such as J. C. Loudon, who argues that "whatever renders the cottager more comfortable and happy at home, will render him a better servant and subject, and in every respect a more valuable member of society."[68] Furthermore, Loudon's position anticipates the allotment movement of the Cottage Garden Association and legislation of the 1880s in which cottage gardening is seen to build moral character because it instills a "habit of reflection" and "produces a love of order and a distaste for low and sordid pleasures," a position that numerous earlier Victorian writers espoused.[69] Lucilla has not thought out her project that carefully and does not imagine it in terms of empowerment. Nonetheless, Oliphant writes with awareness of the larger debate and of the kinds of issues that were part of the discourse on gardens dating back to the 1790s, although they would not necessarily arise in a town such as Carlingford.[70] In this sense, Oliphant's Lucilla Marjoribanks is a true descendant of More's Lucilla Stanley, whose charitable actions were focused on helping the cottagers plant productive and useful gardens.

CONCLUSION

In *Miss Marjoribanks* and in the Carlingford fiction in general, then, gardens raise crucial issues about the culture that they represent. They serve as important signifiers of the social world and of the aspirations of characters, rather than being represented simply for their natural beauty or artful style. Even when the Dissenting minister Mr. Vincent in *Salem Chapel* sees Lady

Western's garden as a paradise, the point is not the garden's beauty but Mr. Vincent's exclusion from the world that it represents. In a crucial passage at the end of that novel, we view this garden from his perspective on her wedding day:

The door of Lady Western's garden was ajar. The minister crossed over and looked in with a wistful, despairing hope ... The house was baking in the spring sunshine – the door open, some of the windows open, eager servants hovering about, an air of expectation over all. With eyes full of memories, the minister looked in at the half-open door, which one time and another had been to him the gate of paradise. Within, where the red geraniums and verbena had once brightened all the borders, were pale crocuses and flowers of early spring – the limes were beginning to bud, the daisies to grow among the grass. The winter was over in that sheltered and sunny place: Nature herself stood sweet within the protecting walls, and gathered all the tenderest sweets of spring to greet the bride in the new beginning of her life.

In contrast to this spring garden joy, the young minister, hopelessly in love with the unattainable Lady Western, experiences the garden's renewal as a "mockery" of his desires.[71] The garden gate, in this instance, represents all that is forbidden to him, not the passageway into a new world.

Like this one, the various gardens of Carlingford suggest a range of meanings for the characters who observe, enjoy, or yearn for them. As we have seen in the Chronicles of Carlingford as a whole, Oliphant links the gardens to the social ambitions and status of her characters, and uses plants, such as the unfortunate geraniums or exotic ferns, to define human relationships more precisely. As constructed spaces, gardens reflect, or occasionally determine, the social activities that take place within, around, and because of them,[72] from Lucilla's moonlit garden parties to Mrs. Woodburn's secret meetings in the arbor. Gardens form part of the object-world that Oliphant imagines in creating the fiction of Carlingford as a typical mid-Victorian country town, already in the midst of the changes that will envelop it.

Epilogue

In the preceding chapters we have traced recurrent themes related to the domesticated landscape in a wide array of texts and visual sources. As we have shown, the garden as constructed by women and reconstructed in their writings and images was an extension of the home, and as such was both constraining and invigorating – a limited space, but one that engaged the hands and the mind in challenging ways. Our consideration of these "disciples of Flora," primarily girls and women of the English middle classes, reveals their use of the carefully cultivated area around the home as a testing ground. Moving outward from the domestic interior, they found opportunities in the garden for moral discernment, intellectual growth, emotional comfort, and charitable action. Even as the garden itself was a transitional zone between the rootedness of home and the mobility of spatial extension, so too were walls, windows, doors, and gates used repeatedly in these texts and images as metaphors for containment but also for exploration and action, whether sanctioned or illicit.

Looking ahead in this brief epilogue from one period of change to another – from the early nineteenth to the early twentieth century – we find many of the same issues appearing, though in different configurations. Gertrude Bell, for example, who followed in the footsteps of the many intrepid Victorian women travelers, wrote about her experiences as a political administrator and archaeologist in the Near East.[1] Her book on Syria, published in 1907, begins with a metaphorical description of leaving the walled garden (which we can construe geographically as the tame island of England, or socially as the claustrophobic small-mindedness of middle-class mores, or in gender terms as the timidity of female existence): "To those bred under an elaborate social order few such moments of exhilaration can come as that which stands at the threshold of wild travel. The gates of the enclosed garden are thrown open, the chain at the sanctuary is lowered, with a wary glance to right and left you step forth, and behold! The immeasurable world." Although Bell goes on to describe this expansion beyond the garden gate as "the world of adventure and of enterprise," she presents her discovery using the biblical language of awe and proclamation: "behold!"[2] Her escape into the larger world reverses, in a way, the expulsion of the original gardeners from Eden, since her curiosity leads to productive intellectual engagement rather than to punishment – unlike Eve, and also unlike the Fairchild children in Mrs. Sherwood's stories, discussed in Chapter 1, who were so often confronted by tempting fruits outside the garden walls but were warned never to "go beyond the bounds."[3]

Bell's garden gate, a threshold between enclosure and exploration, the tame and the wild, returns as a key visual trope in images from around the same time, thus extending the themes of our book several generations later. Frances Hodgson Burnett described the "enchanted" landscape around her childhood home as "the Back Garden of Eden,"[4] and in *The Secret Garden*, published in 1911, the overgrown gate leads to a rich inner garden of transformation, interiority replacing exteriority as the site of greatest risk and potential. In naming her central character Burnett clearly intended a reference to the nursery rhyme "Mistress Mary, quite contrary, / how does your garden grow?"[5] Certainly there is no overt connection between Burnett's Mary and a likely historical source for the rhyme (Mary Tudor, "bloody Mary," and her growing "garden," or cemetery, filled with persecuted Protestants),[6] but the contrariness of the three Marys (Mary Tudor, Mary in the rhyme, and Burnett's Mary) is important for any reader of *The Secret Garden* to keep in mind. In the case of Mary Lennox, however, her discovery of the hidden key and her first forbidden steps through the gate into the overgrown garden result in a transformative healing process for both herself and the sickly Colin. Just as the garden is ordered and tamed, brought back from its wild state, so too is their mental and moral ground renewed through cultivation. Jerry Griswold, in a Bachelardian approach, describes the garden as characterized by what he calls snugness, prompting "a withdrawal associated with a sense of renewal rather than torpor or defeat."[7] Other readers have given a more active role to the garden as a key protagonist in the novel. One early reviewer in 1911 described the "agency of the garden" as a healing force, and Anna Silver's recent analysis personifies the garden as a mother: she proposes that "Mary and Colin are restored to health, 'mothered,' by the nurturant power of a garden."[8]

Charles Robinson's illustrations for the first edition of *The Secret Garden* highlight the change from the overgrown and long-neglected garden to its later blossoming luxuriance, carefully tended by the three children. In the first plate (Fig. 9.1) Mary approaches the gate, pushing aside the concealing branches and vines; her body is tense and expectant as she first glimpses the

Fig. 9.1.   Illustration by Charles Robinson in Frances Hodgson Burnett, *The Secret Garden*.

new terrain through the bars. Although she will be moving inward rather than outward through the gate, the emotional riskiness of her decision reminds us of the dangers inherent in navigating outside of one's socially allotted spaces. Robinson portrays Mary with outstretched arms, in a pose that suggests not only physical action but also openness to what Gertrude Bell called "the world of adventure and of enterprise" – and in fact this scene is reminiscent of Bell's exclamation, "you step forth, and behold!"

This illustration provides a telling contrast with Helen Allingham's turn-of-the-century watercolors, many of which are centered on a woman at the garden gate – thus furthering the idea of the garden as a transitional zone marking the extent of the domesticated landscape (Fig. 9.2). Both Burnett and Allingham idealize rural England, especially the garden at its heart – unlike Bell's frustration with "the enclosed garden" which she envisions as a chained sanctuary – but Allingham's paintings are more conservative in their nostalgic view back at a rapidly disappearing form of country life. Her women often seem caught at the threshold, moving out but looking back, hampered by signs of domestic responsibility: the cottage behind them, the blooming garden, the child in their arms. Even the cats in *A Cottage at Freshwater* underscore the message: although the gate is open, the mother cat sits sedately on the steps, held back by the implied boundary, and only the untrained kitten wanders off. The woman is small and insubstantial in relation to the vegetation all around her, which is luxuriant and fertile but so dense that there seems little room to maneuver. It is an airless space forming a thick band of green across the surface of the painting. The only respite is found in a sliver of sky at the top and a small wedge of the dirt lane in the foreground. She has access to the road – the gate is open – but she stands immobile, more a personification of the home-ground than a purposive agent in her own right. Here we are reminded of the popular Mrs. Ellis and her mid-Victorian ideal of the mother "enclosed, as it were, in the home-garden with her daughters."[9]

Allingham's picturesque cottages were typically painted on site – in this case one of a number of "fine old cottages" on the Isle of Wight, probably painted c. 1890–1910 on her trips there to visit the Tennysons – but the people in the scene were little more than stock figures, added later in the studio. Like Maria Spilsbury and many other nineteenth-century artists and writers, Allingham relied on her work to provide money for her family, especially after her husband's death, but she seems to have returned to the cottage theme not only because it was popular, and thus marketable, but also because she wanted to record what she and others feared was an aspect of English life soon to be lost. One friend described her cottage scenes as

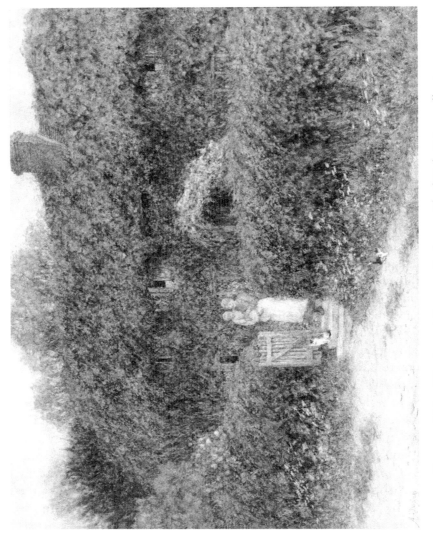

Fig. 9.2. Helen Allingham, *A Cottage at Freshwater, Isle of Wight*. Private collection.

"lasting memorials of the fast-vanishing beauty of our countryside" and, more romantically, as "visions of a lost Fairyland."[10] Allingham and her husband, along with their friends Tennyson, Thomas Carlyle, and the garden writer Gertrude Jekyll, were supporters of William Morris's Society for Protection of Ancient Buildings, founded in 1877. Many of her cottages are still identifiable today, but the realism is partially offset by her occasional revising of the architectural structure (removing an extension or adding a thatched roof) as well as by the addition of figures and even flowers in the garden, using Jekyll's Munstead Wood garden as a model.[11]

A blend of portrait realism and nostalgic fantasy, Allingham's watercolors prolong the Victorian idyll into the new century, unlike Bell's "enclosed garden," which must be escaped in order to enter "the immeasurable world," or Burnett's secret garden, which must be explored and renewed in a way that is similarly both transgressive and healing. All three, then, rely on the garden metaphors of the previous century, but reinvest them with alternative meanings. Bell, so impatient with the enclosed garden, seems especially close to Ruskin's prophecy that the women of England will seek the world outside of their garden gates "where order is more difficult, distress more imminent, loveliness more rare."[12] More free of domestic constraints than Ruskin would have imagined or condoned, Bell's explorer of the "immeasurable world" is one descendant of Smith's "disciples of Flora" who carries her engagement beyond the garden gate, using the domesticated landscape as a springboard for meaningful action.

Notes

INTRODUCTION

1 William Wordsworth, Preface to *Lyrical Ballads*, 1800, *Prose Works* 1:130.
2 John-Joseph Merlin was an inventor who opened Merlin's Mechanical Museum in London. Burnett, *Company of Pianos* 140.
3 Smith, *Rambles Farther* 196.
4 Hunt, "Garden as Cultural Object" 20.
5 Wollstonecraft, *Vindication* 11. See George, *Botany, Sexuality and Women's Writing* 28–35; also 95, for an analysis of female Linnaeans' preference for indigenous plants. See also King, *Bloom*, especially 11–72, for an analysis of the cultural work of botany in the 1790s.
6 More, *Strictures* 158–59.
7 Rousseau, *Letters* 32.
8 Bachelard, *Poetics of Space* 8, 215, 139.
9 Tuan, *Space and Place* 6, 12.
10 Ross, *What Gardens Mean* 169–70. Laura Mulvey, for instance, writing about gender overdetermination in film melodrama, differentiates between "masculine space: an outside, the sphere of adventure, movement and cathartic action" and the feminine space of "emotion, immobility, enclosed space, and confinement." See Mulvey, "Pandora" 55.
11 Hunt, *Greater Perfections* 29, 11.
12 Rose, *Feminism and Geography* 17, 45, 56, 60, 87.
13 Ford, "Landscape Revisited" 151–54.
14 Rose, *Feminism and Geography* 140–41, 149. She cites Elspeth Probyn, who uses Deleuze to complicate the "doubledness of the body": "Rather than the arbitrary meeting of the outside and the inside, of the one and of the other, the double (or what I am calling the doubledness) is more akin to what Deleuze calls 'le pli' ('the pleat,' 'the fold,' 'the doubling up') or 'l'accroc' ('a snag') or 'l'invagination' (the 'invagination' of the one and the other)." Probyn, "This Body" 119.
15 Rose, *Feminism and Geography* 155.
16 Massey, *Space, Place, and Gender* 169–71.
17 Domosh and Seager, *Putting Women in Place* xxi–xxii.
18 *Ibid.* 111.

Notes to pages 7–19

19 Casid's analysis deftly combines a critique of empire with queer theory in Chapter 4, entitled "Some Queer Versions of Georgic," a section that ends with an interpretation of the Ladies of Llangollen's *ferme ornée* in Wales. Casid, *Sowing Empire*, especially 168–90.
20 Taylor and Taylor, *Correspondence* 140.
21 Ellis, *Mothers of England* 202.
22 *Ibid.* 82–84.
23 Bachelard, *Poetics of Space* 155, and Stewart, *On Longing* 68.

1 "IN THE HOME-GARDEN": MORAL TALES FOR CHILDREN

1 Martineau, *Household Education* 159. Edith Cobb considers the affiliation between children and nature as a "bioaesthetic striving" that is a core component of emotional and cultural maturation (*Ecology of the Imagination* 16).
2 Martineau, *Household Education* 159.
3 Yonge, "Children's Literature" 231.
4 Morgan and Richards, *Paradise Out of a Common Field* 169.
5 Ellis, *Mothers of England* 199, 33, 92, 85, 202.
6 James Kincaid, in *Child-Loving*, discusses what he terms "the child botanical" as a common Victorian rhetorical strategy of equating childrearing with botanical cultivation; see also Hines, "He Made *Us*" 25–26.
7 Rose, *Feminism and Geography* 119–20.
8 Tuan, *Space and Place* 6; Rose, *Feminism and Geography* 140–41.
9 Taylor, *Maternal Solicitude* 105.
10 Ariès, *Centuries of Childhood* 415.
11 See, e.g., Locke, *Some Thoughts Concerning Education* 52, 90, 96, 135.
12 *Pleasing Instructor* 6.
13 Bayly, *Life and Letters* 101, 122. The gardener/mentor's control over the plant/child, whether in terms of "domesticating the wild, disciplining the unruly, or gentrifying the common," is emphasized by Kathryn Graham in her study of topiary in children's literature: "Devil's Own Art" 108. See also Briggs, "'Delightful Task!'" 70.
14 Agress proposes that writers such as Ann Martin Taylor, while purporting to be "messiahs to women," often acted inadvertently as "the devil's disciples" to "perpetuate society's biases against women"; *Feminine Irony* 9, 172; also 174–75. She unfortunately confuses Ann Taylor, the better-known children's author, with her mother Ann Martin Taylor, who wrote advice manuals for women.
15 Myers, "Impeccable Governesses" 33.
16 Myers, "Taste for Truth" 118, 120.
17 Edgeworth, *Works* 11:253.
18 Dolan, "Collaborative Motherhood" 110–11.
19 Myers, "Impeccable Governesses" 34, 38.
20 Plumb, "New World" 81.

21 Myers, "Impeccable Governesses" 50, recognized the cruciform shape of the composition and the halo-like hats, and she suggested that "Heroic, even Christlike matrons structure the female mentorial tradition." For an example of the Madonna of Mercy theme, see Piero della Francesca's fifteenth-century version in San Sepolcro.
22 Qtd. in Davidoff and Hall, *Family Fortunes* 397.
23 Wordsworth, *The Prelude* 5:236–37, 1805; Edgeworth, *Early Lessons* 3:258.
24 Summerfield, *Fantasy and Reason* 188, 232. Summerfield's extreme contrast between "fantasy and reason" is evident in his assessment of Blake, whose *Songs of Innocence* "was the only work of genius for children, in its century" (238), and Wollstonecraft: "*Original Stories* has a strong claim to be the most sinister, ugly, overbearing book for children ever published. It is permeated by a grim, humourless, tyrannical spirit of hectoring and unswerving spiritual and mental rectitude – all in the name of healthy growth" (229).
25 See Pickering, *Moral Instruction* viii–ix, and Myers, "Impeccable Governesses" 41; also McCarthy, "Mother of All Discourses" 87, for a summary of this dichotomizing trend in the study of Georgian literature for children. Rowbotham's study of didacticism in Victorian fiction for girls is also relevant; see especially *Good Girls* 103.
26 Smith, *Rambles Farther* 266, 261, 263–64.
27 Smith, *Rural Walks* 1:123–24.
28 Smith, *Rambles Farther* 268.
29 Jacson, *Botanical Dialogues* 32; Ibbetson, "On the Structure and Growth of Seeds" 2.
30 Smith, *Rural Walks* 69–70.
31 Budden, *Chit Chat* 5, 7, 22–24.
32 Budden, *Key to Knowledge* 86, 89.
33 "My Dear Children" 311. This familiar analogy, popularized by John Locke (see *Some Thoughts Concerning Education*, 52, 90, 96, 135), was a commonplace throughout the long eighteenth century, from Sarah Fielding (*Governess* 109) to Jane Taylor (*Contributions of Q.Q.* 1:21) and Mrs. Ellis (*Mothers of England* 92, 99).
34 Taylor, *Rhymes for the Nursery* 22.
35 O'Malley, *Making of the Modern Child* 125, 135.
36 Budden, *Right and Wrong* 4, 6, 3, 164, 170.
37 Tuan, *Space and Place* 22. See Rose for a critique of Tuan's humanistic geography and its universalizing approach to gendered mapping of "front and back, centre and periphery, and closed and open" (*Feminism and Geography* 52).
38 Tuan, *Space and Place* 29.
39 Pickering, *Moral Instruction* 42; More, *Strictures* 1:149–50.
40 Budden, *Always Happy* 58, 142, 164–65.
41 Riley, *Gifts for Good Children* 1:50–51, 114–15.
42 Catlow and Catlow, *Children's Garden* 62–63.
43 [Jerram?], *Lucy and Arthur* 73–82.
44 *Female Aegis* 3–4.

45 "At Home and at School" 572.
46 Budden, *Chit Chat* 174–77.
47 Smith, *Rural Walks* 50. Dolan distinguishes between Mrs. Woodfield's approach and the "finishing school" model ("Collaborative Motherhood" 114).
48 Taylor, *Memoirs* 193–94.
49 Taylor, *Essays in Rhyme* 140–54.
50 Aspinall-Oglander, *Admiral's Wife* 187–88.
51 Wollstonecraft, *Original Stories* 42–47.
52 Wordsworth, *Grasmere Journals* 115; Mitford, *Life* 2:28.
53 Honeyman, "Childhood Bound" 121.
54 Aspinall-Oglander, *Admiral's Wife* 93.
55 Fielding, *Governess* 40, 11–12, 64. Briggs argues that the illustration reflects a central component of Fielding's approach, the replacement of "a masculine and hierarchic model of education with a feminine and democratic one" ("'Delightful Task!'" 68). See also Bree, *Sarah Fielding*, Suzuki, "*Little Female Academy*," and Wilner, "Education and Ideology."
56 Barbauld, *Lessons* 53.
57 McCarthy, "Mother of All Discourses" 93–94.
58 Edgeworth, *Frank* 338–39.
59 Taylor and Taylor, *Original Poems* 2:30.
60 See Taylor and Taylor, *Original Poems* 1:76–78, for the poem, which, being immediately popular, was also published in 1815 as the small pamphlet in which this illustration appears. The image was also used to decorate children's plates and cups, as in Riley, *Gifts for Good Children* 1:25 (#26) and 31 (#65).
61 *Peter Parley's First Present* 48.
62 [Jerram?], *Lucy and Arthur* 141–43.
63 Budden, *Always Happy* 148–49.
64 Martineau, *Deerbrook* 25.
65 Bayly, *Life and Letters* 25.
66 Edgeworth, *Works* 10:9, 13.
67 Bachelard, *Poetics of Space* xxxv; Myers, "Romancing the Moral Tale" 107.
68 Sherwood, *History of the Fairchild Family* 80.
69 *Ibid.* 339–40, 381. For more on Sherwood, see Avery, *Childhood's Pattern* 92–100.
70 Fielding, *Governess* 59.
71 Ellis, *Mothers of England* 102, 135, 191.
72 Fleming, *Complete Marjory Fleming* 31, 69, 12, 6. See also Moffat and Painter, *Revelations* 21, and Alexandra Johnson, "Drama of Imagination."
73 Gorham, *Victorian Girl* 70–72, 93–94.
74 Taylor, *Little Field Daisy* 2.
75 Taylor and Taylor, *Correspondence* 91.
76 Taylor and Taylor, *Snow-Drop* 2–3.
77 Trimmer, review of *Original Poems* 75.
78 Budden, *Right and Wrong* 89, 111.

79 Taylor, *Little Field Daisy* 3.
80 Bachelard, *Poetics of Space* 222, 224. Susan Honeyman also notes the "careful attention to entrances and exits" in children's literature ("Childhood Bound" 125).
81 Fielding, *Governess* 92–93. Mrs. Teachum allows the telling of fairy tales only under certain conditions: when story-time is overseen by the most responsible girl; when the narrative has a clear moral point to it; and when it is told within the safe confines of the arbor.
82 Wakefield, *Juvenile Anecdotes* 108–10.
83 Turner, *Cowslip* 38.
84 Kent, *York House* 19, 180–85.
85 Sherwood, *History of the Fairchild Family* 35, 15, 25, 185, 209.
86 O'Reilly, *Daisy's Companions* 22–24.
87 Wakefield, *Reflections* 34.
88 Fleming, *Complete Marjory Fleming* 121.
89 Wollstonecraft, *Vindication* 137.
90 O'Malley, *Making of the Modern Child* 96.
91 Steward, *New Child* 150.
92 Budden, *Right and Wrong* 43–54, 166.
93 Tuan, *Space and Place* 6, 52–54.
94 Massey, *Space, Place, and Gender* 169.
95 Bachelard, *Poetics of Space* 139.
96 Flint, *Woman Reader* 72.
97 Myers, "Impeccable Governesses" 34.

2 THE "BOTANIC EYE": BOTANY, MINIATURE, AND MAGNIFICATION

1 Bachelard, *Poetics of Space* 155; Stewart, *On Longing* 68. Also interesting is John Mack's recent *The Art of Small Things*.
2 See, for instance, Myers, "Impeccable Governesses," and Ruwe, "Bibliography," for additional essays by Myers. Amies, "Amusing and Instructive Conversations," offers a history and analysis of literature in the dialogue mode.
3 Tonna, *Chapters on Flowers* 1.
4 Loudon, *Botany for Ladies* 281.
5 Southern Faunist, "Letter" 199–200.
6 Wakefield, *Introduction to Botany* 32.
7 Fitton, *Conversations on Botany* 18.
8 See George's analysis of natives and exotics in *Botany, Sexuality and Women's Writing* 153–84.
9 Bellanca, *Daybooks of Discovery* 151, 164–65.
10 Shore, *Journal* 6, 54, 34.
11 Ibid. 62, 89, 103–04.
12 Halstead, *Little Botanist* 5, 9.

13 Henry Phillips's patriotic praise of England's exotics from the corners of the empire would be unfamiliar in most women's texts: "The present Royal Family being greatly attached to the study of Botany … exotic beauties are now seen blended with our natural verdure in every corner of the island" (*History of Cultivated Vegetables* 18).
14 Shteir, *Cultivating Women* 88–89.
15 Jackson-Houlston, "'Queen Lilies'?" 95.
16 Park, *Travels* 225.
17 In *Botanical Rambles*, Atkins also uses the passage from *Travels* to introduce the study of mosses and the minute wonders of plant structure (190–91).
18 Roberts, *Wonders of the Vegetable Kingdom* 167.
19 Pratt, *The Field* 11, 17.
20 See the essays by Nicolson, "Microscope and the English Imagination," Chico, "Minute Particulars," and Arminter, "Sexual Politics"; the last of these analyzes the shift in the microscope from "rare scientific instrument to popular female commodity" (22 and passim); she describes (with illustrations) several of the popular microscopes, including Mr. Wilson's Pocket-Microscope.
21 Nicolson, "Microscope and the English Imagination" 210.
22 Bachelard, *Poetics of Space* 172.
23 Stewart, *On Longing* 54.
24 Bachelard, *Poetics of Space* 150.
25 *Ibid.* 151.
26 Qtd. in *ibid.* 154.
27 Darwin's socio-sexual interpretation permeates the second part of *The Botanic Garden*, "The Loves of Plants." See Bewell, "'Jacobin Plants'," Calè, "Female Band," and Kelley, "Romantic Exemplarity," especially 230–33.
28 Bachelard, *Poetics of Space* 152, 155.
29 See Shteir, *Cultivating Women*, especially 81–103.
30 Jacson, *Botanical Dialogues* 53–54, 239, 2, 60. We have followed Shteir and other sources in spelling the name "Jacson," although it sometimes appears as "Jackson"; her later *The Florist's Manual* is listed in the University of Virginia Library as by Mary Jackson Henry. Also, Jacson's middle name is occasionally spelled "Elizabetha." Since she did not publish under her name but as "a lady," one cannot determine spelling from the publications. See also Percy, "Maria Elizabetha Jacson" 45, and George, *Botany, Sexuality and Women's Writing* 41, note 55, for the varied spelling of her name.

Our allusion to the Proper Lady refers to Mary Poovey's *The Proper Lady and the Woman Writer*, a figure somewhat akin to Virginia Woolf's later Angel in the House from "Professions for Women" (1931), a stereotype borrowed from Coventry Patmore, who also plays havoc with the woman writer.
31 Jacson, *Botanical Dialogues* 139, 65. Her progressive attitude is perhaps more in line with her publication by Joseph Johnson and a printed letter of endorsement in the preface by Erasmus Darwin. Johnson was known for printing left-leaning writers and Darwin for his radical political views. Consider, also,

Rose's recognition of "the everyday [as] the arena through which patriarchy is recreated – and contested" (*Feminism and Geography* 17).

32 As Shteir points out, Jacson is concerned to avoid the scorn of being a learned lady and at times seems to echo the proprieties of conduct literature in an age of "retrenchment" (*Cultivating Women* 117). Yet her discussion of female education is conflicted. After acknowledging that "the world" limits women to "the exercise of their fingers," Hortensia goes on to say that "The world improves, and consequently female education" (*Botanical Dialogues* 239). In this way Jacson critiques the ideology that she seems to support.

33 Jacson, *Botanical Dialogues* 65. Greg Myers points out the fundamental inconsistency for the *reader* of dialogues of popular science (as distinct from the represented participants) in that "The books profess to teach learning by experience, but actually they teach learning from authority," since the reader cannot directly participate in the experiences ("Science for Women and Children" 181). But Jacson does model a process for the reader to adapt that could lead to more open experiences, especially since her text appeals to both young readers and their guardians, who presumably can help guide the processes of thought. As a contemporary review puts it, "we think it so complete an elementary work, that not only the youth of both sexes, but adults also, will consider themselves much indebted to the fair writer for her ingenious labours"; *Analytic Review* 28 (1798): 397–98.

34 Charles Alston claimed in "A Dissertation on the Sexes of Plants" (1771) that Linnaeus was "too smutty for English ears" (qtd. in Bewell, "'Jacobin Plants'" 132) and William Smellie's entry for the first edition of the *Encyclopedia Britannica* in 1773 asserted that "obscenity is the very basis of the Linnaean system" (qtd. in Calè, "Female Band").

35 Jacson, *Botanical Dialogues* 10, 245. For the concept of defamiliarization, see Makaryk, *Encyclopedia* 528–29.

36 *Shelley's Poetry and Prose* 517. The lines from Wordsworth's "Simon Lee" are: "O Reader! had you in your mind / Such stores as silent thought can bring, / O gentle Reader! you would find / A tale in everything" (lines 65–68, *Poetical Works* 3:60).

37 Jacson, *Botanical Dialogues* 228–30, 237.

38 *Ibid.* 32, 68, 245, 4.

39 *Ibid.* 88, 23, 265.

40 *Ibid.* 52–55.

41 *Ibid.* 286.

42 Taylor, *A Day's Pleasure* 41.

43 Jacson, *Botanical Dialogues* 230–32.

44 *Ibid.* 235–36.

45 Stewart, *On Longing* 54.

46 Darwin, *Plan for the Conduct of Female Education* 40–41, 45.

47 Wakefield, *Reflections* 90–91; More, *Strictures* 2:144.

48 Wakefield, *Reflections* 9. See Gates, *Kindred Nature* 66–67, for a discussion of women's difficulties in entering the scientific arena, especially regarding scientific education and professional societies.

49 Her first essays were signed "A. Ibbetson," leading her to be mistaken for a male until she eventually corrected the publisher (not too quickly, however – presumably because she wanted to establish herself first before risking being dismissed as "merely" a woman scientist). The middle-class Ibbsetson, widowed at thirty-three and without children, moved to Devon and devoted her life to her experiments with plant physiology. Essentially self-taught and without mentors or colleagues (in fact, she called herself a "recluse" working "13 out of 24 hours" each day), she relied on first-hand dissections and observations rather than on information received through the numerous botanical books or societies of the period. See Shteir, *Cultivating Women* 120–35, for the first extensive discussion of Ibbetson's work.
50 Ibbetson, "On the Structure and Growth of Seeds" 1.
51 Ibbetson, "Treatise" 51. This "MS Treatise on Botany in the Form of 20 Letters" is in the Botany Library, Natural History Museum, London.
52 Ibbetson, "On the Perspiration" 243, and "On the Structure and Growth of Seeds" 5.
53 Ibbetson, "On the Flower-Buds" 4. This practical focus was particularly important to her later work when she did more applied experiments related to agricultural plants. She did not hesitate to tackle even the most unladylike of subjects, urging the use of liquid manures from the piggery and the house, for example ("On the Action of Lime" 129).
54 Ibbetson, "On the Physiology" 3; "On the Perspiration" 245; and "On the Injurious Effect" 87.
55 Ibbetson, "On the Adapting of Plants" 148.
56 Gates, "Those Who Drew" 193. Lightman, "Depicting Nature," outlines the variety of purposes that visual images in scientific texts could serve during this period, including purely ornamental, rhetorical or persuasive, and authoritative. The last was more typical of male authors, according to Lightman (226), but was certainly also applicable to Ibbetson, as we show here.
57 Ibbetson, "On the Structure and Growth of Seeds" 2, 8.
58 Ibbetson, "Treatise."
59 Shteir, *Cultivating Women* 126.
60 "Monthly Botanical Report" 601.
61 Ibbetson, "Treatise."
62 "On the Interior Buds" 10.
63 Ibbetson, "On the Secret and Open Nectaries" 177.
64 Ibbetson, "Treatise."
65 Ibbetson, "On the Structure and Growth of Seeds" 7, 13; "Treatise."
66 Ibbetson, "On the Structure and Growth of Seeds" 8.
67 Stewart, *On Longing* 54.
68 See especially Ryan's introduction in *The Romantic Reformation* 1–13.
69 The rift between science and religion of course intensifies later in the nineteenth century. See Rauch, who states that "The works of Charles Lyell and Charles Darwin challenged even the most liberal religious interpretations of nature, making it much more difficult to argue for 'design' in the natural world" ("World of Faith" 17).

70 Roberts, *Wonders of the Vegetable Kingdom*, "Preface."
71 Blain *et al.* note that Roberts was learned in "Latin, Greek, Hebrew, and natural history" (*Feminist Companion* 910), so her classical emphasis should not be a surprise.
72 William Withering's *An Arrangement of British Plants According to the Latest Improvements of the Linnæan system* (1796) is the same text that William and Dorothy Wordsworth acquired at Dove Cottage to identify the native plants that Dorothy incorporated into her garden, as we shall see in Chapter 5.
73 Roberts, *Wonders of the Vegetable Kingdom* 26, 12.
74 Hoare, *Poems*, stanza XLIX.
75 Roberts, *Wonders of the Vegetable Kingdom* 86–87.
76 *Ibid.* 83, 12.
77 In *Rambles Farther*, Mrs. Woodfield distinguishes similarly between the botanic eye and that of the landscape painter, commenting that wildflowers "and many other plants are rather the pursuit of the botanist than the landscape painter," since the latter "cannot minutely describe the long tangling branches of the blackberry; the festoons of briony woodbine, nightshade, or wild hop, that creep or flaunt among the rugged hollows" (Smith 99).
78 Seward, *Poetical Works* 3:1–2.
79 Roberts, *Wonders of the Vegetable Kingdom* 119, 124–25. For more on the iron works, see Setzer, "'Pond'rous Engines'," and Coffey, "Protecting the Botanic Garden," who asserts that "Visitors came to Coalbrookdale not in spite of the industrialization, but because of it" (153).
80 Roberts, *Wonders of the Vegetable Kingdom* 165, 216, 212–13.
81 Bachelard, *Poetics of Space* 151.
82 Darwin, *Botanic Garden*, lines 381–84, qtd. in Roberts, *Wonders of the Vegetable Kingdom* 112–13. Roberts does not attribute authorship to any quotations in the text.
83 Roberts, *Wonders of the Vegetable Kingdom* 223.
84 "Tintern Abbey" 49 (Wordsworth, *Poetical Works* 2), and Blake, "Auguries of Innocence" 1.
85 [Marcet], *Conversations on Vegetable Physiology* 206.
86 Bachelard, *Poetics of Space* 7.
87 Stewart, *On Longing* 44.
88 Line 111 (Wordsworth, *Poetical Works* 4).
89 Bachelard, *Poetics of Space* 150, 163.
90 Smith, *Rural Walks* 104. See Judith Pascoe's "Female Botanists" for a detailed analysis of the way that botany permeates Smith's poetry as well as her prose texts.

3 PICTURING THE "HOME LANDSCAPE": THE NATURE OF ACCOMPLISHMENT

1 Edgeworth, *Parent's Assistant* 220–22.
2 Edgeworth and Edgeworth, *Practical Education* 119–25.

3 See Myers, "Dilemmas of Gender," for a discussion of the influence of Edgeworth's father; also Myers, "Reading Rosamond" 59, who observes, "Critics still argue about whether her work was victimized or empowered by her influential, scientific-minded father."
4 Edgeworth, *Rosamond* 2:4, 14–15.
5 Kramer, *Women of Flowers* 152, 204–08, and Blunt and Stearn, *Art of Botanical Illustration* 252. Other women who were drawing teachers as well as active flower illustrators include Mary Gartside, Mary Lawrance, Margaret Meen, Henrietta Moriarty, and Elizabeth Perkins; Bermingham, *Learning to Draw* 215.
6 Hardie, *Water-Colour Painting* 243; Plumb, "New World of Children" 74.
7 Broome, *Fanny and Mary* 5.
8 Kriz, *Idea of the English Landscape Painter* 66–67, and Bermingham, *Learning to Draw* 205; also Catherine King, "What Women Can Make" 61. For more on women flower painters, see Hardie, *Water-Colour Painting* 243 (for Mary Lawrance); Pointon, *Strategies for Showing*, ch. 4 (for Mary Moser); and Bermingham, *Learning to Draw* 211 (for Anne Byrne). For a general summary of some of the differences between eighteenth- and early nineteenth-century drawing manuals, especially a shift from figurative to landscape drawing and from copying earlier designs to imitating nature directly, see Friedman, "Every Lady"; also Bicknell and Monro, *Gilpin to Ruskin* 7–8.
9 Bermingham, *Learning to Draw* 224.
10 Sha, *Visual and Verbal Sketch* 19.
11 Austen, *Emma* 4:43.
12 Sha, *Visual and Verbal Sketch* 80, 85, 93.
13 Shore, *Journal* 87.
14 Bermingham, *Learning to Draw* 159–62; also 217–24 for Mary Gartside's more scientific and experimental use of geometric shapes as a foundation for sketching flowers. See Jackson-Houlston for further discussion of the copy-book approach in early drawing manuals ("'Queen Lilies'?" 94).
15 Kramer, *Women of Flowers* 28, 36, and Bermingham, *Learning to Draw* 205. Margaret Meen's *Exotic Plants from the Royal Gardens at Kew* (1790) and Mary Lawrance's *A Collection of Roses from Nature* (1799) were dedicated to the queen, whose support was also important for Mary Delany and her intricately detailed paper collages of flowers (see Hayden, *Mrs. Delany*, and Moore, "Queer Gardens," especially 61–67).
16 Shore, *Journal* 198. Jane Loudon advised the readers of *The Lady's Country Companion* to employ a maid to carry the sketchpad and stool, thus avoiding "over-fatigue" for a "delicate constitution" (356).
17 Taylor, *Memoirs* 53, 95.
18 Edgeworth, *Memoir* 1:73.
19 See Sha, *Visual and Verbal Sketch* 102, for the statistics. Davidoff and Hall note that while women sometimes exhibited their work, "what these women could not do, except in the most unusual circumstances, was to become professional artists with a commercial reputation in their own right" (*Family Fortunes* 309).

20 Blunt and Stearn, *Art of Botanical Illustration* 220, and Wollstonecraft, *Original Stories* 54.
21 Barbauld, *Selected Poetry* 49, and Ellis, *Mothers of England* 52.
22 Bayly, *Life and Letters* 106, 109.
23 *Elegant Arts* iv.
24 Wollstonecraft, *Original Stories* 76.
25 Budden, *Chit Chat* 72–73.
26 Wakefield, *Reflections* 119.
27 Wakefield, *Introduction* 22–23.
28 Shteir, *Cultivating Women* 86.
29 Bermingham analyzes these etchings at length in the context of theories of the gaze: "As the unconscious object of the gaze she is the equivalent of the landscape she sketches ... Like nature – the nature she embodies – her true role is not that of artist but that of art object" (*Learning to Draw* 194). See also Barnett, *Richard and Maria Cosway* 147.
30 Mellor presents an intriguing alternative reading, proposing that Cosway "domesticates the sublime" by identifying the mother in the easel painting as a personification of Nature. For Mellor, the artist "mediat[es] between nature and culture without the visual interposition of a male mentor or male-authored art" ("British Romanticism" 135).
31 Qtd. in Barnett, *Richard and Maria Cosway* 260.
32 Qtd. in *ibid.* 260–61.
33 Lloyd, *Richard and Maria Cosway* 45.
34 Cunningham, *Lives* 6:10. Cosway became well known as a popular *salon* hostess in the 1780s, attracting such luminaries as the Prince of Wales and Horace Walpole, and among her friends were Jacques-Louis David and Thomas Jefferson. Later, however, she became increasingly religious and distanced from her husband; Lloyd, *Richard and Maria Cosway* 48–50, 67–68.
35 Budden, *Always Happy* 9.
36 Sha argues that with the increase in leisure time came an increase in social fears (that the domestic sphere would be disrupted by women's access to professionalism, for example), which in turn resulted in a narrowing of the definition of appropriate femininity (*Visual and Verbal Sketch* 73). See also Rowbotham, *Good Girls* 13.
37 Elwood, *Memoirs of the Literary Ladies* 2:175, refers to Austen drawing. See *Northanger Abbey* 38 and *The Novels* 6:421 for *Sanditon*. Sha discusses sketching as a character device in *Emma* (*Visual and Verbal Sketch* 145–54).
38 Taylor, *Essays in Rhyme* 121–22.
39 Taylor and Taylor, *Correspondence* 56–58.
40 More, *Works* (1830), 5:325.
41 Bermingham, *Learning to Draw* 145–48.
42 More, *Works* (1856), 1:130–32. See Avery for a discussion of the *Cheap Repository Tracts* (*Childhood's Pattern* 59–68).
43 *Delights of Flower Painting* 7.
44 Barbauld, *Selected Poetry* 95.

45 Wollstonecraft, *Vindication* 143.
46 Burton, *Lectures on Female Education* 118, and Smith, *Minor Morals* 23–24.
47 Smith, *Rural Walks* 2:10–11, 1:70–71.
48 Wakefield, *Reflections* 130–33.
49 Kramer, *Women of Flowers* 35, 116.
50 A Lady, *Floral Knitting Book* v.
51 Howitt, *Sowing and Reaping* 131–32.
52 Shteir, "Fac-Similes of Nature" 658–59.
53 Smith, *Rural Walks* 1:72–74, 82–83, and *Rambles Farther* 101–02.
54 Tuan, *Space and Place* 145.
55 Ford, "Landscape Revisited" 151–55.
56 There is some uncertainty about the birthdate of Maria (whose full name was Rebecca Maria Ann Spilsbury): it is listed as 1777 in Young, *Father and Daughter* 11, and Yeldham, "Spilsbury" 948, but as December 7, 1779, in the family genealogy of her descendant Gavin Taylor. He cites as his source "a school book" by his great-grandmother, whose information came in turn from her father-in-law, Maria's son (email correspondence with Elise Smith, June 13, 2006, and http://homepages.ihug.co.nz/~taylg134/fam00030.html). The earlier birthdate is more likely, however, since she is known to have first exhibited at the Royal Academy in 1792. Our book was unfortunately already in press before the publication of Charlotte Yeldham's *Maria Spilsbury: Artist and Evangelical* (Burlington, VT: Ashgate, 2010), but we are very grateful to her for providing us with the illustration of *After School*, with Sotheby's approval.
57 Qtd. in Young, *Father and Daughter* 24; see also Yeldham, "Spilsbury" 948.
58 Qtd. in Young, *Father and Daughter* 39.
59 *Ibid.* 28.
60 *Ibid.* 28–29, 31–33, and Yeldham, "Spilsbury" 949.
61 Young, "Maria Spilsbury" xlvi.
62 Qtd. in Young, *Father and Daughter* 17, 27.
63 Qtd. in *ibid.* 34–35. Remarkably, Spilsbury continued to exhibit during this time. Her paintings were shown in several venues in Dublin every year from 1814 to 1819 except 1815, between the birth of her two daughters, and 1818, when her son died (Yeldham, "Spilsbury" 949).
64 We are grateful to Gavin Taylor for the quotation from Maria's son Augustus Taylor; email correspondence with Elise Smith, June 16, 2006.
65 For Gainsborough's portrait see Belsey, *Thomas Gainsborough*, fig. 33.
66 Hunt, *Greater Perfections* 20.
67 This small painting measures only 12.4 × 17.5 inches, but she did occasionally work in a larger scale: *The Royal Jubilee, as Celebrated at Great Malvern*, 1809 (location unknown), is 4½ × 5½ feet (Yeldham, "Spilsbury" 949). The identification of the family members is confirmed by an email from Gavin Taylor, August 2, 2007. The painting must have been completed before 1803 when Mr. Taylor died, and it may well date from 1798 when Maria and her father were especially close to the Taylor family, frequently visiting them at their Southampton home (Young, *Father and Daughter* 20).

68 More, *Works* (1856) 1:132.
69 *Domestic Happiness* is the first in Morland's "Laetitia" series, documenting the downfall of the young woman seen at the right in this image of traditional familial order. The domestic/sexual symbolism of Morland's caged bird derives from the Dutch Baroque tradition; see Shefer, *Birds, Cages and Women*.
70 Although the cottage theme was popular in the late eighteenth century, beginning with Gainsborough's 1778 and 1780 exhibitions, it is not clear how Spilsbury would have been aware of any specific work by Gainsborough or his followers. After their RA exhibition Gainsborough's paintings went into private collections (Bermingham, *Sensation and Sensibility* 25–32). The dates of Spilsbury's extant cottage paintings are not known, but Graves lists various works that she exhibited at the RA, including several with rural themes: e.g., *Cottage Children at Supper* (1793), *A Pastoral Scene* (1802), *Children in a Farmyard, Drinking Milk – Morning* (1805), and *A Cottage Door* (1808) (*Royal Academy of Art* 4:221–22). These all date before the Gainsborough retrospective in 1814 at the British Institution with three of his cottage door paintings.
71 This passage was quoted in Rosenthal, "Rough and the Smooth" 53. For more on the issue of eighteenth-century sensibility as a context for Gainsborough's cottage door paintings, see Bermingham, *Sensation and Sensibility*, especially 8–12.
72 For the mood of "uncertainty" or even "impending disaster" in Gainsborough's dramatic landscape settings for these cottage-door paintings, see Asfour and Williamson, "Gainsborough's Cottage-Door Scenes" 100–01.
73 Nead, *Myths of Sexuality* 40.
74 Rose, *Feminism and Geography* 95.
75 Nochlin, *Courbet* 97.
76 Nead, *Myths of Sexuality* 41–42, and pl. 9 for an illustration.
77 For theories about Gainsborough's nursing women, see Sloman, "'Innocence and Health'" 37; Rosenthal, "Gainsborough's Cottage Doors" 81; and Asfour and Williamson, "Gainsborough's Cottage-Door Scenes" 97.
78 Where Morland in such works as *Domestic Happiness* and *The Farmer's Door* offers a parallel to the woman's state in the form of a closed birdcage, Spilsbury seems to reinforce the possibility of meaningful action by including a dovecote on the thatched roof of the cottage in *Family Group* (Fig. 3.11), with a bird flying nearby. Spilsbury dispenses altogether with any overt reference to work in her painting *At the Cottage Door*, in which the two women seem to be simply talking to each other. This may be a charitable visit, however, since the seated woman appears to be dressed in a more rustic style than her standing visitor (sale Phillips, London, June 22, 1999, lot 208; Artnet ID 1910737).
79 *Two Children in a Woodland Glade* was sold at Bonhams, Knightsbridge, April 8, 2008, lot 97 (illustration on Artnet, ID 425472919), and *Portrait of Miss Collier in a Wooded Landscape* was sold at Christie's, London, November 25, 2003, lot 44 (Artnet, ID 423827020). For other portraits of children by Spilsbury, see Graves, *Royal Academy of Art* 4:221–22.
80 "Women's Work."

81 The letters cited in this section are from Hussey to Berkeley, found in the Berkeley Correspondence, vol. 7, Botany Library, Natural History Museum, London.
82 Shteir, "Botany" 33.
83 *Elegant Arts* iv.
84 Wakefield, *Reflections* 9.
85 Review of *Illustrations of British Mycology* 252, and Shteir, *Cultivating Women* 210. Secord's article "Botany on a Plate" provides a useful context for considering Hussey's text and images. She discusses the dichotomy between reason (language) and sensory pleasure (visual imagery) in early nineteenth-century scientific texts (31–32) and notes the ambivalence about viewing images, such as botanical illustrations: while there was a growing desire to be more inclusive and to recruit more novices into the field (56), male scientists also feared weakening the rational basis of scientific knowledge by promoting pleasure.
86 Hussey, *Illustrations* v–vi, and text for pls. 8, 2, and 17.
87 Ibid., text to pl. 68.
88 Ibbetson, "On the Interior Buds" 10, and "Treatise" 15.
89 Hussey, *Illustrations*, text for pls. 17, 49, 36, 72, and 79.
90 Hussey, *Illustrations*, text for pls. 31 and 74.
91 Ibbetson, "Treatise" 10–11, and Hussey *Illustrations*, text for pl. 1.
92 Hussey, *Illustrations*, text for pls. 44 and 77, and viii.
93 Naginski, review of *Scenes in a Library* 200.
94 The first series of plates, financed by subscription, had ninety illustrations; the second series was published in monthly sets of three plates. A two-volume bound edition including all 140 illustrations appeared in 1855.
95 Hare, *Gurneys of Earlham* 1:261.
96 Bermingham illustrates these two sketches but mentions them only briefly as evidence of Louisa Gurney's envy of her older sister's drawing skills; *Learning to Draw* 199.
97 Bachelard, *Poetics of Space* 50.
98 Ibid. 47.

4 COMMANDING A VIEW: THE TAYLOR SISTERS AND THE CONSTRUCTION OF DOMESTIC SPACE

1 Qtd. in Armitage, *Taylors of Ongar* 172.
2 Davidoff, *"Life is Duty"* 7–20, and Davidoff and Hall, *Family Fortunes* 59–69, 172–77.
3 Ross, *What Gardens Mean* 169–70.
4 The Taylor family moved from London to their first house in Lavenham in 1786 and to their second one there in 1793; to Colchester, Essex, in 1795; to their first house in Ongar in 1811, and to their second one there in 1814. When her sister married in 1813, Jane moved in with her brother Isaac before returning to the family home in Ongar in 1816.

The Independent (later Congregational) Church was one of the Protestant dissenting sects whose members were still occasionally persecuted at that time in England, although the Taylors were among the more "prosperous and respectable" dissenters (Summerfield, *Fantasy and Reason* 73); see also Carpenter and Prichard, who describe them as "gently Puritan" (*Oxford Companion* 517).

5 The sisters' mother, Ann Martin Taylor, who wrote domestic advice manuals late in life, recognized the strong feelings of nostalgia for childhood homes by quoting Lawrence Samuel Boyne: "recollection … solaces the imagination and the memory, in the evening of life, as if man, like a plant, were physically attached to the spot on which he blossomed" (*Reciprocal Duties* 95).
6 Taylor et al., *Associate Minstrels* 33–35.
7 Taylor, *Autobiography* 1:265.
8 Taylor, *Memoirs* 38, 209.
9 Bachelard, *Poetics of Space* 5–6, 13.
10 Taylor et al., *Associate Minstrels* 152–54.
11 Taylor, *Contributions of Q.Q.* 254.
12 Taylor, *Autobiography* 1:191, 196.
13 Shore, *Journal* 319–20.
14 Martineau, *Deerbrook* 45 and 596.
15 When they moved away from Colchester Jane took a spray of blossoms (presumably to dry or press) from a beloved laburnum tree which she described as "a friend of mine," "thinking it would be a great pleasure to ruminate over it now and then." But three years after the move she admits never having looked at it or the other nostalgic "relics" (*Memoirs* 271).
16 Taylor, *Autobiography* 1:196–97.
17 Tuan, *Space and Place* 12.
18 Armitage, *Taylors of Ongar* 65.
19 Tuan, *Space and Place* 28.
20 An illustration of this print is found in Davidoff and Hall (*Family Fortunes* 174), where it is identified as the frontispiece in Jane Taylor's *The Contributions of Q.Q.*, a compilation of her writings for the evangelical *Youth's Magazine*. After consultation with a number of libraries, however, we have not been able to find any copy of the book with this illustration.
21 Taylor, *Memoirs* 116.
22 Armitage, *Taylors of Ongar* 69–70.
23 *Ibid.* 74; Taylor, *Autobiography* 2:38, and Taylor, *Memoirs* 286–87.
24 Taylor, *Autobiography* 1:37–38.
25 *Ibid.* 1:102.
26 *Ibid.* 1:198–99.
27 Tuan, *Space and Place* 12, 35, 38.
28 Many years later, she revealed that her increasing deafness was "like living in a house with the blinds always down; so cut off from the world we have lived in" (qtd. in Armitage, *Taylors of Ongar* 119, n. 1).
29 Rose, *Feminism and Geography* 140–41.
30 Massey, *Space, Place, and Gender* 170–71.

31 Taylor, "Aims at Happiness," *Essays in Rhyme* 95–96.
32 Taylor, *Display* 106–07, 112–13.
33 Sha, *Visual and Verbal Sketch* 231, note 54.
34 Taylor, *Essays in Rhyme* 43.
35 *Ibid.* 78–92.
36 Taylor and Taylor, *Original Poems* 1:28–29.
37 Taylor, *Memoirs* 68.
38 Qtd. in Knight, *Jane Taylor* 42, 46.
39 Taylor, *Autobiography* 1:118–19.
40 Taylor, *Memoirs* 240, 188.
41 Taylor, *Contributions of Q.Q.* 1:8.
42 Qtd. in Knight, *Jane Taylor* 86.
43 Taylor, *Memoirs* 76.
44 Qtd. in Knight, *Jane Taylor* 86.
45 Like the Taylors, the artist Mary Delany appreciated her studio window: "There is to my working closet a pleasant window that overlooks the garden, it faces the east, is always dry and warm." But she downplays the significance of her working space, describing it in a letter to a friend, dated October 6, 1750, as "trifling and insignificant" and adding, "Mine fits only an idle mind that wants amusement" (qtd. in Pointon, *Strategies for Showing* 144).
46 Taylor, *Autobiography* 1:199, 201–02.
47 *Ibid.* 1:139.
48 Qtd. in Armitage, *Taylors of Ongar* 165.
49 Taylor, *Autobiography* 1:302, 282, and 24. The borrowed phrase in the letter alludes to the industrious Harry from her poem "The Two Gardens": while "indolent Dick" lazed the morning away in bed, Harry worked diligently in his "neat little garden," full of flowers and vegetables. It seems doubtful, however, that Ann, faced with the multiple tasks of a young mother, felt as satisfied as young Harry who "panted with labour and joy" (Taylor and Taylor, *Original Poems* 1:74).
50 Taylor, *Autobiography* 1:176–77.
51 Smith, *Rambles Farther* 266.
52 Qtd. in Armitage, *Taylors of Ongar* 160.
53 Taylor, *Memoirs* 97, 109.
54 Qtd. in Armitage, *Taylors of Ongar* 156–57.
55 Taylor, *Memoirs* 220.
56 Wilson, "Lost Needles" 179.
57 Davidoff, "Life is Duty" 9.
58 Taylor et al., *Associate Minstrels* 110.
59 Taylor, *Autobiography* 1:321.
60 Taylor, *Memoirs* 94; Taylor, *Autobiography* 1:249, 312.
61 Taylor et al., *Associate Minstrels* 110.
62 Taylor, *Memoirs* 90. The withered leaf was a recurrent motif for Jane. In a lament about growing older she complains that "my mind is hanging as limp as a dead leaf" (*ibid.* 262), and four years before her own early death she

painted a detailed watercolor of a fallen oak leaf and acorn for her sister's album, with a verse, surely self-referential, about "A withered leaf, that faded ere it fell" (Taylor, *Autobiography* 2:30).
63 Taylor, *Autobiography* 1:209.
64 *Ibid.* 2:7–8.
65 Taylor, *Memoirs* 240, 221, 98–101, 144, and 264; see also Knight, *Jane Taylor* 96–97.
66 Taylor, *Autobiography* 1:210.
67 Taylor, *Memoirs* 240.
68 Sha, *Visual and Verbal Sketch* 19.

5 DOROTHY WORDSWORTH: GARDENING, SELF-FASHIONING, AND THE CREATION OF HOME

1 We are aware of the vexing problem of referring to Dorothy Wordsworth as "Dorothy" but have opted to use first names for both her and William since this seems the clearest and least awkward approach.
2 Wordsworth and Wordsworth, *Letters* 274–75. On the subject of Wordsworth and domesticity, see Kurt Heinzelman's "The Cult of Domesticity" and Judith W. Page's "Gender and Domesticity."
3 Wordsworth and Wordsworth, *Letters* 295.
4 See Noyes, *Wordsworth and the Art of Landscape*, for a good summary of the outlines and progress of the garden at Town End, especially 101–11. Also, Buchanan's recent book *Wordsworth's Gardens* includes numerous photographs and diagrams. But both Noyes and Buchanan view the garden as Wordsworth's, meaning of course William's. Labbe, in contrast, sees Dorothy's role as primary: "In the province of the Grasmere garden, [Dorothy] Wordsworth assumes the authority, deciding on plants, borders, herbs, and requiring only William's *help*" (*Romantic Visualities* 84).
5 Wallace writes about the relationship between Dorothy's domestication of outdoor spaces and her interest in women walkers in "'Inhabited Solitudes.'" Although Wallace focuses on travel and walking in particular, her argument that Dorothy Wordsworth domesticates the wild anticipates ours. See also Fay's *Becoming Wordsworthian* for a fascinating Kristevan reading of Dorothy Wordsworth's domestic spaces, including nests and bowers (92–108 and passim).
6 Snyder, "Mother Nature's Other Natures" 145. See also Nabholtz, "Dorothy Wordsworth," and Davis, "Structure of the Picturesque," on Dorothy Wordsworth and the picturesque.
7 Bellanca makes a similar point when she argues that "Dorothy Wordsworth's landscape representations are not reducible to or containable by the picturesque because they are materially rooted and locally invested" (*Daybooks of Discovery* 132).

8 See particularly Bell's analysis of women as "commonplace" gardeners whose practice runs counter to the "monumental" qualities of the landscape park ("Women Create Gardens" 491). This is not to say that all early women gardeners eschewed larger landscape design. See Bending, for instance, on the case of Lady Mary Coke ("Miserable Reflections" 44).
9 Wordsworth, *Poetical Works* 3:1, line 14, and Wordsworth and Wordsworth, *Letters* 274.
10 There is a sense in which the garden itself – or gardens in general – are miniaturized versions of the larger world, as Mack suggests (*Art of Small Things* 84–94). As we shall see in Chapter 7, Fanny Price's potted plants and Elizabeth Kent's *flora domestica* are really just miniature gardens.
11 Appleton, *Experience of Landscape* 73.
12 Labbe, *Romantic Visualities* 18–19.
13 Bachelard, *Poetics of Space* xxxi.
14 Rose, *Feminism and Geography* 56.
15 Dorothy lost her mother when she was six and her father when she was twelve. After her mother's death, she was taken from the nuclear family and raised by various (often unsympathetic) relatives. See Gittings and Manton, *Dorothy Wordsworth*, and Gill, *William Wordsworth*, for additional biography and interpretation, as well as Worthen, *The Gang*, for a perspective on the close family circle. More recently, Frances Wilson, *Ballad*, has examined Dorothy's relationship with the family.
16 Wordsworth and Wordsworth, *Letters* 93.
17 *Ibid.* 521.
18 Page references to the Grasmere journals are to Moorman's edition, but we also quote Woof's helpful notes to her edition where appropriate.
19 Wordsworth, *Grasmere* 118.
20 *Ibid.* 119.
21 Levin, *Dorothy Wordsworth and Romanticism* 21.
22 Worthen in *The Gang* offers a compelling analysis of Mary as a wildflower planted in the Grasmere garden; see especially 207–13.
23 Wordsworth, *Grasmere* 129. Susan Ford describes the "female gaze" as "seek[ing] to reveal aspects of the landscape which other ways of looking have chosen to ignore, for example the detail of the scene or its place in everyday life" ("Landscape Revisited" 153).
24 Wordsworth, *Grasmere* 25.
25 *Ibid.* 83, 164–65. Our reading here is indebted to both Mellor's analysis of "feminine romanticism" as espousing an "ethics of care" (*Romanticism and Gender* 1–15) and Snyder's analysis of nature not as a mother but as itself in need of care ("Mother Nature's Other Natures" 146). See also Harrison's argument that gardening is based on a "vocation of care" (*Gardens*, especially 1–13).
26 Ritvo, "At the Edge of the Garden" 367–68.
27 Wordsworth, *Grasmere* 115.

28 Scott, *Lady of the Lake* I.xii, lines 5–6, and Wordsworth, *Poetical Works* 4:58, line 9.

29 In reading male Romantics' use of the bower, Labbe sees it as a "regression that is nonetheless valuable for restorative powers" (*Romantic Visualities* 94) in such poems as Coleridge's "Lime-Tree Bower" or Keats's "La Belle Dame." Crawford makes the similar point that "During the romantic period especially, the conventions of the bower were used to anatomize the process of poetic productivity" (*Poetry, Enclosure, and the Vernacular Landscape* 226). In such poems as "Lines Written in Early Spring" and in his letters, however, William Wordsworth seems to accept a less conflicted and ambivalent view of the bower than either Labbe or Crawford suggests.

30 Woof concludes that the Bower was the "first step towards the 'seat with a summer shed on the highest platform in this our little domestic slip of mountain'" (Wordsworth, *Grasmere* 227). Worthen interprets the "Indian shed" alluded to in "A Farewell" (26) as indication that the Wordsworths actually finished the summer house in the spring of 1802 (*The Gang* 206), but Dorothy's later letter to Lady Beaumont corroborates Woof's claim that the shed was not finished until 1804–05, although it does seem to have been begun.

31 Wordsworth, *Grasmere* 122.

32 Bachelard, *Poetics of Space* 155.

33 Wordsworth, *Grasmere* 129 (published as "A Farewell" in 1815).

34 *Ibid.* 142.

35 Bachelard, *Poetics of Space* 103.

36 Wordsworth, *Grasmere* 142. There is a page missing from the journal, which, as Mary Moorman speculates, "must have described the rebuilding by the swallows of their nest" (*ibid.*).

37 *Ibid.* 145–46, 161.

38 Worthen, *The Gang* 209.

39 Wordsworth, *Grasmere* I, 32.

40 Wordsworth, *Poetical Works* 2:23–25, lines 33–40.

41 Hunt, *Greater Perfections* 11.

42 Wordsworth, *Grasmere* 25.

43 Murdoch, *Discovery of the Lake District* 81. Some would question the claim of uniqueness: Daniels, for instance, comments that Constable's roughly contemporary garden had similar components to Repton's flower garden ("Love and Death" 437).

44 Mitford, *Life* 2:27–29.

45 Daniels, "Love and Death" 437–38.

46 Wordsworth and Wordsworth, *Letters* 93.

47 Dorothy Wordsworth was not alone is embracing a mixed style of gardening, as evidenced by women gardeners of the eighteenth century (noted in Bell, "Women Create Gardens"). And as Charlesworth points out in his introduction to Cobbett's *The English Gardener*, Cobbett's praise of the mixed or herbaceous flower border in 1829 indicates "its popularity in the years before 1829" (*The English Garden* 193).

48 Jacson, *Florist's Manual* 5, 7. Later in the text Jacson qualifies her distinction between a botanist's and a florist's approach to gardening: "to the classical Botanist variety and rarity are of the first value; hence the gardens of the classical botanist and general florist differ, even in first principles" (50–51).
49 *Ibid.* 16–18.
50 Wordsworth, *Prose Works* 1:161–62.
51 Jacson, *Florist's Manual* 23.
52 Wordsworth, *Grasmere* 109.
53 Mitford, *Our Village* 180.
54 Abercrombie and Withering are listed in Shaver and Shaver (*Wordsworth's Library* 3, 276). The Wordsworths' copy of *British Plants*, with marginal notes by Dorothy and William, is now housed at the Wordsworth Library in Grasmere. Abercrombie's practical guide is arranged according to the months of the year, and each section begins with the kitchen garden.
55 The interest in exotics is usually interpreted as an upper-class phenomenon because such acquisitions and collections required means and money, as we shall see in Chapter 7. Henry Phillips notes in 1822 that during George III's reign "not less than 6756 rare exotic plants were introduced into these kingdoms" (*History of Cultivated Vegetables* 18). Tobin analyzes "the culture of collecting" exotic plants in *Colonizing Nature* and the class implications of such connoisseurship. However, there is also evidence that exotics were viewed in anti-Jacobin circles as associated with foreign, radical elements. In George Walker's anti-Jacobin novel *The Vagabond*, "They [the lower classes] seem to have liberty enough; they are treading down my fine flower garden like an herd of swine: there goes all my exotic shrubs: – I believe they are a troop of Goths and Vandals, who pay no regard to science" (2:98). We thank Stephen Bending for this reference to *The Vagabond*.
56 Worthen analyzes the Wordsworths' unconventional behavior (*The Gang* 76–81).
57 Wordsworth and Wordsworth, *Letters* 117.
58 Vlasopolos also notes the similarity to *Pride and Prejudice* after aptly stating the situation thus: "We look to the experience of artists in their youth in the great metropolises of London or Paris for the *vie de bohème*, the rebellion against middle-class strictures about the organization of family life and gendered spheres, but we have not yet looked for it in the hills and valleys of the Lake District" ("Texted Selves" 124).
59 Hunt, *Greater Perfections* 215, 51.
60 Wordsworth and Wordsworth, *Letters* 624.
61 Wordsworth, *Prose Works*, 2:211–12.
62 Williamson, *Polite Landscapes* 150.
63 Throughout, we refer to Walker's edition of *Recollections*, the text of which is adopted from John Campbell Shairp's 1894 edition.
64 Wordsworth and Wordsworth, *Letters* 598.
65 Walker 19, in Wordsworth, *Recollections*.
66 See Walker's introduction for a thoughtful analysis of the crafting of the *Recollections* and its publication history (18–26).

67 Levin, *Dorothy Wordsworth* 73.
68 Brownstein, "Private Life" 60.
69 Wordsworth, *Recollections* 2.
70 *Ibid.* 55.
71 Domosh and Seager, *Putting Women in Place* xxii.
72 Wordsworth, *Recollections* 83.
73 *Ibid.* 49.
74 Snyder, "Mother Nature's Other Natures" 147–48.
75 Wordsworth, *Recollections* 94.
76 *Ibid.* 54.
77 Bohls, *Women Travel Writers* 179. She grounds her argument in terms of the tradition of male appropriation of the "actual or imaginative" landscape, arguing that "The process of framing and composing constitutes an exercise of power, a non-reciprocal mode of vision whose effect is to display and reinforce mastery" (*ibid.* 87).
78 *Ibid.* 206.
79 Lines 3, 65–66. We use Susan Levin's texts of Dorothy Wordsworth's poems, found in "Appendix One" of her book, *Dorothy Wordsworth* 175–237.
80 *Ibid.* lines 11–12.
81 Shore, *Journal* 319–21.
82 Bachelard, *Poetics of Space* 6.
83 Wordsworth, *Grasmere* 17.
84 Wordsworth, *Tour of the Continent* 245.

6 "WORK IN A SMALL COMPASS": GARDENING MANUALS FOR WOMEN

1 Waters, *Garden in Victorian Literature* 242–45.
2 Bilston, "Queens of the Garden" 5–6.
3 Even before Jacson, periodicals for women such as Eliza Haywood's *Female Spectator* (1744–46), the *Lady's Magazine; or, Polite Companion for the Fair Sex* (1759–63), and Charlotte Lennox's *Lady's Museum* (1760–61) included articles on gardening. Haywood, e.g., encouraged women to learn from their gardeners how to perform such tasks as grafting, adding that it was not "in the least beneath the dignity of the greatest lady to assist his work: it requires the utmost gentleness and delicacy to cut the little scion exactly" (4 [1745]:47–48).
4 Loudon, *Gardening for Ladies* iv.
5 *Ibid.* xi.
6 Geoffrey Taylor, *Some Nineteenth Century Gardeners* 27, 38, and Bilston, "Queens of the Garden" 4.
7 Jane was called on to assist her horticulturist husband in many ways with his projects, often in a secretarial capacity, but judging from the sales figures for her books and the number of editions, her own success as an author was remarkable: e.g., 1,350 copies of *Instructions in Gardening for Ladies* sold on

the day it was published (Shteir, "Loudon" 474; also Bermingham, *Learning to Draw* 214).
8. Loudon, *Gardening for Ladies* xi, 37.
9. Loudon, *Ladies' Companion* 375.
10. Jacson, *Florist's Manual* 10. For more on her own gardens, see Percy, "Maria Elizabetha Jacson" 47, 49–50, 54.
11. Johnson, *Every Lady* 2, 4. She may have been influenced here by J. C. Loudon's statement that "*Cottage-gardens*, in a moral and political point of view, are of obvious importance; attaching the cottager to his home and to his country, by inducing sober, industrious, and domestic habits" (*Encyclopaedia of Gardening* 1225).
12. A Lady, *Every Lady's Guide* 45. This anonymous book was attributed to Louisa Johnson by an early cataloguer at the Royal Horticultural Society library, but recent correspondence with the library confirms that there is no evidence for this attribution.
13. Jacson, *Florist's Manual* 11, 33–34.
14. Hibberd, *Rustic Adornments* 190.
15. Jacson, *Florist's Manual* 34, and Loudon, "Suburban Garden" 81. See Mitford for other references to flowers as pets (*Life* 2:167 and *Our Village* 179).
16. Kent, *Flora Domestica* 49, 139.
17. Massey, *Space, Place, and Gender* 169.
18. This information is from a memoir by James Luckcock (1761–1835) entitled "My House and Garden: Lime Grove, Edgbaston"; Birmingham Reference Library 375948 (cited by Davidoff and Hall, *Family Fortunes* 371).
19. Yonge, *Herb of the Field* 33.
20. Loudon, *Ladies' Companion* 404, 356.
21. Flora, "On the Means of Improving" 72–73.
22. Loudon, "My Letter-Bag" 57.
23. The first edition of Jacson's *Florist's Manual* was dedicated to Lady Broughton (Percy, "Maria Elizabetha Jacson" 49).
24. For more on the development of the terrace, particularly recommended by Repton, see Davidoff *et al.*, "Landscape with Figures" 160; Burton, *Early Victorians* 272; and Loudon, *Suburban Gardener* 738–40.
25. Loudon, *Lady's Country Companion* 194.
26. Hibberd, *Rustic Adornments* 341.
27. Loudon, *Lady's Country Companion* 17, 129–30, 29.
28. *Ibid.* 141.
29. Loudon, *Ladies' Companion* 210.
30. Loudon, *Lady's Country Companion* 354.
31. Loudon, "Ladies' Companion" 8.
32. Loudon, *Amateur Gardener* 95, and *Ladies' Companion* 176, 370–71.
33. Qtd. in Colvin and Nelson, "'Building Castles of Flowers'" 68.
34. Ellis, *Women of England* ix, 32.
35. Johnson, *Every Lady* 7, 23.
36. Loudon, *Gardening for Ladies* 73.
37. Taylor, *Contributions of Q.Q.* 1:253–57.

38 Loudon, *My Own Garden* 1.
39 Loudon, *Gardening for Ladies* 16.
40 Johnson, *Every Lady* 11–12.
41 More, *Strictures* 2:185–86.
42 Loudon, *My Own Garden* 16; also Johnson, *Every Lady* 39.
43 *Young Lady's Book* 24, 27.
44 Loudon, *Ladies' Companion* 216.
45 Johnson, *Every Lady* 2.
46 Wollstonecraft, *Vindication* 125
47 Johnson, *Every Lady* 4.
48 Mitford, *Life* 2:45.
49 Johnson, *Every Lady* 89.
50 More, *Cœlebs* 146, 126. Comparable benefits were voiced by male authors, from Gilbert Brookes in *The Complete British Gardener*, published in 1779 (vii, ix) to Shirley Hibberd in *Rustic Adornments for Homes of Taste*, 1856 (327–28), but in the case of ladies Hibberd was careful to suggest that gardening need not make them unduly "strong-minded": "a rosary stocked with plants raised wholly by one fair hand, would be a triumph, not of strong-mindedness and blue stocking-ism, but of feminine patience and ingenuity, applied to a work of artistic taste and high ornament" (*ibid.* 489).
51 Qtd. in Colvin and Nelson, "'Building Castles of Flowers'" 60.
52 A foreman gardener in the early Victorian period would typically make 15–25 shillings a week, or £39–65 a year (Geoffrey Taylor, *Some Nineteenth Century Gardeners* 57). See also "On the Wages of Gardeners" (1843).
53 Loudon, *Ladies' Companion* 219.
54 Loudon, "Floral Calendar" 160.
55 Davidoff and Hall, *Family Fortunes* 191.
56 Budden, *Always Happy* 144–45.
57 Loudon, "Suburban Garden" 81.
58 Loudon, *Lady's Country Companion* 6, 134, 141.
59 Howe, *Lady with Green Fingers* 91.
60 Davidoff and Hall, *Family Fortunes* 393.
61 A Lady, *Every Lady's Guide* 4–8.
62 Qtd. in Davidoff and Hall, *Family Fortunes* 460.
63 Cobbett, *English Housekeeper* 382–83.
64 Gorham, *Victorian Girl* 79.
65 P. E., "The Vine" 73.
66 Gorham, *Victorian Girl* 93–94.
67 P. E., "Ripe Cherries" 34–35.
68 Loudon, *Greenhouse Companion* 1.
69 Davidoff and Hall, *Family Fortunes* 191–92.
70 Drury and Lewis, *Victorian Garden Album* 42, 65.
71 Atkins, *Botanical Rambles* 93, 4.
72 Barbauld, *Stories of the Months* 66–67, 14–15.
73 Broome, *Fanny and Mary* 7, 20–21, 40.

74 Shore, *Journal* 39.
75 Loudon, *My Own Garden* 1, 5.
76 Loudon, *Gardening for Ladies* 15–20.
77 Loudon, *Encyclopaedia* 718.
78 Loudon, *Amateur Gardener* 30.
79 *Young Lady's Book* 35–36.
80 *New Female Instructor* 16, 14.
81 Qtd. in Davidoff and Hall, *Family Fortunes* 374.
82 Wakefield, *Reflections* 173–75.
83 Loudon, *Lady's Country Companion* 239.
84 *Ibid.* 21–22. Loudon herself had taken a more traditional approach in *The Ladies' Flower-Garden of Ornamental Annuals* (1842), particularly recommending annuals for a lady's garden because of "the easiness of their culture," unlike trees and vegetables which "require too much strength and manual labour." The shift in tone may well have been due to a different readership, more accustomed to rural life, for *The Lady's Country Companion*.
85 "Carnation and Piccotee" 145–46.
86 Mackenzie, "Gardening Practiced by the Fair Sex" 725.
87 P.P., "Ladies Turned Gardeners" 742.
88 "Ladies [sic] Gardeners" 759.
89 Lover of Gardening, "On the Best Method of Growing" 48.
90 Also included are various initials and devices borrowed from Freemasonry, including the eye and rainbow at the top, the compass and square (signifying submission and moral rectitude), and the pruning knife (suggesting the lopping off of vice and the cultivation of mental and moral virtues). Information on the Free Gardeners can be found at http://freemasonry.bcy.ca/Writings/gardeners.html, http://sites.scran.ac.uk/shelf/free, and the Friendly Societies Research Group Newsletter (10 [May 2003]). We are particularly grateful to Philip Norman, Volunteer Curator at the Museum of Garden History (now the Garden Museum), where this banner is located. From what we have been able to discover these societies did not include women in the period under discussion, although by the late nineteenth century there were some chapters open only to women.
91 Loudon, *Ladies' Companion* 256. Johnson's list was shorter, and included only what she deemed "*essential* to a lady's garden" (italics in the original). She noted that the knife was "sufficient for all the purposes of a flower garden" (*Every Lady* 11).
92 Loudon, *Ladies' Companion* 69.
93 Loudon, *Gardening for Ladies* 18–19.
94 Loudon, *Lady's Country Companion* iv.
95 Taylor, *Some Nineteenth Century Gardeners* 56.
96 Davidoff *et al.*, "Landscape with Figures" 157.
97 Loudon, *Encyclopaedia* 1017.
98 Perhaps under the influence of his wife, whom he married in 1830, J. C. Loudon intended his later book on *The Suburban Gardener, and Villa Companion*

(1838) to be especially adapted for "the instruction and amusement of ladies" (2). According to him lower-class women could be expected to hoe, weed, and water (*Encyclopaedia* 1226), but middle-class women should be assistants to their husbands in the garden rather than active gardeners in their own right. At peak seasons he did allow them to help with watering or collecting insects (*Suburban Gardener* 208, 260).

99 *Transactions of the Horticultural Society of London* 4 (1822): 69, and 5 (1824): n.p.

100 "On the Disposition of Flowers in Masses" (*Floricultural Cabinet and Florists' Magazine* 14 [1846]: 4–5), "Remarks on the Sensitive Plant" (14 [1846]: 255–57), "Propagation of the Calampelus Scaber" (15 [1847]: 43–44), "On Blooming the Large White Datura (Brugmansia Suaveolens) in a Very Dwarf Manner" (15 [1847]: 211), "The Hydrangea Hortensis as an Open-Air Border Flower" (16 [1848]: 110–11), "To Stay the Bleeding of Plants" (16 [1848]: 285), and "On Cultivating Plants in Dwelling Rooms, Windows, &c." (16 [1848]: 310).

101 Jacson, *Florist's Manual* 47, 23.

102 Johnson, *Every Lady* i–ii, 90.

103 Ibid. 8–9, 81–82, 96.

7 "UNBOUGHT PLEASURE": GARDENING IN *CŒLEBS IN SEARCH OF A WIFE* AND *MANSFIELD PARK*

1 Roberts, *Memoirs* 1.3:268.

2 Austen, *Letters* 119. More paraphrases Adam's words from *Paradise Lost* (4:628) and the narrator's description of Mulciber's fall (1:742–43); Austen alludes to lines from William Cowper's *The Task*: "Laburnam rich / In streaming gold; syringa, iv'ry pure" ("The Winter Walk at Noon" 6:149–50).

3 On the trajectory of More's career, her popularity, and her developing commitment to evangelical Christianity, see Stott: "In her time she was better known than Mary Wollstonecraft, and her books outsold Jane Austen's many times over ... Her *Cheap Repository Tracts* (aided by a little help from her friends) had a wider circulation than Thomas Paine's *Rights of Man*" (*Hannah More* vii). On the general connection between More, conduct books, and "persistent garden metaphors," see Labbe, *Romantic Visualities*, especially 72–80.

4 Although there are few examples from Austen's fiction of attention to the cultivation of specific plants, gardens nonetheless play a significant role, often with key scenes taking place in the garden or in the nearby shrubbery. Not much has been done with gardens in Austen per se, but there has been important work on landscape and responses to the natural world in Austen's work. For instance, in *The Improvement of the Estate*, Duckworth established Austen's relationship to landscape parks and estates. Deresiewicz has argued in *Jane Austen and the Romantic Poets* that there is a greater responsiveness to the natural world in the later novels. Although Wenner's focus is on landscapes and not on specific plants and gardens, she develops the connection

between women characters and natural landscapes; see especially *Prospect and Refuge* 1–12.
5 See, for instance, Krueger, *Reader's Repentance* 94–124; Elliott, *Angel Out of the House* 54–80; and Tobin, *Superintending the Poor* 74–97, on More's place in relation to traditions of philanthropy.
6 Elliott, *Angel Out of the House* 55. Mellor develops her position about More in *Mothers of the Nation* 13–38, as well as in "Hannah More." See also Myers, "Reform or Ruin."
7 See Fabricant on the objectification of women in garden history, particularly in the early eighteenth century ("Binding and Dressing" 121). Also relevant is Labbe's analysis of the enfranchised "male eye" in landscape aesthetics (*Romantic Visualities* xii). See especially ch. 1, "Engendering Landscape Perception," where Labbe analyzes the male Romantic preference for lofty eminences.
8 More, *Strictures* 2:27.
9 Compare Ford's "feminist reappraisal" of landscape, which contrasts the focus on the garden with the "grand sweep of the masculinist gaze" ("Landscape Revisited" 112).
10 Williams, *Keywords* 81.
11 Labbe, *Romantic Visualities* 72.
12 Woolf, *A Room of One's Own* 112.
13 More, *Cœlebs* 203.
14 *Paradise Lost* 12:623.
15 *Ibid.* 9:233.
16 Snook, "Eve and More," argues that More deliberately misquotes passages from *Paradise Lost* in order to assert her own ideas.
17 *Paradise Lost* 12:581–85.
18 *Ibid.* 4:241–42.
19 More, *Coelebs* 217.
20 *Ibid.* 146–47.
21 *Ibid.* 166.
22 See Tobin, *Superintending the Poor* 84–85.
23 More, *Memoirs* 2:4.103 (March 24, 1803).
24 More, *Cœlebs* 215. We see a similar attitude in other literature of the period, including botanical texts. In Atkins's *Botanical Rambles*, for instance, Caroline's condescension toward the poor (34) seems endorsed by the author, who (like Maria Spilsbury in Chapter 3) reiterates the myth of cottage happiness, seemingly without irony.
25 More, *Cœlebs* 216.
26 *Paradise Lost* 4:306.
27 More, *Cœlebs* 138.
28 *Ibid.* 178.
29 *Ibid.*
30 *Ibid.* 165.

31 This notion of nature as a representation of the divine, albeit a religious commonplace, is a constant theme in More's writing. See, for instance her correspondence with William Pepys in 1784, *Memoirs* 1:276–80.
32 More, *Cœlebs* 178.
33 Wordsworth, *Prose Works* 1:128.
34 Both More and Wordsworth, in turn, echo Cowper's warning against luxury and excess in "The Winter Evening," from *The Task*: "Increase of pow'r begets increase of wealth, / Wealth luxury, and luxury excess" (4:579–86).
35 Addison, *Spectator*, no. 411, 3:278.
36 More, *Cœlebs* 110, 20.
37 Several scholars have noted that More's stance is not necessarily opposed to Wollstonecraft's feminism. More's critique of accomplishments, as well as her support of educational achievement in women, links her to Wollstonecraft. See Myers, "Reform or Ruin," and Mellor, *Mothers of the Nation*, as well as Demers, *World* 81–88.
38 Mellor, *Mothers of the Nation* 14.
39 More, *Cœlebs* 126, 183–84, 75.
40 Austen, *Mansfield Park* 41.
41 Duckworth, *Improvement of the Estate* 54.
42 See *ibid.*, particularly ch. 1 on *Mansfield Park*, 33–80. For a lively reading of improvement in terms of gender, bawdy humor, and the body, see Heydt-Stevenson, *Austen's Unbecoming Conjunctions* 137–58.
43 Williams, *Keywords* 133.
44 On the connection between Austen, particularly *Mansfield Park*, and *Cœlebs*, see Waldron, *Jane Austen*, ch. 4, "The Frailties of Fanny" 84–111, and "Introduction" xxvii–xxviii. It is clear from Austen's letters that she read the very popular *Cœlebs*. See Prior, *Hannah More's Coelebs*, for a survey of the readership and reviews.
45 More, *Cœlebs* 59.
46 *Ibid.* 178.
47 *Ibid.* 77.
48 Fabricant, "Binding and Dressing" 127.
49 More, *Cœlebs* 235.
50 *Ibid.*
51 Williamson, *Polite Landscapes* 117.
52 Bell, "Women Create Gardens." More, *Cœlebs* 172. See Ross, *What Gardens Mean* 63–66, for an analysis of the significance of Stourhead, and Atkins, *Botanical Rambles* 196–97, for a similar temple.
53 Doody, "Introduction" xix.
54 Tuite sees *Catharine* as more closely connected to *Northanger Abbey* – a revision of the naïve but sympathetic heroine, as the earlier Catharine becomes Catherine Morland (*Romantic Austen* 27). Wenner connects *Mansfield Park* to *Catharine* and identifies Fanny's enclave as a metaphorical "cottage" within the larger estate, an idea related to our suggestion that Fanny inherits Catharine's bower (*Prospect and Refuge* 72).

55 Austen, *Catharine* 222.
56 Austen, *Letters* 172 (letter 67; January 30, 1809).
57 Waldron, *Jane Austen* 86, 89–90.
58 Tuite, *Romantic Austen* 34.
59 Austen, *Catharine* 187.
60 Tuite also suggests this interest in rooms in *Romantic Austen* 202, note 19. Laird follows Williamson, whom he quotes as first suggesting that the landscape garden is the "'mirror, of the new, easier pattern of social relationships'" (Williamson, *Polite Landscapes* 110–11; also qtd. in Laird, *Flowering of the Landscape Garden* 391, note 81). Williamson, in fact, sees the eighteenth-century development of French doors on the ground floor as a way that the outdoor space was more immediately connected to the interior as an extension of the living area (*Polite Landscapes* 111).
61 Abercrombie, *Garden Vade Mecum* 1–2.
62 Repton, *Observations* 100–02.
63 Austen, *Catharine* 199.
64 Austen, *Mansfield Park* 107. On the subject of gardens, meditation, and female retirement in the eighteenth century, see Stephen Bending's "Mrs. Montagu's Contemplative Bench."
65 Hunt, *Greater Perfections* 11.
66 Kent, *Flora Domestica* xxxii.
67 Austen, *Mansfield Park* 107.
68 Mitford, *Life* 2:27. In *Flora*, Brent Elliott offers a history of the geranium (see especially 181 and 136–41). In *A Little History*, Jenny Uglow relates this history through Mary Capel, who in the mid-seventeenth century "corresponded with leading botanists, including Sir Hans Sloane of the Chelsea Physic Garden, and [at] Badminton she created a special botanic garden, where a specialty was the mass of 'geraniums' from South Africa: one of her introductions was the ivy-leaved geranium, *Pelargonium peltatum*" (109).
69 Smith, *Conversations Introducing Poetry* 67.
70 Loudon, *Lady's Country Companion* 18.
71 Twining, "A Few Words" 286, 293.
72 Austen, *Mansfield Park* 106.
73 Deresiewicz, *Jane Austen* 107.
74 Bachelard, *Poetics of Space* 155.
75 Mack, *Art of Small Things* 84.
76 See Skinner, for instance, who views the nest-like East room as a "source of oneiric inspiration" ("Exploring Space" 134), as well as Wenner (*Prospect and Refuge* 72).
77 Bachelard, *Poetics of Space* 103.
78 Austen, *Mansfield Park* 218. Laird discusses the function of the shrubbery as a "spot for private walks and intimate talks" (*Flowering of the Landscape Garden* 18).
79 Austen, *Emma* 361.
80 Austen, *Mansfield Park* 219.

81 *Ibid.* 263, 271, 93, 144.
82 See Duckworth's reading of this scene in *The Improvement of the Estate*, especially 52–55, as well as Heydt-Stevenson's analysis in *Austen's Unbecoming Conjunctions*, especially 148–52.
83 Austen, *Mansfield Park* 52–54.
84 For an analysis of the related topic of landscaping as a "technique of empire," see Casid, *Sowing Empire*, especially xxi–xxiii.
85 Wiltshire, *Jane Austen and the Body* 73.
86 Austen, *Northanger Abbey* 178.
87 Austen, *Mansfield Park* 166.

8 MARGARET OLIPHANT'S CHRONICLES OF CARLINGFORD AND THE MEANING OF VICTORIAN GARDENS

1 The Chronicles of Carlingford consist of *The Executor* (1861), *The Rector* and *The Doctor's Family* (published in one volume in 1863), *Salem Chapel* (1863), *The Perpetual Curate* (1864), *Miss Marjoribanks* (1866), and *Phoebe Junior* (1876). For the publication history of this series, see Colby, *Equivocal Virtue* 38–74.
2 See Jay, *Mrs. Oliphant*, and Jay's introduction to *Miss Marjoribanks*, as well as Langland, *Nobody's Angels*, and Schaub, "Queen of Air." Both Jay and Schaub see Oliphant as self-consciously destabilizing gender and class; Langland argues that the character Lucilla Marjoribanks herself is a "sophisticated semiotician" (Langland, *Nobody's Angels* 164). Tange convincingly concludes that both Lucilla and Oliphant subvert the system: "characters like Lucilla Marjoribanks stand metonymically for Oliphant herself: 'mak[ing] it a point to give in to the prejudices of society' may be a strategy that a woman employs in order to pave the way for resistance against the restrictive conventions that derive from such prejudices" ("Redesigning Femininity"166). For various perspectives on Oliphant's attitude toward social and cultural norms, see the essays in Trela.
3 Schaub, "Queen of Air" 201–02.
4 Bilston ("Queens of the Garden" 2–3) follows Weltman, "'Be No More Housewives'," in arguing that Ruskin promotes an expanded view of women's sphere. Bilston proposes that gardening manuals actually "furthered the Ruskinian vision of the garden as not-home, as a broader and even public realm for women's activity, in a variety of ways" ("Queens of the Garden" 2).
5 We should acknowledge, though, that Ruskin did pursue an interest in gardens and botany at various points in his life. See Hilton, for instance, for comments on Ruskin's project for the grounds around Brantwood on Lake Coniston (*John Ruskin* 217) or on his practical focus on agriculture and gardening in relation to his work for the Guild of St. George (*ibid.* 335–39). Also, scattered throughout his letters to the students at the Winnington School are references to flowers and gardening (Burd, *Winnington Letters* 514). We thank Elizabeth Helsinger for sharing her expertise on Ruskin.

6 Tange, "Redesigning Femininity" 163.
7 Tange, "Redesigning Femininity," also sees the feminine power of the drawing room, which extends into the social and political world, as complicating the public/private binary. More on the Victorian drawing room can be found in Flanders, *Inside the Victorian Home*, ch. 5. Gardens function in a similar way, as we have argued in previous chapters and as Bilston, "Queens of the Garden," posits in relation to women's gardening texts.
8 Morgan and Richards emphasize the relationship of the drawing room to the garden: "The drawing room was an emphatically feminine room, which was always given a sunny aspect and the best view. As the ladies received carriage calls and took afternoon tea, they were able to enjoy the glowing colours of the parterre at its best" (*Paradise Out of a Common Field* 25).
9 Hunt, *Greater Perfections* 11, 215.
10 Hunt, "Garden" 19–20.
11 *Ibid.* 20, 27.
12 Rose, *Feminism and Geography* 17.
13 Elliott, *Victorian Gardens* 20.
14 Waters notes that the word "trim" is Trollope's favorite adjective for the garden "and a term much favored by garden writers. Though 'trim' has a cluster of significations, Trollope consistently applies it to tidy, tasteful, well-tended arrangements" (*Garden in Victorian Literature* 12).
15 Hibberd, *Rustic Adornments* 333, 359.
16 *Ibid.* 189.
17 Jacson, *Florist's Manual* 11, and Hibberd, *Rustic Adornments* 334.
18 Hibberd, *Rustic Adornments* 341.
19 See, for instance, Colby, *Equivocal Virtue* 42, or Fitzgerald, "Introduction" iv.
20 Oliphant, *Doctor's Family* 58–59.
21 Oliphant, *Perpetual Curate* 10.
22 Oliphant, *Salem Chapel* 437.
23 Oliphant, *Rector* 3.
24 Oliphant, *Perpetual Curate* 102, 5.
25 Oliphant, *Miss Marjoribanks* 173.
26 Oliphant, *Rector* 3.
27 Readers will recall that this character was "Lady Western" in *Salem Chapel*. Oliphant apparently misremembers the name in *Phoebe Junior*, referring to the character as "Lady Weston."
28 Oliphant, *Phoebe Junior* 126–28.
29 *Ibid.* 24–25.
30 Hibberd, *Town Garden* 6.
31 Hibberd, *Rustic Adornments* 134.
32 See the discussion of the Victorian fern craze, in which Mrs. Morgan is an excellent fictional participant, in Merrill, *Romance of Victorian Natural History*.
33 Hibberd, *Rustic Adornments* 135.
34 Oliphant, *Perpetual Curate* 514.

35 Oliphant, *Miss Marjoribanks* 27–28, 32.
36 Mitford, *Life* 27.
37 Oliphant, *Miss Marjoribanks* 134.
38 *Ibid.* 32–33.
39 Hibberd, *Rustic Adornments* 362.
40 Oliphant's husband Francis Wilson Oliphant (Frank), who died tragically from consumption in Italy, had been an artist of painted glass. Following her husband's death, Margaret Oliphant was befriended by other artists. Although she herself did not embrace the bohemian life, she did not share Lucilla's smug rejection of unconventional artistic feeling. See Jay, in Oliphant, *Miss Marjoribanks*, especially 15–17.
41 Johnson, *Every Lady* 28.
42 In addition to the novel itself, see Tobin, *Superintending the Poor* 74–97, for an analysis of More's place in traditions of philanthropy.
43 Oliphant, *Miss Marjoribanks* 2: chs 22–23.
44 *Ibid.* 194.
45 *Ibid.* 200.
46 *Ibid.* 199, 202–03.
47 *Ibid.* 204–05.
48 Waters, *Garden in Victorian Literature* 53–54.
49 There are several ironic allusions to cottages in *Sense and Sensibility*, including the narrator's comment in ch. 6: "As a house, Barton Cottage, though small, was comfortable and compact; but as a cottage it was defective, for the building was regular, the roof was tiled, the window shutters were not painted green, nor were the walls covered with honeysuckle" (65).
50 Elliott, *Victorian Gardens* 63.
51 Helsinger, *Rural Scenes* 121.
52 Hunt, "Garden" 19.
53 Oliphant, "Mary Russel Mitford" 659.
54 Onslow, *Women of the Press* 91.
55 Mitford, *Our Village* 9.
56 Oliphant, *Miss Marjoribanks* 286.
57 *Ibid.* 177.
58 Numerous botanical and horticultural writers praise mignonette. In *Flora Domestica*, Kent notes: "People have not been satisfied, however, with growing this little-darling in pots; it is more frequently seen cradled in the sunshine, in boxes the whole length of the window it is placed" (246). Jane Loudon refers to mignonette as "delightfully fragrant" (*Gardening for Ladies* 289).
59 Oliphant, *Miss Marjoribanks* 443.
60 Oliphant goes on to write an ironic and unromantic short story, "Queen Eleanor and Fair Rosamond," in *A Widow's Tale and Other Stories* (1898), in which she subverts the legend (see Rubik, "Subversion of Cliches" 52–53).
61 Oliphant, *Miss Marjoribanks* 484.
62 *Ibid.* 486.
63 *Ibid.* 494.

64 Helsinger does not make this comment about "Of Queens' Gardens" in the context of Oliphant, but her assessment of the inherent contradictions in Ruskin's argument is relevant to our discussion here ("Authority" 127). Compare Helsinger's reading of Ruskin with Tange's reading of *Miss Marjoribanks*: "the novel demonstrates the irony of identifying women as domestic Queens but denying them any sphere of public or political action" ("Redesigning Femininity" 175).
65 Homans, *Royal Representations* 82.
66 For an analysis of Lucilla's marriage and extended sphere at the end of the novel, see Cohen, especially the comment that "Lucilla's retreat from the public world of parliamentary politics to a private one of marriage to her cousin Tom does not clearly return Lucilla to a separate sphere" ("Maximizing Oliphant" 109).
67 Austen, *Emma* 361.
68 Loudon, *Encyclopaedia of Gardening* 1203.
69 These particular quotations are from William Paul's speech to the Cottage Gardens Association (Charlesworth, *English Garden* 299).
70 Charlesworth (*English Garden* 177) traces this concern for cottage gardens as compensation for enclosure back to Quaker writers in the 1790s as well as such books as Cobbett's *Cottage Economy* (1822).
71 Oliphant, *Salem Chapel* 436–38.
72 Hunt, *Greater Perfections* 215.

EPILOGUE

1 See Birkett, *Spinsters Abroad* 48, and Domosh and Seager, *Putting Women in Place* 122.
2 Bell, *Syria* 1.
3 Sherwood, *History of the Fairchild Family* 185.
4 Burnett, *One I Knew* 26.
5 Ch. 2 in *The Secret Garden* is entitled, "Mistress Mary, Quite Contrary."
6 Opie and Opie, *Oxford Dictionary of Nursery Rhymes* 355, and Loades, *Mary Tudor* 8.
7 Griswold, "Snugness" 149.
8 Lundin, "Cultural Work" 157, and Silver, "Domesticating Bronte's Moors" 193. See also Lundin, "Cultural Work" 155, 157, for Burnett's love of gardening, and Thwaite, "Biographer Looks Back" 28–29, for her home at Maytham Hall as the possible inspiration for *The Secret Garden*.
9 Ellis, *Mothers of England* 202.
10 Qtd. in *Marley Collection* 14.
11 *Ibid.* 65, 12, 14–16.
12 Ruskin, "Of Queens' Gardens" 88.

Works cited

Abercrombie, John. *The Garden Vade Mecum, or Compendium of General Gardening.* 1790. Dublin: J. Jones, 1790. Eighteenth Century Collections Online. June 14, 2009. http://galenet.galegroup.com.
Addison, Joseph. *The Spectator by Joseph Addison, Richard Steele, and Others.* 4 vols. Ed. G. Gregory Smith. 1907. New York: E. P. Dutton, 1950.
Agress, Lynne. *The Feminine Irony: Women on Women in Early-Nineteenth-Century English Literature.* London: Associated University Presses, 1978.
Amies, Marion. "Amusing and Instructive Conversations: The Literary Genre and its Relevance to Home Education." *History of Education* 14 (1985): 87–99.
Appleton, Jay. *The Experience of Landscape.* London: John Wiley, 1975.
Ariès, Philippe. *Centuries of Childhood: A Social History of Family Life.* Trans. Robert Baldick. New York: Alfred A. Knopf, 1962.
Armintor, Deborah Needleman. "The Sexual Politics of Microscopy in Brobdingnag." *Studies in English Literature* 47 (Summer 2007): 619–40.
Armitage, Doris Mary. *The Taylors of Ongar.* Cambridge: W. Heffer & Sons, 1939.
Asfour, Amal, and Paul Williamson. "Gainsborough's Cottage-Door Scenes: Aesthetic Principles, Moral Values." *Sensation & Sensibility: Viewing Gainsborough's Cottage Door.* Ed. Ann Bermingham. New Haven and London: Yale University Press, 2005. 97–119.
Aspinall-Oglander, Cecil. *Admiral's Wife, Being the Life and Letters of The Hon. Mrs. Edward Boscawen from 1719 to 1761.* London: Longmans, Green and Co., 1940.
"At Home and at School." *All the Year Round* October 8, 1859: 572.
Atkins, Lucy Sarah (later Wilson). *Botanical Rambles; Designed as an Early and Familiar Introduction to the Elegant and Pleasing Study of Botany.* London: Baldwin, Cradock, and Joy, 1822.
Austen, Jane. *Catharine and Other Writings.* Eds. Margaret Anne Doody and Douglas Murray. New York: Oxford University Press, 1998.
  Emma. Ed. Kristin Flieger Samuelian. Peterborough, ON: Broadview, 2004.
  Jane Austen's Letters. 3rd edn. Ed. Deirdre Le Faye. New York: Oxford University Press, 1997.
  Mansfield Park. 1814. Ed. Claudia Johnson. New York: Norton, 1998.
  Northanger Abbey. 2nd edn. Ed. Claire Grogan. Peterborough, ON: Broadview, 2002.

Persuasion. Ed. Linda Bree. Peterborough, ON: Broadview, 2000.
Sense and Sensibility. 1811. Ed. Kathleen James-Cavan. Peterborough, ON: Broadview, 2001.
The Novels of Jane Austen. Ed. R. W. Chapman. 6 vols. London: Oxford University Press, 1954.
Avery, Gillian. *Childhood's Pattern: A Study of the Heroes and Heroines of Children's Fiction, 1770–1950*. London: Hodder and Stoughton, 1975.
Bachelard, Gaston. *The Poetics of Space*. Trans. Maria Jolas. Boston: Beacon, 1964. Trans. of *La Poétique de l'espace*. 1958.
Barbauld, Anna Letitia. *Lessons for Children of Three Years Old*. 1778. Philadelphia: Warner, 1818.
Selected Poetry and Prose. Eds. William McCarthy and Elizabeth Kraft. Peterborough, ON: Broadview, 2002.
Stories of the Months. 1850. Boston: Edward Livermore, 1853.
Barnett, Gerald. *Richard and Maria Cosway: A Biography*. Tiverton: Westcountry Books, and Cambridge: Lutterworth, 1995.
Bayly, [Mary]. *The Life and Letters of Mrs. Sewell*. 4th edn. London: James Nisbet, 1889.
Bell, Gertrude Lowthian. *Syria: The Desert and the Sown*. New York: Dutton & Co., 1907.
Bell, Susan Groag. "Women Create Gardens in Male Landscapes: A Revisionist Approach to Eighteenth Century English Garden History." *Feminist Studies* 16 (Fall 1990): 471–91.
Bellanca, Mary Ellen. *Daybooks of Discovery: Nature Diaries in Britain, 1770–1870*. Charlottesville and London: University of Virginia Press, 2007.
Belsey, Hugh. *Thomas Gainsborough: A Country Life*. Munich: Prestel, 1988.
Bending, Stephen. "'Miserable Reflections on the Sorrows of My Life': Letters, Loneliness, and Gardening in the 1760s." *Tulsa Studies in Women's Literature* 25 (Spring 2006): 31–47.
"Mrs. Montagu's Contemplative Bench: Bluestocking Gardens and Female Retirement." *Huntington Library Quarterly* 69.4 (2006): 555–80.
Bermingham, Ann. *Learning to Draw: Studies in the Cultural History of a Polite and Useful Art*. New Haven and London: Yale University Press, 2000.
ed. *Sensation and Sensibility: Viewing Gainsborough's Cottage Door*. New Haven and London: Yale University Press, 2005.
Bewell, Alan. "'Jacobin Plants': Botany as Social Theory in the 1790s." *Wordsworth Circle* 20 (Summer 1989): 132–39.
Bicknell, Peter, and Jane Munro. *Gilpin to Ruskin: Drawing Masters and Their Manuals, 1800–1860*. Cambridge: Fitzwilliam Museum, 1988.
Bilston, Sarah. "Queens of the Garden: Victorian Women Gardeners and the Rise of the Gardening Advice Text." *Victorian Literature and Culture* 36 (2008): 1–19.
Birkett, Dea. *Spinsters Abroad: Victorian Lady Explorers*. Oxford: Blackwell, 1989.
Blain, Virginia, Patricia Clements, and Isobel Grundy, eds. *The Feminist Companion to Literature in English: Woman Writers from the Middle Ages to the Present*. New Haven: Yale University Press, 1990.

Blake, William. *The Complete Poetry and Prose of William Blake.* Newly rev. edn. Ed. David Erdman. New York: Doubleday, 1988.

Blunt, Wilfred, and William T. Stearn. *The Art of Botanical Illustration.* Rev. edn. Woodbridge: Antique Collectors' Club, 1994.

Bohls, Elizabeth A. *Women Travel Writers and the Language of Aesthetics, 1716–1818.* New York: Cambridge University Press, 1995.

Bradley, Martha. *The British Housewife, or, The Cook, Housekeeper's and Gardiner's Companion.* 1756. Facsimile edn. 6 vols. Blackawton: Prospect Books, 1996.

Bree, Linda. *Sarah Fielding.* New York: Twayne, 1996.

Briggs, Julia. "'Delightful Task!' Women, Children, and Reading in the Mid-Eighteenth Century." *Culturing the Child, 1690–1914.* Ed. Donelle Ruwe. Lanham, MD: Scarecrow Press, 2005. 67–82.

Brookes, Gilbert. *The Complete British Gardener: Containing Full Directions for Every Thing Necessary to be Done in the Fruit, Flower, and Kitchen Garden, Throughout the Year.* London: Fielding and Walker, 1779.

Broome, Charlotte Anne. *Fanny and Mary; or Juvenile Views of Happiness.* London: Harvey and Darton, 1821.

Brownstein, Rachel Meyer. "The Private Life: Dorothy Wordsworth's Journals." *Modern Language Quarterly* 34 (1973): 48–63.

Buchanan, Carol. *Wordsworth's Gardens.* Lubbock: Texas Tech University Press, 2001.

[Budden, Maria Elizabeth]. *Always Happy! Or, Anecdotes of Felix and His Sister Serena.* 1814. 9th edn. London: John Harris, n.d.

Chit Chat, or Short Tales in Short Words. 1825. 5th edn. London: John Harris, 1841.

A Key to Knowledge; or, Things in Common Use Simply and Shortly Explained. 1814. New York: W. B. Gilley, 1816.

Right and Wrong. 1815. 4th edn. London: John Harris, 1825.

Burd, Van Akin. *The Winnington Letters: John Ruskin's Correspondence with Margaret Alexis Bell and the Children at Winnington Hall.* Cambridge, MA: Harvard University Press, 1969.

Burke, Edmund. *A Philosophical Enquiry into the Origin of Our Ideas of the Sublime and the Beautiful.* 1757. Ed. James T. Boulton. Notre Dame: University of Notre Dame Press, 1968.

Burnett, Frances Hodgson. *The One I Knew the Best of All.* 1893. London: Frederick Warne & Co., 1974.

The Secret Garden. London: Heinemann, 1911.

Burnett, Richard. *Company of Pianos.* London: Third Millennium, 2006.

Burton, Elizabeth. *The Early Victorians at Home, 1837–1861.* London: Longman, 1972.

Burton, John. *Lectures on Female Education and Manners.* Dublin: J. Milliken, 1794.

Bury, [Priscilla Susan]. *A Selection of Hexandrian Plants, Belonging to the Natural Orders Amaryllidae and Liliaceae.* London: Robert Havell, 1831–34.

Calè, Luisa. "'A Female Band Despising Nature's Law': Botany, Gender and Revolution in the 1790s." *Romanticism on the Net* 17 (February 2000). February 1, 2008. http://users.ox.ac.uk/~scat0385/17botany.html.

"The Carnation and Piccotee, and Their Cultivation by Ladies." *Gardener and Practical Florist* 1 (1843): 145–46.
Carpenter, Humphrey, and Mari Prichard. *The Oxford Companion to Children's Literature*. Oxford and New York: Oxford University Press, 1984.
Casid, Jill H. *Sowing Empire: Landscape and Colonization*. Minneapolis: University of Minnesota Press, 2004.
Catlow, Agnes, and Maria. *The Children's Garden and What They Made of It*. London: Cassell, Petter, & Galpin, 1865.
Charlesworth, Michael, ed. *The English Garden: Literary Sources and Documents*. Vol. 3: *1772–1910*. Mountfield: Helm Information, 1993.
Chico, Tita. "Minute Particulars: Microscopy and Eighteenth-Century Narrative." *Mosaic* 39 (2006): 143–61.
Cobb, Edith. *The Ecology of the Imagination in Childhood*. London: Routledge & Kegan Paul, 1977.
Cobbett, Anne. *The English Housekeeper*. 1835. Wakefield: E. P. Publishing, 1973.
Coffey, Donna. "Protecting the Botanic Garden: Seward, Darwin, and Coalbrookdale." *Women's Studies* 31 (2002): 141–64.
Cohen, Monica. "Maximizing Oliphant: Begging the Question and the Politics of Satire." *Victorian Women Writers and the Woman Question*. Ed. Nicole Diane Thompson. New York: Cambridge University Press, 1999. 99–115.
Colby, Vineta, and Robert A. *The Equivocal Virtue: Mrs. Oliphant and the Victorian Literary Market Place*. Hamden, CT: Archon Books, 1966.
Coleridge, Samuel Taylor. *Coleridge: Poetical Works*. New York: Oxford University Press, 1967.
Colvin, Christina, and Charles Nelson. "'Building Castles of Flowers': Maria Edgeworth as Gardener." *Garden History* 16.1 (Spring 1988): 58–70.
Cosway, Maria. *Progress of Female Dissipation*. London: R. Ackermann, 1800.
Progress of Female Virtue. London: R. Ackermann, 1800.
Cowper, William. *The Task and Selected Other Poems*. Ed. James Sambrook. New York: Longman, 1994.
Crawford, Rachel. *Poetry, Enclosure, and the Vernacular Landscape, 1700–1830*. New York: Cambridge University Press, 2002.
Cunningham, Allan. *The Lives of the Most Eminent British Painters, Sculptors, and Architects*. 6 vols. London: John Murray, 1829–33.
Curtis, William. *Flora Londinensis*. London: printed for the author and B. White, 1777–98.
Daniels, Stephen. "Love and Death across an English Garden: Constable's Paintings of His Family's Flower and Kitchen Gardens." *An English Arcadia: Landscape and Architecture in Britain and America*. Huntington Library Quarterly 55 (Summer 1992): 433–57.
Darwin, Erasmus. *The Botanic Garden, A Poem*. 1791. 4th edn. London: J. Johnson, 1799.
 A Plan for the Conduct of Female Education, in Boarding Schools. 1797. New York: Johnson, 1968.
Davidoff, Leonore. *"Life is Duty, Praise and Prayer": Some Contributions of the New Women's History*. London: LLRS Publications, 1981.

Davidoff, Leonore, and Catherine Hall. *Family Fortunes: Men and Women of the English Middle Class 1780–1850*. Rev. edn. London and New York: Routledge, 2002.

Davidoff, Leonore, Jean L'Esperance, and Howard Newby. "Landscape with Figures: Home and Community in English Society." *The Rights and Wrongs of Women*. Eds. Ann Oakley and Juliet Mitchell. Harmondsworth: Penguin, 1976.

Davis, Robert Con. "The Structure of the Picturesque: Dorothy Wordsworth's Journals." *Wordsworth Circle* 9 (1978): 45–49.

The Delights of Flower Painting. 2nd edn. London: D. Voisin, 1756.

Demers, Patricia. *The World of Hannah More*. Lexington: University Press of Kentucky, 1996.

Deresiewicz, William. *Jane Austen and the Romantic Poets*. New York: Columbia University Press, 2004.

Dolan, Elizabeth A. "Collaborative Motherhood: Maternal Teachers and Dying Mothers in Charlotte Smith's Children's Books." *Women's Writing* 16.1 (May 2009): 109–25.

Domosh, Mona, and Joni Seager. *Putting Women in Place: Feminist Geographers Make Sense of the World*. New York and London: Guilford Press, 2001.

Doody, Margaret Anne. Introduction. *Catharine and Other Writings*. Ed. Margaret Anne Doody and Douglas Murray. New York: Oxford University Press, 1998.

Drury, Elizabeth, and Philippa Lewis. *The Victorian Garden Album*. London: Collins & Brown, 1993.

Duckworth, Alistair M. *The Improvement of the Estate: A Study of Jane Austen's Novels*. 1971. Baltimore: Johns Hopkins University Press, 1994.

Edgeworth, Maria. *Early Lessons*. 5th edn. 4 vols. London: R. Hunter, 1824.

Frank. New York: Harper & Bros., 1836.

A Memoir of Maria Edgeworth, with a Selection from Her Letters by the Late Mrs. Edgeworth. Eds. "Her Children." 3 vols. London: Joseph Masters and Son, 1867.

The Parent's Assistant or Stories for Children. 1796. Rev. edn. New York: Hurd and Houghton, 1869.

Rosamond, A Sequel to Early Lessons. 2 vols. London: R. Hunter and Baldwin, Cradock, and Joy, 1821.

Works of Maria Edgeworth. 13 vols. Boston: Parker, 1825.

Edgeworth, Maria, and Richard Lovell Edgeworth. *Practical Education*. 1798. 1st American edn. 2 vols. New York: Browne Stansbury, 1801.

Elegant Arts for Ladies. London: Ward & Lock, 1856.

Elliott, Brent. *Flora: An Illustrated History of the Garden Flower*. Buffalo, NY: Firefly Books, 2001.

Victorian Gardens. Portland, OR: Timber Press, 1986.

Elliott, Dorice Williams. *The Angel Out of the House: Philanthropy and Gender in Nineteenth-Century England*. Charlottesville: University Press of Virginia, 2002.

Ellis, [Sarah Stickney]. *The Mothers of England: Their Influence and Responsibility.* 1843. New York: D. Appleton, 1844.
— *The Women of England, Their Social Duties, and Domestic Habits.* New York: D. Appleton, 1839.
Elwood, [Anna Katharine]. *Memoirs of the Literary Ladies of England.* 2 vols. London: Henry Coburn, 1843.
Everard, Anne. *Flowers from Nature, with the Botanical Name, Class, and Order; and Instructions for Copying.* London: Joseph Dickinson, 1835.
Fabricant, Carole. "'Binding and Dressing Nature's Loose Tresses': The Ideology of Augustan Landscape Design." *Studies in Eighteenth Century Culture* 8 (1979): 109–35.
Fay, Elizabeth A. *Becoming Wordsworthian: A Performative Aesthetic.* Amherst: University of Massachusetts Press, 1995.
The Female Aegis; or, the Duties of Women from Childhood to Old Age. London: Sampson Low, 1798.
Fielding, Sarah. *The Governess, or Little Female Academy.* 1749. London and New York: Pandora, 1987.
Fitton, Sarah. *Conversations on Botany.* London: Longman, Hurst, Rees, Orme, & Brown, 1817.
Fitzgerald, Penelope. Introduction. *The Rector and The Doctor's Family.* New York: Virago, 1986.
Flanders, Judith. *Inside the Victorian Home: A Portrait of Domestic Life in Victorian England.* New York and London: W. W. Norton, 2003.
Fleming, Marjory. *The Complete Marjory Fleming: Her Journals, Letters & Verse.* Ed. Frank Sidgwick. New York: Oxford University Press, 1935.
Flint, Kate. *The Woman Reader, 1837–1914.* Oxford: Clarendon, 1993.
Flora. "On the Means of Improving the General Appearance of Small Gardens, By Introducing Plants Not in Common Cultivation." *Ladies' Magazine of Gardening* 1 (1842): 72–73.
Ford, Susan. "Landscape Revisited: A Feminist Reappraisal." *New Words, New Worlds: Reconceptualising Social and Cultural Geography.* Ed. Chris Philo. Lampeter: Social and Cultural Geography Study Group of the Institute of British Geographers, 1991. 151–55.
Friedman, Joan. "Every Lady Her Own Drawing Master." *Apollo* 105 (April 1977): 262–67.
Gates, Barbara T. *Kindred Nature: Victorian and Edwardian Women Embrace the Living World.* Chicago: University of Chicago Press, 1998.
— "Those Who Drew and Those Who Wrote: Women and Victorian Popular Science Illustration." *Figuring It Out: Science, Gender, and Visual Culture.* Eds. Ann B. Shteir and Bernard V. Lightman. Lebanon, NH: Dartmouth College Press, 2006. 192–213.
George, Sam. *Botany, Sexuality and Women's Writing 1760–1830: From Modest Shoot to Forward Plant.* New York: Manchester University Press, 2007.
Gill, Stephen. *William Wordsworth: A Life.* Oxford: Clarendon, 1989.
Gittings, Robert, and Jo Manton. *Dorothy Wordsworth.* Oxford: Clarendon, 1985.

Gorham, Deborah. *The Victorian Girl and the Feminine Ideal.* Bloomington: Indiana University Press, 1982.

Graham, Kathryn V. "The Devil's Own Art: Topiary in Children's Fiction." *Children's Literature* 33 (2005): 94–114.

Graves, Algernon. *The Royal Academy of Art: A Complete Dictionary of Contributors and Their Work from its Foundation in 1769 to 1904.* 4 vols. London: Kingsmead Reprints, 1970.

Griswold, Jerry. "Snugness: The Robin in Its Nest." *In the Garden: Essays in Honor of Frances Hodgson Burnett.* Ed. Angelica Shirley Carpenter. Lanham, MD: Scarecrow Press, 2006. 147–52.

Halstead, Caroline A. *The Little Botanist, or Steps toward the Attainment of Botanical Knowledge.* London: John Harris, 1835.

Hardie, Martin. *Water-Colour Painting in Britain. Vol. 3: The Victorian Period.* Eds. Dudley Snelgrove, Jonathan Mayne, and Basil Taylor. New York: Barnes and Noble, 1968.

Hare, Augustus J. C. *The Gurneys of Earlham.* 2 vols. London: George Allen, 1895.

Harrison, Robert Pogue. *Gardens: An Essay on the Human Condition.* Chicago: University of Chicago Press, 2008.

Hayden, Ruth. *Mrs. Delany, Her Life and Her Flowers.* New York: New Amsterdam Books, 1980.

Heckle, Augustin. *The Lady's Drawing Book.* London: T. Bowles, 1753.

Heinzelman, Kurt. "The Cult of Domesticity: Dorothy and William Wordsworth at Grasmere." *Romanticism and Feminism.* Ed. Anne K. Mellor. Bloomington: Indiana University Press, 1988. 52–78.

Helsinger, Elizabeth. "Authority, Desire, and the Pleasures of Reading." *Sesame and Lilies.* Ed. Deborah Epstein Nord. New Haven: Yale University Press, 2002. 113–41.

Rural Scenes and National Representation: Britain, 1815–50. Princeton: Princeton University Press, 1997.

Heydt-Stevenson, Jill. *Austen's Unbecoming Conjunctions: Subversive Laughter, Embodied History.* New York: Palgrave Macmillan, 2005.

Hibberd, Shirley. *Rustic Adornments for Homes of Taste and Recreations for Town Folk in the Study and Imitation of Nature.* Intro. John Sales. 1856. London: Century Hutchinson, 1987.

The Town Garden: A Manual for the Management of City and Suburban Gardens. London: Groombridge & Sons, 1855.

Hilton, Tim. *John Ruskin: The Later Years.* New Haven: Yale University Press, 2000.

Hines, Maude. "'He Made *Us* Very Much Like the Flowers': Human/Nature in Nineteenth-Century Anglo-American Children's Literature." *Wild Things: Children's Culture and Ecocriticism.* Eds. Sidney I. Dobrin and Kenneth B. Kidd. Detroit: Wayne State University Press, 2004. 16–30.

Hoare, Sarah. *Poems on Conchology and Botany.* London: Simpkin & Marshall; Bristol: Wright and Bagnall, 1831.

Homans, Margaret. *Royal Representations: Queen Victoria and British Culture, 1837–1876.* Chicago: University of Chicago Press, 1998.

Honeyman, Susan E. "Childhood Bound: In Gardens, Maps, and Pictures." *Mosaic: A Journal for the Comparative Study of Literature* 34.2 (June 2001): 117–32.

Hooke, Robert. *Micrographia, or Some Physiological Descriptions of Minute Bodies made by Magnifying Glasses with Observations and Inquiries Thereupon.* 1665. New York: Dover, 1961.

Howe, Bea. *Lady with Green Fingers: The Life of Jane Loudon.* London: Country Life, 1961.

Howitt, Mary. *Sowing and Reaping; or, What Will Come Of It?* London: D. Appleton, 1841.

Hunt, John Dixon. "The Garden as Cultural Object." *Denatured Visions: Landscape and Culture in the Twentieth Century.* Eds. Stuart Wrede and William Howard Adams. New York: Museum of Modern Art, 1991. 19–32.

Greater Perfections: The Practice of Garden Theory. Philadelphia: University of Pennsylvania Press, 2000.

Hurdis, James. *The Village Curate: A Poem.* 1788. Newburyport, MA: W. & J. Gilman, 1808.

Hussey, Mrs. T. J. [Anna Maria]. Berkeley Correspondence. Vol. 7. Botany Library, Natural History Museum, London.

Illustrations of British Mycology. Vol. 1. London: Reeve, Benham and Reeve, 1847–55.

Ibbetson, Agnes. "MS Treatise on Botany in the Form of 20 Letters." MSS IBB. Botany Library, Natural History Museum, London.

——. "On the Action of Lime upon Animal and Vegetable Substances." *Annals of Philosophy* 14 (July–December 1819): 125–29.

——. "On the Adapting of Plants to the Soil, and Not the Soil to the Plants." *Letters and Papers on Agriculture, Planting, &c. Selected from the Correspondence of the Bath and West of England Society* 14 (1816): 136–59.

——. "On the Flower-Buds of Trees Passing through the Wood, as Noticed by Cicero and Pliny." *Philosophical Magazine and Journal* 59 (1822): 3–8.

——. "On the Injurious Effect of Burying Weeds." *Annals of Philosophy* 12 (August 1818): 87–91.

——. "On the Interior Buds of All Plants." *Journal of Natural Philosophy, Chemistry and the Arts* 33 (1812): 1–10.

——. "On the Perspiration Alleged to Take Place in Plants." *Philosophical Magazine and Journal* 59 (1822): 243–48.

——. "On the Physiology of Botany." *Philosophical Magazine and Journal* 56 (1820): 3–9.

——. "On the Secret and Open Nectaries of Various Flowers." *Journal of Natural Philosophy, Chemistry and the Arts* 33 (November 1812): 171–79.

——. "On the Structure and Classification of Seeds." *Journal of Natural Philosophy, Chemistry and the Arts* 27 (November 1810): 174–84.

——. "On the Structure and Growth of Seeds." *Journal of Natural Philosophy, Chemistry, and the Arts* 7 (September 1810): 1–17.

Jackson-Houlston, Caroline. "'Queen Lilies'? The Interpenetration of Scientific, Religious and Gender Discourses in Victorian Representations of Plants." *Journal of Victorian Culture* 11.1 (2006): 84–110.

[Jacson, Maria Elizabeth]. *Botanical Dialogues, between Hortensia and Her Four Children, Charles, Harriet, Juliette and Henry.* London: J. Johnson, 1797.

Jacson, Maria Elizabeth. *The Florist's Manual; or, Hints for the Construction of a Gay Flower Garden.* 1816. New edn. London: Henry Colburn, 1827.

Jay, Elisabeth. *Mrs Oliphant: "A Fiction to Herself," A Literary Life.* New York: Oxford University Press, 2001.

[Jerram, Jane Elizabeth Holmes?]. *Lucy and Arthur: A Book for Children.* London: James Burns, [1840?].

Johnson, Alexandra. "The Drama of Imagination: Marjory Fleming and Her Diaries." *Infant Tongues: The Voice of the Child in Literature.* Eds. Elizabeth Goodenough, Mark A. Heberle, and Naomi Sokoloff. Detroit: Wayne State University Press, 1994. 80–109.

Johnson, Louisa. *Every Lady Her Own Flower Gardener: Addressed to the Industrious and Economical.* 1839. Canberra: Mulini, 1999.

Kelley, Theresa M. "Romantic Exemplarity: Botany and 'Material' Culture." *Romantic Science: The Literary Forms of Natural History.* Ed. Noah Heringman. Albany: State University of New York Press, 2002.

Kent, Anna. *York House.* London: Francis Westley, 1820.

Kent, Elizabeth. *Flora Domestica, or, The Portable Flower-Garden.* 1823. London: Whittaker, Treacher & Co., 1831.

Kincaid, James. *Child-Loving: The Erotic Child and Victorian Culture.* New York: Routledge, 1994.

King, Amy M. *Bloom: The Botanical Vernacular in the English Novel.* New York: Oxford University Press, 2003.

King, Catherine. "What Women Can Make." *Gender and Art.* Ed. Gill Perry. New Haven and London: Yale University Press, 1999. 61–86.

Knight, Mrs. H. C. *Jane Taylor: Her Life and Letters.* London: Thomas Nelson & Sons, 1880.

Kramer, Jack. *Women of Flowers: A Tribute to Victorian Women Illustrators.* New York: Stewart, Tabori & Chang, 1996.

Kriz, Kay Dian. *The Idea of the English Landscape Painter: Genius as Alibi in the Nineteenth Century.* New Haven and London: Yale University Press, 1997.

Krueger, Christine. *The Reader's Repentance: Women Preachers, Women Writers, and Nineteenth-Century Social Discourse.* Chicago: University of Chicago Press, 1992.

Labbe, Jacqueline M. *Romantic Visualities: Landscape, Gender, and Romanticism.* London: Macmillan, 1998.

"Ladies [sic] Gardeners." *Gardeners' Chronicle* November 12, 1842: 759.

A Lady. *Every Lady's Guide to Her Own Greenhouse, Hothouse, and Conservatory.* London: W. S. Orr, 1851.

The Floral Knitting Book: or, the Art of Knitting Imitations of Natural Flowers. London: Groombridge and Sons, n.d.

Laird, Mark. *The Flowering of the Landscape Garden: English Pleasure Grounds, 1720–1800.* Philadelphia: University of Pennsylvania Press, 1999.

Langland, Elizabeth. *Nobody's Angels: Middle-Class Women and Domestic Ideology in Victorian Culture.* Ithaca: Cornell University Press, 1995.

Lawrance, Mary. *A Collection of Roses from Nature.* London: published by the author, 1799.

Sketches of Flowers from Nature. London: published by the author, 1801.

Levin, Susan M. *Dorothy Wordsworth and Romanticism.* New Brunswick: Rutgers University Press, 1987.

Lightman, Bernard. "Depicting Nature, Defining Roles: The Gender Politics of Victorian Illustration." *Figuring It Out: Science, Gender, and Visual Culture.* Eds. Ann B. Shteir and Bernard V. Lightman. Lebanon, NH: Dartmouth College Press, 2006. 214–39.

Lindley, John. [Editor's Note]. *Gardeners' Chronicle* November 12, 1842: 759.

Lloyd, Stephen. *Richard and Maria Cosway: Regency Artists of Taste and Fashion.* Edinburgh: Scottish National Portrait Gallery, 1995.

Loades, David. *Mary Tudor: The Tragical History of the First Queen of England.* Richmond: National Archives Press, 2006.

Locke, John. *Some Thoughts Concerning Education.* Vol. 37, Part 1. Harvard Classics. New York: P. F. Collier & Son, 1909–14. www.bartleby.com/37/1/. 2001. 07 July 2006.

Loudon, Jane. *The Amateur Gardener.* 1847. Rev. W. Robinson. London: Frederick Warne, [1869].

Botany for Ladies; or, A Popular Introduction to the Natural System of Plants. London: John Murray, 1842.

"Floral Calendar." *Ladies' Magazine of Gardening* 1 (1842): 160.

Gardening for Ladies. 1840. 6th edn. London: John Murray, 1843.

Gardening for Ladies; and Companion to the Flower-Garden. 1st American edn., from the 3rd London edn. New York: Wiley & Putnam, 1846.

"The Ladies' Companion." *Ladies' Companion at Home and Abroad* December 29, 1849: 8.

The Ladies' Companion to the Flower-Garden. 1841. Rept. in *Gardening for Ladies; and Companion to the Flower-Garden.* 1st American edn., from the 3rd London edn. New York: Wiley & Putnam, 1846.

The Ladies' Flower-Garden of Ornamental Annuals. London: William Smith, 1840.

The Lady's Country Companion; or, How to Enjoy a Country Life Rationally. 1845. Ed. Nicolas Barker. Bungay: Paradigm Press for the National Trust, 1984.

"My Letter-Bag." *Ladies' Companion at Home and Abroad* January 19, 1850: 57.

My Own Garden; or the Young Gardener's Year Book. London: Kerby and Son, 1855.

"The Suburban Garden." *Ladies' Companion at Home and Abroad* February 2, 1850: 81.

Loudon, John Claudius. *An Encyclopaedia of Gardening.* 1822. 2 vols. Rev. edn. London: Longman, Rees, Orme, Brown, Green, and Longman, 1835. Facsimile edn. New York and London: Garland, 1982.

The Greenhouse Companion. 3rd edn. London: Whittaker, Treacher, 1832.

"Notes on Gardens and Country Seats. Hoole House, the Rev. Peploe W. Hamilton; Occupied by Lady Broughton." *Gardener's Magazine and Register of Rural and Domestic Improvement* 14 (August 1838): 353–63.

The Suburban Gardener, and Villa Companion. London: Longmans, Orme, Brown, Green, and Longmans, 1838. Facsimile edn. New York and London: Garland, 1982.

A Lover of Gardening. "On the Best Method of Growing the *Phlox drummondii*." *Ladies' Magazine of Gardening* 1 (1842): 48–49.

Lundin, Anne. "Cultural Work: The Critical and Commercial Reception of *The Secret Garden*, 1911–2004." In the Garden: *Essays in Honor of Frances Hodgson Burnett*. Ed. Angelica Shirley Carpenter. Lanham, MD: Scarecrow Press, 2006. 153–68.

Mack, John. *The Art of Small Things*. Cambridge, MA: Harvard University Press, 2007.

Mackenzie, Peter. "Gardening Practiced by the Fair Sex." *Gardeners' Chronicle* October 29, 1842: 725.

Makaryk, Irena R., ed. *Encyclopedia of Contemporary Literary Theory: Approaches, Scholars, Terms*. Toronto: University of Toronto Press, 1997.

Maling, Miss E. A. *In-Door Plants and How to Grow Them*. London: Smith and Elder, 1862.

[Marcet, Jane.] *Conversations on Vegetable Physiology; Comprehending the Elements of Botany, with Their Application to Agriculture*. Adapted to the use of schools, by Rev. J. L. Blake. 1st American edn. Boston: Crocker & Brewster, 1830.

The Marley Collection of Watercolours by Helen Allingham. London: Christie, Manson & Woods, 1991.

Martineau, Harriet. *Deerbrook*. 1839. Ed. Valerie Sanders. London: Penguin, 2004.

Household Education. 1848. Boston: Houghton, Osgood & Co., 1880.

Massey, Doreen. *Space, Place, and Gender*. Minneapolis: University of Minnesota Press, 1994.

McCarthy, William. "Mother of All Discourses: Anna Barbauld's Lessons for Children." *Culturing the Child, 1690–1914*. Ed. Donelle Ruwe. Lanham, MD: Scarecrow Press, 2005. 85–111.

Meen, Margaret. *Exotic Plants from the Royal Gardens at Kew*. London: n.p., 1790.

Mellor, Anne. "British Romanticism, Gender, and Three Women Artists." *The Consumption of Culture, 1600–1800: Image, Object, Text*. Eds. Ann Bermingham and John Brewer. New York: Routledge, 1997. 121–42.

"Hannah More, Revolutionary Reformer." October 12, 2004. www.adam-matthew-publications.co.uk/collect/e001.htm.

Mothers of the Nation: Women's Political Writing in England, 1780–1830. Bloomington: Indiana University Press, 2002.

Romanticism and Gender. New York: Routledge, 1993.

Merrill, Lynn L. *The Romance of Victorian Natural History*. New York: Oxford University Press, 1989.

Milton, John. *Complete Poems and Major Prose*. Ed. Merritt Y. Hughes. Upper Saddle River, NJ: Prentice Hall, 1957.

Mitford, Mary Russell. *The Life of Mary Russell Mitford: Told by Herself in Letters to Her Friends*. Ed. Rev. A. G. K. L'Estrange. 2 vols. New York: Harper & Bros., 1870.

Our Village. 1824. New York: Prentice Hall, 1987.

Moffat, Mary Jane, and Charlotte Painter, eds. *Revelations: Diaries of Women*. New York: Random House, 1974.

"Monthly Botanical Report." *Monthly Magazine, or, British Register* 31.214 (July 1, 1811): 601–02.

Moore, Lisa L. "Queer Gardens: Mary Delany's Flowers and Friendship." *Eighteenth-Century Studies* 39.1 (2005): 49–70.

More, Hannah. *Cœlebs in Search of a Wife*. 1808. Bristol: Thoemmes Press, 1995.

The Complete Works of Hannah More. 2 vols. New York: J. C. Derby, 1856.

Memoirs of the Life of Mrs. Hannah More. 2 vols. Ed. William Roberts. London: R. R. Seeley & W. Burnside, 1836.

Strictures on the Modern System of Female Education. 1799. 2 vols. Oxford and New York: Woodstock Books, 1995.

The Works of Hannah More. 11 vols. London: T. Cadell, 1830.

Morgan, Joan, and Alison Richards. *A Paradise Out of a Common Field: The Pleasures and Plenty of the Victorian Garden*. New York: Harper & Row, 1990.

Mulvey, Laura. "Pandora: Topographies of the Mask and Curiosity." *Sexuality and Space*. Ed. Beatriz Colomina. Princeton: Princeton Papers on Architecture, 1992. 53–72.

Murdoch, John. *The Discovery of the Lake District: A Northern Arcadia and its Uses*. London: Victoria and Albert Museum, 1984.

"My Dear Children." *Child's Companion; or, Sunday Scholar's Reward* 7 (1829): 311.

Myers, Greg. "Science for Women and Children: The Dialogue of Popular Science in the Nineteenth Century." *Nature Transformed: Science and Literature, 1700–1900*. Eds. John Christie and Sally Shuttleworth. Manchester: Manchester University Press, 1989. 171–200.

Myers, Mitzi. "The Dilemmas of Gender as Double-Voiced Narrative; or, Maria Edgeworth Mothers the Bildungsroman." *The Idea of the Novel in the Eighteenth Century*. Ed. Robert W. Uphaus. East Lansing, MI: Colleagues Press, 1988. 67–96.

"Impeccable Governesses, Rational Dames, and Moral Mothers: Mary Wollstonecraft and the Female Tradition in Georgian Children's Books." *Children's Literature* 14 (1986): 31–58.

"Reading Rosamond Reading: Maria Edgeworth's 'Wee-Wee Stories' Interrogate the Canon." *Infant Tongues: The Voice of the Child in Literature*. Eds. Elizabeth Goodenough, Mark A. Heberle, and Naomi Sokoloff. Detroit: Wayne State University Press, 1994.

"Reform or Ruin: 'A Revolution in Female Manners.'" *Studies in Eighteenth Century Culture* 11 (1982): 199–216.

"Romancing the Moral Tale: Maria Edgeworth and the Problematics of Pedagogy." *Romanticism and Children's Literature in Nineteenth-Century England*. Ed. James Holt McGavran, Jr. Athens and London: University of Georgia Press, 1991. 96–128.

"'A Taste for Truth and Realities': Early Advice to Mothers on Books for Girls." *Children's Literature Association Quarterly* 12.3 (1987): 118–24.

Nabholtz, John R. "Dorothy Wordsworth and the Picturesque." *Studies in Romanticism* 3 (Winter 1964): 118–28.

Naginski, Erika. Review of *Scenes in a Library: Reading the Photograph in the Book, 1843–1875*, by Carol Armstrong; *Learning to Draw: Studies in the Cultural History of a Polite and Useful Art*, by Ann Bermingham; and *Parallel Lines: Printmakers, Painters, and Photographers in Nineteenth-Century France*, by Stephen Bann. *Art Bulletin* 85.1 (March 2003): 196–202.

Nead, Lynda. *Myths of Sexuality: Representations of Women in Victorian Britain*. Oxford: Blackwell, 1988.

The New Female Instructor, or Young Woman's Guide to Domestic Happiness. London: Thomas Kelly, 1834.

Nicolson, Marjorie Hope. "The Microscope and the English Imagination." 1935. *Science and Imagination*. 1956. Hamden, CT: Archon, 1976.

Nochlin, Linda. *Courbet*. New York: Thames & Hudson, 2007.

Noyes, Russell. *Wordsworth and the Art of Landscape*. Bloomington: Indiana University Press, 1968.

Oliphant, Margaret. "Mary Russel [sic] Mitford." *Blackwood's* 75 (June 1854): 658–70.

Miss Marjoribanks. 1866. Ed. Elisabeth Jay. New York: Penguin, 1998.

The Perpetual Curate. 1864. New York: Virago, 1987.

Phoebe Junior. 1876. Ed. Elizabeth Langland. Peterborough, ON: Broadview, 2002.

The Rector and The Doctor's Family. 1863. New York: Virago, 1986.

Salem Chapel. 1863. New York: Virago, 1986.

O'Malley, Andrew. *The Making of the Modern Child: Children's Literature and Childhood in the Late Eighteenth Century*. New York and London: Routledge, 2003.

Onslow, Barbara. *Women of the Press in Nineteenth-Century Britain*. New York: St. Martin's, 2000.

"On the Wages of Gardeners." *Gardener and Practical Florist* 1 (1843): 19–21.

Opie, Iona, and Peter, eds. *The Oxford Dictionary of Nursery Rhymes*. 2nd edn. Oxford: Oxford University Press, 1997.

[O'Reilly, Mrs. Robert]. *Daisy's Companions; or, Scenes from Child Life*. London: Bell & Daldy, [1860?].

P. E. "Ripe Cherries." *Child's Companion* 2 (August 1824): 33–40.

"The Vine." *Child's Companion* 1 (March 1824): 72–80.

P. P. "Ladies Turned Gardeners." *Gardeners' Chronicle* November 5, 1842: 742.

Page, Judith W. "Gender and Domesticity." *The Cambridge Companion to Wordsworth*. Ed. Stephen Gill. New York: Cambridge University Press, 2003. 125–41.

"Reforming Honeysuckles: Hannah More's *Cœlebs in Search of a Wife* and the Politics of Women's Gardens." *Keats–Shelley Journal* (2006): 11–36.

Park, Mungo. *Travels in the Interior of Africa*. 1799. Ware: Wordsworth Editions, 2002.

Parkinson, Thomas. *Flower Painting Made Easy*. London: Robert Sayer, 1775.

Pascoe, Judith. "Female Botanists and the Poetry of Charlotte Smith." *Re-Visioning Romanticism: British Women Writers, 1776–1837*. Eds. Carol Shiner Wilson and Joel Haefner. Philadelphia: University of Pennsylvania Press, 1994. 193–209.

Paul, William. "Address to the Cottage Gardens Association, 9 December 1882." *The English Garden: Literary Sources and Documents*. Vol. 3. Ed. Michael Charlesworth. Mountfield: Helm Information, 1993. 297–305.

Percy, Joan. "Maria Elizabetha Jacson and her *Florist's Manual*." *Garden History* 20.1 (Spring 1992): 45–56.

Peter Parley's First Present for Very Young Children. London: Darton and Clark, [between 1836 and 1847].

Phillips, Henry. *History of Cultivated Vegetables; Comprising Their Botanical, Medicinal, Edible, and Chemical Qualities; Natural History; and Relation to Art, Science, and Commerce*. 2 vols. London: Henry Colburn and Co., 1822.

Pickering, Samuel F. *Moral Instruction and Fiction for Children, 1749–1820*. Athens and London: University of Georgia Press, 1993.

The Pleasing Instructor. London: Religious Tract Society, [c. 1850].

Plumb, J. H. "The New World of Children in Eighteenth-Century England." *Past & Present* 67 (May 1975): 65–95.

Pointon, Marcia. *Strategies for Showing: Women, Possession, and Representation in English Visual Culture, 1665–1800*. Oxford and New York: Oxford University Press, 1997.

Poovey, Mary. *The Proper Lady and the Woman Writer: Ideology as Style in the Works of Mary Wollstonecraft, Mary Shelley, and Jane Austen*. Chicago: University of Chicago Press, 1984.

Pratt, Anne. *The Field, the Garden, and the Woodland*. 1838. 3rd edn. London: C. Cox, 1847.

Prior, Karen Swallow. *Hannah More's* Coelebs in Search of a Wife: *A Review of Criticism and a New Analysis*. Studies in British Literature 74. Lewiston: Edwin Mellen Press, 2003.

Probyn, Elspeth. "This Body Which Is Not One: Speaking an Embodied Self." *Hypatia* 6 (1991): 111–24.

Rauch, Alan. "A World of Faith on a Foundation of Science: Science and Religion in British Children's Literature: 1761–1878." *Children's Literature Association Quarterly* 14 (1989): 13–19.

Repton, Humphry. *Observations on the Theory and Practice of Landscape Gardening*. London: J. Taylor, 1803.

Review of *Botanical Dialogues* by Maria Elizabeth Jacson. *Analytic Review* 28 (1798): 397–98.

Review of *Illustrations of British Mycology*, by Anna Maria Hussey. *Journal of Botany* (1886): 252.

Riley, Noel. *Gifts for Good Children: The History of Children's China*. 2 vols. Ilminster: Richard Dennis, 1991.

Ritvo, Harriet. "At the Edge of the Garden: Nature and Domestication in Eighteenth- and Nineteenth-Century Britain." *An English Arcadia: Landscape and Architecture in Britain and America*. Huntington Library Quarterly 55 (Summer 1992): 363–75.

Roberts, Mary. *The Wonders of the Vegetable Kingdom Displayed: In A Series of Letters*. London: G. and W. B. Whittaker, 1822.

Roberts, William. *Memoirs of the Life of Mrs. Hannah More*. 3rd edn. 2 vols. London: R. K. Seeley and W. Burnside, 1836.

Rose, Gillian. *Feminism and Geography: The Limits of Geographical Knowledge*. Minneapolis: University of Minnesota Press, 1993.

Rosenthal, Michael. "Gainsborough's Cottage Doors: A Matter of Modernity." *Sensation & Sensibility: Viewing Gainsborough's Cottage Door*. Ed. Ann Bermingham. New Haven and London: Yale University Press, 2005. 77–95.

——— "The Rough and the Smooth: Rural Subjects in Later-Eighteenth-Century Art." *Prospects for the Nation: Recent Essays in British Landscape, 1750–1880*. Eds. Michael Rosenthal, Christiana Payne, and Scott Wilcox. New Haven and London: Yale University Press, 1997. 37–59.

Ross, Stephanie. *What Gardens Mean*. Chicago: University of Chicago Press, 1998.

Rousseau, Jean-Jacques. *Letters on the Elements of Botany, Addressed to a Lady*. Trans. Thomas Martyn. 5th edn. London: B. and J. White, 1796.

Rowbotham, Judith. *Good Girls Make Good Wives: Guidance for Girls in Victorian Fiction*. Oxford: Blackwell, 1989.

Rubik, Margaret. "The Subversion of Clichés in Oliphants's Fiction." *Margaret Oliphant: Critical Essays on a Gentle Subversive*. Ed. D. J. Trela. Selinsgrove, PA: Susquehanna University Press, 1995. 49–65.

Ruskin, John. "Of Queens' Gardens." *Sesame and Lilies*. 1865. Ed. Deborah Epstein Nord. New Haven: Yale University Press, 2002. 68–93.

Ruwe, Donelle. "A Bibliography of Mitzi Myers's Scholarly Work." *Culturing the Child: 1690–1914: Essays in Honor of Mitzi Myers*. Ed. Donelle Ruwe. Lanham, MD: Children's Literature Association and Scarecrow Press, 2005.

Ryan, Robert. *The Romantic Reformation: Religious Politics in English Literature, 1789–1824*. New York: Cambridge University Press, 1997.

Salzmann, C. G. *Elements of Morality*. Trans. Mary Wollstonecraft. London: J. Johnson, 1791.

Schaub, Melissa. "Queen of Air or Constitutional Monarch? Idealism, Irony, and Narrative Power in *Miss Marjoribanks*." *Nineteenth-Century Literature* 55.2 (September 2000): 195–225.

Scott, Walter. *The Lady of the Lake: A Poem*. 7th edn. Edinburgh: John Ballantyne, 1810.

Secord, Anne. "Botany on a Plate: Pleasure and the Power of Pictures in Promoting Early Nineteenth-Century Scientific Knowledge." *Isis* 93 (2002): 28–57.

Setzer, Sharon. "'Pond'rous Engines' in 'Outraged Groves': The Environmental Argument of Anna Seward's 'Colebrook Dale'." *European Romantic Review* 18 (January 2007): 69–82.

Seward, Anna. *The Poetical Works of Anna Seward: With Extracts from Her Literary Correspondence*. 3 vols. Ed. Walter Scott. Edinburgh: Ballantyne and Co.; London: Longman, Hurst, Rees, and Orme, 1810.

Sha, Richard C. *The Visual and Verbal Sketch in British Romanticism*. Philadelphia: University of Pennsylvania Press, 1998.

Shaver, Chester L., and Alice C. *Wordsworth's Library: A Catalogue*. New York: Garland, 1979.

Shefer, Elaine. *Birds, Cages and Women in Victorian and Pre-Raphaelite Art*. New York: Peter Lang, 1990.

Shelley, Percy Bysshe. *Shelley's Poetry and Prose*. Eds. Donald H. Reiman and Neil Fraistat. 2nd edn. New York: Norton, 2002.

Sherwood, [Mary Martha]. *History of the Fairchild Family*. 1818. New York: Frederick A. Stokes, n.d.

Shore, Emily. *Journal of Emily Shore*. Ed. Barbara Timm Gates. Charlottesville and London: University Press of Virginia, 1991.

Shteir, Ann B. "Botany in the Breakfast Room: Women and Early Nineteenth-Century British Plant Study." *Uneasy Careers and Intimate Lives: Women in Science, 1789–1979*. Eds. Pnina G. Abir-Am and Dorinda Outram. New Brunswick and London: Rutgers University Press, 1987. 31–43.

Cultivating Women, Cultivating Science: Flora's Daughters and Botany in England 1760–1860. Baltimore and London: Johns Hopkins University Press, 1996.

"'Fac-Similes of Nature': Victorian Wax Flower Modelling." *Victorian Literature and Culture* 35 (2007): 649–61.

"Loudon [nee Webb], Jane." *The Oxford Dictionary of National Biography*. Oxford and New York: Oxford University Press, 2004. 474–75.

Silver, Anna K. "Domesticating Brontë's Moors: Motherhood in *The Secret Garden*." *Lion and the Unicorn* 21.2 (1997): 193–203.

Skinner, John. "Exploring Space: The Constellations of *Mansfield Park*." *Eighteenth-Century Fiction* 4 (January 1992): 125–48.

Sloman, Susan. "'Innocence and Health': Nursing Women in Gainsborough's Cottage-Door Paintings." *Sensation & Sensibility: Viewing Gainsborough's Cottage Door*. Ed. Ann Bermingham. New Haven and London: Yale University Press, 2005. 37–51.

Smith, Charlotte. *Conversations Introducing Poetry*. London: John Sharp, 1815.

Minor Morals Interspersed with Sketches of Natural History, Historical Anecdotes, and Original Stories. 1798. London: A. K. Newman, 1823.

Rambles Farther: A Continuation of Rural Walks: In Dialogues. Intended for the Use of Young Persons. 2 vols. in 1. Dublin: P. Wogan et al., 1796.

Rural Walks: In Dialogues. Intended for the Use of Young Persons. 2 vols. London: T. Cadell and W. Davies, 1795.

Smith, Elise L. "Centering the Home-Garden: The Arbor, Wall, and Gate in Moral Tales for Children." *Children's Literature* 36 (2008): 24–48.

Snook, Edith. "Eve and More: The Citation of *Paradise Lost* in Hannah More's *Coelebs in Search of a Wife*." *English Studies in Canada* 26.2 (June 2000): 127–54.

Snyder, William. "Mother Nature's Other Natures: Landscape in Women's Writing." *Women's Studies* 21 (1992): 143–62.

Southern Faunist. Letter to the editor. *Gentleman's Magazine* 71.1 (1801): 198–200.

Steward, James Christen. *The New Child: British Art and the Origins of Modern Childhood, 1730–1830*. Berkeley: University of California Press, 1995.

Stewart, Susan. *On Longing: Narratives of the Miniature, the Gigantic, the Souvenir, the Collection*. Durham, NC: Duke University Press, 1993.

Stott, Anne. *Hannah More: The First Victorian*. New York: Oxford University Press, 2003.

Summerfield, Geoffrey. *Fantasy and Reason: Children's Literature in the Eighteenth Century*. Athens: University of Georgia Press, 1984.

Suzuki, Mika. "*The Little Female Academy* and *The Governess*." *Women's Writing* 1.3 (1994): 325–39.

Tange, Andrea Kaston. "Redesigning Femininity: Miss Marjoribanks's Drawing-Room of Opportunity." *Victorian Literature and Culture* 36 (2008): 163–86.

[Taylor, Ann]. *The Autobiography and Other Memorials of Mrs Gilbert, Formerly Ann Taylor*. Ed. Josiah Gilbert. 2 vols. London: Henry S. King, 1874.

Taylor, Ann. "My Mother." Pamphlet edn. London: William Darton Jr., 1815.

[Taylor, Ann, and Jane]. *Original Poems for Infant Minds*. 1804–05. 2 vols. Rpt. in *Original Poems for Infant Minds [two volumes] and Rhymes for the Nursery*. New York and London: Garland, 1976.

  Rhymes for the Nursery. 1806. Rpt. in *Original Poems for Infant Minds [two volumes] and Rhymes for the Nursery*. New York and London: Garland, 1976.

  The Snow-Drop: A Collection of Rhymes for the Nursery. New Haven: S. Babcock, [1841].

[Taylor, Ann, Jane, et al.]. *The Associate Minstrels*. London: Thomas Conder, 1810.

Taylor, Geoffrey. *Some Nineteenth Century Gardeners*. Tiptree: Anchor Press, 1951.

Taylor, Jane. *The Contributions of Q. Q.* 2 vols. London: B. J. Holdsworth, 1824.

  A Day's Pleasure: To Which Are Added Reflections on a Day's Pleasure, and Busy Idleness. New York: Mahlon Day, 1830.

  Display: A Tale for Young People. 1815. New York: Robert Carter, 1847.

  Essays in Rhyme, on Morals and Manners. London: Taylor and Hessey, 1816.

[Taylor, Jane]. *The Little Field Daisy*. New York: Mahlon Day, n.d. [before 1844].

  Memoirs and Poetical Remains of the Late Jane Taylor, with Extracts from her Correspondence. Ed. Isaac Taylor, Jr. Boston: Crocker and Brewster, 1826.

Taylor, Mrs. [Ann Martin]. *Maternal Solicitude for a Daughter's Best Interests*. 1813. 2nd American edn. Boston: James Loring, 1827.

  Reciprocal Duties of Parents and Children. London: Taylor and Hessey, 1818.

Taylor, Mrs. [Ann Martin], and Jane. *Correspondence between a Mother and Her Daughter at School*. 2nd edn. London: Taylor and Hessey, 1817.

Thwaite, Ann. "A Biographer Looks Back." *In the Garden: Essays in Honor of Frances Hodgson Burnett*. Ed. Angelica Shirley Carpenter. Lanham, MD: Scarecrow Press, 2006. 17–31.

Tobin, Beth Fowkes. *Colonizing Nature: The Tropics in British Arts and Letters, 1760–1820*. Philadelphia: University of Pennsylvania Press, 2005.
Superintending the Poor: Charitable Ladies and Paternal Landlords in British Fiction, 1770–1860. New Haven: Yale University Press, 1993.
Tonna, Charlotte Elizabeth. *Chapters on Flowers*. London: R. B. Seeley and W. Burnside, 1836.
Trela, D. J., ed. *Margaret Oliphant: Critical Essays on a Gentle Subversive*. Selinsgrove, PA: Susquehanna University Press, 1995.
Trimmer, Sarah. Review of *Original Poems for Infant Minds*, by Ann and Jane Taylor. *Guardian of Education* 4 (1805): 77–82.
Tuan, Yi-Fu. *Space and Place: The Perspective of Experience*. Minneapolis and London: University of Minnesota Press, 1977.
Tuite, Clara. *Romantic Austen: Sexual Politics and the Literary Canon*. New York: Cambridge University Press, 2002.
Turner, Elizabeth. *The Cowslip, or More Cautionary Stories in Verse*. 1811. New York: Allen Brothers, 1869.
Tusser, Thomas. *A Hundreth Good Pointes of Husbandrie*. 1557. Renascence Editions. February 7, 2009. http://darkwing.uoregon.edu/~rbear/tusser1.html.
Twining, Elizabeth. "A Few Words about Window-Gardens." In *Nature's Name: An Anthology of Women's Writing and Illustration, 1780–1930*. Ed. Barbara T. Gates. Chicago: University of Chicago Press, 2002. 285–95.
Uglow, Jenny. *A Little History of British Gardening*. New York: North Point, 2004.
Vlasopolos, Anca. "Texted Selves: Dorothy and William Wordsworth in the Grasmere Journals." *a/b: Auto/Biography Studies* 14 (Summer 1999): 118–36.
Wakefield, Priscilla. *An Introduction to Botany, in a Series of Familiar Letters*. 1796. Boston: J. Belcher and J. W. Burditt, 1811.
Juvenile Anecdotes, Founded on Facts. Philadelphia: Johnson and Warner, 1809.
Reflections on the Present Condition of the Female Sex. 1798. New York and London: Garland, 1974.
Waldron, Mary. "Introduction." *Cœlebs in Search of a Wife*. 1808. Bristol: Thoemmes, 1995.
Jane Austen and the Fiction of Her Time. New York: Cambridge University Press, 1999.
Walker, George. *The Vagabond*. 3rd edn. Vol. 2. London: Printed for G. Walker, and Lee and Hurst, 1799. Eighteenth Century Collections Online. June 18, 2009. http://galenet.galegroup.com.
Wallace, Anne. "'Inhabited Solitudes': Dorothy Wordsworth's Domesticating Walkers." *Nordlit: Arbeidstidsskrift i litteratur* 1 (1997): 99–126. December 9, 2006. www.hum.uit.no/nordlit/1/wallace.html.
Waters, Michael. *The Garden in Victorian Literature*. Aldershot: Scolar Press, 1988.
Weltman, Sharon Arnofsky. "'Be No More Housewives but Queens': Queen Victoria and Ruskin's Domestic Mythology." *Remaking Queen Victoria*. Eds. Margaret Homans and Adrienne Munich. New York: Cambridge University Press, 1997. 105–22.

Wenner, Barbara Britton. *Prospect and Refuge in the Landscape of Jane Austen.* Burlington, VT: Ashgate, 2006.
Whiting, J. B. *Manual of Flower Gardening for Ladies.* London: David Bogue, 1849.
Williams, Raymond. *Keywords: A Vocabulary of Culture and Society.* New York: Oxford University Press, 1976.
Williamson, Tom. *Polite Landscapes: Gardens and Society in Eighteenth-Century England.* Baltimore: Johns Hopkins University Press, 1995.
Wilner, Arlene Fish. "Education and Ideology in Sarah Fielding's *The Governess.*" *Studies in Eighteenth-Century Culture* 24 (1995): 307–27.
Wilson, Carol Shiner. "Lost Needles, Tangled Threads: Stitchery, Domesticity, and the Artistic Enterprise in Barbauld, Edgeworth, Taylor, and Lamb." *Re-Visioning Romanticism: British Women Writers, 1776–1837.* Eds. Carol Shiner Wilson and Joel Haefner. Philadelphia: University of Pennsylvania Press, 1994. 167–90.
Wilson, Frances. *The Ballad of Dorothy Wordsworth.* New York: Farrar, Straus and Giroux, 2008.
Wiltshire, John. *Jane Austen and the Body: "The Picture of Health."* New York: Cambridge University Press, 2002.
Wollstonecraft, Mary. *Original Stories from Real Life, with Conversations Calculated to Regulate the Affections, and Form the Mind to Truth and Goodness.* London: J. Johnson, 1791.
  A Vindication of the Rights of Woman. Ed. Miriam Kramnick. New York: Penguin, 1975.
"Women's Work: Portraits of 12 Scientific Illustrators from the 17th to the 21st Century." *Linda Hall Library of Science, Engineering & Technology.* 2005. May 22, 2008. www.lindahall.org/events_exhib/exhibit/index.shtml.
Woolf, Virginia. "Professions for Women." 1931. *Virginia Woolf: Women and Writing.* Ed. Michèle Barrett. New York: Harcourt Brace, 1979. 57–63.
  A Room of One's Own. 1929. Intro. Susan Gubar. New York: Harcourt Brace, 2005.
Wordsworth, Dorothy. *The Grasmere Journals.* Ed. Pamela Woof. New York: Oxford University Press, 1991.
  The Journals of Dorothy Wordsworth. 2nd edn. Ed. Mary Moorman. New York: Oxford University Press, 1976.
  Recollections of a Tour Made in Scotland. Ed. and intro. Carol Kyros Walker. New Haven: Yale University Press, 1997.
  Tour of the Continent. 1820. *Journals of Dorothy Wordsworth.* 2 vols. Ed. Ernest de Selincourt. New York: Macmillan, 1941.
Wordsworth, William. *The Poetical Works of William Wordsworth.* Ed. Ernest de Selincourt and Helen Darbishire. 5 vols. Oxford: Clarendon, 1940–49.
  The Prelude, 1798, 1805, 1850. Eds. Jonathan Wordsworth, M. H. Abrams, and Stephen Gill. New York: Norton, 1979.
  The Prose Works of William Wordsworth. 3 vols. Eds. W. J. B. Owen and Jane Worthington Smyser. Oxford: Clarendon, 1974.

Wordsworth, William, and Dorothy. *The Letters of William and Dorothy Wordsworth: The Early Years, 1787–1805*. 2nd edn. Ed. Ernest de Selincourt. Rev. Chester L. Shaver. Oxford: Clarendon, 1967.

Worthen, John. *The Gang: Coleridge, the Hutchinsons and the Wordsworths in 1802*. New Haven: Yale University Press, 2001.

Yeldham, Charlotte. "Spilsbury, (Rebecca) Maria Ann." *The Oxford Dictionary of National Biography*. Vol. 51. Oxford and New York: Oxford University Press, 2004. 948–49.

Yonge, [Charlotte]. "Children's Literature of the Last Century." *Macmillan's Magazine* (July 1869): 229–37.

Yonge, Charlotte M. *The Herb of the Field*. 1853. Rev. edn. London: Macmillan, 1887.

The Young Lady's Book: A Manual of Elegant Recreations, Exercises, and Pursuits. 1829. New York: Elibron, 2001.

Young, Ruth. *Father and Daughter: Jonathan and Maria Spilsbury*. London: Epworth Press, 1952.

"Maria Spilsbury, 1777–1820. A Woman Artist of the Regency." *Country Life* (May 28, 1938): xliv–xlvi.

Index

Abercrombie, John
   The Garden Vade Mecum 217
   The Gardener's Pocket Journal 153
"accomplishments" 79–81, 91, 210
Adams, Henry Charles
   Geraniums 220
Addison, Joseph 210
Allingham, Helen
   A Cottage at Freshwater 253
   watercolors 253–55
Amateur Gardening 182
Appleton, Jay
   The Experience of Landscape 141
arbors 17, 31–38, 235
   communal 37
   at school 31
   see also bowers; grottos
art education 81, 91
Atkins, Lucy Sarah
   Botanical Rambles 53, 184
Austen, Jane 201
   Catharine, or the Bower 214–19
      and *Cœlebs in Search of a Wife* (More) 215–16
   Mansfield Park 10, 211, 214–16, 226
      and garden workers 224–26
      and "improvement" 225
      and indoor gardens 219–24
      and personal development 201, 211, 215, 227
   Northanger Abbey 91, 226
   Sanditon 91
"authorities" on botany 62, 63–64

Bachelard, Gaston 8, 74, 75, 113, 119, 141, 147, 160
   analysis of nests 222
   The Poetics of Space 3, 42, 59, 147
Baldwin, Samuel
   Sketching from Nature 83

Barbauld, Anna Letitia
   Lessons for Children of Three Years Old 25, 32
   Stories of the Months 186
   "To a Lady, With Some Painted Flowers" 92
Bell, Gertrude 250, 255
Bell, Susan Groag
   gendered gardens 214
Bellanca, Mary Ellen 53
Bermingham, Ann 81
Bilston, Sarah
   "Queens of the Garden" 163
Blake, William
   Songs of Innocence 19, 258n24
Bohls, Elizabeth 159
Boscawen, Fanny
   journal of 31
botanical texts 8, 50, 60
   by women 50–55, 60
botany 6, 61, 66–67, 68
   a study suitable for women 55, 67
bowers 37–38, 145–47, 215–24, 227, 274n29
   and bedrooms 216
   indoors 222–23
Broome, Charlotte Anne
   Fanny and Mary 81, 187
Brownstein, Rachel 156
Budden, Maria Elizabeth 28, 90
   Always Happy 26, 37, 179
   Chit Chat 23, 87
   Key to Knowledge 24
   Right and Wrong 25, 42
   on self-control 47
Burke, Edmund 7
   A Philosophical Enquiry into the Origin of Our Ideas of the Sublime and Beautiful 92
Burnett, Frances Hodgson
   The Secret Garden 251, 255
Bury, Priscilla
   A Selection of Hexandrian Plants 86

Index

Casid, Jill H.
  Sowing Empire: Landscape and Colonization 7
Catlow, Agnes and Maria
  The Children's Garden and What They Made of It 27
charity
  see philanthropy
children
  and flowers 15
  garden as training ground for 17, 27
  girls 41, 62, 183–89
  and mothers 18–22
  nature's functions for 23
children's books 3, 8, 15–22
  authors of 15
  garden imagery in 22
  and virtues 46–49
The Child's Companion 183
class 3, 19, 24, 28–31, 178, 191, 194, 196
  boundaries of 245
  and "improvement" 211
  markers of 19, 228–31, 235–38
  and situation of houses 232, 234, 238–40
classicism 71
classification, language of 63
Cobbett, Anne
  The English Housekeeper 183
Cockburn, Edwin
  The Return from Market 104
Colebrook Dale 73
Coleridge, Samuel Taylor 145
"commanding a view" 130
consumerism 209–10
Cosway, Maria 266n34
  illustrations by 88
  Princess Amelia (portrait) 83
  professional life of 90
Cosway, Richard 90
Cowper, William 209, 211–12
Cunningham, Richenda Gurney
  sketchbook of 113
Curtis, William
  Flora Londinensis 63

Daniels, Stephen
  on women's gardening 151
Darwin, Erasmus
  The Botanic Garden: The Economy of Plants 74
  Plan for the Conduct of Female Education 67
Davidoff, Leonore 116, 132
Davidoff, Leonore, and Catherine Hall 178, 184
defamiliarization 62

Delany, Mary 271n45
The Delights of Flower Painting 92
Deresiewicz, William 222
domesticity 27, 34–38, 132, 165–73, 174
Domosh, Mona, and Joni Seager
  Putting Women in Place: Feminist Geographers Make Sense of the World 6
Doody, Margaret Anne 214
drawing 79–81, 87
  of flowers 81, 92–94
  of landscapes 92
  as an occupation 93
  sketching 81–94, 265n14
  teachers of 265n5
drawing manuals 81–87
Duckworth, Alistair 211, 280n4, 284n82
  The Improvement of the Estate 211

Edgeworth, Maria 19, 32, 86, 173, 177
  The Parent's Assistant 79
  Rosamond 80, 83
  "Simple Susan" 37
Edgeworth, Maria, and Richard Lovell Edgeworth
  Practical Education 80
education 2–3, 18, 80, 91, 262n32
  in the arts 81, 91
Elegant Arts for Ladies 87
Elliott, Brent 243
  Victorian Gardens 230
Elliott, Dorice Williams 202
Ellis, Sarah 8, 38, 174
  The Mothers of England 7, 15
empire, the 261n13
Enlightenment, the 75
epistolary writing 71
Every Lady's Guide to Her Own Greenhouse 180
exotics 51, 154, 226, 261n13, 275n55
  geraniums 219–21, 236

Fabricant, Carole 212
fairy tales 260n81
The Female Aegis; or, the Duties of Women from Childhood to Old Age 28
Fielding, Sarah
  The Governess 31, 43
Fitton, Sarah
  Conversations on Botany 53, 56
Fleming, Marjory
  journal of 39
Flint, Kate 49
The Floricultural Cabinet and Florists' Magazine 195

flowers
    and children 15
    painting of 81
        see also drawing
    sexualized 59
Ford, Susan 94
    "Landscape Revisited: A Feminist
        Reappraisal" 5
Free Gardeners 192, 279n90
Freemasonry 279n90
fungi 108–11

Gainsborough, Thomas 102–04, 268n70
The Gardener and Practical Florist 191
gardening 163, 173, 212, 224–26, 230–32,
        274n47
    benefits of 173–77
        health 174, 221–24
        mental 175, 222–24
        moral 175
        spiritual 176, 203, 205–07
    and domesticity 165–73, 174
    by girls 183–89
        see also children
    by men 172, 177–80
    by women 151, 177, 180–83, 184, 189–93,
        195–98
        and dirt 110
        and dress 194
        functions of 163
        lady gardeners 178–80, 235
        and manual labor 171–73, 189–93, 280n98
        as supervisors 180
        and tools for 193–95
        and watering 184
gardening manuals 3, 10, 178
    for and by women 163–65
gardens
    boundaries of 17, 116
        fences 42–46
        gates 17, 42–45, 249, 250
        walls 17, 30
    cottage 240–46
    indoor 219–24
    open 239
    "rooms" of 217
    secret 251, 255
    walled 232–33, 239, 245
    window gardens 221
    windows onto 123–25, 128–30, 166, 169–70
gaze
    theories of the 266n29
gender 27–28, 32, 104, 178, 184, 190–93, 196
    boundaries of 245

gendered gardens 214
    inversion of roles 209
    and masculinity 190–91
    and separate spheres 202–04, 213–14,
        228–31, 235–38
George, Sam
    *Botany, Sexuality and Women's Writing
        1760–1830* 6
geraniums 219–21, 236
Gilbert, Josiah 133
greenhouses 166, 226, 234
Grew, Nehemiah 63
Griswold, Jerry 251
grottos 38

habitat theory 141
Hall, Catherine
    see Davidoff, Leonore, and Catherine Hall
Halstead, Caroline A.
    *The Little Botanist, or Steps toward the
        Attainment of Botanical Knowledge* 55
Heckle, Augustin
    The Lady's Drawing Book 82
Helsinger, Elizabeth 243, 247, 287n64
Hibberd, Shirley 166
    Rustic Adornments for Homes of Taste 170,
        231–32, 238
    The Town Garden 236–38
Hoare, Sarah
    Poems on Conchology and Botany 72
Homans, Margaret 247
"home landscapes" 96
homes 30, 117–23, 141
    nostalgia for 76, 270n5
    see also Taylor, Ann; Taylor, Jane;
        Wordsworth, Dorothy
Howitt, Mary
    Sowing and Reaping 93
Hunt, John Dixon 2–4, 98, 149, 155, 219, 238, 243
    "The Garden as Cultural Object" 230
    *Greater Perfections: The Practice of Garden
        Theory* 4, 230
Hurdis, James
    The Village Curate 57
Hussey, Anna Maria 9, 79, 106–13, 115
    artistic abilities of 111
    botanical studies of 108
    on collecting 109
    use of scientific language 110
    writings of 108, 111
        Illustrations of British Mycology 106, 108
        "Matrimony" 108
Hutchinson, Mary 143
    marriage to William Wordsworth 147, 148

Index

Ibbetson, Agnes 67–71, 109
  articles published by 68
  illustrations by 68
  methods of study 69
  on observation and confidence 68
  and the study of botany 110
  "Treatise on Botany" 68
  writing style of 69
imagination in study 64, 75
"improvement" 211–14, 225, 227, 247
  and class 211
instructional texts 3, 7, 81–87

Jackson-Houlston, Caroline 55
Jacson, Maria Elizabeth
  Botanical Dialogues 60–67
  The Florist's Manual 152, 163, 196
Jerram, Jane
  Lucy and Arthur 27
Johnson, Joseph 261n31
Johnson, Louisa 174, 175–77
  Every Lady Her Own Flower Gardener 164, 196–98, 240

Kent, Anna
  York House 44
Kent, Elizabeth
  Flora Domestica 11, 163, 166, 219

Labbe, Jacqueline 203
  Romantic Visualities 141
Laird, Mark 217
landscape poetry 208
landscapes 94–105, 214
  see also nature
Lawrance, Mary
  Sketches of Flowers from Nature 83
Lawson, William
  Country Housewife's Garden 213
Levin, Susan 143, 156
Lindley, John
  Ladies' Botany 192
Linnaeus 63, 73
Loudon, Jane 3, 173, 175, 179, 195, 221
  Botany for Ladies 51
  Gardening for Ladies 172, 174, 180, 189, 194
  "Implements" 193
  Instructions in Gardening for Ladies 164–65
  Ladies' Companion at Home and Abroad 172
  The Ladies' Companion to the Flower-Garden 169, 177
  The Lady's Country Companion 171, 179
  My Own Garden 189
  success as an author 276n7
Loudon, John Claudius 248
  An Encyclopaedia of Gardening 194
Luckcock, James 169, 182

Mack, John 222
Mackenzie, Peter
  "Gardening Practiced by the Fair Sex" 191
magnification 50–55, 66
  see also microscopes; miniature
Maling, E. A.
  In-Door Plants 236
Marcet, Jane
  Conversations on Vegetable Physiology 75
Martineau, Harriet
  Deerbrook 37, 120
  Household Education 15
Massey, Doreen 125, 169
  Space, Place, and Gender 6
melancholia 121
Mellor, Anne 202, 210, 266n30, 273n25
microscopes 58–60, 69
  see also miniature
Milton, John
  Paradise Lost 203, 204–08
miniature 50–51, 62, 76, 222
Mitford, Mary Russell 151, 176, 220
  Our Village 243–44
Montagu, Elizabeth 30
monumentalism 214
More, Hannah 9, 151, 201
  Cœlebs in Search of a Wife 10, 176, 208–11, 227
  and Austen 215–16
  on the consumer economy 209–10
  and "improvement" 212–14
  on literature and landscape 208
  and *Paradise Lost* 204–08
  and philanthropy 201, 202–08, 227
  and separate spheres 202–04, 213–14
  on education for women 91
  Strictures on the Modern System of Female Education 2, 202
  "The Two Wealthy Farmers" 91
Morland, George
  The Happy Cottagers 104
mothers
  "an Enlightenment mother" 32
  and children 18–22
  and daughters 15, 34
Mulvey, Laura 256n10
Murdoch, John 151
Myers, Mitzi 18–19, 22, 37, 47, 49, 202, 258n21

Naginski, Erika 111
nature 23, 87–94, 132–36, 154, 156–57
　domestication of 126, 145–46, 156–59, 166–69
The New Female Instructor 190
Nicolson, Marjorie Hope
　"The Microscope and the English Imagination" 58

observation 66–67, 68
Oliphant, Margaret
　Chronicles of Carlingford 3, 11, 228–32, 248
　The Doctor's Family 232
　"The Latest Lawgiver" 228
　"Mary Russel [sic] Mitford" 243
　Miss Marjoribanks 228–29, 234, 248
　　and the cottagers 248
　　country estate in 246
　　drawing room in 238
　　open gardens in 239
　　philanthropy in 238–43, 245, 247–48
　　walled gardens in 232–33, 239, 245
　The Perpetual Curate 233, 237
　Phoebe Junior 235
　The Rector 233, 235
　Salem Chapel 233, 248
O'Malley, Andrew
　The Making of the Modern Child 25
O'Reilly, Mrs. (Robert)
　Daisy's Companions 45
ornamentality 151
　of girls and women 62
　of plants and women 51
　of women 51, 92

parents as educators 18
Park, Mungo 72
　Travels in the Interior of Africa 55–58
passions, the 46–49
patriarchy 230
personal development 201, 211, 215, 227
philanthropy 201, 202–08, 212, 222, 227
　in *Miss Marjoribanks* (Oliphant) 238–43, 245, 247–48
picturesque, the 94, 125–28, 134, 140, 158, 159
　domesticated 126
plants
　exotics 51, 154
　ferns 237
　potted 169, 184, 219, 236
　seeds 74
　sexualized 62
Pratt, Anne
　The Field, the Garden, and the Woodland 58

Probyn, Elspeth 256n14
puberty 39, 80

religion 55–58, 71, 126
　Adam and Eve 192
　creation 72
　Eve 203, 204–08, 212
　and the Garden of Eden 75
　and science 263n69
Repton, Humphry 151, 211–12, 217, 231, 274n43, 277n24
rhetoric of apology 112, 164
Ritvo, Harriet 145
Roberts, Mary
　The Wonders of the Vegetable Kingdom Displayed 56, 71–75
Robinson, Charles
　illustrations for *The Secret Garden* (Burnett) 251
Romantics, the 75
Rose, Gillian 125, 230
　Feminism and Geography 5
Ross, Stephanie
　What Gardens Mean 4, 117
Rousseau, Jean-Jacques
　Letters on the Elements of Botany, Addressed to a Lady 2, 6, 61
Ruskin, John
　interest in gardens and botany 284n5
　"Of Queens' Gardens" 228, 247

Salzmann, C. G.
　Elements of Morality 19
Schaub, Melissa 228
Scotland 156–60
Scott, Sir Walter
　The Lady of the Lake 146
Seager, Joni
　see Domosh, Mona, and Joni Seager
"seeing" 62–64
　and children's education 61
　see also observation
sensibility 102
Seward, Anna
　"Colebrooke Dale" 73
Sewell, Anna 37
Sewell, Mary Wright
　Thoughts on Education 87
sexualization
　of flowers 59
　of plants 62
Sha, Richard 82, 126, 266n36
Sherwood, Mary Martha 44
　History of the Fairchild Family 27, 37

Index

Shore, Emily 53–55, 82, 85, 120, 160, 188–89
Shteir, Ann B. 55, 60, 88, 94, 108
   Cultivating Women, Cultivating Science 6, 50
Silver, Anna 251
Smith, Charlotte 221
   Rambles Farther 1, 22, 42
   Rural Walks 1, 23, 29, 42, 76, 93, 94
Snyder, William 140, 158
Spilsbury, Jonathan 95
Spilsbury, Maria 9, 79, 94–105, 115
   framing 98
   "home landscapes" 96
   marriage to John Taylor 96
   paintings by
      After School 105
      cottage door paintings 101
      Family Group before a Thatched Cottage 102
      Four Children in a Landscape 105
      Group Portrait at a Drawing Room Table 105
      Group Portrait in a Wooded Landscape 97
      Patron's Day at the Seven Churches, Glendalough 96
      Two Children in a Woodland Glade 105
   professional life of
      exhibition of paintings 96, 267n63
      sale of paintings 96
Stewart, Susan
   On Longing 8, 59
sublime, the 73, 133
Summerfield, Geoffrey
   Fantasy and Reason 22

Tange, Andrea Kaston 229
Taylor, Ann 116–17, 132–36
   homes
      of childhood 117–23
      Colchester 119–20, 124
      images of 123
      Lavenham 121
      Ongar 121, 124
   marriage and writing 130–31
   and nature 132–36
   portrait by father 118
   private study 128–30
      in the attic 129
   and windows 123–25
      with ivy around 125–26
   work and domesticity 132
   workroom 124
   writings of
      Autobiography 9
      "Domestic Recollections" 123
      "The Flower and the Lady, About Getting Up" 24
      "The Little Field Daisy" 39
      "To Memory" 117
      "My Mother" 34, 133
      poem for sister, Jane 118
   see also Taylor, Jane, and Ann Taylor
Taylor, Ann Martin
   concern for plants 131
   nostalgia for childhood homes 270n5
Taylor, Ann Martin, and Jane Taylor
   Correspondence between a Mother and Her Daughter at School 7, 39, 91
Taylor, Jane 116–17, 132–36
   homes
      of childhood 117–23
      Colchester 119–20, 124
      images of 123
      Lavenham 121
      Ongar 121
   and nature 132–36
   and the picturesque 125–28, 134
   portrait by father 118
   private study
      in the attic 128
   sketches 85, 92
   and the sublime 133
   and windows 123–25, 128–30
      with ivy around 125–26
   work and domesticity 132
   and writing 131–32
   writings of
      "Accomplishment" 91
      "Birth-Day Retrospect" 119
      "Busy Idleness" 65
      "Come and Play in the Garden" 42
      Display: A Tale for Young People 125
      "The English Girl" 34
      "The Industrious Boy" 126
      Memoirs and Poetical Remains 9
      "On Visiting an Old Family Residence" 119
      "Poetry and Reality" 126
      "Spring Flowers" 120
      "Twinkle, twinkle little star" 133
      "The Violet to the Rose" 30
      "The World in the House" 30
Taylor, Jane, and Ann Taylor
   Original Poems 34
Taylor, John 96
Taylor family, the 269n4

teachers 18
see also education
terrace, the 170
terrarium 238
Thomson, James 208
Tobin, Beth Fowkes
   Colonizing Nature: The Tropics in British Arts and Letters, 1760–1820, 7
Tonna, Charlotte Elizabeth
   Chapters on Flowers 51
Tuan, Yi-Fu 25, 49, 125
   Space and Place: The Perspective of Experience 3
Tuite, Clara 216
Turner, Elizabeth
   The Cowslip, or More Cautionary Stories in Verse 44
Twining, Elizabeth
   "A Few Words about Window-Gardens" 221

virtues 30, 34–38, 46–49, 67
   feminine 26
   industry 24–27, 65, 110, 128
   modesty 28
   morality 30
   neatness 27–28, 174, 240
   self-control 47
   simplicity 28
   usefulness 65, 90

Wakefield, Priscilla
   An Introduction to Botany 51, 88
   "The Little Wanderer" 43
   Reflections on the Present Condition of the Female Sex 88, 190
Waldron, Mary 215
Walker, Carol Kyros 156
Waters, Michael 243
   The Garden in Victorian Literature 163, 230
Whiting, J. B.
   Manual of Flower Gardening for Ladies 181
wildflowers 28–30, 52, 53, 144–45, 264n77
Williams, Raymond 211
Williamson, Tom 155, 213
Wilson, Carol Shiner 132
window gardens 221
Withering, William 71
   An Arrangement of British Plants 153
Wollstonecraft, Mary 87, 175
   Original Stories from Real Life 19, 31, 46, 258n24
   A Vindication of the Rights of Woman 2, 92

women 17, 23, 80, 92
   education of 91, 262n32
   farmers 190
   objectification of 281n7
   and professionalism 86, 90, 112, 115
   and the rhetoric of apology 112, 164
Woolf, Virginia 129, 203, 261n30
Wordsworth, Dora
   illustration of Dove Cottage 149
Wordsworth, Dorothy 3, 10, 189, 243
   and bowers 145–47
      at Town End 146
   Continental tour 161–62
   death of brother, John 156
   and domestication
      of nature 156–57
      of the Scottish landscape 157–59
   and the garden 143–45, 149–55
      as a text 149, 153
   gardening books consulted 153
   and home 141
      at Rydal Mount 160
      at Town End (Dove Cottage), Grasmere 139–40, 146, 160
   and objects of refuge 140–42
   and the picturesque 140
   and small spaces 140
   summer-huts and sheds 156–57
      shelter at "The Hollins" 142
   and the wilderness 145–46, 154
   and William's marriage 147
   writings of
      "Grasmere – A Fragment" 160
      The Grasmere Journals 142–49
      Recollections of a Tour of Scotland 156–60
Wordsworth, William
   and bowers 274n29
   courtship of and marriage to Mary Hutchinson 143, 147
   Town End (Dove Cottage), Grasmere 139–40
   writings of
      A Guide through the District of the Lakes 155
      "Lines Written in Early Spring" 146
      Lyrical Ballads 153, 209
      "Tintern Abbey" 222
Worthen, John 148

Yonge, Charlotte 169
Young, Mary
   commonplace book of 22
The Young Lady's Book 189

CAMBRIDGE STUDIES IN NINETEENTH-CENTURY
LITERATURE AND CULTURE

General editor
Gillian Beer, *University of Cambridge*

Titles published

1. The Sickroom in Victorian Fiction: The Art of Being Ill
Miriam Bailin, *Washington University*

2. Muscular Christianity: Embodying the Victorian Age
edited by Donald E. Hall, *California State University, Northridge*

3. Victorian Masculinities: Manhood and Masculine Poetics in Early Victorian
Literature and Art
Herbert Sussman, *Northeastern University, Boston*

4. Byron and the Victorians
Andrew Elfenbein, *University of Minnesota*

5. Literature in the Marketplace: Nineteenth-Century British Publishing
and the Circulation of Books
edited by John O. Jordan, *University of California, Santa Cruz*
and Robert L. Patten, *Rice University, Houston*

6. Victorian Photography, Painting and Poetry
Lindsay Smith, *University of Sussex*

7. Charlotte Brontë and Victorian Psychology
Sally Shuttleworth, *University of Sheffield*

8. The Gothic Body:
Sexuality, Materialism and Degeneration at the *Fin de Siècle*
Kelly Hurley, *University of Colorado at Boulder*

9. Rereading Walter Pater
William F. Shuter, *Eastern Michigan University*

10. Remaking Queen Victoria
edited by Margaret Homans, *Yale University*
and Adrienne Munich, *State University of New York, Stony Brook*

11. Disease, Desire, and the Body in Victorian Women's Popular Novels
Pamela K. Gilbert, *University of Florida*

12. Realism, Representation, and the Arts in Nineteenth-Century Literature
Alison Byerly, *Middlebury College, Vermont*

13. Literary Culture and the Pacific
Vanessa Smith, *University of Sydney*

14. Professional Domesticity in the Victorian Novel: Women, Work and Home
Monica F. Cohen

15. Victorian Renovations of the Novel: Narrative Annexes and the Boundaries of Representation
Suzanne Keen, *Washington and Lee University, Virginia*

16. Actresses on the Victorian Stage: Feminine Performance and the Galatea Myth
Gail Marshall, *University of Leeds*

17. Death and the Mother from Dickens to Freud: Victorian Fiction and the Anxiety of Origin
Carolyn Dever, *Vanderbilt University, Tennessee*

18. Ancestry and Narrative in Nineteenth-Century British Literature: Blood Relations from Edgeworth to Hardy
Sophie Gilmartin, *Royal Holloway, University of London*

19. Dickens, Novel Reading, and the Victorian Popular Theatre
Deborah Vlock

20. After Dickens: Reading, Adaptation and Performance
John Glavin, *Georgetown University, Washington DC*

21. Victorian Women Writers and the Woman Question
edited by Nicola Diane Thompson, *Kingston University, London*

22. Rhythm and Will in Victorian Poetry
Matthew Campbell, *University of Sheffield*

23. Gender, Race, and the Writing of Empire: Public Discourse and the Boer War
Paula M. Krebs, *Wheaton College, Massachusetts*

24. Ruskin's God
Michael Wheeler, *University of Southampton*

25. Dickens and the Daughter of the House
Hilary M. Schor, *University of Southern California*

26. Detective Fiction and the Rise of Forensic Science
Ronald R. Thomas, *Trinity College, Hartford, Connecticut*

27. Testimony and Advocacy in Victorian Law, Literature, and Theology
Jan-Melissa Schramm, *Trinity Hall, Cambridge*

28. Victorian Writing about Risk: Imagining a Safe England in a Dangerous World
Elaine Freedgood, *University of Pennsylvania*

29. Physiognomy and the Meaning of Expression in Nineteenth-Century Culture
Lucy Hartley, *University of Southampton*

30. The Victorian Parlour: A Cultural Study
Thad Logan, *Rice University, Houston*

31. Aestheticism and Sexual Parody 1840–1940
Dennis Denisoff, *Ryerson University, Toronto*

32. Literature, Technology and Magical Thinking, 1880–1920
Pamela Thurschwell, *University College London*

33. Fairies in Nineteenth-Century Art and Literature
Nicola Bown, *Birkbeck, University of London*

34. George Eliot and the British Empire
Nancy Henry, *The State University of New York, Binghamton*

35. Women's Poetry and Religion in Victorian England: Jewish Identity and Christian Culture
Cynthia Scheinberg, *Mills College, California*

36. Victorian Literature and the Anorexic Body
Anna Krugovoy Silver, *Mercer University, Georgia*

37. Eavesdropping in the Novel from Austen to Proust
Ann Gaylin, *Yale University*

38. Missionary Writing and Empire, 1800–1860
Anna Johnston, *University of Tasmania*

39. London and the Culture of Homosexuality, 1885–1914
Matt Cook, *Keele University*

40. Fiction, Famine, and the Rise of Economics in Victorian Britain and Ireland
Gordon Bigelow, *Rhodes College, Tennessee*

41. Gender and the Victorian Periodical
Hilary Fraser, *Birkbeck, University of London* and Judith Johnston and Stephanie Green, *University of Western Australia*

42. The Victorian Supernatural
edited by Nicola Bown, *Birkbeck College, London* Carolyn Burdett, *London Metropolitan University* and Pamela Thurschwell, *University College London*

43. The Indian Mutiny and the British Imagination
Gautam Chakravarty, *University of Delhi*

44. The Revolution in Popular Literature: Print, Politics and the People
Ian Haywood, *Roehampton University of Surrey*

45. Science in the Nineteenth-Century Periodical: Reading the Magazine of Nature
Geoffrey Cantor, *University of Leeds* Gowan Dawson, *University of Leicester* Graeme Gooday, *University of Leeds* Richard Noakes, *University of Cambridge* Sally Shuttleworth, *University of Sheffield* and Jonathan R. Topham, *University of Leeds*

46. Literature and Medicine in Nineteenth-Century Britain from Mary Shelley to George Eliot
Janis McLarren Caldwell, *Wake Forest University*

47. The Child Writer from Austen to Woolf
edited by Christine Alexander, *University of New South Wales* and Juliet McMaster, *University of Alberta*

48. From Dickens to Dracula: Gothic, Economics, and Victorian Fiction
Gail Turley Houston, *University of New Mexico*

49. Voice and the Victorian Storyteller
Ivan Kreilkamp, *University of Indiana*

50. Charles Darwin and Victorian Visual Culture
Jonathan Smith, *University of Michigan-Dearborn*

51. Catholicism, Sexual Deviance, and Victorian Gothic Culture
Patrick R. O'Malley, *Georgetown University*

52. Epic and Empire in Nineteenth-Century Britain
Simon Dentith, *University of Gloucestershire*

53. Victorian Honeymoons: Journeys to the Conjugal
Helena Michie, *Rice University*

54. The Jewess in Nineteenth-Century British Literary Culture
Nadia Valman, *University of Southampton*

55. Ireland, India and Nationalism in Nineteenth-Century Literature
Julia Wright, *Dalhousie University*

56. Dickens and the Popular Radical Imagination
Sally Ledger, *Birkbeck, University of London*

57. Darwin, Literature and Victorian Respectability
Gowan Dawson, *University of Leicester*

58. 'Michael Field': Poetry, Aestheticism and the *Fin de Siècle*
Marion Thain, *University of Birmingham*

59. Colonies, Cults and Evolution: Literature, Science and Culture in Nineteenth-Century Writing
David Amigoni, *Keele University*

60. Realism, Photography and Nineteenth-Century Fiction
Daniel A. Novak, *Lousiana State University*

61. Caribbean Culture and British Fiction in the Atlantic World, 1780–1870
Tim Watson, *University of Miami*

62. The Poetry of Chartism: Aesthetics, Politics, History
Michael Sanders, *University of Manchester*

63. Literature and Dance in Nineteenth-Century Britain: Jane Austen to the New Woman
Cheryl Wilson, *Indiana University*

64. Shakespeare and Victorian Women
Gail Marshall, *Oxford Brookes University*

65. The Tragi-Comedy of Victorian Fatherhood
Valerie Sanders, *University of Hull*

66. Darwin and the Memory of the Human
Cannon Schmitt, *University of Toronto*

67. From Sketch to Novel
Amanpal Garcha, *Ohio State University*

68. The Crimean War and the British Imagination
Stefanie Markovits, *Yale University*

69. Shock, Memory and the Unconscious in Victorian Fiction
Jill L. Matus, *University of Toronto*

70. Sensation and Modernity in the 1860s
Nicholas Daly, *University College Dublin*

71. Ghost-Seers, Detectives, and Spiritualists:
Theories of Vision in Victorian Literature and Science
Srdjan Smajić, *Furman University*

72. Satire in an Age of Realism
Aaron Matz, *Scripps College, California*

73. Thinking About Other People in Nineteenth-Century British Writing
Adela Pinch, *University of Michigan*

74. Tuberculosis and the Victorian Literary Imagination
Katherine Byrne, *University of Ulster, Coleraine*

75. Urban Realism and the Cosmopolitan Imagination:
Visible City, Invisible World
Tanya Agathocleous, *Hunter College, City University of New York*

76. Women, Literature, and the Domesticated Landscape:
England's Disciples of Flora, 1780–1870
Judith W. Page, *University of Florida* and Elise L. Smith,
Millsaps College, Mississippi

CPSIA information can be obtained at www.ICGtesting.com
Printed in the USA
LVOW02s2324150414

381904LV00005B/55/P

9 781107 420236